Tools and Technologies for the Development of Cyber–Physical Systems

Sergey Balandin
FRUCT Oy, Finland

Ekaterina Balandina
Tampere University, Finland

A volume in the Advances in Computer and
Electrical Engineering (ACEE) Book Series

Published in the United States of America by
IGI Global
Engineering Science Reference (an imprint of IGI Global)
701 E. Chocolate Avenue
Hershey PA, USA 17033
Tel: 717-533-8845
Fax: 717-533-8661
E-mail: cust@igi-global.com
Web site: http://www.igi-global.com

Library of Congress Cataloging-in-Publication Data

Names: Balandin, Sergeĭ I., editor. | Balandina, Ekaterina, 1988- editor.
Title: Tools and technologies for the development of cyber-physical systems
  / Sergey Balandin, Ekaterina Balandina, editors.
Description: Hershey, PA : Engineering Science Reference, an imprint of IGI
  Global, [2020] | Includes bibliographical references and index. |
  Summary: "This book discusses recent advancements of cyber-physical
  systems and its application within the health, information, and computer
  science industries"-- Provided by publisher.
Identifiers: LCCN 2019035513 (print) | LCCN 2019035514 (ebook) | ISBN
  9781799819745 (hardcover) | ISBN 9781799819752 (paperback) | ISBN
  9781799819769 (ebook)
Subjects: LCSH: Human-machine systems. | Cooperating objects (Computer
  systems) | Internet of things.
Classification: LCC TA167 .T65 2020 (print) | LCC TA167 (ebook) | DDC
  620.8/2--dc23
LC record available at https://lccn.loc.gov/2019035513
LC ebook record available at https://lccn.loc.gov/2019035514

This book is published in the IGI Global book series Advances in Computer and Electrical Engineering (ACEE) (ISSN: 2327-039X; eISSN: 2327-0403)

British Cataloguing in Publication Data
A Cataloguing in Publication record for this book is available from the British Library.

The views expressed in this book are those of the authors, but not necessarily of the publisher.

For electronic access to this publication, please contact: eresources@igi-global.com.

Advances in Computer and Electrical Engineering (ACEE) Book Series

Srikanta Patnaik
SOA University, India

ISSN:2327-039X
EISSN:2327-0403

MISSION

The fields of computer engineering and electrical engineering encompass a broad range of interdisciplinary topics allowing for expansive research developments across multiple fields. Research in these areas continues to develop and become increasingly important as computer and electrical systems have become an integral part of everyday life.

The **Advances in Computer and Electrical Engineering (ACEE) Book Series** aims to publish research on diverse topics pertaining to computer engineering and electrical engineering. **ACEE** encourages scholarly discourse on the latest applications, tools, and methodologies being implemented in the field for the design and development of computer and electrical systems.

COVERAGE

- Digital Electronics
- VLSI Design
- VLSI Fabrication
- Computer Science
- Qualitative Methods
- Microprocessor Design
- Optical Electronics
- Power Electronics
- Applied Electromagnetics
- Analog Electronics

IGI Global is currently accepting manuscripts for publication within this series. To submit a proposal for a volume in this series, please contact our Acquisition Editors at Acquisitions@igi-global.com or visit: http://www.igi-global.com/publish/.

Titles in this Series

For a list of additional titles in this series, please visit:https://www.igi-global.com/book-series/advances-computer-electrical-engineering/73675

Novel Approaches to Information Systems Design
Naveen Prakash (Indraprastha Institute of Information Technology, Delhi, India) and Deepika Prakash (NIIT University, India)
Engineering Science Reference • © 2020 • 299pp • H/C (ISBN: 9781799829751) • US $215.00

IoT Architectures, Models, and Platforms for Smart City Applications
Bhawani Shankar Chowdhry (Mehran University of Engineering and Technology, Pakistan) Faisal Karim Shaikh (Mehran University of Engineering and Technology, Pakistan) and Naeem Ahmed Mahoto (Mehran University of Engineering and Technology, Pakistan)
Engineering Science Reference • © 2020 • 291pp • H/C (ISBN: 9781799812531) • US $245.00

Nature-Inspired Computing Applications in Advanced Communication Networks
Govind P. Gupta (National Institute of Technology, Raipur, India)
Engineering Science Reference • © 2020 • 319pp • H/C (ISBN: 9781799816263) • US $225.00

Pattern Recognition Applications in Engineering
Diego Alexander Tibaduiza Burgos (Universidad Nacional de Colombia, Colombia) Maribel Anaya Vejar (Universidad Sergio Arboleda, Colombia) and Francesc Pozo (Universitat Politècnica de Catalunya, Spain)
Engineering Science Reference • © 2020 • 300pp • H/C (ISBN: 9781799818397) • US $215.00

Handbook of Research on New Solutions and Technologies in Electrical Distribution Networks
Baseem Khan (Hawassa University, Hawassa, Ethiopia) Hassan Haes Alhelou (Tishreen University, Syria) and Ghassan Hayek (Tishreen University, Syria)
Engineering Science Reference • © 2020 • 439pp • H/C (ISBN: 9781799812302) • US $270.00

Major Applications of Carbon Nanotube Field-Effect Transistors (CNTFET)
Balwinder Raj (National Institute of Technical Teachers Training and Research, Chandigarh, India) Mamta Khosla (Dr. B. R. Ambedkar National Institute of Technology, Jalandhar, India) and Amandeep Singh (National Institute of Technology, Srinagar, India)
Engineering Science Reference • © 2020 • 255pp • H/C (ISBN: 9781799813934) • US $185.00

Neural Networks for Natural Language Processing
Sumathi S. (St. Joseph's College of Engineering, India) and Janani M. (St. Joseph's College of Engineering, India)
Engineering Science Reference • © 2020 • 227pp • H/C (ISBN: 9781799811596) • US $235.00

701 East Chocolate Avenue, Hershey, PA 17033, USA
Tel: 717-533-8845 x100 • Fax: 717-533-8661
E-Mail: cust@igi-global.com • www.igi-global.com

Table of Contents

Detailed Table of Contents

Chapter 1
    Man Tianxing, ITMO University, Russia
    Vasiliy Yurievich Osipov, Saint Petersburg Institute for Informatics and Automation of
        Russian Academy of Sciences (SPIIRAS), Russia
    Ildar Raisovich Baimuratov, ITMO University, Russia
    Natalia Alexandrovna Zhukova, Saint Petersburg Institute for Informatics and Automation of
        Russian Academy of Sciences (SPIIRAS), Russia
    Alexander Ivanovich Vodyaho, Saint Petersburg Electrotechnical University (LETI), Russia
    Sergey Vyacheslavovich Lebedev, Saint Petersburg Electrotechnical University (LETI),
        Russia

In the chapter, the problem of cyber-physical systems monitoring based on the processing and evaluation of the data received from the observed objects is considered. The main attention is paid to finding a suitable way to reduce the synthesis complexity of the observed objects models and monitoring processes. The authors propose a multilevel automatic synthesis technology that formalizes such models to multilevel relatively finite automata. The architecture of cyber-physical monitoring systems using this technology is presented.

Chapter 2
    Alexey Kashevnik, St. Petersburg Institute for Informatics and Automation of Russian
        Academy of Sciences (SPIIRAS), Russia
    Nikolay Teslya, St. Petersburg Institute for Informatics and Automation of Russian Academy
        of Sciences (SPIIRAS), Russia

The chapter presents an approach to agent indirect interaction in smart space based on the publication/ subscription mechanism. It is proposed to describe every agent with an ontology and support the ontology matching between ontologies of different agents in smart space to enrich the semantic interoperability between them. When the agents reach the semantic interoperability, they are aimed to create a coalition to perform a task. The task is described by ontology and the agents determine what they can propose to implement it. Group of agents that can perform the task together is called coalition. The considered case study describes the mobile robot interaction for the case of joint obstacle overcoming by the 6WD robot with lifting chassis, quadrocopter that scans an obstacle, and knowledge base service that contains algorithms for obstacle overcoming.

Chapter 3

Sergey Lebedev, Saint Petersburg Electrotechnical University (LETI), Russia
Michail Panteleyev, St. Petersburg Electrotechnical University (LETI), Russia

Evolution of cyber-physical systems (CPS) and extension of their application areas complicate, among other things, their software design and development. This requires improvements in programming techniques used to build CPS. One of the important tasks arising in complex CPS is a situation assessment (SA) based on data received from diverse sources. In the chapter, an ontology-driven approach for CPS SA software design and development automation is proposed. The approach is based on the JDL data fusion model and flexible enough to be applied for any class of CPS applications. In contrast to known approaches, ontologies are used not only for domain knowledge representation but also for SA calculation process formalization. It provides a higher level of automation of SA software synthesis and, in the end, increases design and development efficiency.

Chapter 4

Valentin Olenev, St. Petersburg State University of Aerospace Instrumentation, Russia
Yuriy Sheynin, St. Petersburg State University of Aerospace Instrumentation, Russia
Irina Lavrovskaya, St. Petersburg State University of Aerospace Instrumentation, Russia
Ilya Korobkov, St. Petersburg State University of Aerospace Instrumentation, Russia
Lev Kurbanov, St. Petersburg State University of Aerospace Instrumentation, Russia
Nadezhda Chumakova, St. Petersburg State University of Aerospace Instrumentation, Russia
Nikolay Sinyov, St. Petersburg State University of Aerospace Instrumentation, Russia

This chapter presents an approach for the design and simulation of embedded networks for spacecraft. The chapter provides an analysis of existing simulation tools for the on-board and local area networks. The authors overview the main abilities of the existing software and then propose the computer-aided design system for SpaceWire onboard networks design and simulation. This CAD system supports the full on-board network design and simulation flow, which begins from the network topology automated generation and finishes with getting the network structure, configuration and parameters setting, simulation results, and statistics – SpaceWire Automated Network Design and Simulation (SANDS). The authors describe formal theories, algorithms, methods, and approaches, which are used to solve general issues that appear in developing of onboard networks. The chapter covers topics of fault-tolerance in onboard networks, discusses routing problems, and approaches to organize deadlock-free routing. The authors propose schedule creation algorithms for STP ISS protocol and consider network simulation issues.

Chapter 5

Konstantin Nedovodeev, St. Petersburg State University of Aerospace Instrumentation, Russia

Yuriy Sheynin, St. Petersburg State University of Aerospace Instrumentation, Russia

Alexey Syschikov, St. Petersburg State University of Aerospace Instrumentation, Russia

Boris Sedov, St. Petersburg State University of Aerospace Instrumentation, Russia

Vera Ivanova, St. Petersburg State University of Aerospace Instrumentation, Russia

Sergey Pakharev, St. Petersburg State University of Aerospace Instrumentation, Russia

The chapter considers VIPE development environment with the main emphasis on its formal ground. The detailed description of a formal VIPE model of computation (MoC) and the semantics of language constructs let the reader reason about the behavior of the constructs in question. The authors propose a rigorous description of program transformations applied to the program while it is compiled. The program after all the transformations is a correct one from the view of the host MoC. Its behavior meets the programmer's expectations even when it includes fragments, which belong to a guest MoC. Techniques for translation of the guest MoC (OpenVX) constructs into the host MoC (VIPE) constructs were proposed. The approach described here leads to the end program that is fully conformant to the host MoC. In addition, the whole toolset is at the programmer's disposal, namely visual editor, compiler, runtime, and analysis tools. They stay applicable to the program, some parts of which are now guest MoC constructs.

Chapter 6

Andrey Kuzmin, Penza State University, Russia

Maxim Safronov, Penza State University, Russia

Oleg Bodin, Penza State University, Russia

Victor Baranov, Penza State University, Russia

This chapter describes a design of prototype of mobile heart monitoring system based on the Texas Instruments ADS1298R ECG front end and NRF52832 wireless data transmission chip. The described design and technical details allow developing a new mobile heart monitoring system consisting of ECG recording device, mobile computer (smartphone or tablet). The algorithm for ECG recovery using a reverse filter, whose parameters are determined by means of bioimpedance measurement, is described. The new algorithm of J-point detection is described and examined on the test ECG database. The detection rate is from 88% to 93%. It will allow mobile monitoring system to inform the user about any signs of dangerous heart condition in ECG. The chapter also describes experimental results of wireless protocol bandwidth and contact break detection. The results confirm the efficiency of the proposed technical solutions to mobile heart monitoring for wide range of applications from sports and fitness to monitoring for medical reasons.

Alexander Yu. Meigal, Petrozavodsk State University, Russia
Dmitry G. Korzun, Petrozavodsk State University, Russia
Alex P. Moschevikin, Nanoseti LTD, Petrozavodsk State University, Russia
Sergey Reginya, Petrozavodsk State University, Nanoseti LTD, Russia
Liudmila I. Gerasimova-Meigal, Petrozavodsk State University, Russia

The chapter summarizes the authors' development on the concept of "at-home lab" (AHL). The concept employs the methods of artificial intelligence (AI), smart internet of things (IoT) technologies, and data mining techniques. The aim is at support for patients with Parkinson's disease and aged people to continuously monitor and evaluate their motor and cognitive status using own smartphone (in particular, IMU as wearable sensor, apps for testing cognitive status, camera for motor tracking). In addition, other devices in the IoT environment can participate in creating the information assistance support for people. This chapter presents and discuss the AHL concept as a further development step of AI in respect with human evolution (NeoNeoCortex). The focus is on evolutionary, environmental, and biological aspects of AI.

Andrew Ponomarev, St. Petersburg Institute for Informatics and Automation of Russian
Academy of Sciences (SPIIRAS), Russia
Nikolay Shilov, St. Petersburg Institute for Informatics and Automation of Russian Academy
of Sciences (SPIIRAS), Russia

The chapter addresses two problems that typically arise during the creation of decision support systems that include humans in the information processing workflow, namely, resource management and complexity of decision support in dynamic environments, where it is impossible (or impractical) to implement all possible information processing workflows that can be useful for a decision-maker. The chapter proposes the concept of human-computer cloud, providing typical cloud features (elasticity, on demand resource provisioning) to the applications that require human input (so-called human-based applications) and, on top of resource management functionality, a facility for building information processing workflows for ad hoc tasks in an automated way. The chapter discusses main concepts lying behind the proposed cloud environment, as well as its architecture and some implementation details. It is also shown how the proposed human-computer cloud environment solves information and decision support demands in the dynamic and actively developing area of e-tourism.

Chapter 9

Svetlana E. Yalovitsyna, Institute of Linguistics, Literature, and History, Karelian Research
Centre of the Russian Academy of Sciences, Russia
Valentina V. Volokhova, Petrozavodsk State University, Russia
Dmitry G. Korzun, Petrozavodsk State University, Russia

The chapter presents the authors' study on the smart museum concept. Semantic Web technology and ontology modeling methods are applied to construct advanced digital services, supporting the study and evolution of museum collections. The concept aims at significant increase of the information impact of museum exhibits by providing augmented annotations, identifying semantic relations, assisting the visitors to follow individual trajectories in exposition study, finding relevant information, opening the collection to knowledge from visitors. A museum collection is advanced to a knowledge base where new information is created and evolved by museum visitors and personnel. The chapter discusses reference information assistance services, which are oriented for use as mobile applications on users' smartphones. The proof-of-the-concept case study is the History Museum of Petrozavodsk State University. The pilot implementation demonstrates the feasibility of the smart museum concept in respect to the user mobility, service personalization, and collaborative work opportunity.

Chapter 10

Imed Saad Ben Dhaou, Qassim University, Saudi Arabia & The University of Monastir,
Tunisia
Aron Kondoro, University of Dar es Salaam, Tanzania
Syed Rameez Ullah Kakakhel, University of Turku, Finland
Tomi Westerlund, University of Turku, Finland
Hannu Tenhunen, Royal Institute of Technology, Sweden

Smart grid is a new revolution in the energy sector in which the aging utility grid will be replaced with a grid that supports two-way communication between customers and the utility company. There are two popular smart-grid reference architectures. NIST (National Institute for Standards and Technology) has drafted a reference architecture in which seven domains and actors have been identified. The second reference architecture is elaborated by ETSI (European Telecommunications Standards Institute), which is an extension of the NIST model where a new domain named distributed energy resources has been added. This chapter aims at identifying the use of IoT and IoT-enabled technologies in the design of a secure smart grid using the ETSI reference model. Based on the discussion and analysis in the chapter, the authors offer two collaborative and development frameworks. One framework draws parallels' between IoT and smart grids and the second one between smart grids and edge computing. These frameworks can be used to broaden collaboration between the stakeholders and identify research gaps.

Chapter 11

Dmitry Namiot, Lomonosov Moscow State University, Russia
Manfred Sneps-Sneppe, Ventspils University of Applied Sciences, Latvia

This chapter describes proposals for organizing university programs on the internet of things (IoT) and cyber-physical systems. The final goal is to provide a structure for a basic educational course for the internet of things and related areas. This base (template) could be used both for direct training and for building other courses, including those that are more deeply specialized in selected areas. For related areas, the authors see, for example, machine-to-machine communications and data-driven cities (smart cities) development. Obviously, the internet of things skills are in high demand nowadays, and, of course, IoT models, architectures, as well as appropriate data proceedings elements should be presented in the university courses. The purpose of the described educational course is to cover information and communication technologies used in the internet of things systems and related areas. Also, the authors discuss big data and AI issues for IoT courses and highlight the importance of data engineering.

Preface

The book consists of a set of chapters that present and discuss major issues and hottest topics of the development of cyber-physical systems. The cyber-physical systems enable fusion and cooperative interaction of the physical and virtual worlds. The data fusion enables advanced solutions for service intelligence to be constructed to deliver properties such as adaptation, personalization, and proactive delivery of the services. This research topic is huge and consists of multiple aspects and the book provides a snapshot of the most interesting research and development challenges in the field.

The first chapter opens the discussion by defining the problem of cyber-physical systems monitoring based on the processing and evaluation of the data received from the observed objects. The main focus of this chapter is on how to reduce the synthesis complexity of the observed objects models and monitoring processes. The chapter presents a multilevel automatic synthesis technology that formalizes the model of multilevel relatively finite automata. Then architecture of a cyber-physical monitoring system created on top of the proposed technology is presented.

The second chapter is devoted to a technology for indirect interaction of agents in smart spaces. The presented case study for this technology shows a cyber-physical-social system that implementing joint actions in the physical space by coordinating interaction of the physical devices with each other and humans in a smart space. This case illustrates how to describe every agent with ontology and support the ontology matching between different ontologies in smart space to enrich the semantic interoperability between them. It also clearly illustrates how to use this technology in practice.

The third chapter presents integration of information processing capabilities and network communications of various devices within the framework of the cyber-physical systems. In particular you can read about enhancements and improvements to the programming techniques that are required to support efficient design of cyber-physical systems. The chapter discusses principles of ontology-driven design and development of situation assessment software in cyber-physical systems. Ontologies provide the ability to flexibly and quickly focus on the domain of a specific application. The approach allows reducing the time needed for designing and developing the software. The software framework to solve this problem is considered. An example of building a situation assessment system for cyber-physical system to ensure the security of public events is considered to illustrate the proposed approach.

The next two chapters introduce the key low-level aspects of the problem domain. The fourth chapter discusses general questions of the embedded networks design and simulation. This topic is really crucial as evolution of microelectronics has led to the growth of systems complexity, size and creation of the large on-board networks. The chapter provides an example of a universal software tool for designing and simulation of the complex onboard networks.

The fifth chapter further dives into the topic by presenting the model-based techniques and tools for programming embedded multicore platforms. The main elements of the presented technology are AGP-models of computation, namely: general, special, language of parallel abstract machine. Computations in the abstract machine are defined as operation of an interpreted parallel program schema. The chapter provides proofs of theorems and propositions that help to illustrate how the correctness for each step of the analysis and transformation is ensured.

The next group of chapters turns the discussion into analysis of the use case examples. The sixth chapter particularly addresses issues related to power supply and data transfer methods for implantable medical devices. The presented use case addresses the unsolved problem of modern health care - the risk of sudden cardiac death. This risk affects both the elderly people with known heart disease, and young people who have no idea about their health problems. To reduce the risk of sudden cardiac death it is necessary to improve portable systems recording and processing of ECG, both in hardware and software by improving the methods and means of processing, applying them in free movement conditions. Discussion on the corresponding challenges and opportunities can be found in the chapter.

The seventh chapter also addresses the e-health group of use cases by dealing with prototyping mobile heart monitoring system. The chapter summarizes development on the concept of at-home lab. The concept employs methods of Artificial Intelligence, smart Internet of Things technologies, and data mining techniques. The use case is a service for supporting patients with Parkinson's disease and aged people by providing continuous monitoring and evaluation of their motor and cognitive status using personal smartphone as an individual data processing hub. The chapter presents and discusses the at-home lab concept as a further development step of AI in respect with human evolution. The focus is on evolutionary, environmental and biological aspects of AI.

The eighth chapter addresses another application domain – e-tourism. The chapter addresses two challenges that typically arise during the construction of human-machine computational systems. The first challenge is proper organization of the resource management. The second challenge is dealing with complexity of decision support in dynamic environments. The chapter discusses a human-computer cloud architecture that addresses both these problems. The environment includes two parts: the platform that provides a unified resource management environment, and the decision support software running on top of the platform that allows to automatically decompose tasks to subtasks and distribute them among human participants.

The next chapter summarizes experience of our team in the smart museum concept development. The discussed semantic approach provides high flexibility in processing and presenting the content of museum collections. The chapter provides an overview of the existing IoT-enabled smart museum solutions. Then there is a discussion and analysis of the key problems of semantic layer construction on top of a museum information system. Then we elaborate appropriate models of Semantic Web applied for creation of the semantic layer. It is followed by discussion on various ranking algorithms than can be used to search the most relevant information in the museum collection. Finally, the chapter summarizes the key solutions and recommendations to be applied for the smart museum concept and provides an overview of possible future research directions.

Chapter 10 describes the application of IoT technologies at the five domains of the smart grid: operations, customer, generation, distribution, and transmission. The utility grid is experiencing a drastic transformation towards adopting two-way communications. Smart-grid is the new generation of the utility grid that is driven by arduous factors such as the need to reduce carbon dioxide, increase the grid efficiency, decrease the cost of operation and maintenance, etc. IoT has enabled new forms of services and architectures such as advanced smart metering infrastructure, distributed intelligence, demand-response program, volt/var optimization, home energy management system, and substation automations. Those functions and services are enabled by key technologies such as multi-agent systems, fog/cloud computing, middleware, and communication technologies. Notwithstanding, IoT has enabled the realization of the smart-grid, privacy and security remain one big challenge.

As a conclusion for the book we provide chapter that discusses education in the field of the Internet of things and cyber-physical systems as a part of the university program. In particular the main focus of presented discussion can be formulated by the question - what exactly and why should be included in the course/courses of master's level training on the topics of the Internet of Things and cyber-physical systems. The chapter is resulted in a detailed proposal for the content of the corresponding courses.

The proposed book structure provides the reader with well-balanced theoretical and practical overview of the subject, enhanced by deep inside for selected topics. The book is meant for students and researchers interested in the research trends and development tools for the cyber-physical systems. The book provides enough materials to prepare a course or seminar on advances in cyber-physical systems development.

Chapter 1
Advanced Technology for Cyber–Physical System Monitoring

Man Tianxing
https://orcid.org/0000-0003-2187-1641
ITMO University, Russia

Vasiliy Yurievich Osipov
https://orcid.org/0000-0001-5905-4415
*Saint Petersburg Institute for Informatics and
Automation of Russian Academy of Sciences
(SPIIRAS), Russia*

Ildar Raisovich Baimuratov
ITMO University, Russia

Natalia Alexandrovna Zhukova
*Saint Petersburg Institute for Informatics and
Automation of Russian Academy of Sciences
(SPIIRAS), Russia*

Alexander Ivanovich Vodyaho
*Saint Petersburg Electrotechnical University
(LETI), Russia*

Sergey Vyacheslavovich Lebedev
https://orcid.org/0000-0002-0045-6310
*Saint Petersburg Electrotechnical University
(LETI), Russia*

ABSTRACT

In the chapter, the problem of cyber-physical systems monitoring based on the processing and evaluation of the data received from the observed objects is considered. The main attention is paid to finding a suitable way to reduce the synthesis complexity of the observed objects models and monitoring processes. The authors propose a multilevel automatic synthesis technology that formalizes such models to multilevel relatively finite automata. The architecture of cyber-physical monitoring systems using this technology is presented.

INTRODUCTION

The Cyber-Physical System (CPS) is a multi-dimensional complex system that implements real-time perception, dynamic control and information service for large engineering systems through 3C (Computation, Communication, Control) technologies. These systems can contain a considerable number of

DOI: 10.4018/978-1-7998-1974-5.ch001

interconnected objects. The CPSs make different decisions and controls based on monitoring the real-time state of the observed systems through a large number of sensors. However, the data obtained by the underlying physical components are redundant, massive, and uncertain (Wolf, W. H. 2009). These systems typically are not smart enough to extract information from large amounts of input data.

To address these critical issues, in recent years, researches have been focused on intelligent cyber-physical monitoring systems (CPMS) that are CPS systems with intelligent abilities oriented on solving monitoring tasks. Such systems are based on models, methods, and technologies of artificial intelligence (AI). They can analyze and interpret acquired data and activate proper reaction/control mechanisms to guarantee the quality of monitoring results.

In the researches about the building of CPSs, most of the attention is paid to the synthesis of programs (Gulwani, S., et al. 2017). There is no known effective solution for the synthesis of models of complex observed objects. The modern approaches to model synthesis don't allow synthesizing models that allow solving CPS monitoring tasks. For now, the most reliable way to solve the synthesis problem is to develop the ideas of model synthesis within the symbolic approach.

Model synthesis in CPS can be based on models and methods proposed in (Osipov V. Yu., 2016). It assumes building single-level models using deductive synthesis methods. However, it cannot be directly used for model synthesis in CPS because of the high computational complexity. The complexity can be significantly reduced due to the transition from single-level to multi-level models. Attempts to build such multilevel models in program systems revealed a considerable number of problems. To solve them it is necessary to state the problem, to develop formal models and methods, define new technology of data processing and evaluation. It is expected that new multilevel systems can overcome the drawbacks of existing single level systems.

In this chapter, the general ideas of multilevel monitoring are considered. These ideas are translated into a multilevel automatic synthesis technology which includes new methods for multilevel synthesis of objects and systems, processes and programs for monitoring based on the results of data processing. For processing monitoring data, a new ontology-based knowledge model is proposed. At last, the architecture of the CPS monitoring system using the proposed technology is presented.

BACKGROUND

Cyber-physical systems operate alongside, for the benefit of, and supported by humans. The approaches to modeling and reasoning about human involvement in socio-cyber-physical systems (SCPS) have become a popular topic (Calinescu, R. C., et al. 2019). Zavyalova, Y. V., et al. (2017) combined this concept with the cyber-medicine system to discuss the development of smart spaces-based socio-cyber-medicine systems. Smirnov, A., et al. (2017, June) addressed context-aware decision support in agent-based environments for smart space-based systems and human-computer cloud services. This method deal well with the highly decentralized up-to-date data sets arriving from various resources located in socio-cyber physical systems.

Most of the existing monitoring systems use intelligent components that are aimed to solve analytical tasks and visualize data (Albahri, O. S. 2018). By now a considerable number of such components have been developed, including Zabbix Monitoring (Dalle Vacche, A. 2015), Pentaho Reports (Gorman, W. 2009), Google Analytics (Plaza, B. 2009) and so on (Nasle, A. 2017; Luo, H. 2015).

Recently some new monitoring systems have been developed. Most of them are problem-oriented systems. Chakravarthi, M. K., etc. (2015) presented an accelerometer-based static gesture recognition and mobile monitoring system using neural networks. Bello, J. P., et al. (2018) proposed a system for the monitoring, analysis, and mitigation of urban noise. The project includes a distributed network of both sensors and people for large-scale noise monitoring. Dejan Dovžan, et al. (2015) proposed the implementation of an evolving fuzzy model in a monitoring system for a waste-water treatment process. The method uses basic evolving mechanisms to add and remove clusters and the mechanism to adapt the clusters' and local models' parameters. Nguyen, T. (2017, May) proposed a modeling and simulation-based engineering approach that can address the challenges of large and complex Socio-CPS. The proposed approach relies on constraints models that specify envelopes of required or assumed behaviors, and that can be applied at any phase of the system lifecycle.

The complexity and the diversity of the observed objects and system made the researchers focus their attention on building reconfigurable monitoring systems that can act operatively. Vangheluwe, H. (2018, May) presented the concept of Multi-paradigm Modeling (MPM) for CPS. It proposes to model every part and aspect of such complex systems explicitly, at the most appropriate level(s) of abstraction, using the most appropriate modeling formalism(s). To help guarantee system quality and compliance during both design time and runtime adaptations, Anda, A. (2018, August) proposed to translate goal and feature models to mathematical functions used to validate the possible design and adaptation alternatives both during simulations at design time and adaptations at runtime.

Building a reconfigurable system is an effective solution to the CPS monitoring problem. Stefanov, K., etc. (2015) proposed a dynamically reconfigurable distributed modular monitoring system that allows different parts of the monitoring system to process only the data needed for the task assigned to these parts. Mamun, M. A. A., et al. (2016) presented a theoretical model and implementation of a real-time intelligent bin status monitoring system using rule-based decision algorithms. The elementary concept is that smart bins collect their status when any changes occur and transmit the status data to a server via an intermediate coordinator. A set of applications in the server presents the updated bin status in real-time.

The principal limitation for the further development of existing systems is their weak capabilities to synthesize the models of the observed objects and to synthesize the processes and programs for monitoring on the base of initial data received from the observed objects. These limitations are caused by the high complexity of the processes of synthesis. Nowadays three approaches that can be used for model synthesis: emergence, symbolic and hybrid (Kotseruba, I. & Tsotsos, J.K. (2018)).

Emergent methods for synthesizing models of observed objects and their characteristic processes involve the use of learning neural networks. According to these methods, the signals received from the observed objects are transformed in a certain way to match the input of the neural network. Then the signals are associatively processed by the neural network in accordance with the rules of its functioning. Note that neural networks in self-learning phase synthesize models of perceived events (signals) within themselves. These models can be formed in neural networks in the form of associatively memorized spatio-temporal relationships. In the future, these models can be used to solve filtering and signal recognition problems, predicting events, controlling external devices and other tasks., The possibilities of synthesizing event models by neural networks depend on their structures and methods of intellectual information processing, approaches to implementing these networks. The most promising for the synthesis of the models of observed objects are recurrent neural networks (RNN).

However, most of such networks are not applicable for deep and quick processing of continuous streams of heterogeneous signals. In particular, the Hopfield Neural Networks process the information deeply, but not quickly (S.Haykin (2006)). Known real-time Recurrent Neural Networks operate quickly, but don't implement deeply associative processing (Pentti Haikonen (2009); Günther Palm (2013) Jerome Feldman (2013); Anne Treisman (1996); S.Haykin (2006)). Recently new ideas of building recurrent neural networks for deep operational processing have been proposed (Osipov V.&Osipova M. (2018); Osipov V.& Nikiforov V. (2018); Osipov V. (2016); Osipov V. (2017)). The RNNs are recurrent neural networks with controlled elements. The layers of these networks can be endowed with various logical structures. The networks also provide control of associative signal interactions. There is every indication that new networks will be successfully applied to model synthesis, but they need reducing the complexity of their software and hardware implementation.

Symbolic methods can also be used for model synthesis. Many researchers have been working in this field. A considerable number of symbolic systems have been developed, including SOAR (Laird, John E. 2012), MIDAS (B. F. Gore. et al. 2009), Disciple (Michael Glodek. et al. 2015), ICARUS (Perlovsky L. I. 2007), ARCADIA (G. Tecuci, M. et al. 2000). The common drawbacks of these systems are the weakness of self-learning ability, lack of association ability and others. Within the symbolic approach, it is proposed to use a multilevel data fusion model as the backbone of symbolic systems (P. Langley and D. Choi. 2006; W. Bridewell &P. F. Bello. 2015). These ideas have significantly extended the potential capabilities of the symbolic approach, but still, symbolic systems lack flexibility. As a result, they are able to solve only specific tasks.

The above methods are effective when the observed object has a single level, simple structure. However, it is still a challenge of CPS monitoring to synthesis the models of complex observed objects. A general and low complexity approach is required. In this chapter, we propose a multilevel automatic synthesis technology to solve the CPS monitoring problem.

PROBLEM OF CPS MONITORING

The physical objects under monitoring usually have a complex internal structure. They contain dozens, hundreds, and sometimes thousands of elements that are related to each other. They are linked and constantly interacting. Interactions lead to heterogeneity of objects in general. Sometimes the objects can be elements of other objects. The environment can have a significant impact on the state and behavior of these objects.

Common (General, Usual) object models are built under difficult conditions: lack of general information about the objects and the environment, absence of models of related objects, limited resources for data collection and processing. These situations make it difficult to the formed models.

The complexity of solving monitoring problems in CPMS significantly depends on characteristics of the input data. The main properties of the data are the following.

- **The structural complexity of the data stream.** Both active and passive means of observation are used for data collection. These means can be embedded in the object or located at significant distances. The collected data is organized in the form of streams. Such streams have a complex internal structure. In many cases, it is difficult to detect the structure. Usually, streams come in real time and have large volumes.

- **Multidimensionality of data, multiple relations between data elements.** The data received from the objects are the results of measurements of the parameters values. Parameters characterize the elements of the objects. There are many dependencies between the parameters, including unobvious ones.
- **Lack of direct information about the objects.** Commonly it is possible to get only indirect information about the states of the objects through observing its separate parameters. The characteristics of the objects can be restored based on the results of parameters measurements.

Gathered data about the objects and the environment can be used to build models of the objects that reflect their current state. Requirements to the output models define target models of the objects. Target models also take into account existing restrictions such as admissible modeling time, accuracy and reliability of models, available resources, etc. The processes and programs of object monitoring should allow building target object models given current object models.

Formally the monitoring problem can be defined in the following way. It is necessary to build processes and programs of monitoring using models of observed objects:

$$PR \,/\, PRG : O'(D) \rightarrow O^{*},$$

where O' - current object models, O^{*} - target object models, D - data about the object and the environment, PR - processes of monitoring, PRG - programs of monitoring. Processes define additional data that should be gathered about the objects. The programs are files with the commands to sensors to measure the required parameters.

CPS MONITORING CONCEPT

CPS Monitoring Basics

CPS monitoring based on building models of the observed objects assumes four main steps: gathering data about the observed object and processing of gathered data, synthesis of object models using the results of data processing, building models of monitoring processes taking into account the parameters of the synthesized models, building monitoring programs for data gathering according to monitoring processes.

Step 1: Gathering data about the observed object and processing of gathered data. Initial data received from the objects are presented in a form of data streams. Data processing assumes the transformation of initial heterogeneous data to the homogeneous form, revealing informational elements from the streams and their identification. Usually, it is hard to guarantee the quality of the results of data processing because of the complexity of the process. An evaluation process based on information criteria is used to provide feedback on the processing results. According to the feedback processes of data processing can be rebuilt.

Step 2: For building models, the obtained data elements are bind. Data elements and revealed links between them are presented using formal structures. These structures are considered as current models of objects.

Step 3: Having a current model and a target model possible transitions between them are investigated. In order to build transitions, the data received from the object is used. If the required data is not available, it should be gathered. Thus, the sets of additional expected data are defined. According to the processes for monitoring are build.

Step 4: Monitoring programs are generated on the base of monitoring processes. Programs are transmitted to the technical devices for execution. The new data allow the rebuilding of the current model. Then the steps are repeated.

The results of CPS monitoring can be estimated using various performance indicators such as the duration of the control cycle, the time and accuracy of the synthesis of programs and processes for managing monitoring tools. The effectiveness of individual monitoring tools and the processes they implement can be assessed both by their own indicators and by indicators of the systems of which they are an integral part.

It is worth noting that such a monitoring process is more suitable for complex observed objects. The interaction and processing process for simple objects is simpler and easier to be implemented. This paper assumes that the observed objects are complex and have multiple levels of structure.

CPS Monitoring Model

The structure of the proposed CPS model is shown in Figure 1.

The model consists of four main elements: repository, automata models of observed objects management (AMOM), automata models of monitoring processes and programs management (APPM), automata for monitoring management (AMM).

Repository. Repository contains synthesized current and target models of the observed object, models of monitoring processes, monitoring programs. It also contains models of gathered data and other data, required for monitoring management.

Automata models of observed objects management. It is an engine that processes data about the object and the environment, builds the models of the object or rebuilds them using the results of data processing. Input data for the automata are initial data streams received from the object. Output data are the models of the object, that reflect its current state. AMOM also defines the target models according to the requirements of end users.

Automata models of monitoring processes and programs management. Input data for the automata are current and target models of the observed object. The automata compare this two models and reveals possible transitions from current model to the target. To make the transitions additional data can be required. Gathering data requires new monitoring processes. Defined monitoring processes are the then converted to monitoring programs.

Automata for monitoring management. The automata manage the activities of the AMOM and AMPM. All input signals from the external world are coming to the entrance of AMM. It can be requests from end users, information that the new data about the observed objects is available, information about the changes in the environment and other. Signals can also come from AMOM and AMPM. The automata is functioning in the following way. It defines the processes of objects monitoring and activates both automata. When AMM gets new signals it can activate new processes in AMOM or AMPM. AMOM is activated each time new data is received. It rebuilds the models of the objects. AMPM is activated

Figure 1. CPS monitoring model

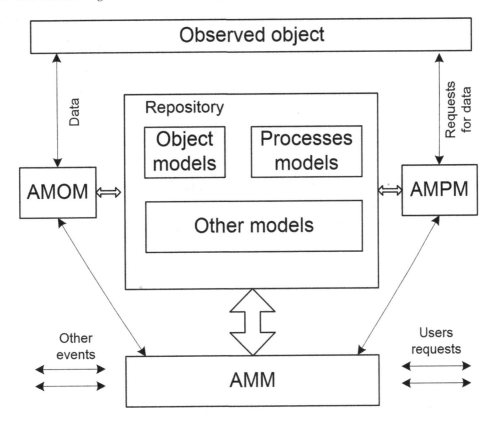

when the current or target model changes. If the models don't match AMPM defines new processes for data gathering.

CPS Monitoring Process

CPS monitoring process assumes that synthesis is executed at multiple levels and the synthesized models have multilevel structure. These levels can be the following: 'level of objects parameters', 'level of objects nodes and aggregates', 'level of objects subsystems and systems', 'level of the whole object'. It is admissible to define many other levels. Their number and composition completely depends on the monitoring tasks and conditions in which they are solved.

Multilevel structure of the objects allows describe them at different levels of granularity. At each level data is represented in its own feature spaces. The tasks of building models are considered at many levels. At high levels, rough solutions are formed. Their inconsistency is taken into account at lower levels.

The CPS monitoring process relies upon the technologies of data processing and its results evaluation. Building different data representations assumes using different data processing techniques. To choose a technique it is necessary to consider the requirements to data representations that are build and the conditions of data processing. The results of data processing are estimated. In case of the inappropriate results other techniques are used for data processing.

The implementation of a technology for building the described CPS monitoring process will provide a set of advantages. First, it has high potential to reduce the computational complexity. This possibility is ensured by the multilevel approach to modeling. Second, the technology allows performing system analyses of objects states. It is provided due to describing observed objects through dependencies between their elements. Third, it has a very intelligent working mechanism. It is achieved through the capabilities of the technology to build, rebuild models of the objects and manage the processes of model building.

To implement technology, it is required to develop new multilevel models and methods of synthesis, new models for data processing and new criteria for data processing results estimation.

MODELS AND METHODS FOR MULTILEVEL SYNTHESIS

Multilevel Models of Observed Objects, Monitoring Processes and Programs

The multilevel model of the observed object can be described as set of five parameters:

```
<Model>::= {<Sets of input data> <Sets of output data> <State of the model>
<Transitions between model states>},
<State of the model>:: = {<General state of the model> <Current structure of
the model>},
<Current structure>:: = {<Elements> <Links>}.
```

Sets of input data are the fragments of data streams received from the observed objects. Sets of output data define data elements that can be reached from the current state of the model having input data.

The state of the model is defined as the general state of the model and the current structure of the model. General state of the model is defined according to the states of its elements. The structure of the model reflects the structure of the observed object. It describes the object as the set of data elements and links between them. In the structure multiple levels are defined. Data elements refer to different levels of the structure. The elements of the higher levels can be described with the set of elements at lower levels. The links are defined between separate elements and group of elements. They reflect internal relationships intrinsic to the object.

The transitions from one state of the model to the other can be described with different functions that characterize the behavior of the observed objects.

For the parameters of the model admissible sets of their values are defined. These sets are rebuild at each step of model synthesize.

The parameters and the admissible sets of the parameters are defined at each level of the model.

The models of the objects can be described in the form of relatively finite operational automata.

The model of the processes of monitoring can be defined as

```
<Monitoring process model>::= {<Set of data elements>[<Data processing param-
eters>]},
<Data element>:: = {<Identifier> <Parameters of data gathering>}.
```

Monitoring process model defines the set of data elements that are required to synthesize the target model of the object. For each data element parameters for its gathering are defined. They can be frequency, accuracy of measurements and etc. In a number of cases there is a need to preprocess gathered data before transferring it. Such preprocessing allows reduce the amount of transferred data.

For formal representation of the models of the processes graphs of work streams can be used (Rudnitckaia, J. 2015).

Monitoring process model can be defined for different levels of objects models.

Models of the monitoring programs depends on the program language perceived by physical devices. Usually scripting languages are used.

Models of the received data describe initial data and results of its processing. They can be defined in a following way:

```
<Data model>::={<Initial data> <Data representations>},
<Data representation>::= {<Data representation description> <Data elements
representation>},
< Data representation description >::= {<Feature space> <Parent representa-
tions> <Processing technique>}.
```

Data representation assumes that the data about the objects is described in a new feature space. Both initial data and existing data representations can be transformed to a new feature space. If existing representations are used for building a new one, then they are considered as parent representations. Transformation from one feature space to another is performed using one of the data processing techniques. Thus, data model is multilevel structure that contains multiple data representations.

Models of the received data and are represented in the form of ontologies.

The data that is required for managing the processes of model synthesis is the data referred to the domain of data processing and analyses. These data allow build data processes for processing gathered data. It is also represented in the form of ontologies.

Method of Models Synthesis

The method of models assumes combined usage of inductive and deductive synthesis. Inductive synthesis allows build local models of objects using fragments of received data streams. Deductive synthesis allows generalize local models and build on the base of them global models.

The synthesized models are represented in the form of multilevel relatively finite automata (Osipov, V. Y., et al. 2017; Osipov, V. Y., et al. 2017, May). Each level of automata is characterized by the sets of input data elements d_a, output data elements d_c, internal states d_b, transition functions between internal states F_b, output functions F_c and the corresponding sets of the admissible values of the parameters DA, DB, DC, FB, FC. For the automata states and functions predicates can be defined.

Transition functions define conditions for linking data elements from the sets of input data with the elements from the sets of output data. For these conditions statuses S can be defined. A condition can be considered as pre condition, post condition or main condition. Functions can be of different kinds z and different types v.

For multilevel automata models admissible sets of parameters are defined at multiple levels: DA^i, DB^i, DC^i, FB^i, FC^i, where i is the level, $i \in \left[0, \overline{L}\right]$, L - the number of levels. The lowest level is the zero level. At this level the parameters of the automata are defined using initial data.

Method of Inductive Synthesis of Models of the Observed Objects

The task of inductive synthesis is to build local models of objects in the form of multilevel automata. Inductive synthesis involves the processing of particular examples and the transition to a common solution. A local model M is build using a fragment of data stream received from the object during time interval Ts. The process of building model assumes building a set of models for subintervals of time interval Ts. For building each of the models initial data is processed in order to reveal data elements and links between them. The parameters of automata models of objects for subintervals are defined according to revealed data elements and links. Predicates of automata states and functions reflect the conditions in which the elements and links have been observed in initial data.

The result local model for the whole time interval Ts is constructed on the base of models build for subintervals. According to the structure of the model M statuses for transition and output functions are defined. They set relations between different functions.

The pseudo code of the method of inductive synthesis is the following:

Method of Deductive Synthesis of Models of the Observed Objects

The task of deductive synthesis assumes building global models of objects on the base of local models.

Global models reflect the state and the behavior of the object at piecewise stationary time intervals. Within piecewise stationary time interval Tp object state and behavior can change several times.

Within the global model links between elements of local models are defined. The links are characterized by functions of different kinds and types. Synthesized global models of the observed objects are presented in the form of multilevel automata.

Global models can be considered at different scales. The scale s of a model depends on the length of the time interval for which the model is build.

Method Description: The pseudo code of the method of deductive synthesis is the following:

Method of Synthesis of Models of Monitoring Processes and Programs

The method of synthesis of monitoring processes assumes building sequences of transitions between two states of the object defined in the form of local models. The first model is the current model of the object, the second model is the target model of the object. A theorem on the existence of the target model is formulated. To proof the theorem direct inference is used. The inference is based on the elements and functions defined in global models. In the conditions, when the required sequence was not found, the possibility of changing the target models can be considered.

For formal representation of the monitoring processes a workflow model is used. Within this model each process is described by the set of data elements {ds} defined in the current model of the object, the set of data elements {dw} defined in the target model of the object and transition functions Fzv that

Table 1.

function InductiveSynthesis	
1	**inputs:** prosessingResults, computationConditions
2	**outputs:local model M**
3	//Build separate models for subintervals of Ts
4	$[t_1,...,t_N] = split(Ts)$
5	$[M_1,...,M_N] = initializeModels(N)$
6	**for each** j in $[1,...,N]$ **do**
7	**for each** l in $[0,...,L]$ **do**
8	{l -> [element]} = *extractElements*(prosessinResults)
9	{l -> [relations]} = *extractRelations*(prosessinResults)
10	Mj::{l -> [da]j} = *computeInputElements*({l -> [element]}[l])
11	Mj::{l -> [db]j} = *computeOutputElements*({l -> [element]}[l])
12	Mj::{l -> [dc]j} = *computeInternalStates*({l -> [element]}[l])
13	Mj::{l -> [Fb]j} = *computeTransitionFunctions*({l->[relation]}[l])
14	Mj::{l -> [Fc]j} = *computeOutputFunctions*({l->[relation]}[l])
15	Mj::[C]j = *computeConditions*(computationConditions)
16	**end**
17	**end**
18	//Build model for interval Ts on the base of separate models
19	**for each** l in $[0,...,L]$ **do**
20	M::{l -> [da]} = *computeInputElements*([$M_1,...,M_N$]::{l -> [da]}[l])
21	M::{l -> [db]} = *computeOutputElements*([$M_1,...,M_N$]::{l -> [db]}[l])
22	M::{l -> [dc]} = *computeInternalStates*([$M_1,...,M_N$]::{l -> [dc]}[l])
23	M::{l -> [Fb]} = *computeTransitionFunctions*([$M_1,...,M_N$]::{l -> [Fb]}[l])
24	M::{l -> [Fc]} = *computeOutputFunctions*([$M_1,...,M_N$]::{l -> [Fc]}[l])
25	**end**
26	**for each** l in $[0,...,L]$ **do**
27	{l -> [DA]} = *computeAdmissibleInputElements*(M::{l -> [da]}[l])
28	{l -> [DB]} = *computeAdmissibleOutputElements*(M::{l -> [db]}[l])
29	{l -> [DC]} = *computeAdmissibleInternalStates*(M::{l -> [dc]}[l])
30	{l -> [FB]} = *computeAdmissibleTransitionFunctions*(M::{l -> [Fb]}[l])
31	{l -> [FC]} = *computeAdmissibleOutputFunctions*(M::{l -> [Fc]}[l])
32	**for each** k in $[1,...,L]$ **do**
33	[links] = computeLevelLinks(k-1, k)
34	{l -> [FBx]} = *computeXAdmissibleTransitionFunctions*([links])
35	{l -> [FCx]} = *computeXAdmissibleOutputFunctions*([links])
36	**end**
37	**end**
38	//Define status for transition and output functions
39	**for each** z in $[1,...,Z]$ **do**
40	**for each** v in $[1,...,V]$ **do**
41	**for each** l in $[0,...,L]$ **do**
42	{FB -> l -> s^i_{zn}}= *computeFunctionstatus*({l -> [FB]}[l])
43	**end**
44	**end**
45	end

Table 2.

function DeductiveSynthesis **is**	
1	**inputs:** local models, Tp, funTypes, funKinds, Ms
2	**outputs: model M**
1	M = initializeGlobalModel(maxLevel) /* max level of local models Ms */
2	M.vsFuns = cartesianProduct(funTypes, funKinds) /* array of functions, where each function is a function of type v and kind z */
3	M.Tp = Tp
4	/* identify transition functions to link elements within one level of global model */
5	**for each** l **in** [1..maxLevel] **do**
6	**for each** f **in** [0.. M.vsFuns.lenth] **do**
7	M.vzLevelLinkingFuns[l] = unionOf(vzLevelLinkingFuns[l], testFunctionOnLinkingElements(elements[l], M.vsFuns[f])) /* elements of local models */
8	**End**
9	**for each** i **in** [0..vzLevelLinkingFuns[l].length] **do**
10	M.Parameters[l][i] = findParameters(vzLevelLinkingFuns[l][i])
11	**end**
12	**End**
13	/* parameterize transition functions to link elements within different levels */
14	**for each** l **in** [1..maxLevel] **do**
15	**for each** k **in** [1..maxLevel] **do**
16	**if** l != k **do**
17	**for each** f **in** [1.. M.vsFuns.lenth] **do**
18	M.vzInterLevelLinkingFuns[l] = unionOf(vzInterLevelLinkingFuns[l], testFunctionOnLinkingElements(elements[l], elements[k], M.vsFuns[f]))
19	**end**
20	**end**
21	**end**
22	**for each** i **in** [0..vzInterLevelLinkingFuns[l].length] **do**
23	M.Parameters[l][i] = findParameters(vzInterLevelLinkingFuns[l][i])
24	**end**
25	**end**
26	/* define conditions for identified transition functions */
27	**for each** l **in** [1..maxLevel] **do**
28	M.vzLinkingFun[l] = unionOf(vzLevelLinkingFuns[l], vzInterLevelLinkingFuns[l])
29	**for each** i **in** [0..vzLinkingFun[l].length] **do**
30	M.funConditions[l][i] = computeConditions(vzLinkingFun[l][i])
31	**end**
32	**end**
33	/* compute admissible sets for global automata model */
34	
35	**for each** l **in** [0.. maxLevel] **do**
36	M.DA[l] = *computeAdmissibleInputElements*(M.da[l])
37	M.DB[l] = *computeAdmissibleOutputElements*(M.db[l])
38	M.DC[l] = *computeAdmissibleInternalStates*(M.dc[l])
39	M.FB[l] = *computeAdmissibleTransitionFunctions*(M.Fb[l])

continued on following page

Table 2. Continued

40	M.FC[l] = *computeAdmissibleOutputFunctions*(M.Fc[l])
41	**for each** k **in** [1.. maxLevel] **do**
42	**if** k != l **do**
43	links = computeInterLevelLinks(l, k)
44	M.FBx[l][k] = *computeExtendedAdmissibleTransitionFunctions*(links)
45	M.FCx[l][k] = *computeExtendedAdmissibleOutputFunctions*(links)
46	**end**
47	**end**
48	**end**
49	/* scale global model */
50	**if** Ms.length > 0 **do** /* if there are some previous global models */
51	**for** m **in** [0..Ms] **do**
52	**if** isContain(M.Tp, m.Tp) **do**
53	M.SpecFb = computeTransitionFunctions(M.Elements, m.elements)
54	M.SpecFb.v = 'specification function'
55	**end**
56	**if** isContain(m.Tp, M.Tp) **do**
57	M.GeneralFb = computeTransitionFunctions(M.Elements, m.elements)
58	M.SpecFb.v = generalization function'
59	**end**
60	**end**
61	**end**
62	**return** M

reflect links between elements of the models: Fzv(dzve) ->(dzva), where $e = \begin{bmatrix} 1, Ez \end{bmatrix}$ indicates elements of the models that are required to achieved an element indicated as dzva.

Method Description: The pseudo code of the method of synthesis of models of monitoring processes is the following:

The models of the programs are built on the base of the models of monitoring processes. They are extracted from the results of the proof of the theorem on the existence of the target model using backward inference.

The representation of monitoring programs is similar to representation of monitoring processes, but transition functions are substituted with program structure elements.

The resulting program is a sequence of program structure elements that can be converted to program code written using scripting languages.

MODEL FOR MONITORING DATA PROCESSING

The synthesis of models is based on the results of data processing. The processes of data processing can be specified only for some certain conditions. When the conditions change, the processes must be rebuilt. Due to the complexity of the processes effective data processing requires usage of knowledge.

Table 3.

function FindAchievableElements(maxLevel, M, CurrentM, TargetM) is	
1	**for each** l **in** [maxLevel..0] **do**
2	**for each** i **in** [0..M.funConditions[l].length] **do**
3	**if** checkCondition(M.funConditions[l][i]) == **true do**
4	elementPairs = cartesianProduct(CurrentM.Elements[l], TargetM.Elements[l])
5	**for each** j **in** [0..elementPairs.length]
6	**if** profTransition(M.vzLinkingFun[l][i](elementPairs[j].first, elementPairs[j].second) == **true do**
7	M.AchievedFrom[l] = add(M.AchievedFrom[l], elementPairs[j].first)
8	M.AchievedTo[l] = add(M.AchievedTo[l], elementPairs[j].first)
9	M.AchievedWith[l] = add(M.AchievedWith[l], M.vzLinkingFun[l][i])
10	M.AchivedWhile[l] = add(M.AchivedWhile[l], checkCondition[l][i])
11	remove(M.NonProven[l+1], elementPairs[j].second)
12	**else**
13	M.NonProven[l]= add(M.NonProven[l], elementPairs[j].second)
14	**end**
15	**if** M.NonProven[l].length != 0 && maxLevel != 0 **do**
16	FindAchievableElements(maxLevel-1, M, CurrentM, TargetM)
17	**end**
18	**return** M

We represent the knowledge about data processing in a form of a model (Tianxing, M., & Zhukova, N. 2018). It describes and links the data characteristics, users' requirements and corresponding data processing solutions.

Basic Structure of the Model for Monitoring Data Processing

The knowledge model is used to select the appropriate solution for data processing based on the characteristics of the monitoring data and users' requirements. In order to ensure the integrity of the set of processing schemes, we integrate the existing taxonomies of data processing algorithms (Abanda, A., et al. 2019; Susto, G. A., et al. 2018). In addition, data pre-processing techniques and data representation methods are also described in the model as important parts of data processing knowledge. It also includes fundamental mathematics knowledge about data processing for presenting the details of related algorithms. The monitoring data are described in the model as corresponding data features. Logical relationships are defined to make the knowledge model more functional.

Structure of the Model

Within the knowledge model, dataset characteristics and task requirements define the conditions for algorithm selection. Suitable models, measures and algorithms are selected based on these conditions. Description of the algorithms contains information that allows defining their parameters and executing

Figure 2. Basic Structure of the model for monitoring data processing (ML-Algorithm: machine learning algorithm)

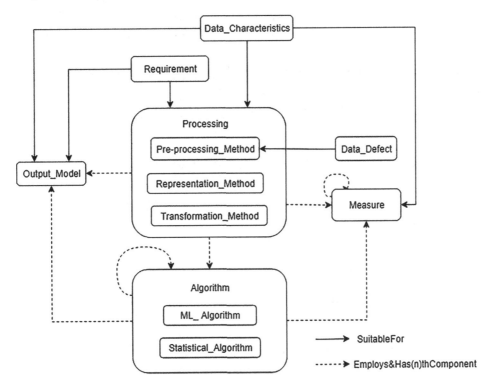

them. In this model, we use "component" to indicate the actions of a process, such as algorithms, output models, measures etc. The results of processing are estimated using information measures. In case the results don't meet the requirements, then other algorithms are selected.

The structure of the knowledge model is shown in Figure 2.

In order to use enable the knowledge model in practical applications, the model is represented as an ontology.

The ontological model contains several main classes:

- **Processing:** This is the main class of the ontology. Pre-processing methods, representation methods, and transformation methods are the subclasses of this class.
- **Algorithm:** The algorithms used in the processes of data processing and related statistical knowledge are described in this class. It provides a variety of taxonomies to classify these algorithms so that they can be evaluated from different perspectives. ML_Algorithm presents the machine learning algorithms which are usually used to transform the data into knowledge (object model). And Statistical_Algorithm presents the basic models and functions of statistics. They are the main components of ML algorithms which can explain the Algorithmic details to users.
- **Data_characteristics/Data_Defect:** These two classes are used to describe the processed data in the ontology. Data_Defect is corresponding to the pre-processing methods. And Data_Characteristics contains various information about data such as size, correlation, redundancy etc. The selection of suitable algorithms depends on this information.

- **Requirement:** This class describes the users' requirements to the results of data processing.
- **Output_Model/Measure**: The models and measures are the cores of data processing processes, so they are the main factors why processes possess different performance for different situations. These two classes can help the user choose suitable algorithms for data processing.

These classes describe the knowledge about data processing. It is a comprehensive and extendable description that allow receive enough information to build and rebuild data processing processes.

In this knowledge model, object property and data property are used for description of logic and knowledge.

- Object properties that describe logic relations are as follow:
  - subclassOf is a typical relation in ontology and taxonomy. It makes the hierarchy of algorithms and data clearer. Many taxonomies are integrated into the ontology of data processing using this relation;
  - employ is used to link the methods and algorithms in class Processing/Algorithm to measures, models, and other algorithms.
  - has(n)thComponent is used to link the methods and algorithms and their components to describe the processes. The processing sequence of the components is presented by assigning the value of n.
  - suitableFor is used to provide advice about solution selection by linking the solutions (Processing/Algorithm) with the situation (Data and Requirement). The relation "suitableFor" is based on the theory base and the previous experimental results (Bagnall, A., et al. 2017; Fawaz, H. I., et al. 2019; Lhermitte, S., 2011).
- Data property is used to describe the value and range of the parameters of classes. They clarity the restrictions of values on the class to distinguish them from each other.

Workflow for Data Processing

On the base of object property defined in the ontology, a user can choose the suitable solution for data processing. As Figure 3 shows, the workflow of building processes for monitoring data processing using the suggested model is as follow:

1. Obtain user requirements and extract the characteristics of the data set
2. Convert them into the entries in ontology
3. Get the corresponding set of suitable algorithms
4. Extract the intersection of the sets
5. If the intersection does not exist, Plan A is to delete the least important entry and then performs step 4; Plan B is directly to select the algorithms which are suitable for the most important condition.
6. Output the selected algorithms.
7. (Optional) Describe the selected algorithm based on the outward links(*has(n)thComponent*).

Since the data characteristics connect their available solutions with the object property *suitableFor* in the ontology, users don't need check all the candidate algorithms.

Figure 3. The workflow of building data processing processes

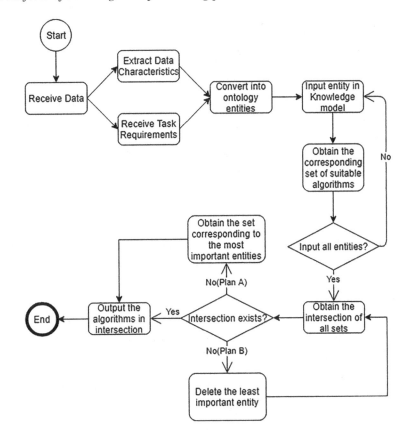

Main Features of the Model

The distinguishing features of the proposed knowledge model are the following

- This model contains knowledge about data processing for different kinds of data types. This is appropriate for the situation of data processing in CPS monitoring. The monitoring data comes from different sensors so that they have different characteristics. There are no perfect algorithms which are suitable for all the situations. So, the model can support the process of choosing suitable algorithms for each situation in CPS monitoring.
- This model contains hundreds of machine learning algorithms and data preprocessing methods and provides measurement functions, representation methods and mathematics models for data processing. It contains as much knowledge as possible about all types of data processing.
- This model is based on ontology technology so that it is easy to extend when a new machine learning algorithm is proposed, or new data characteristics are considered.
- It can be released for anyone to use and improve. Currently, it is similar to a framework that continues to enrich its content as one uses it.
- This model can provide suggestions for the entire process including preprocessing methods and data processing algorithms. It makes up for the lack of overview of preprocessing techniques.

Figure 4. CPMS exploitation scheme

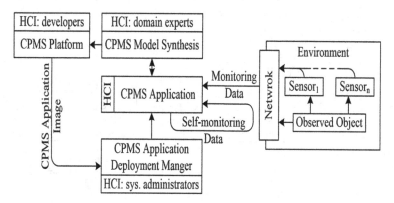

- With the description of the process of the algorithms and methods, user could understand the algorithmic details. This is useful for the non-experts.

Data Processing Indicators

For a comprehensive assessment of the effectiveness of data processing in CPS monitoring, various indicators can be used. They can refer to initial data, results of data processing and the model of the process of data processing (Zhukova, N. et al. 2019). They are based on Kolmogorov complexity (Kolmogorov, A. N. 1965), Shannon entropy (Shannon, C. E. 1948), Hartley entropy (Hartley, R. V. L. 1928).

The effectiveness of data processing can also be estimated at the level of solving monitoring tasks. At this level the indicators can be the average time, accuracy and quality of output results, their complexity, reliability, integrity, required material and human resources.

CPMS ARCHITECTURE

CPMS Exploitation Scheme

A general scheme of CPMS application exploitation is presented in Figure 4.

CPMS Application is a process executing in a particular runtime environment. It receives results of monitoring through a *Network* infrastructure from an observed object's operating *Environment* and from the *Observed Object* itself. Also, it receives *Self-Monitoring Data* including the ones produced by the runtime environment. Through *HCI* (Human-Computer Interaction) it interacts with different categories of users: analysts, decision makers, executors, etc. If CPMS application encounters with an "anomaly" monitoring data that cannot be handled by the application itself, it sends it to *CPMS Model Synthesis*. The letter produces new models that can be directly sent back. Or the model can be sent to *CPMS Platform* if some complex computation should be implemented based on synthesized models. The platform builds an executable *CPMS Application Image* that is deployed by the *CPMS Application Manager*.

Figure 5. CPMS application architecture and general algorithm

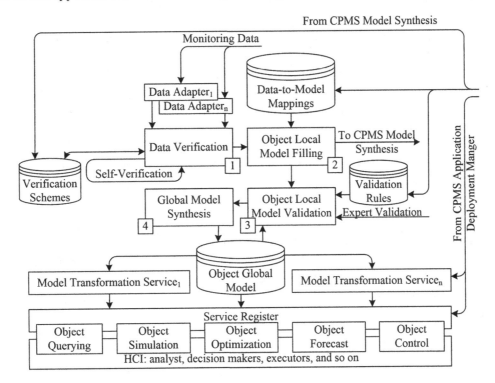

The environment forms an operating context for the observed object: defines a set of constraints for its behavior and directly interacts with it. The environment can be equipped with different kinds of sensors that collect data about the object: visual, audio, and so on. The object also can send some data including those that cannot be directly monitored by environment sensors. All data is sent through the network. There are boundary cases when the object does not send data at all and all information comes from the environment and vice versa.

Based on received monitoring data CPMS application tries to compute models of a user interest. Access to these models is provided through different services forming the HCM system. The most obvious example is querying models by experts.

If received data cannot be interpreted by CPMS application, i.e. no known model can be built (or filled with data), then the "anomaly" data is sent to CPMS model synthesis system that builds new models or corrects known one. If the resulting model just describes the object state and does not suggest any computations, and if it can be filled with data using existing application algorithms then it can be re-sent to CPMS application.

Otherwise, it is sent to the CPMS platform module that generates all necessary instruments and services exploited while the usage of models. These are packed into the CPMS application image that is sent to the CPMS application deployment manager that updates the running application.

CPMS Application Architecture

CPMS application architecture and the general algorithm of its operation are represented in Figure 5.

Main stages of algorithm are represented with numbered rectangles. The work of algorithm starts with receiving *Monitoring Data* from the environment and the observed object(s) (in Figure 5 it is called just *Object* not to clutter up the view)

At the first stage, the received data are verified with the help of schema if the operation is applicable to the kind of data. In the case of self-described data then self-verification is used. The schema can be provided by experts or can be mined from data. If the data are successfully verified it is sent to the next step. Otherwise, two cases are possible. The first one is when the scheme for the data is known, but cannot be applied. Then an error is produced. The second one is when there is no scheme at all. Then it is also sent to the next stage.

At the second stage, the *Object Local Model* is filled with data. To represent models created on the stage some single language is used to gain advantages of unification. The language should be expressive enough. One of the best candidates is an OWL language based on description logic (Krötzsch, Simancik, & Horrocks, 2012). It comes from a realm of so-called Semantic Web. The language has a number of dialects with different levels of expressivity, has a wide community and technological support, and allows building linked knowledge bases.

To fill a model a set of *Data-to-Model mappings* are used that define how data should be organized to satisfy the model: separate pieces of data are transformed to object model elements, their attributes, and connections between them. From this point of view, the process can be represented as a process of filling theory model (TBox, theory box – in term of description logic) with concrete data (ABox, assertion box). If no mapping has been found then the data is unknown, or "anomaly" one, and it is sent to *CPMS Model Synthesis* module.

At the third stage, the object local model is validated against some predefined constraints. These constraints can be somehow extracted (mined) from the data and represented in a form of special *Validation Rules*. In the case of OWL, the restrictions can be represented with OWL axioms, SWRL rules, SPARQL-quires, SHACL or SPIN constraints. The local model can be validated against the current global model of the object: that new state does not contradict to the current state. Also, an expert can be engaged to manually check the model, but the last variant creates a bottleneck within the overall system functioning.

Received validation inconsistencies can be considered as errors or as new data for the object model modification.

At the fourth stage, the object local model is integrated with a previously built model to form an *Object Global Model* that reflects the evolution of the object in time and space.

The global model can be directly used by a number of existing user services. Or it can be transformed with an appropriate *Model Transformation Service* to a new model. These transformations are necessary in cases when the initial form of the model cannot be used because of some reasons. The main one is when there are no appropriate (in terms of performance, usability, simplicity, maintainability, and so on) methods of the model interpretation.

The initial or transformed models are interpreted by different services proving useful functionality to a user: querying, simulation, control, optimization, forecast, and so on.

Errors that can be made at different stages of CPMS working as well as the received results (see paragraph on the evaluation of received results in data processing) are the subjects of self-monitoring.

Figure 6. CPMS model synthesis general algorithm

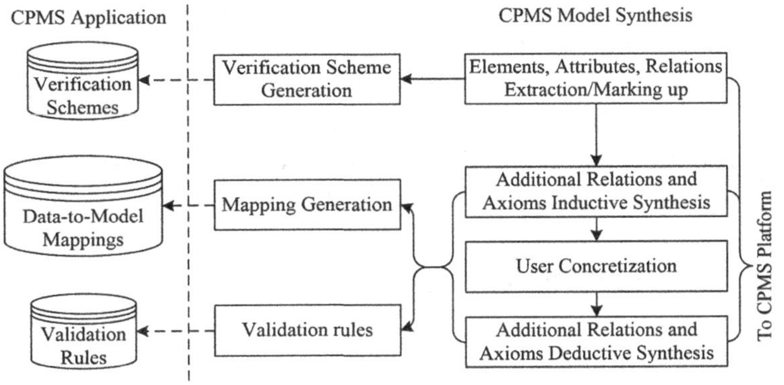

It can be seen from the presented description that CPMS application architecture reminds JDL data fusion (Blasch, 2016) or situation awareness model (Endsley, 2016). The main difference as compared with these models is the interaction with CPMS Model Synthesis module that can lead to the whole CPMS application modification.

CPMS Model Synthesis

The concepts of model synthesis are described in the section – model and methods for multilevel synthesis. The common idea is to extract separate elements of interest from data, their attributes, interconnections, and axioms (restrictions). The general algorithm is represented in Figure 6.

At the first stage of the algorithm, separate elements, their attributes are extracted. Some of this work can be done by an expert – manual marking up. Based on this information, schemes for data verification can be generated and sent to CPMS Application.

At the next stage, some additional relations and axioms are synthesized based on different induction methods: when some hypotheses are built upon data sets.

The received structures can be concretized by a user (expert), e.g. if a positive correlation is found, the user can specify its concrete type.

On the base of this information some additional relations and axioms can be generated as the properties of elements specified by the user.

The generated elements, attributes, relations, and axioms are used to generate data-to-model mappings and validation rules. Also, they are sent to the CPMS Platform to generate programming artifacts.

CPMS Platform

CPMS Platform is used when object models cannot be fully expressed in the frame of chosen general language (e.g. OWL). E.g. there are complex functional dependencies.

The goal of the CPMS Platform is twofold: 1) to generate/choose a transformation that can be used to turn the object model written in the general language to a model in a more appropriate language; 2) to generate/choose service that will implement or interpret the model.

Also, inductive and deductive techniques can be used. In the first case, the "procedural" hypotheses are generated based on separate findings (positive and negative examples). In the second case, proof that the model satisfies some restrictions is fulfilled.

The concrete artifacts of the platform depend upon the chosen architectural approach. The CPMS application can be built as, e.g. a bunch of services or, more specifically, as a multi-agent system. Or it can be a more tightly coupled application. The letter case can, in theory, provide higher performance characteristics, but on the other hand, it needs a more complex deployment process.

CPMS Application Deployment Manager

The manager is used to deploy the newly generated element. As it was said at the end of the previous paragraph the deployment depends upon the chosen architectural approach. In a case of loosely coupled architectures (services, agents) it will be necessary mostly to publish new services so that they can be found at the appropriated stages of CPMS application functioning.

In the case of tightly coupled application, it will be necessary to reconfigure necessary links between separate modules. With a high probability, it may need the restart of the whole system that is not always acceptable.

APPLICATIONS

Authors have applied the proposed technology for several CPS problems. The complexity will be significantly reduced due to considering multi-level objects models instead of single level models. And reconfigurable programs are developed.

In (Osipov, V., et al. 2019, July), authors used the method of automatic synthesis of multilevel automata models to assess the state of patients with surgical pathology in a cavernous sinus during the postoperative period in the operating room and in the cardio-resuscitation unit. As a result, the dependencies among the states of the patients in different studied groups were identified. Usually there is not a uniform cross-cutting method to analyze the data. Non-computer professional researchers spend a lot of time to find the most suitable solution. The proposed technique provides a viable framework to help them analyze and obtain information about objects from different perspectives.

In (Osipov, V., et al. 2017), the approach of multilevel program synthesis was used for generating behavioral programs for smart devices working in sensor networks. The suggested approach was tested on the problem of diagnostic and equipment repairing digital cable TV networks. The implementation is based on an ontological approach. The ontology was used for describing the subject domain and defining repairing instructions using information about parameters that have values different from the reference. The defined sequence of instruction was used for forming scripts. These scripts were loaded into the receiver where they were executed in order to realize diagnostic and repair.

An example which described the solution of the "No Video" problem supported in a monitoring of one of the cable TV operators was presented. The multilevel description of analyzed processes allows divide complex problems into smaller ones, for solving which one can find relatively simple solutions.

CONCLUSION

In this chapter, we propose a new technology for solving problem of CPS monitoring. Existing technologies have been able to solve the modeling problem of simple objects. Our focus is on monitoring complex objects. In particular, it is highly efficient for observation objects with multiple levels of structure. The technology assumes synthesis of object models on the base of the results of data processing. New methods for model synthesis have been developed, new model for data processing has been proposed.

New models and methods develop a multilevel approach to model synthesis. With this approach, the models of the observed objects are synthesized at multiple levels. Due to that, the synthesis of models is reduced to solving a small number of simple problems. Low complexity of each problem is determined by a small number of analyzed conditions.

The model for data processing allows choose appropriates method of initial data processing. It contains knowledge about machine learning algorithms and conditions of their applications. For this data representation methods, mathematical models, data features and output features are also considered in the model. Multiple relations are defined between the elements of the model. With the analysis of data processing algorithms, this technique can provide multi-level descriptions of the states of the observed objects as well as intra- and inter-level dependencies.

This architecture for CPS monitoring has a high intelligence potential. The reconfigurable capability helps the systems to build, rebuild models of the objects and manage the processes of model building.

REFERENCES

Abanda, A., Mori, U., & Lozano, J. A. (2019). A review on distance based time series classification. *Data Mining and Knowledge Discovery*, *33*(2), 378–412. doi:10.100710618-018-0596-4

Albahri, O. S., Albahri, A. S., Mohammed, K. I., Zaidan, A. A., Zaidan, B. B., Hashim, M., & Salman, O. H. (2018). Systematic review of real-time remote health monitoring system in triage and priority-based sensor technology: Taxonomy, open challenges, motivation and recommendations. *Journal of Medical Systems*, *42*(5), 80. doi:10.100710916-018-0943-4 PMID:29564649

Anda, A. (2018, August). Modeling Adaptive Socio-Cyber-Physical Systems with Goals and SysML. In *2018 IEEE 26th International Requirements Engineering Conference (RE)* (pp. 442-447). IEEE. 10.1109/RE.2018.00059

Bagnall, A., Lines, J., Bostrom, A., Large, J., & Keogh, E. (2017). The great time series classification bake off: A review and experimental evaluation of recent algorithmic advances. *Data Mining and Knowledge Discovery*, *31*(3), 606–660. doi:10.100710618-016-0483-9 PMID:30930678

Bello, J. P., Silva, C., Nov, O., Dubois, R. L., Arora, A., Salamon, J., & ... . (2018). Sonyc: A system for the monitoring, analysis and mitigation of urban noise pollution. *Communications of the ACM*.

Blasch, E. (2016). *JDL Model (III) Updates for an Information Management Enterprise*. Academic Press.

Bridewell, W., & Bello, P. (2015). *Incremental Object Perception in an Attention-Driven Cognitive Architecture*. CogSci.

Calinescu, R. C., Camara Moreno, J., & Paterson, C. (2019). Socio-Cyber-Physical Systems: Models, Opportunities, Open Challenges. *5th International Workshop on Software Engineering for Smart Cyber-Physical Systems.*

Chakravarthi, M. K., Tiwari, R. K., & Handa, S. (2015). Accelerometer based static gesture recognition and mobile monitoring system using neural networks. *Procedia Computer Science, 70,* 683-687.

Dalle Vacche, A. (2015). *Mastering Zabbix.* Packt Publishing Ltd.

Dovžan, D., Logar, V., & Skrjanc, I. (2015). Implementation of an evolving fuzzy model (efumo) in a monitoring system for a waste-water treatment process. *IEEE Transactions on Fuzzy Systems, 23*(5), 1761–1776. doi:10.1109/TFUZZ.2014.2379252

Endsley, M. R. (2016). *Designing for situation awareness: An approach to user-centered design.* CRC Press. doi:10.1201/b11371

Fawaz, H. I., Forestier, G., Weber, J., Idoumghar, L., & Muller, P. A. (2019). Deep learning for time series classification: A review. *Data Mining and Knowledge Discovery, 33*(4), 917–963. doi:10.100710618-019-00619-1

Feldman, J. (2013). The neural binding problem(s). *Cognitive Neurodynamics, 7*(1), 1–11. doi:10.100711571-012-9219-8 PMID:24427186

Glodek, M., Honold, F., Geier, T., Krell, G., Nothdurft, F., Reuter, S., ... Biundo, S. (2015). Fusion paradigms in cognitive technical systems for human–computer interaction. *Neurocomputing, 161,* 17–37. doi:10.1016/j.neucom.2015.01.076

Gore, B. F., Hooey, B. L., Wickens, C. D., & Scott-Nash, S. (2009, July). A computational implementation of a human attention guiding mechanism in MIDAS v5. In *International conference on digital human modeling* (pp. 237-246). Springer. 10.1007/978-3-642-02809-0_26

Gorman, W. (2009). *Pentaho Reporting 3.5 for Java Developers.* Packt Publishing Ltd.

Gulwani, S., Polozov, O., & Singh, R. (2017). Program synthesis. *Foundations and Trends® in Programming Languages, 4*(1-2), 1-119.

Haikonen, P. O. (2009). The role of associative processing in cognitive computing. *Cognitive Computation, 1*(1), 42–49. doi:10.100712559-009-9006-y

Hartley, R. V. L. (1928, July). Transmission of Information. *Bell System Technical Journal.*

Haykin, S. (2006). Cognitive radar: A way of the future. *IEEE Signal Processing Magazine, 23*(1), 30–40. doi:10.1109/MSP.2006.1593335

Haykin, S. (Ed.). (2006). *Nonlinear methods of spectral analysis* (Vol. 34). Springer Science & Business Media.

Kolmogorov, A. N. (1965). Three approaches to the quantitative definition of information'. *Problems of Information Transmission, 1*(1), 1–7.

Krötzsch, M., Simancik, F., & Horrocks, I. (2012). *A description logic primer.* arXiv preprint arXiv:1201.4089

Laird, J. E. (2012). *The Soar cognitive architecture.* MIT Press. doi:10.7551/mitpress/7688.001.0001

Langley, P., & Choi, D. (2006). Learning recursive control programs from problem solving. *Journal of Machine Learning Research, 7*(Mar), 493–518.

Lhermitte, S., Verbesselt, J., Verstraeten, W. W., & Coppin, P. (2011). A comparison of time series similarity measures for classification and change detection of ecosystem dynamics. *Remote Sensing of Environment, 115*(12), 3129–3152. doi:10.1016/j.rse.2011.06.020

Luo, H. (2015). *Wearable mini-size intelligent healthcare system.* U.S. Patent No. 9,044,136. Washington, DC: U.S. Patent and Trademark Office.

Mamun, M. A. A., Hannan, M. A., Hussain, A., & Basri, H. (2016). Theoretical model and implementation of a real time intelligent bin status monitoring system using rule based decision algorithms. *Expert Systems with Applications, 48*(C), 76–88. doi:10.1016/j.eswa.2015.11.025

Nasle, A. (2017). *Real-time predictive systems for intelligent energy monitoring and management of electrical power networks.* U.S. Patent No. 9,557,723. Washington, DC: U.S. Patent and Trademark Office.

Nguyen, T. (2017, May). A modeling & simulation based engineering approach for socio-cyber-physical systems. In *2017 IEEE 14th International Conference on Networking, Sensing and Control (ICNSC)* (pp. 702-707). IEEE.

Osipov, V. (2016, July). Space-time structures of recurrent neural networks with controlled synapses. In *International Symposium on Neural Networks* (pp. 177-184). Springer. 10.1007/978-3-319-40663-3_21

Osipov, V. (2017). Structure and basic functions of cognitive neural network machine. In *MATEC Web of Conferences* (Vol. 113, p. 02011). EDP Sciences. 10.1051/matecconf/201711302011

Osipov, V., & Nikiforov, V. (2018, June). Formal aspects of streaming recurrent neural networks. In *International Symposium on Neural Networks* (pp. 29-36). Springer. 10.1007/978-3-319-92537-0_4

Osipov, V., & Osipova, M. (2018). Space–time signal binding in recurrent neural networks with controlled elements. *Neurocomputing, 308*, 194–204. doi:10.1016/j.neucom.2018.05.009

Osipov, V., Stankova, E., Vodyaho, A., Lushnov, M., Shichkina, Y., & Zhukova, N. (2019, July). Automatic Synthesis of Multilevel Automata Models of Biological Objects. In *International Conference on Computational Science and Its Applications* (pp. 441-456). Springer. 10.1007/978-3-030-24296-1_35

Osipov, V., Vodyaho, A., & Zhukova, N. (2017). About one approach to multilevel behavioral program synthesis for television devices. *International Journal of Computers and Communications, 11*, 17-25.

Osipov, V. Y. (2016). Automatic synthesis of action programs for intelligent robots. *Programming and Computer Software, 42*(3), 155–160. doi:10.1134/S0361768816030063

Osipov, V. Y., Vodyaho, A. I., Zhukova, N. A., & Glebovsky, P. A. (2017, May). Multilevel automatic synthesis of behavioral programs for smart devices. In *2017 International Conference on Control, Artificial Intelligence, Robotics & Optimization (ICCAIRO)* (pp. 335-340). IEEE. 10.1109/ICCAIRO.2017.68

Osipov, V. Y., Zhukova, N. A., Vodyaho, A. I., Kalmatsky, A., & Mustafin, N. G. (2017). Towards building of cable TV content-sensitive adaptive monitoring and management systems. *Int. J. Comput. Commun, 11*, 75–81.

Palm, G. (2013). Neural associative memories and sparse coding. *Neural Networks, 37*, 165–171. doi:10.1016/j.neunet.2012.08.013 PMID:23043727

Perlovsky, L. I. (2007). Cognitive high level information fusion. *Information Sciences, 177*(10), 2099–2118. doi:10.1016/j.ins.2006.12.026

Plaza, B. (2009, September). Monitoring web traffic source effectiveness with Google Analytics: An experiment with time series. *Aslib Proceedings, 61*(5), 474–482. doi:10.1108/00012530910989625

Rudnitckaia, J. (2015). Process Mining. Data science in action. University of Technology, Faculty of Information Technology.

Shannon, C. E. (1948). A mathematical theory of communication. *The Bell System Technical Journal, 27*(3), 379–423. doi:10.1002/j.1538-7305.1948.tb01338.x

Smirnov, A., Kashevnik, A., Ponomarev, A., & Shilov, N. (2017, June). Context-aware decision support in socio-cyberphysical systems: From smart space-based applications to human-computer cloud services. In *International Conference on Practical Applications of Agents and Multi-Agent Systems* (pp. 3-15). Springer. 10.1007/978-3-319-59930-4_1

Stefanov, K., Voevodin, V., Zhumatiy, S., & Voevodin, V. (2015). Dynamically reconfigurable distributed modular monitoring system for supercomputers (dimmon). *Procedia Computer Science, 66*, 625–634. doi:10.1016/j.procs.2015.11.071

Susto, G. A., Cenedese, A., & Terzi, M. (2018). Time-series classification methods: Review and applications to power systems data. In *Big data application in power systems* (pp. 179–220). Elsevier. doi:10.1016/B978-0-12-811968-6.00009-7

Tecuci, G., Boicu, M., Bowman, M., Marcu, D., Shyr, P., & Cascaval, C. (2000). An experiment in agent teaching by subject matter experts. *International Journal of Human-Computer Studies, 53*(4), 583–610. doi:10.1006/ijhc.2000.0401

Tianxing, M., & Zhukova, N. (2018). An Ontology of Machine Learning Algorithms for Human Activity Data Processing. *Learning, 10*, 12.

Treisman, A. (1996). The binding problem. *Current Opinion in Neurobiology, 6*(2), 171–178. doi:10.1016/S0959-4388(96)80070-5 PMID:8725958

Tsotsos, J. K., Kotseruba, I., Rasouli, A., & Solbach, M. D. (2018). Visual attention and its intimate links to spatial cognition. *Cognitive Processing, 19*(1), 121–130. doi:10.100710339-018-0881-6 PMID:30094803

Vangheluwe, H. (2018, May). Multi-paradigm modeling of cyber-physical systems. In *Proceedings of the 4th International Workshop on Software Engineering for Smart Cyber-Physical Systems* (pp. 1-1). ACM.

Wolf, W. H. (2009). Cyber-physical systems. *IEEE Computer, 42*(3), 88–89. doi:10.1109/MC.2009.81

Zavyalova, Y. V., Korzun, D. G., Meigal, A. Y., & Borodin, A. V. (2017). Towards the development of smart spaces-based socio-cyber-medicine systems. *International Journal of Embedded and Real-Time Communication Systems*, 8(1), 45–63. doi:10.4018/IJERTCS.2017010104

Zhukova, N., Baimuratov, I., Than, N., & Mustafin, N. (2019, April). The Information Estimation System for Data Processing Results. In *Proceedings of the 24th Conference of Open Innovations Association FRUCT* (p. 117). FRUCT Oy.

Chapter 2
Ontology–Based Coalition Creation by Autonomous Agents in Smart Space:
An Approach and Case Study

Alexey Kashevnik
iD https://orcid.org/0000-0001-6503-1447

St. Petersburg Institute for Informatics and Automation of Russian Academy of Sciences (SPIIRAS), Russia

Nikolay Teslya
iD https://orcid.org/0000-0003-0619-8620

St. Petersburg Institute for Informatics and Automation of Russian Academy of Sciences (SPIIRAS), Russia

ABSTRACT

The chapter presents an approach to agent indirect interaction in smart space based on the publication/subscription mechanism. It is proposed to describe every agent with an ontology and support the ontology matching between ontologies of different agents in smart space to enrich the semantic interoperability between them. When the agents reach the semantic interoperability, they are aimed to create a coalition to perform a task. The task is described by ontology and the agents determine what they can propose to implement it. Group of agents that can perform the task together is called coalition. The considered case study describes the mobile robot interaction for the case of joint obstacle overcoming by the 6WD robot with lifting chassis, quadrocopter that scans an obstacle, and knowledge base service that contains algorithms for obstacle overcoming.

DOI: 10.4018/978-1-7998-1974-5.ch002

INTRODUCTION

Last years, there are a lot of research and development in the topic of mobile robotics and coalition creation by mobile robots (Li et al., 2019; Kirichek, Paramonov, Vladyko, & Borisov 2016; Du, He, Chen, Xiao, Gao, & Wang, 2017). They are actively used for different tasks such as scouting, technological accidents and catastrophes consequences liquidation, counterterrorism operations and patrolling (Teja, Harsha, Siravuru, Shan, Krishna, 2015; Reddy, Kalyan, Murthy, 2015). Often robots are used for manipulating an object when a human cannot achieve it in some reasons. At the moment in the world there are a lot of mobile robots developed that can implement simple tasks. However, these robots alone usually cannot implement complex tasks that requires joint actions from several robots. In this case, automation of coalition creation is an actual and promising task. When a task is determined the robots should interact with each other, understand each other, and create a coalition for joint task solving.

The paper presents an approach to ontology-based mobile robot interaction for coalition creation. The approach is based on such concepts as cyber-physical-social systems (Zeng et al., 2017), mobile robotics, ontology modeling (Carvalho, Almeida, Fonseca, Guizzardi, 2017), semantic interoperability models (Ganzha et al., 2017), and context management (Snidaro, García, Llinas, 2015). The core concept is the cyber-physical-social system where the physical devices are interacted in smart space with each other and with human for implementing joint actions in physical space. Cyber-physical-social systems tightly integrate physical, information (cyber), and social spaces based on interactions between them in real time. This kind of systems relies on communication, computation and control infrastructures for the three spaces with various resources:

- Acting resources (mobile robots, sensors, actuators) that implements actions in physical space;
- Information resources (robot control blocks, user mobile devices, services, computation resources, etc.) that operate in information space;
- Social resources (human) that form tasks in social space.

For interaction in the cyber-physical-social system the smart space technology is used, which allows to provide information sharing between different services of the system. This technology (Cook & Das, 2007; Balandin & Waris, 2009) aims to the seamless integration of different devices by developing ubiquitous computing environments, where different services can share information with each other, make different computations and interact for joint tasks solving (Korzun, Balandin, Kashevnik, Smirnov, & Gurtov, 2017). In the considered approach, the main goal of smart space technology is to provide ontology-based information sharing for the cyber-physical-social system.

In scope of the presented in the paper an approach the context-based model for mobile robots interaction, the ontological model of mobile robot, and the method for robot ontology matching have been developed as well as a case study for task performing by the group of mobile robots for obstacle overcoming. The presented case study has been implemented both: using LEGO Mindstorms EV3 robotic kit as well as models of robots developed using the ROS system and Gazebo modelling environment. The ontologies in the considered scenarios formally represents knowledge as a set of concepts within a domain, using a shared vocabulary to denote the types, properties, and interrelationships of those concepts. The context is defined as any information that can be used to characterize the situation of an entity. An entity is a person, place or object that is considered relevant to the interaction between a user and an application, including the user and application themselves (Dey, Salber, & Abowd, 2001).

Authors propose a case study for robot and human coalition formation for joint task performing. There are two types of robots and human participating in the considered scenario: 6WD manipulator robot with extendable & lifting chassis, measurement flying robot, and human operator that controls the robot if it does not have a possibility to move automatically in case of obstacles. While performing a task the manipulating robot tends to face obstacles on its path. If the robot can not overcome it the human expert takes a control and help with obstacle overcoming. For understand the obstacle parameters manipulating robot creates a coalition with measuring robot which reaches the obstacle, implements measurements, and provide the information to the manipulating robot. Each robot consists of several blocks with pairs of wheels and is equipped with ultrasonic sensors. The open source Smart-M3 platform is used for organization of the smart space infrastructure for robots interaction. The use of this platform enables to significantly simplify further development of the system, include new information sources and services, and to make the system highly scalable. The Smart-M3 platform consists of two main parts: information agents and kernel (Honkola, Laine, Brown, & Tyrkko, 2010). The kernel consists of two elements: Semantic Information Broker (SIB) and information storage. Information agents are software entities, installed on mobile devices of the smart space users and other devices, which host smart space services. The Smart-M3 platform allows to organize ontology-based information and knowledge sharing for various participants based on publication subscription mechanism and provides possibilities to develop different kinds of application aimed at ontology-based interaction of agents for joint tasks solving (Smirnov, Kashevnik, & Ponomarev, 2015; Smirnov et al., 2014; Smirnov, Kashevnik, Shilov, & Teslya, 2013; Smirnov, Shilov, Kashevnik, & Teslya, 2012).

It should be mentioned that authors consider process of coalition creation by mobile robots and human and support the process of their interaction. Presented ontology-based approach is aimed at semantic interoperability support between them. Communication of the mobile robots as well as synchronization of their behavior is not related to this paper. For the case study we used Wi-Fi network that have been used to support the discussed scenario.

The paper extends the previous authors work related to coalition creation in human-robot systems (Kashevnik, Smirnov, & Teslya, 2018) by the following main features.

- The mobile robot ontology has been developed to describe the main robot capabilities and constraints during the for mobile robots and human interaction. The ontology is based on definitions and abbreviations from Suggested Upper Merged Ontology (SUMO) proposed by (IEEE-SA Standards Board, 2015).
- The ontology matching method based on background knowledge sources application that has to be adapted from (Smirnov et al., 2010) and (Smirnov, Teslya, & Shilov, 2017) for interaction of mobile robots for coalition creation.

The rest of the paper is organized as follows. The next section describes related work in the area of mobile robot interaction. Then authors present context-based coalition creation approach. After that mobile robot ontology model is described. Next, authors propose the method for robot ontology matching. After that a case study is shown. Finally, the conclusion summarizes the paper.

BACKGROUND

One of the main enabling technology for robot joint work is a multi-agent system. With this technology robots are viewed as intelligent agents connected through network. Intelligence is provided by the use of ontologies to represent knowledge and ensure interoperability between various agents. Agents act independently from each other, exchanging information about their actions or their results (Gyrard et.al., 2017). In addition to agents there are services in MAS that process information (i.e. store it, provide semantic search (Nadim et.al., 2018; Serena et.al., 2017). That allows to organize fairly complex interaction algorithms applicable in various problem areas, for example, in manufacturing (Ciotera et.al., 2017) or research automation.

Nowadays, the main interest of researchers in the topic of joint activities of autonomous agents are concentrated around the following issues: organization of a coalition, exchange of information between coalition members, distribution of tasks and resources between coalition members.

In the process of coalition organization, two major areas can be distinguished: centralized organization and decentralized (Koes et al., 2005). The centralized coalition organization is defined by the presence of a control center at which decisions are made on the composition of the coalition, the distribution of tasks, and a plan for solving the problem is formed. In this case, the control center can be represented as a separate computing device that performs only the functions of the coordinator, and a robot that performs tasks along with the rest (Yu & Cai, 2009). The structure of the coalition in this case can be multi-level hierarchical, in which robots at each underlying level obey only one center of their superior level (Qian & Cheng, 2018). The decentralized organization of the coalition usually implies the absence of a decision-making center, often focusing on bio-inspired methods of organizing joint work, such as swarm and flock (Liang, & Xiao, 2009 and Verma et al., 2017). At the same time, robots are considered equal in hierarchy and are guided by the same algorithms during the decision making process.

The exchange of information between coalition members is an important task for coalition problem solution. This issue is urgent since joint task performing requires the notification of the coalition participants about the current member state that helps organizing coordinated actions, or monitoring the implementation of the plan (Smirnov et al., 2015). The information exchange can be organized through a common centralized repository on a separate device or by the distribution of information between coalition members (Tosello et al., 2016). The combination of two approaches with the utilization of smart spaces is considered that requires the creation of a common information repository that provides links to resources presented by coalition members, which makes information distributed among all participants (Hartanto & Eich, 2014). There are also solutions based on peer2peer networks and a distributed ledger that provide quick distribution of information between all participants, while duplicating all the information on the device of each participant (Ferrer, 2018, Shabanov & Ivanov, 2019). Distributed ledger-based solutions also provide information protection against rewriting, which can be useful during organization a coalition with the requirement to ensure trust between participants without a single certification center (Shabanov & Ivanov, 2019).

The type of coalition organization also influences how tasks and resources are distributed among coalition members. Centralized coalitions with hierarchical structure usually organize their work through centralized planning when a task arrives. At upper-level nodes, a work plan is built taking into account the capabilities of down-level nodes and coalition resources. It this plan the executors and the procedure for solving problems are fixed (Ivanov, 2018). This ensures that the stages of the plan and the entire plan are completed by a certain date with an accurate forecast of the expenditure of resources and the payment of winnings, if this is provided for by the conditions of the task. However, this solution is not flexible, because an emergency leads to a deviation from the plan, with the need for its correction or complete replanning. Decentralized coalitions are based on the adaptation of participants to current conditions, with the absence of a single plan for solving the problem (Xue et al., 2019, Alkilabi et al., 2017). This provides the flexibility to solve the problem under conditions of frequent changes in the composition of the coalition or available resources, but in other hand it limits the ability to predict the time moment of finishing the task (Li et al., 2019).

Also, special attention should be paid to imitation and visual modeling of the robot interaction, since this approach greatly simplifies hypothesis testing by reducing the cost of development, as well as visually present the results of the proposed approaches. Some researchers develop their own visualizations, displaying robots with conventional signs, since the tasks under consideration do not require detailed design of the robot (Koes, 2005, Liang & Xiao, 2010). For the detailed visualization, the Gazebo modeling environment is most often used in combination with the control code of the robot operating system (ROS) for controlling a virtual robot (Barbosa et al., 2019, Tagliabue et al, 2019, Klug et al., 2019).

Summarizing the areas of research considered, it can be noted that currently main attention now is paid to the creation of decentralized coalitions of robots for joint task performing. The distribution of tasks and resources between them is carried out based on decentralized planning to adapt the task context change, while robots take part in the problem based on existing functionality and available resources, such as battery power or device maintenance period. The interaction and exchange of information between robots is carried out through a common repository, but recent studies are biased towards decentralization based on the peer2peer model and the use of distributed ledgers.

COALITION CREATION APPROACH BY AUTONOMOUS AGENTS

Coalition creation process in cyber-physical-social systems requires semantic interoperability support between potential participants: mobile robots and human. The process is based on cyber-physical systems concept that is aimed at tightly integration of the physical and cyber spaces based on interactions between these spaces in real time. Mobile robots and human are exchange information with each other in information space while their physical interaction occurs in physical space. Moreover, social space joins the human that can participate in the interaction process. Human access to the information space using the smartphones. It is needed to create the model of problem domain and support the interaction of potential participants based on this model. One of the possible approaches to problem domain modelling is to use ontologies. The ontology formally represents knowledge as a set of concepts within a domain, using a shared vocabulary to denote the types, properties, and interrelationships of those concepts. For current situation modelling and reducing the search space in the coalition creation process the utilization of context management technology is proposed. The aim of this technology is a context model creation that is based on ontology of problem domain and information about current situation in physical space. Context is defined as any information that can be used to characterize the situation of an entity. An entity is a person, place or object that is considered relevant to the interaction between a user and an application, including the user and application themselves (Dey, Salber, & Abowd, 2001). Context is suggested being modeled at two levels: abstract and operational. These levels are represented by abstract and operational contexts, respectively. The process of coalition creation based on abstract and operational contexts is shown in Figure 1 (adapted from Kashevnik, Smirnov, & Teslya, 2018).

Figure 1. Abstract and operational contexts for coalition creation of mobile robots

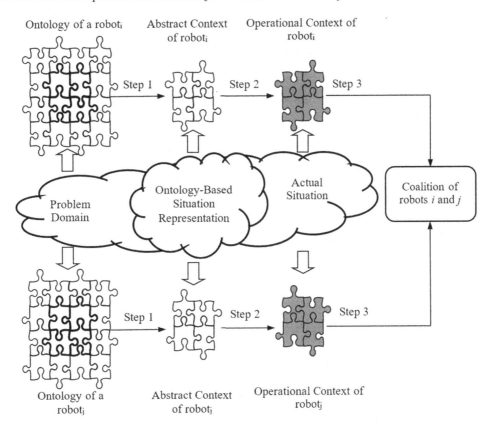

Abstract context is an ontology-based model of a potential coalition participant related to the current task. Abstract context is build based on integrating information and knowledge relevant to the current problem situation. Operational context is an instantiation of the domain constituent of the abstract context with data provided by the contextual resources. Thereby the coalition creation is implemented in three steps. The first step includes the abstract context creation that covers the selection of knowledge relevant to the task from the potential coalition participant ontology. The second step includes the process of concretization of these knowledge by information accessible in information space for operational context formation. The operational context is published in information space and becomes accessible for other potential coalition participants. On the third step, the coalitions of mobile robots and human are created based on their operational context intersections (see Figure 2 adapted from Smirnov, Kashevnik, Petrov, & Parfenov, 2017).

Information space is organized based on blackboard architecture that provides possibilities for potential coalition participants to implement indirect interaction. Thereby, virtual coalition is created in information space and then physical coalition appears in physical space (mobile robots and human implement the joint task). Interaction of potential coalition participants in information space is implemented using the ontology-based publish/subscribe mechanism that provides possibilities for mobile robots and human publishing their information and knowledge and subscribing on interesting information using ontologies. When a mobile robot or human registers to be a potential coalition participant it uploads the own ontology to the information space.

Figure 2. Reference model for mobile robot and human interaction for coalition formation

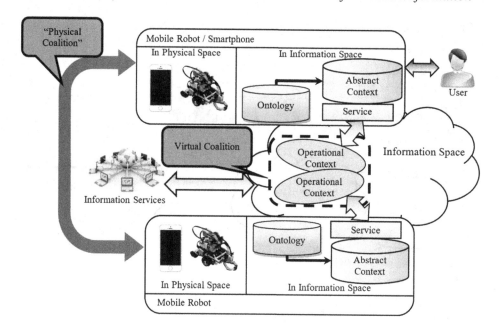

This ontology formalizes the main robot capabilities and constraints that have to be satisfied to use the capabilities. The human mobile device is used to represent him/her in information space, describes the human capabilities and tasks to be implemented. Mobile device also contains the human profile that provide to the information space the human preferences. Thereby, the interoperability for robot and human interaction is supported based on open information space and ontology-based publish/subscribe mechanism. A potential coalition participant can participate in joint task if the ontology in information space is matched with own ontology. More details about the ontology matching see in the section "Ontology Matching Method".

AN ONTOLOGY FOR THE MOBILE ROBOT MODELLING

Communication between mobile robot and human in cyber-physical-social system requires the designing of ontologies that describe the mobile robots, their competencies and constraints that have to be satisfied to get these competencies. With the growing complexity of behaviors that robots are expected to perform as well as the need for multi-robot and human-robot collaboration, the need for a standard and well-defined knowledge representation is becoming more evident (Schlenoff et al., 2012). Authors are determined the following packages that need to be developed for the robot ontologies:

- Device: describes devices such as sensors and actuators;
- Control strategy: controls the autonomous systems for navigation;
- Perception: uses sensor information for state estimation and world representation;
- Motion planning: plans motion (actions) in the perceived world;

Figure 3. Cyber-physical-social system ontology

- Knowledge representation: represents knowledge related to particular problems and solutions in order to make decisions.

Schlenoff & Messina, 2005 identify the requirements definition related to the robots' ontology development. These requirements have been taken into account for ontology construction.

The main concept in the ontology is a class "Robot" that is described by three common categories of information:

- Physical Characteristics (describes physical and structural aspects of a robot);
- Functional Characteristics (describes possible behavior of the robot);
- Operational Considerations (describes the interactions of the robot with the human and with other robots).

Developed cyber-physical-social system ontology (Figure 3) is based on definitions and abbreviations from Suggested Upper Merged Ontology (SUMO) proposed by (IEEE-SA Standards Board, 2015) (see Figure 4). The top level of the robot ontology consists from the 62 classes and two types of relationships between them: *"is_a"* and *"associate with"*. The ontology describes the main processes that is appeared during the coalition creation for joint task solving by mobile robots.

The developed ontology consists of three main sections: class "Physical Space", class "Information Space", and class "Social Space". Class "Physical Space" describes the physical space objects, class "Information Space" describes the control and computational services as well as information services, and class "Social Space" includes a description of people competencies involved to human-computer interaction.

Let's consider in detail class "Physical Space". The class contains a description of physical objects and includes the following subclasses: "Collection", "Device", and "Environment". Class "Collection" characterizes a set of devices that are participants in a cyber-physical-social system (for example, robots). Class "Device" is a description of devices that operate in the physical space and consists of the following subclasses: "Connect_Interface", "Battery", "Hull", "Motor", "Sensor", "Switch", and "Whell".

Figure 4. The Suggested upper merged ontology (SUMO) ontology
(IEEE-SA Standards Board, 2015)

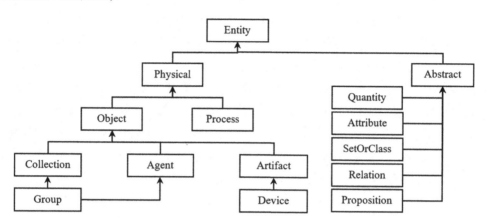

Class "Connect_Interface" characterizes connection type that is used to implement the interaction between objects. A subclass of the class is class "Wirelessinterface". This class describes the options for a wireless interface; it includes subclasses "Bluetooth" and "WiFi".

Class "Motor" describes characteristics of motors used to operate the devices. Class "Sensor" characterizes device sensors. Subclasses of the class "Sensor" describe various types sensors mounted to mobile robots: class "DistanceSensor", class "HeatSensor", "LightSensor", and class "TouchSensor". Class "Wheel" contains wheels characteristics of mobile robots. Class "Battery" defines power supplies installed to mobile robot platform. Class "Environment" defines the parameters of the environment in which the robots are operated.

Class "Information Space" describes objects of information space and consists of the following subclasses: "CompetenceProfile", "Configuration", "Context", "Policy", "Interaction", "Process", "Agent", "Human_Profile", "Resource", and "Resource_profile". Class CompetenceProfile describes the competencies of human and robot. The class consists of a subclass "History", containing statistics of the robot operation. The class also includes a description of the results of the executed scripts. Class "Agent" describes the software that manages "Resource" and "Device". Class "Configuration" contains description of the set of settings and components that should be taken into account in the information space. Class "Context" contains a variety of information that characterizes the environment in which objects of the cyber-physical-social system are located. The class consists of subclasses: "ResourceContext", which determines the specifics of the device environment, "EnvironmentContext", which includes information about the external environment. The EnvironmentContext class is subclassed as "Spatial" and "Temporal".

Class "Spatial" describes the space and includes subclass "Location". The class describes location of system objects in space. Class "Temporal" defines time characteristics and includes a subclass "Time", which defines the time intervals associated with script execution.

Class "Human_profile" contains a description of the competencies of a person, as one of the objects of the cyber-physical-social system. Class "Human_Profile" includes a subclass "Competency". The class describes the basic properties that can characterize an expert person: "Opportunities", "Proficiency_level", "Capabilities", "Skills", and "Knowledge". Class "Opportunities" defines the capabilities of an expert. Class "Proficiency_level" contains information about the qualifications of an expert. Class

"Capabilities" defines the characteristics that an expert should meet. Class "Skills" is the skills that expert should meet to accomplish a task.

Class "Interaction" describes the types of interactions "HumanInteraction" and "CollectionInteraction". Class "CollectionInteraction" describes the interaction of several robots, and "HumanInteraction" describes the interaction of a robot and a human.

Class "Policy" defines the rights and capabilities of system objects. The class contains subclass "Autorization". Class "Autorization" defines the rules for authorizing objects in the system.

Class "Process" contains a description of the processes that can be executed by the system. Class "Process" includes a subclass "Scenario" containing scripts that can be executed by system objects.

NEURAL NETWORK BASED ONTOLOGY MATCHING

Artificial neural network is an outstanding technology that can also be used in ontology matching process. Two main approaches can be overviewed for ANN utilization: i) based on feature extraction for concept and context of ontologies and ii) based on weight calculation for combination of several classic matching methods, like linguistic or context-based. For the first approach type ontology concepts, their characteristics and context (nearest neighbors with characteristics and relation descriptions) are transformed to input vector of neural network (Manjula Shenoy, 2013). Network learning process is based on training NN to classify ontology concepts for each ontology (Xiang et.al., 2015). After the training phase the NN is able to detect which ontology the provided concept belongs to and therefore to find similarities between ontologies by calculating the probability that some concept belongs to ontology. The second type is based on the existing approaches to ontology matching and use them separately to get initial estimation of ontologies concepts similarity (Ali Khoudja et.al., 2019; Djeddi et.al., 2013). To get the integrated similarity coefficient the neural network is trained to weight result from the each of used methods and therefore calculate overall coefficient.

The general scheme of the developed method is based on expanding the ontology matching process developed by the authors earlier by adding background knowledge hidden in the vector space of words. The vector space reflects the semantics of the problem domain by using latent factors as word vector dimensions factors. By the learning process the latent factors are evaluated based on word context (nearest words and constructions) to reflect the meaning of the word in context.

Words vector space is implemented with matrix with size of dictionary and number of vector features. This matrix is also called embedded and can be used as embedded layer in neural networks for classification. The neural network uses a vector space of words as a hidden level to evaluate similarity of words used in ontology concept descriptions (like name of concept and parameters) The method accepts the ontologies O_1 and O_2 in the OWL format as an input and returns the result of the comparison in the form of an alignment matrix for ontology concepts A as well as its visualization in the form of a bipartite graph. The basic scheme of the method is based on the use of entities labels and the context of the concepts of these ontologies.

The work of the method can be divided into three stages (see Figure 5). The first stage is related to the processing of initial ontologies, during which the abstract and operational contexts are identified, as well as the problem area of each ontology is extracted. At the second stage, the mapping of processed ontologies based on methods using matching patterns and concept contexts takes place. To improve the

Figure 5. Proposed ontology matching method

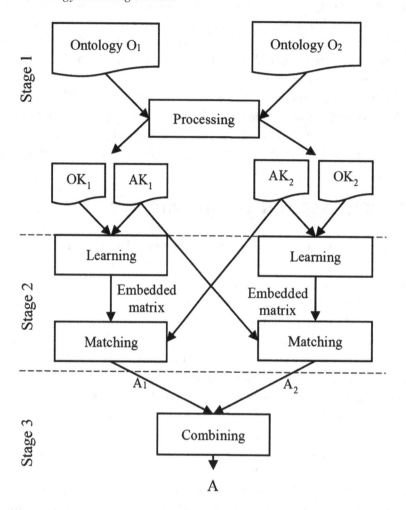

quality of comparison methods different sources of background knowledge are used. The work of the matching methods at the second stage is performed in parallel and independently with the formation of intermediate matrices of ontology concepts. At the third stage of work, the composition of intermediate correspondence matrices is carried out with the formation of the final matrix, which is the result of the work of the developed ontology matching method.

Let consider in detail each of the stages. The first stage is the processing of the initial ontologies. Since these methods are used primarily to build topic models of texts, ontologies need to be converted into a textual representation, for which information from the operational context is used. The texts in this case are all the labels of the concepts of ontologies and the text parameters of the entity instances, collected in the so-called "bag of words".

The second stage is the comparison. Since the proposed method implies cross-matching of ontologies, at the second stage two sub-stages can be distinguished, associated with the matching of each ontologies.

When searching for correspondence between concepts, the matching ontologies O_1 and O_2 are transmitted to the neural network. From each ontology, the string characteristics of the concepts are retrieved - the labels of the concepts, their properties, relationships. A pre-trained vector word model is loaded into the hidden layer of the neural network. Then the neural network is additionally trained using first O_1 ontology concepts to recognize their belonging to a given ontology. The training is based on the fact that for each ontology concept its semantic proximity with neighboring concepts and links with them are checked. If the value of the output neurons does not correspond to the context of the concept, the corresponding vectors are recalculated. Upon completion of the learning process, concepts from the O_2 ontology are fed to the input of the neural network and are checked to which concepts from the O_1 ontology they most fully correspond (the value of the activation function is checked, which lies in the range [0, 1], where 0 is the lack of correspondence, 1 is full compliance). The maximum value of the activation function and its corresponding concepts are recorded in the intermediate matrix of ontology correspondence A_1. After checking all the concepts from the ontology O_2 in a similar way, the ontologies are replaced - the network is retrained to recognize the concepts from the ontology O_2 and checks the consistency of the concepts from the ontology O_1.

The configuration of neural network on these sub-stages reflects the used Word2Vec model for word representation as a vector. The input layer has a dimension of dictionary of due to all words in space are processed to a dictionary and has unique ID in it. In this case the input vector is a binary vector that reflects position of the word in the dictionary. The hidden layer of the neural network stores a vector model of titles and can be represented by a matrix of size [m, n], where m is the number of words in the model dictionary, and n is the size of the word vector. The neurons of the output layer contain the sigmoid activation function (Elfwing et al., 2018), which activates neurons depending on the value of the vector in hidden layer. This allows to calculate the nearest vectors that represent words and measure the similarity metrics.

Learning for a hidden layer of a neural network requires processing of a large corpora of natural language texts. Examples of such cases are encyclopedias articles, electronic libraries, and news or messages archives. An obvious advantage of this approach is control over the learning process, which consists in using only domain-specific texts. However, the learning process takes a significant amount of time (from 12 hours when using one device with CPU and without graphics accelerators) or requires significant computational resources (with graphics accelerators, or parallelization of computations on several devices).

The learning process can be skipped when using a previously trained vector word model containing the semantics of the problem areas of the ontologies under consideration. Such a model will contain a large number of words, but due to the dimension of the vector space it will require very large volume and RAM size. The model used can be further trained on the context of ontology concepts (neighboring concepts, relationships between concepts, characteristics of concepts), so that it most fully reflects the semantics for a specific ontology. During training, the presence of ontology terms in the vector model is checked. If the word vector is present in the vector model, then for neighboring concepts and ontology properties, the elements of the corresponding vectors are adjusted to bring them together in vector space. Adjustment is carried out by the backward propagation method by calculating the difference between the expected output of the neural network and the real output and applying the difference to the vectors of the hidden layer inside the neural network. In the case of the absence of a vector in the vocabulary, it is added to the model along with the corresponding output neuron, after which the elements are calculated for the new vector also on the basis of the back propagation of the error. The use of a pre-trained vector word model is necessary in order to exclude a situation in which there is no vector representation of the concept label from the compared ontology. If the label of the concept is not in the model, then it will be ignored, since the capabilities of the neural network are limited to the names included in the dictionary. One of the possible solutions to this problem is the stemming (search for the basis of the word) and lemmatization (bringing the word form to the normal (vocabulary) form) of words, followed by the search for the corresponding forms in the vector model. The trained vector model of words can also be saved for future use in order to reduce the learning time of the neural network for the ontology studied.

At the third stage, the intermediate comparison results are combined in the final alignment matrix by calculating the average value of each coefficient $A = \frac{1}{2}(A_1 + A_2)$. The choice of simple arithmetic average is due to the equivalence of matching procedures.

Presented approach based on the use of a neural network for implementing the model of the vector space of words allows to partially extract the background knowledge and utilize it to analyze the names of ontology concepts. It helps to avoid fuzziness in ontology concept names caused by possible mistypes or by using synonyms to name the concepts as well as speed up the matching process in compare to using dictionaries or thesauri.

CASE STUDY

The proposed case study is a good example of cyber-physical-social system that includes automated robots and human that can take control in case the robot cannot perform a task automatically. During the scenario the manipulating robot should go to the destination. If the robot finds an obstacle that has to be overcoming to complete the task, it publishes the context information to smart space (location, available time). Then measuring robots get notification about obstacle found and decide to create a coalition with the manipulating robot to perform together the obstacle overcoming task. Then the measuring robot participated in coalition implements the obstacle scanning and publish obstacle parameters to the smart space. The manipulating robot searches the algorithm to overcome this type of obstacle in smart space. In case of this algorithm is available to use, the robot implements corresponding actions to overcome the obstacle. Otherwise, the human operator gets notification that he/she should control the robot manually since the obstacle cannot be overcoming automatically. For this purpose, an adaptive context-based robot control interface for the smartphone has been developed [Kashevnik et al., 2018].

If more than one human operator is required to control the manipulating robot the control interface provides possibilities to distribute robot control functionality between group of human, e.g., driver, manipulator, and expert. Prototypes of the manipulating robot and the measuring robot have been developed based on the Lego Mindstorms EV3 kit as well as scenario modelling has been implemented using Gazebo and robotic operation system. Lego Mindstorms EV3 kit allows to easily design robots with required functionality for education purposes. Gazebo and robotic operation system provides possibilities to simulate real engines and sensors in the modelling environment. Figure 6 shows the manipulating robot prototype and Figure 7 presents the design of measuring robot prototype constructed for the presented above scenario (figures are adapted from Smirnov, Kashevnik, Petrov, & Parfenov, 2017).

In order to overcome obstacles, the robot was constructed from several blocks. Due to the design the robot could climb an obstacle gradually. First, it lifted and fixed the front block, then basing on the front and back blocks it raised the middle one. All blocks were equipped with a pair of drive wheels; in addition, the middle block had a pair of wheels without a drive for balance. An ultrasonic sensor for measuring the distance to objects was also mounted on the central block.

Figure 6. The manipulating robot prototype

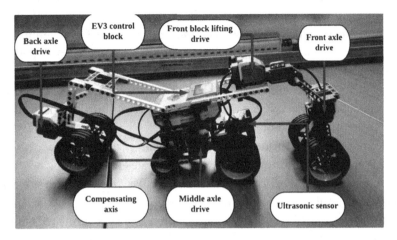

Figure 7. Measuring robot prototype

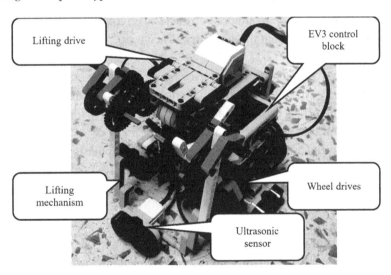

Figure 8. Implementation of the scenario for gazebo and robotic operation system

Smart-M3 information sharing platform is used for information space implementation in the considered case study. It information storage in the form of RDF-ontologies, in which information is presented as a set of triples of "subject-predicate-object". A triple subject describes an entity such as an object, a device, or a person. The triple is described that the entity has a property, or it performs an action. A triples object describes an entity, which the subject is associated with, that is its function or property. The object of one triple may be the subject of another one. A triples predicate describes the type of relationship between subject and object. It can determine the type of functions performed by the subject, or the correlation between subject and object.

A simple example of a triple stored in the ontology is < *"robot", "task", "goToLocation"* >. The subject *"robot"* describes a robot, which information in the triple relates to, the predicate *"task"* defines what this information is, and the object *"goToLocation"* is a particular *"task"* for the subject *"robot"*. At the same time *"goToLocation"* is also a subject in the triple < *"goToLocation", "coordinates", "40; 200"* >.

Devices connected to the information space based on Smart-M3 platform are able to "subscribe" to a triple to get notification when the needed information is published in the information space. In the case of a new triple satisfying pattern all devices, which are subscribed to triples of this pattern, are notified.

Figure 9 (adapted from Smirnov, Kashevnik, Petrov, & Parfenov, 2017) shows the scenario for coalition creation for forward moving and encountered obstacles overcoming. The presented diagram shows five main components of the system that implements the scenario.

- Smartphone application publishes tasks to perform and shows the status of performance.
- Image processing service is designed to retrieve information about an object or area from a photo.
- Information space is an infrastructure to information sharing by mobile robots.
- The manipulating robot that overcome an obstacle.
- Measuring robot that measure the obstacle found by the manipulating robot.

When starting each robot publishes information about its functions and limitations from its own ontology in the information space. Moreover, while executing tasks a robot publishes information about its location and the current task.

For example, a user publishes task "Go to location" to the smart space. Since a robot is free, that is, it does not perform any other tasks, its interaction service determines whether the robot is to perform published task. For this purpose, the service follows the information about the task and about other robots. If the robot is the closest one to the point, it proceeds to the task.

When the robot detects an obstacle in the way, it automatically stops and publish in information space information about the obstacle. If there is no information about such an obstacle, the user takes control over the manipulating robot. As a result, the commands that are to be done in order to overcome this obstacle are consistently being published in the information space. After overcoming the obstacle, the robot continues to perform the task and finds the second obstacle that is similar to the first one. Since the information about it is already in the obstacles templates database, the robot overcomes it without the user's help.

To estimate proposed ontology matching method for using in robot communication the simple use case was implemented. The neural network was build based on TensorFlow 2.0 framework and use pre-trained word2vec model to speed-up the process. The model is based on Google News text corpora and contains about 3 million words and phrases with vector dimension for each entry equal to 300 components (the embedded matrix, provided by the model, requires about 3Gb of HDD space to store). Ontologies was

Figure 9. The scenario of coalition creation for forward moving and encountered obstacles overcoming

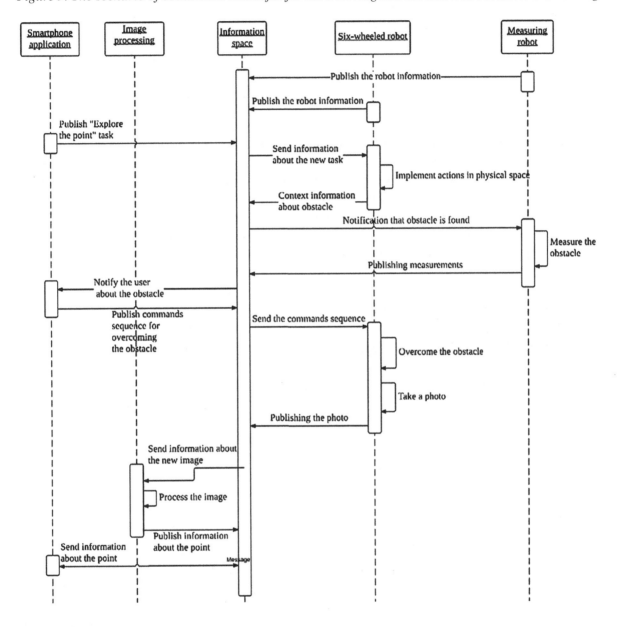

processed with owlready2 library for Python 3.7. For each concept names, characteristics and relations names was extracted. Each name and characteristic were cross-checked between ontologies using neural network and highest similarity values was stored as similarity coefficients for ontologies concepts. The accuracy was estimated using OAEI dataset for conferences ontologies and compared with other approaches on the same dataset. The evaluation result is presented in Table 1.

Table 1. Evaluation of ontology matching with word2vec-based NN

Metric	Proposed Approach	ALOD2Vec	StringEquiv	AML
Precision	0.79	0.71	0.8	0.84
Recall	0.65	0.5	0.43	0.66
F1-measure	0.36	0.59	0.56	0.74

SOLUTIONS AND RECOMMENDATIONS

The following main technologies has been used to solve the task of ontology-based coalition formation by autonomous agents: semantic interoperability support, ontology utilization, context modelling, multi-level self-organization, ontology matching, artificial neural networks, and vector representation of words. The next is the justification for their use and recommendations for the application of the developed methods and models in solving similar tasks (see Table 1).

FUTURE RESEARCH DIRECTIONS

Technologies of coalition formation by autonomous agents is urgent task and emerging trend last years. Nowadays, a lot of possible solutions are proposed to solve this kind of task based on various concepts, like centralized hierarchical coalition formation with static planning or decentralized coalition with common storage of tasks and resources for joint task solving. Some approaches are use an ontology-based description of robots and tasks to provide interoperability between them. However, there are still open questions to solve in this field of research. The following open problems have been identified (see details in Table 2).

CONCLUSION

This chapter considers the problem of mobile robot coalition creation for joint task performing. The approach is based on semantic interoperability support based on proposed ontology matching method, context model, and reference model for coalition creation of mobile robot as well as on ontology management technique and resource interaction support based on shared space. Smart-M3 information sharing platform has been used to implement the sharing space concept. The case study has been implemented based on Lego Mindstorms EV3 robotic construction platform as well as using Robotic Operation System and Gazebo. The scenario of obstacle overcoming by the 6WD manipulating robot has been considered. Manipulating robot creates the coalition with measurement robot(s) and human(s) (if needed) and perform the task of obstacle overcoming.

Table 2. Solutions spectrum for ontology-based coalition creation

#	Solution	Comment
1	Semantic interoperability support	Semantic interoperability support for autonomous agents is a key point of coalition creation since each agent can provide own vision of problem domain. There are known standard protocols and standards exist that can be used for resource interaction.
2	Ontology utilization	An ontology is a domain vocabulary completed with a set of precise definitions, or axioms, that constrain the meanings of the terms sufficiently to enable consistent interpretation of the data that use that vocabulary. Utilization of such vocabulary for description of the problem domain allows to formalize the autonomous agents and their contexts to ensure interoperability during joint task solving.
3	Context modelling	The problem domain ontology allows to identify of the user and task contexts. Context is a description of a situation in which the resource is located and contains all the information that can be used to describe this situation. Task context is a slice of the problem domain ontology that is related to the task. The agent's context is a slice of problem domain ontology that is related to the user.
4	Multi-level self-organization	Self-organization solution assumes of creating and maintaining a logical network structure on top of a dynamically changing physical network topology. Proposed multi-level self-organization solution allows to support the self-organization of the autonomous agents during coalition formation in different levels and provides policies from the upper level to the lower.
5	Ontology matching	Ontology matching solution is aimed to match two ontologies that formally describe different autonomous agents to support the semantic interoperability between them. Such matching provides possibilities for agents to "understand" each other and interact for coalition creation and task performing in case of absence of common ontology.
6	Artificial neural networks	The use of an artificial neural network allows to solve the ontology matching task for the case of weak formalization of the problem domain. Once having trained a neural network, the result of training can be used for various situations. In the case of minor changes in the compared ontologies (due to the variability of the operational context), the trained neural network will still give the correct result, albeit with less confidence due to the neural network flexibility. It should be noted that with significant changes in ontologies (for example, changing the abstract context) the neural network requires retraining.
7	Vector representation of words	The use of the vector representation of words allows to expand the possibilities of finding matches between ontology concepts based on the analysis of the semantics of the terms used to describe the concept. Since the vector space displays the meaning of a word in relation to its context, the detection of synonyms and concepts similar in meaning to a specific context is simplified. However, it should be noted that the use of vector representation of words requires a significant expenditure of resources both in the formation of vectors and in utilization.

ACKNOWLEDGMENT

The research is funded by the Russian State Research #0073-2019-0005. The neural network-based ontology matching method has been developed due to RFBR grant ## 17-29-07073. An ontology for mobile robot modelling has been developed in scope of RFBR grant 19-07-00670.

Table 3. Open problems: coalition formation by autonomous agents

#	Open Problem	Comment
1	Ontology usage and ontology matching methods	Ontology management is a powerful approach that allows to formally describe interacting resources in machine readable form with purposes of semantic interoperability between them. It is quite useful for providing autonomous agents interoperability, however there are open questions of how the ontology have to be built. If the resources are created on top of common ontology the matching between them is a simple task but the coverage of ontology will be highly limited by existing concepts of common ontology. If the ontologies have been created by different experts the ontology will describe the problem aria in very detail, but the matching becomes a complicated task. The successfulness of the matching depends on the several factors including the qualification of the ontology engineers. But it is possible to imagine the cases where the ontologies will not be matched, and the service will not be constructed. In this case the experts should be attracted to implement this process manually.
2	Multi-level self-organization	Knowledge-based interaction of the services requires a higher computation complexity in contrast to the usual one based on exchange the predefined structures of data. Knowledge based computation requires additional tasks such as ontology matching and requires to exchange more information. In this case the applicability of such approach strongly depends on the scenario. The developed should thing and choose between speed and universalism.
3	Task definition and distribution	Task definition in a formal form requires additional background from the agent who specifies it. These detail can provide a lot of information about how the certain task can be resolved therefore the task description is still open task. It is important to provide enough information to solve the task but keep away the information that is insufficient or even adversely affecting on the success of task solving. At the same time there are a lot of approaches to distribute task between coalition participants and the question of which approach is better is still open. For the proposed model one of the existing approaches to task distribution have to be chosen or an own approach have to be developed and evaluated.

REFERENCES

Ali Khoudja, M., Fareh, M., & Bouarfa, H. (2019). A New Supervised Learning Based Ontology Matching Approach Using Neural Networks. In Á. Rocha & M. Serrhini (Eds.), *Smart Innovation, Systems and Technologies* (Vol. 111, pp. 542–551). Cham: Springer International Publishing.

Alkilabi, M. H. M., Narayan, A., & Tuci, E. (2017). Cooperative object transport with a swarm of e-puck robots: Robustness and scalability of evolved collective strategies. *Swarm Intelligence*, *11*(3-4), 185–209. doi:10.100711721-017-0135-8

Baader, F., Calvanese, D., McGuinness, D., Nardi, D., & Patel-Schneider, P. (2003). *The description logic handbook: theory, implementation, and applications.* New York, NY: Cambridge University Press.

Baca, J., Pagala, P., Rossi, C., & Ferre, M. (2015). Modular robot systems towards the execution of cooperative tasks in large facilities. *Robotics and Autonomous Systems*, *66*, 159–174. doi:10.1016/j.robot.2014.10.008

Balandin, S., Boldyrev, S., Oliver, I., Turenko, T., Smirnov, A., Shilov, N., & Kashevnik, A. (2012). *Method and apparatus for ontology matching.* US Patent 2012/0078595 A1.

Barbosa, F. S., Duberg, D., Jensfelt, P., & Tumova, J. (2019). Guiding Autonomous Exploration With Signal Temporal Logic. *IEEE Robotics and Automation Letters*, *4*(4), 3332–3339. doi:10.1109/LRA.2019.2926669

Chand, P., & Carnegie, D. A. (2013). Mapping and exploration in a hierarchical heterogeneous multi-robot system using limited capability robots. *Robotics and Autonomous Systems*, *61*(6), 565–579. doi:10.1016/j.robot.2013.02.009

Ciortea, A., Mayer, S., & Michahelles, F. (2018). Repurposing manufacturing lines on the fly with multi-agent systems for the Web of Things. In *Proceedings of the 17th International Conference on Autonomous Agents and MultiAgent Systems* (pp. 813-822). International Foundation for Autonomous Agents and Multiagent Systems.

De Mola, F., & Quitadamo, R. (2006). Towards an Agent Model for Future Autonomic Communications. *Proceedings of the 7th WOA 2006 Workshop From Objects to Agents*.

Dey, A., Salber, D., & Abowd, G. (2001). A Conceptual Framework and a Toolkit for Supporting the Rapid Prototyping of Context-Aware Applications. *Human-Computer Interaction*, *16*(2), 97–199. doi:10.1207/S15327051HCI16234_02

Djeddi, W. E., & Khadir, M. T. (2013). Ontology alignment using artificial neural network for large-scale ontologies. *International Journal of Metadata, Semantics and Ontologies*, *8*(1), 75–92. doi:10.1504/IJMSO.2013.054180

Elfwing, S., Uchibe, E., & Doya, K. (2018). Sigmoid-weighted linear units for neural network function approximation in reinforcement learning. *Neural Networks*, *107*, 3–11. doi:10.1016/j.neunet.2017.12.012 PMID:29395652

Fernández, J. L., Sanz, R., Benayas, J. A., & Diéguez, A. R. (2004). Improving collision avoidance for mobile robots in partially known environments: The beam curvature method. *Robotics and Autonomous Systems*, *46*(4), 205–219. doi:10.1016/j.robot.2004.02.004

Ferrer, E. C. (2018, November). The blockchain: a new framework for robotic swarm systems. In *Proceedings of the Future Technologies Conference* (pp. 1037-1058). Springer.

Gyrard, A., Patel, P., Datta, S. K., & Ali, M. I. (2017). Semantic web meets internet of things and web of things. In *Proceedings of the 26th International Conference on World Wide Web Companion* (pp. 917-920). International World Wide Web Conferences Steering Committee. 10.1145/3041021.3051100

Hartanto, R., & Eich, M. (2014, April). Reliable, cloud-based communication for multi-robot systems. In *2014 IEEE International Conference on Technologies for Practical Robot Applications (TePRA)* (pp. 1-8). IEEE.

Horrocks, I. (2008). Ontologies and the semantic web. *Communications of the ACM*, *51*(12), 58–67. doi:10.1145/1409360.1409377

Iqbal, A., Ullah, F., Anwar, H., Kwak, K. S., Imran, M., Jamal, W., & Rahman, A. (2018). Interoperable Internet-of-Things platform for smart home system using Web-of-Objects and cloud. *Sustainable Cities and Society*, *38*, 636–646. doi:10.1016/j.scs.2018.01.044

Ivanov, D. (2018, September). Decentralized planning of intelligent mobile robot's behavior in a group with limited communications. In *International Conference on Intelligent Information Technologies for Industry* (pp. 418-427). Springer.

Jantsch, E. (1975). *Design for Evolution*. New York: George Braziller.

Kashevnik, A., Kalyazina, D., Parfenov, V., Shabaev, A., Baraniuc, O., Lashkov, I., & Khegai, M. (2018). Ontology-Based Human-Robot Interaction: An Approach and Case Study on Adaptive Remote Control Interface. In *Interactive Collaborative Robotics, Third International Conference on Interactive Collaborative Robotics (ICR 2018)*. Leipzig, Germany: Springer International Publishing.

Kashevnik, A., Smirnov, A., & Teslya, N. (2018). Ontology-Based Interaction of Mobile Robots for Coalition Creation. *International Journal of Embedded and Real-Time Communication Systems, 9*(2), 63–78. doi:10.4018/IJERTCS.2018070105

Klug, C., Schmalstieg, D., Gloor, T., & Arth, C. (2019). A complete workflow for automatic forward kinematics model extraction of robotic total stations using the denavit-hartenberg convention. *Journal of Intelligent & Robotic Systems, 95*(2), 311–329. doi:10.100710846-018-0931-4

Koes, M., Nourbakhsh, I., Sycara, K., Koes, M., Sycara, K., Nourbakhsh, I., & Jennings, N. R. (2005, July). *Heterogeneous multirobot coordination with spatial and temporal constraints* (Vol. 5). AAAI.

Kubicek, H., & Cimander, R. (2009). Three dimensions of organizational interoperability: Insights from recent studies for improving interoperability frame-works. *European Journal of ePractice, 6*.

Kubicek, H., Cimander, R., & Scholl, H. (2011). Organizational Interoperability in E-Government: Lessons from 77 European Good-Practice Cases. Academic Press.

Li, B., Moridian, B., Kamal, A., Patankar, S., & Mahmoudian, N. (2019). Multi-robot mission planning with static energy replenishment. *Journal of Intelligent & Robotic Systems, 95*(2), 745–759. doi:10.100710846-018-0897-2

Li, W., Li, Z., Li, Y., Ding, L., Wang, J., Gao, H., & Deng, Z. (2019, November). Semi-autonomous bilateral teleoperation of six-wheeled mobile robot on soft terrains. *Mechanical Systems and Signal Processing, 133*, 106234. doi:10.1016/j.ymssp.2019.07.015

Liang, X., & Xiao, Y. (2009). Studying bio-inspired coalition formation of robots for detecting intrusions using game theory. *IEEE Transactions on Systems, Man, and Cybernetics. Part B, Cybernetics, 40*(3), 683–693. doi:10.1109/TSMCB.2009.2034976 PMID:19933008

López, J., Pérez, D., Paz, E., & Santana, A. (2013). WatchBot: A building maintenance and surveillance system based on autonomous robots. *Robotics and Autonomous Systems, 61*(12), 1559–1571. doi:10.1016/j.robot.2013.06.012

Manjula Shenoy, K., Shet, K. C., & Dinesh Acharya, U. (2013). NN based ontology mapping. *Communications in Computer and Information Science, 296*, 122–127.

Meulpolder, M., Pouwelse, J., Epema, D., & Sips, H. (2009). BarterCast: A practical approach to prevent lazy freeriding in P2P networks. *IEEE International Symposium on Parallel & Distributed Processing*.

Nadim, I., Elghayam, Y., & Sadiq, A. (2018, April). Semantic discovery architecture for dynamic environments of Web of Things. In *2018 International Conference on Advanced Communication Technologies and Networking (CommNet)* (pp. 1-6). IEEE. 10.1109/COMMNET.2018.8360269

Negash, B., Westerlund, T., & Tenhunen, H. (2019). Towards an interoperable Internet of Things through a web of virtual things at the Fog layer. *Future Generation Computer Systems, 91*, 96–107. doi:10.1016/j.future.2018.07.053

Ono, K., & Ogawa, H. (2014). Personal Robot Using Android Smartphone. *Procedia Technology, 18*, 37–41. doi:10.1016/j.protcy.2014.11.009

Qian, B., & Cheng, H. H. (2018). Bio-Inspired Coalition Formation Algorithms for Multirobot Systems. *Journal of Computing and Information Science in Engineering, 18*(2), 021010. doi:10.1115/1.4039638

Rodić, A., Jovanović, M., Stevanović, I., Karan, B., & Potkonjak, V. (2015). *Building Technology Platform Aimed to Develop Service Robot with Embedded Personality and Enhanced Communication with Social Environment*. Digital Communications and Networks.

Serena, F., Poveda-Villalón, M., & García-Castro, R. (2017, June). Semantic discovery in the web of things. In *International Conference on Web Engineering* (pp. 19-31). Springer.

Shabanov, V., & Ivanov, D. (2019, March). Organization of Information Exchange in Coalitions of Intelligent Mobile Robots. In *2019 International Conference on Industrial Engineering, Applications and Manufacturing (ICIEAM)* (pp. 1-5). IEEE. 10.1109/ICIEAM.2019.8743043

Smirnov, A., Kashevnik, A., & Shilov, N. (2015). *Cyber-Physical-Social System Self-Organization: Ontology-Based Multi-level Approach and Case Study*. 2015 IEEE 9th International Conference on Self-Adaptive and Self-Organizing Systems, Cambridge, MA.

Smirnov, A., Kashevnik, A., Shilov, N., Balandin, S., Oliver, I., & Boldyrev, S. (2010). On-the-Fly Ontology Matching in Smart Spaces: A Multi-Model Approach. *Proceedings of the Third Conference on Smart Spaces*, 72-83. 10.1007/978-3-642-14891-0_7

Smirnov, A., Kashevnik, A., Teslya, N., Mikhailov, S., & Shabaev, A. (2015, April). Smart-M3-based robots self-organization in pick-and-place system. In *2015 17th Conference of Open Innovations Association (FRUCT)* (pp. 210-215). IEEE. 10.1109/FRUCT.2015.7117994

Tagliabue, A., Kamel, M., Siegwart, R., & Nieto, J. (2019). Robust collaborative object transportation using multiple mavs. *The International Journal of Robotics Research, 38*(9), 1020–1044. doi:10.1177/0278364919854131

Tosello, E., Fan, Z., Castro, A. G., & Pagello, E. (2016, July). Cloud-based task planning for smart robots. In *International Conference on Intelligent Autonomous Systems* (pp. 285-300). Springer.

Verma, D., Desai, N., Preece, A., & Taylor, I. (2017, May). A block chain based architecture for asset management in coalition operations. In *Ground/Air Multisensor Interoperability, Integration, and Networking for Persistent ISR VIII* (Vol. 10190, p. 101900Y). International Society for Optics and Photonics. doi:10.1117/12.2264911

Xiang, C., Jiang, T., Chang, B., & Sui, Z. (2015). ERSOM: A structural ontology matching approach using automatically learned entity representation. In *Conference Proceedings - EMNLP 2015: Conference on Empirical Methods in Natural Language Processing* (pp. 2419–2429). 10.18653/v1/D15-1289

Xue, F., Tang, H., Su, Q., & Li, T. (2019). Task Allocation of Intelligent Warehouse Picking System based on Multi-robot Coalition. *Transactions on Internet and Information Systems (Seoul)*, *13*(7).

Yu, L., & Cai, Z. (2009, August). Robot exploration mission planning based on heterogeneous interactive cultural hybrid algorithm. In *2009 Fifth International Conference on Natural Computation* (Vol. 5, pp. 583-587). IEEE. 10.1109/ICNC.2009.15

Zhang, T., & Ueno, H. (2007). Knowledge model-based heterogeneous multi-robot system implemented by a software platform. *Knowledge-Based Systems*, *20*(3), 310–319. doi:10.1016/j.knosys.2006.04.019

Zhu, Y., Zhang, T., Song, J., & Li, X. (2013). A hybrid navigation strategy for multiple mobile robots. *Robotics and Computer-integrated Manufacturing*, *29*(4), 129–141. doi:10.1016/j.rcim.2012.11.007

KEY TERMS AND DEFINITIONS

Abstract Context: The ontology-based description of the task appearing in the IoT environment taking in the account the current situation.

Context: Any information that can be used to characterize the situation of a resource of IoT environment.

Internet of Things (IoT): The internetworking of physical entities represented by devices that enable these entities to collect and exchange data for a achieving a common goal.

Ontology: Formally represents knowledge as a set of concepts within a domain, using a shared vocabulary to denote the types, properties, and interrelationships of those concepts.

Ontology Matching: Set of techniques combined together for identified the similar elements in two ontologies.

Operational Context: The instantiation of the domain constituent of the abstract context with data provided by the contextual resources.

Semantic Interoperability: An understanding of the meaning of the information exchanged between software components.

Chapter 3
Ontology–Driven Design and Development of Situation Assessment Software in Cyber–Physical Systems

Sergey Lebedev

(iD) https://orcid.org/0000-0002-0045-6310

Saint Petersburg Electrotechnical University (LETI), Russia

Michail Panteleyev

St. Petersburg Electrotechnical University (LETI), Russia

ABSTRACT

Evolution of cyber-physical systems (CPS) and extension of their application areas complicate, among other things, their software design and development. This requires improvements in programming techniques used to build CPS. One of the important tasks arising in complex CPS is a situation assessment (SA) based on data received from diverse sources. In the chapter, an ontology-driven approach for CPS SA software design and development automation is proposed. The approach is based on the JDL data fusion model and flexible enough to be applied for any class of CPS applications. In contrast to known approaches, ontologies are used not only for domain knowledge representation but also for SA calculation process formalization. It provides a higher level of automation of SA software synthesis and, in the end, increases design and development efficiency.

INTRODUCTION

The integration of information processing capabilities and network communications of various devices has been actively developed in recent years within the framework of the concepts of "Cyber-Physical Systems" (CPS) and "Internet of Things" (IoT). Examples of such systems vary in a very wide range – from intelligent vehicles to advanced manufacturing systems, in such diverse sectors as energy, agri-

DOI: 10.4018/978-1-7998-1974-5.ch003

culture, smart cities, public security and others (Greer, Burns, Wollman, & Griffor, 2019; Yang, Yang, & Plotnick, 2013)

According to ITU-T Y.2060 recommendation IoT architecture includes four levels (Guth et al., 2018):

- Device Layer;
- Network Layer;
- Service support and Application support Layer;
- Application Layer.

In recent years, a considerable progress has been made in the realm of development of wireless access technologies for sensor networks and IoT networks (LoRa, Wi-Fi HaLoW, ZigBee, Sigfox, and etc) (Fujino, Ogawa, & Minowa, 2016; Kocakulak & Butun, 2017; Lazarescu, 2017; Lea, 2018).

Nowadays the creation of technologies that helps to increase the efficiency of CPS/IoT design processes at the Application Layer becomes relevant.

As CPS/IoT complexity is increasing, the number of sensor nodes is growing and the volume of data from these nodes is going up, the Application Layer task of situation assessment (SA) is becoming increasingly important. Within different domains (e.g. mass event security) SA exploiting perceived data is used to support decision-making processes. In this context, a consideration of CPS/IoT from the position of People in the Loop (Petrov et al., 2018) concept becomes crucial.

The key features of the current stage of CPS/IoT development are the transition to the mass practical use of such systems and their complications both in quantitative (increasing the number of interacting nodes) and in qualitative (complicating data processing algorithms) terms. Given these trends, a lot of attention has recently been paid to the development of platforms for CPS/IoT (Guth et al., 2018; Meiling, Purnomo, Shiraishi, Fischer, & Schmid, 2018).

An important intelligent function of CPS/IoT systems is data fusion from many sources including real-time situation assessment (SA). As systems become more and more complex the value of this function increases significantly. Given this, an urgent task at present is to create platform solutions that allow situation assessment software to be effectively implemented for a wide range of applications.

The article discusses the approach, formal models and methods for automating processes of designing and developing software for SA systems (SAS) using ontologies. Ontologies provide the ability to flexibly and quickly focus on the domain of a specific application. The approach allows reducing the time needed for designing and developing SAS software. The software framework to solve this problem is considered. An example of building a situation assessment system for CPS to ensure the security of public events is considered to illustrate the proposed approach.

BACKGROUND

In recent years, CPSs have been rapidly evolving and have been found to have extensive use in widespread application areas (Greer et al., 2019). Therefore significant attention has been put on CPS platforms allowing replication of single applications and effective implementation of concrete applied CPS (Guth et al., 2018).

There are a wide number of questions that are discussed within the context of CPS platform development. In (Theodoropoulos et al., 2017) issues on building scalable software and hardware solutions for CPS supporting parallel programming are discussed. In (Sun, Yang, & Zhou, 2017) classification of CPS platforms into three categories based on the software architecture is suggested: based on components, based on services, and based on agents. For each category, several design approaches, key challenges, and solutions are considered.

Issues on semantic integration of models and instruments with the aim of their reuse while the development of commercial and open instruments for CPS based on OpenMETA solution are discussed in (Sztipanovits et al., 2018). OpenMETA includes two key platforms: one for model and one for instrument integration.

In (Lovas et al., 2018) an approach allowing creating and controlling scalable virtual CPS platforms is proposed. The solution is based on two types of demands: one is concerning a framework used to form a sensor network and one is concerning a model tools configuration used to forecast the behavior of production systems.

Within the context of various CPS, one of the most important functions is SA that is used to integrate diverse data received from multiple sources (sensors, detectors, channels) and to build a semantically meaningful situation model based on this data. In (Alcaraz, Cazorla, & Lopez, 2017; Alcaraz & Lopez, 2013) a concept of global SA (WASA) is considered. Also, an approach to the construction of such systems is proposed. In (Y. Wang, Tan, Wang, & Yin, 2012) an architecture for CPS perception control within a realm of traffic monitoring and control is proposed. The architecture is used to build solutions for preventing traffic accidents but can also be used for other tasks. In (Yang et al., 2013) a situation awareness based on IoT for emergency response is presented. Several questions on social data fusion within a CPS platform are discussed in (P. Wang, Yang, Li, Chen, & Hu, 2019).

Platform solutions for SA should be created based on some wide adopted theoretical models. One such model orientated on an operator's cognitive processes is a situation awareness model proposed by Endsley (Endsley, 2016). Another widespread model currently used for construction information systems including SA functionality is a reference JDL Data Fusion model (Blasch, 2017). A thorough review of SA models and their comparison can be found in (Foo & Ng, 2013).

In recent years Semantic Web technologies and, in particular, an OWL language have found use as a unified conceptual base for the development of cross-domain CPS platforms. Examples of platforms using Semantic Web technologies are considered in (Bonte et al., 2017; Seiger, Huber, Heisig, & Assmann, 2016)

The usage of formal models codified with ontologies is also considered as a perspective instrument for building SAS. The main idea behind the approach is a desire to reduce as much as possible the volume of procedural programming and substitute it with the wide use of declarative knowledge. According to the approach, a domain is described with a set of axioms and rules. Some extra assertions are added to the set reflecting the current state of the environment. After this, a procedure of logical inference is launched that derive new facts about the environment. There are several examples of using Semantic Web technologies for SA – (Baumgartner et al., 2014; Hongfei, Hongjian, Hongli, & Ying, 2016; Kokar, Matheus, & Baclawski, 2009; Pai, Yang, & Chung, 2017).

Increased automation of CPS and, in particular, SAS software development can be reached through an application of the model-driven approach. The approach enables a cross-cutting transition from a domain description to several program artifacts. Theoretically, the approach is close to works on the inductive and deductive synthesis of programs, where some kind of logic is used to generate software (Tyugu, Matskin, & Penjam, 1999).

The development of these ideas in connection with descriptive logic (OWL ontologies) within the context of the model-driven approach is considered perspective as it allows increasing the level of automation of CPS and SAS software design and development processes.

ONTOLOGY-DRIVEN DESIGN AND DEVELOPMENT OF SAS SOFTWARE

Ontology Engineering

As ontologies play an important role in the proposed approach, some important concepts from the realm of Semantic Web are discussed in the paragraph: ontological languages, instruments, and libraries used for the proposed approach. Also, a SPARQL-base rule system is described. The system is used for inter-ontology transition in accordance with the model-driven approach.

In the Semantic Web domain, a variety of languages, instruments, and libraries to work with ontologies are being designed and developed. For ontology representation metadata model/scheme RDF/RDFS and OWL languages are used. OWL language is based on description logic and extends RDF/RDFS.

OWL is used to describe a problem domain in the form of so-called subject-predicate-objects triples. The subject and the object are usually expressed with ontological classes and class instances. Predicates are expressed with ontological properties. There are two types of properties: data property and object property. The letter is used to set binary relations between objects. In the context of the paper (binary) relation and object property are used as synonyms.

SPARQL language is a query language that is used to work with ontologies. To some extent, it is similar to the SQL language used for relational databases. SPARQL provides different query types and constructs to get data from ontologies and to build new ontological fragments. Typical SPARQL query comprises two parts: an action-part (select, construct, ask, insert) that is used to form a query result; and a "where"-part that is used to match triples in the ontology.

Another one important language is SPIN – the SPARQL Inferencing Notation[1]. It is the language that is used to fix constraints and rules based on SPARQL-queries. Constraints can be used to put and check some restrictions on classes, instances, and their links. Rules can be used to build new ontological entities or to modify the existing ontology-based on its current state. The language also defines some additional constructs including those to codify some common use cases.

With the help of SPIN constructs, a SPARQL-query is attached as a rule or a constraint to an ontological class. So when an instance of the class is asserted the query is called. If the query represents a rule and the rule constructs some new instances of classes with attached rules then these rules are also called. Eventually, a rule chain emerges. Also, there is a successor of SPIN language – SHACL, Shapes Constraint Language[2].

There are a number of editors that can be used for ontology building and editing, e.g. Protégé[3] and TopBraid Composer[4]. TopBraid editor is implemented as an Eclipse plugin. One of the significant advantages of this editor is that it supports SPIN and SHACL languages including special GUI forms and an in-build engine for processing constraints and rules specified in those languages. To work with the engine out from a program code a special TopBraid API[5] can be used.

Figure 1. A mass event use case

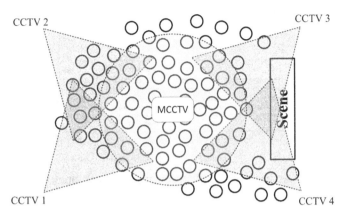

To visualize ontology fragments presented in the paper a data.world[6] integration called Ontodia[7] is used. It provides a GUI to visualize OWL graph fragments. To use the integration it is necessary to upload data containing ontology to be visualized.

To work with ontologies out of a program code Jena API[8] can be used. API provides the means to load and save ontologies, to run SPARQL queries, to construct ontologies in an object-oriented manner.

Data Fusion Use Case: Role of SAS

One of the key functions of CPS is building a high-level model of a monitored environment. The model allows forecasting environment evolution and making reasonable decisions. Within the data fusion model, a situation assessment system (SAS) is responsible for the construction of the model. The obtained state is also called situational awareness.

Let's consider a data fusion process and the role of SAS in detail. To make the discussion more clear an illustrative use case from a realm of public mass events (festivals, sports games, music concerts, demonstrations and so on) will be used. The example will be used within the whole paper.

Some typical mass event scenario is presented in Figure 1. The scenario is applicable to music concerts, football matches open broadcasting, political performance, and so on.

In front of the open space, there is a scene where some performance is taking place. People (designated with circles) are mainly located opposite the stage, but some of them are around the stage.

One of the tasks to be solved when conducting a mass event is to provide public security. For this purpose a special information system can be used for monitoring and early detection of dangerous situations including: a threat of a terrorist incident, a clash of conflicting groups (football fans, supporters of opposite socio-political parties and so on), individual antisocial manifestations, unforeseen unintended events (like fires, a sudden decline in health and so on).

According to the JDL data fusion model, the system's calculation process will be the following – Figure 2, where solid-line arrows designate control links, dotted lines with hollow tips designate data links, HCI is an abbreviation for human-computer interaction.

There are the following levels:

Figure 2. JDL Model

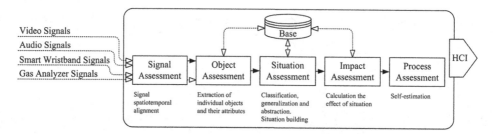

The zeroth level is a signal assessment level: receiving and spatiotemporal synchronization of signals. Signals can be transmitted from a variety of sensors. In Figure 2 a video system is presented as an example: stationary closed-circuit television (CCTV) and mobile (drone-based) closed-circuit television (MCCTV). Also, data from wearable devices can be used such as smartphones, fitness-trackers, police video cameras, and so on. Of course, sensors provide not only video data but other types of data as well – audio, geo, health information, etc. In some cases, special types of sensors can be used such as gas one to detect smoke or gas poisoning.

The first level is an object assessment level: extraction of objects and their attributes from signals. In the considered use case, individual persons or indistinguishable groups of people can be extracted from video signals. Also, separate features can be extracted, including clothes and things (bags, bottles, and so on); age; distinctive behavioral patterns and emotional conditions; attributes of some processes like smoke, open fire, firework. Separate sound events can be extracted from audio signals – like explosions, cries, fan chants.

The second level is a situation assessment level (SA). The goal of SA is to classify, abstract and generalize received object data while construction of a restricted set of situations for which it is known what variants of the decisions can be made or variants of actions can be performed. SA is a kind of ascending process from concrete and individual to general and abstract.

For example, based on extracted features of clothes (colors, inscriptions) an individual affiliation to a known fan group is found. Individual persons are joined to the group based on a number of specific movement patterns. Based on gestures, chants, and pulse changes (if data from fitness-tracker is available) of separate participants, the group is characterized as emotionally excited, aggressive. Another group and its location are detected. It is found that the second group has a hostile attitude to the first group (e.g. based on existing police historical reports). Also, it is found based on mutual movement that these two groups have an intention to clash.

As a result, a problem situation arises that needs different (police, ambulance) services attention. Also, the probability and severity of the problem situation can be estimated, e.g. based on the group size, armament (bottles, street furniture, etc.), and so on.

The third level is an impact assessment level. The possible effects of the conflict are calculated based on the computed problem situations. Using these results the mode and the scale of emergency services can be defined.

The fourth level is a process assessment level. The effectiveness and performance of data fusion processes are estimated at this level. Based on these estimations these processes can be tuned or modified.

Figure 3. SAS Computation Architecture

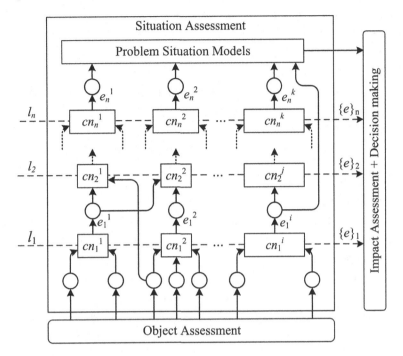

So the role of SAS is to build a problem high-level integrated situation model based on separate objects and their features. Problem situations can be used to forecast environment states, participant intentions, and, in the end, to make a reasonable decision. Essentially SA is a process of calculation of unseen elements and their interconnections based on separately perceived elements.

Let's consider the SAS architecture.

Situation Awareness System Architecture

The most straightforward approach to software development is a so-called "ad hoc" approach. According to the approach, a system is developed exclusively for the domain in mind and for the given set of scenarios. The approach has the following disadvantage. If there is a need to modify or extend the system it will be necessary to invest practically the same volume of labor that was spent at the creation of the system. In other words, one will have to repeat the work once again.

An alternative approach is supposed to separate domain-independent and domain-specific parts. The domain-independent part can be freely transferred to a new domain.

It is suggested to consider an architecture of SAS based on a dataflow model as a domain-independent part, see Figure 3.

The dataflow is a graph composed of computation nodes ("black boxes") performing specific calculations based on data received from and passing results to some other nodes. The idea of dataflow computation is thoroughly developed within the concept of flow-based programming (Morrison, 2010). The advantages of the dataflow model are the following: the model provides "natural" parallelization because separate nodes do not share data (Johnston, Hanna, & Millar, 2004); there a number of scalable high-performance frameworks based on the concepts of this model such as Apache Beam[9], Apache Spark[10], Apache Storm[11], Apache Flink[12], and others; the SA process as an ascending computation process can be naturally represented in terms of this model.

The process of SA is divided into computation levels $(l_1, ..., l_n)$. Each level is linked with a set of computation nodes – cn_i^j, where i is the number of node's level, j is the number of the node among other nodes of the same level. Each node implements some function specified by a user or a developer. The function used to compute a domain object or a relation – a domain element e.

Nodes receive data from nodes located on the lower levels and transfer data to nodes located on higher levels. Nodes of the first level receive data from the downstream system – from the object assessment level of the data fusion model. At the highest levels of SA, a set of problem situations is formed that is transferred to the impact assessment level of the data fusion model or to some servicers supporting or implementing a decision-making process.

Relatively to some concrete node it is distinguished: donor nodes – a set of nodes that provide input data for the considered node; acceptor nodes – a set of nodes that use output data of the considered node as its input data; and independent nodes – a set comprising of nodes having no links with the considered node (in the first place, the set includes nodes located on the same level).

Let's illustrate the dataflow with the previously represented example. The nodes of the first level of SAS receive data describing separate participants of a mass event and their clothes attributes. These nodes compute the affiliation of an individual to some known organization based on the provided attributes. On the next level, separate individuals are joined into a crowd based on their mutual location. And so on accordingly to the example. On the highest level, the problem situation is constructed – an armed group of people threatens the lives and property of others.

The common principles of the presented architecture are independent of the domain. The specificity of domain manifests itself in the following details:

- A concrete SAS computation architecture structure: the number of computation nodes and levels, the configuration of inter-node connections;
- Domain content: a set of algorithms used to implement node functions, a set of objects received from the downstream system, a set of calculated elements including a set of problem situations.

The listed items define the scope and the content of a tailoring a domain-independent part to domain specificity. And thus define the scope and the content of the design and development processes of SAS software.

To make the domain tuning efficient it is necessary to support it with an instrument set.

Ontology-Driven Approach to Design and Development of SAW Software

To build the said instrument the authors propose to use an ontology-driven approach to design and development of software. The approach provides automation of transition from a formal domain model (ontology) as an initial stage of the design process to program implementation of SAS as a final stage of the development process through a number of intermediate stages.

In Figure 4 the general scheme of the approach is presented, where rectangles with numbers in circles designate an ordered sequence of stages (actions), rounded rectangles designate created and transferred artifacts.

Figure 4. The Proposed Approach

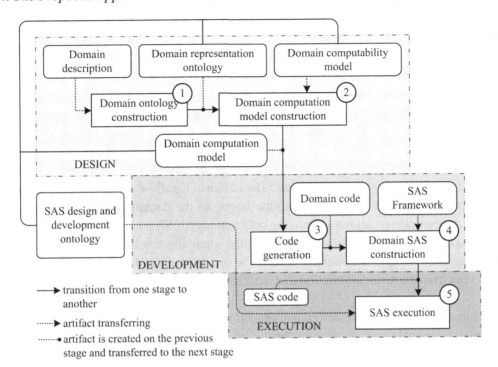

The proposed approach covers the main stages of the software product life cycle: design, development, and execution. Let's consider each stage separately.

In accordance with the model-driven approach design process consists of: 1) building some initial models; 2) transition from initial models to target model through a number of intermediate models. In that way, the process is simplified to be controlled more easily. Note, that ontologies are considered as a way to formally codify a model in OWL. In the proposed approach an initial model is the domain ontology, the target model – is the domain dataflow ontology. Domain-independent elements used on the design stage to automate model transitions are grouped in SAS design and development ontology (SAS Ontology).

The design process starts with an informal domain description. The description is formalized as a domain-specific ontology based on *representation ontology*.

The transition from the domain ontology to dataflow ontology is suggested to be done in two steps:

1. Set computability dependencies among separate domain ontology elements, i.e. between classes and relations;
2. Link and order separate commutability dependencies so that each dependency will be associated with some computation node located on a concrete computation level, see Figure 3.

To set computability dependencies the authors suggest using a set of predefined schemes. Elements of these schemes are formalized in the proposed computability ontology, see Figure 4. The schemes are discussed in "Domain-Independent SAS Ontology" paragraph. These schemes allow the automation of the second step while transitioning to the domain dataflow ontology.

Created computability dependencies are fixed in *the domain computability ontology*. On the second stage (see Figure 4), *the domain dataflow ontology* is constructed based on the previously received ontology: separate computability dependencies are associated with computability nodes which are ordered in a dataflow process. The lowest level is formed with nodes using only data from the object assessment level; the next level is formed with nodes using data from the object assessment level and data calculated with the nodes of the first level and so on.

The generated dataflow ontology is passed to the development stage where it is used to generate domain-specific program code. The generated code is integrated into the domain-independent framework. The framework implements a general logic of the dataflow process.

On the final step, nodes' calculation functions are implemented by a programmer.

The advantage of the approach is as follows. The obtained dataflow ontology can be used not only on the development stage but also on the runtime stage. As the domain dataflow ontology fixes the computability dependencies it allows initializing only that part of SA software which is supported with some real data. It makes sense in so-called open worlds, where the number and diversity of objects are constantly changing making it necessary to change the structure of the dataflow.

It can be seen from the given description that dataflow process is represented in the following forms:

1.   In the ontological form on the design and execution stages;
2.   As a program model (a set of program classes) on the development stage;
3.   And as a program dataflow (s set of instances of program classes) on the execution stage.

All these representations fit the common dataflow model depicted in Figure 3.

The application of ontologies not only for the domain model description but also for building and implementing the dataflow process is a distinctive feature of the proposed approach that allows:

1.   To lift the conceptual level of the design process up to the level of domain model engineering and so make it less coupled with software concepts;
2.   To partially automate considered transitions. On the design stage, dataflow ontology is automatically generated. And so does the domain-specific code on the development stage. On the execution stage, the program structure of the dataflow process is generated based on the dataflow ontology.

SAS Ontology and SAS framework are domain-independent parts of the instrument. Let's consider them in detail.

Ontology-Driven Instrument for Design and Development of SAW Software

Domain-Independent SAS Ontology

As it was said the design process is the process of ontologies transformation. It starts with domain ontology that is transformed into the domain computability ontology that, in its turn, is transformed into the domain dataflow ontology (computation ontology). These transformations are based on the corresponding domain-independent ontologies joined in SAS Ontology. Based on the elements of this ontology the authors proposed a set of rules to automate transformations.

Let's consider these ontologies.

Figure 5. Elements of the computability ontology

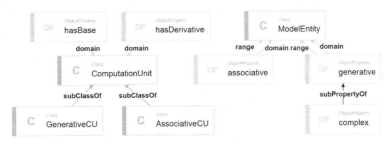

Figure 6. Codification of associative relation

Domain ontology is mostly built using the representation means provided by OWL. The provided representational ontology includes a couple of abstract elements to designate domain elements.

As it has been said the transition from the domain ontology to the domain computability ontology is comprised of fixing computability dependencies between separate domain elements with elements of the special schemes represented in computability ontology. The elements of the ontology are represented in Figure 5 and are discussed below.

Generally, computability dependency is a link between known/computed elements and unknown elements that should be computed. Such a link can be represented as a function dependency $f(x) = y$. Taking into account the chosen formalization language, i.e. OWL, the authors have proposed the mechanism that derives these dependencies from OWL axioms defining the domain. For now, the mechanism exploits only axioms that define the domain and range of object properties.

To use the chosen axioms two basic types of computability relations are proposed: associative and generative relation – so that any domain relation can be inherited from one of these relations.

Each computability relation is interpreted with a corresponding function, represented in Equation (1) and in Equation (2).

$$r(D, R) \rightarrow r_a(D, R) \rightarrow f(D, R) = r(D, R) \tag{1}$$

$$r(D, R) \rightarrow r_g(D, R) \rightarrow f(D) = <R, r(D, R)> \tag{2}$$

where r – a domain relation, r_a – an associative relation, r_g – a generative relation, D – a relation/function domain set, R – a relation/function range set, f – a calculation function.

An associative relation defines a function that on the base of two known (perceived or previously calculated) objects calculates the unknown relation between these objects. E.g., if we have extracted an

Figure 7. Codification of generative relation

Figure 8. Codification of a composite associative relation

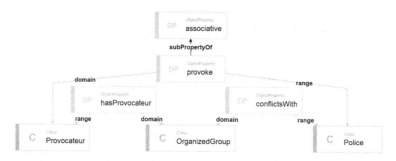

object describing a person in specific clothes and also know that there are some groups with some particular attributes then we may compute with which group the person is affiliated with or, in other words, to classify the person. Figure 6 represents the codification of the described computability dependency.

A generative relation defines a function that on the base of known (previously computed) object calculates the unknown object and sets a relation between them. E.g., we classify a group of individuals as an organized group based on predefined behavioral patterns. Then we may suppose that the group has a leader that is not "seen" at the current moment (but we may take some additional actions to find him/her out). Figure 7 represents the codification of the described computability dependency.

Besides these two basic interpretations, Equation (1) and Equation (2), there are four additional interpretations based on them. The first two of them are defined for a relation composition (in OWL language *owl:propertyChainAxiom* construct is used to represent object property compositions):

$$r(D_1, R_2) = r_2(D_2, R_2) \circ r_1(D_1, R_1) \to r_a(D_1, R_2) \to f(r_2(D_2, R_2), r_1(D_1, R_1)) = r(D_1, R_2) \tag{3}$$

$$r(D_1, R_2) = r_2(D_2, R_2) \circ r_1(D_1, R_1) \to r_g(D_1, R_2) \to f(r_1(D_1, R_1)) = <R_2, r_2(D_2, R_2), r(D_1, R_2)> \tag{4}$$

where $R_1 = D_2$.

Functions defining basic interpretations accept only objects as arguments. But it can be seen from Equation (2) that relation is also a possible result and so there is a need to be able to use it as a function argument. For this purpose, relation composition interpretations, Equation (3) and Equation (4), are proposed.

Figure 9. Codification of a composite generative relation

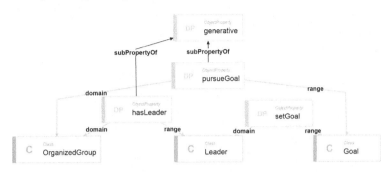

Figure 10. Codification of a complex object

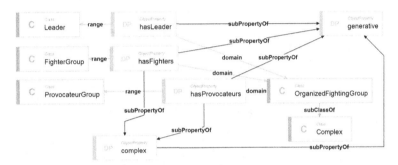

The interpretation represented in Equation (3) is an associative composition that allows linking two objects through another common object. E.g. it is known that some group has provocateurs. Also, it is known that the group is conflicting with the police. So, we may make an assumption, i.e. compute a composite relation *provoke = conflictsWith ∘ hasProvocateur⁻¹*, that provocateurs will provoke the police into conflict, see Figure 8.

The interpretation represented in Equation (4) defines a generative composition that generates a third object based on the knowledge that there are two objects interlinked with the relation. E.g. it is known that some organized group has a leader. Then it is possible to assume that the leader has set a goal that must be pursued by the group. In other words, it is possible to compute the goal as a new object and link it with two previously known objects – the leader and the group, see Figure 9.

And there also proposed two interpretations that define complex object generation:

$$r_1(D_1, R_c), \ldots, r_n(D_n, R_c) \rightarrow r_c(D_1, R_c), \ldots, r_c(D_n, R_c) \rightarrow f(D_1, \ldots, D_n) = \langle R_c, r_1(D_1, R_c), \ldots, r_n(D_1, R_c) \rangle \tag{5}$$

$$r(D, R_c)^n \rightarrow r_c(D, R_c)^n \rightarrow f(D^n) = \langle R_c, r(D, R_c)^n \rangle \tag{6}$$

Figure 11. Computation unit example

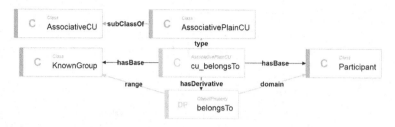

Figure 12. Domain-independent dataflow ontology

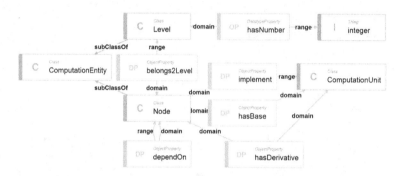

The complex interpretation represented in Equation (5) allows treating a case when some object can be generated only when a complex structure of objects exists. As a result, the complex object is created and linked with all initial objects. E.g. an organized battle group of fans is created only in a case when a leader, a sub-group of provocateurs, and a sub-group of fighters are known, see Figure 10.

The complex interpretation represented in Equation (6) allows treating a case when some object can be generated only when a group of objects of the same class exists. As a result, the complex object is created and linked with all initial objects. E.g. in such a manner a group can be created based on separate individuals having some common attributes.

The user should designate (through class inheriting) a set of classes which instances are received from the downstream system (*Percepted* class is used) and a set of classes which instances will be known a priory (*Known* class is used).

Based on fixed by a user computability dependencies (or relations) a set of computability units – instances of *ComputationUnit* class – is automatically generated with the help of rules included in domain-independent computability ontology. Computation units help to explicitly represent dependencies. Each calculation unit is defined as a set of basic objects (linked with *hasBase* relation) that forms function arguments and a set of derivative objects (linked with *hasDerivative* relation) that forms the function value. E.g. in Figure 11 a computation unit is represented that has been built for an associative relation *belongs_to*. A set of base elements consists of instances of known groups and "seen" individual participants; a set of derivative (computed) elements consists of the said instances linked with the relation.

Figure 13. An example fragment of domain dataflow ontology

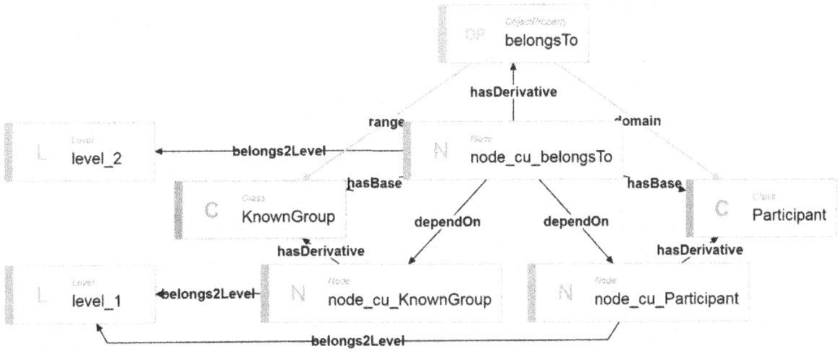

At this step, the building of the domain computability ontology is finished. On the next step, an automated transition to the domain dataflow ontology is taken place. The automation is done with the help of rules.

The elements of domain-independent dataflow ontology are represented in Figure 12. These elements are used to codify a domain dataflow and discussed below.

Based on the information on computation units linked with percepted and known elements, nodes of the first level are created. These nodes do not have base elements and their derivative elements are instances of mentioned classes. The nodes can be seen as adapters to said systems.

Then provided rules choose computation units which base elements constitute a subset of currently fixed set of derivative elements. In other words, these base elements are computed by generated computation nodes.

For every such computation unit, a computation node (*Node*) is generated, which picks base (*hasBase*) and derivative (*hasDerivative*) elements of the computation unit. Also, the created node is linked with those nodes that provide base elements – donor nodes, and the node itself becomes an acceptor for them. The node is linked to a computation level (*Level*) which number is greater on one than the number of the max donor's level. E.g. nodes that depend only on the first level nodes are linked to the second level.

The levels are generated as follows. At the very beginning, the first level is unconditionally created. As the first node is linked to this level the next one is generated, and so on.

As nodes of the second level are generated they form a set of available donors with the nodes of the first level. The dataflow generation process continues until a node or a level can be generated

An example of the generated domain dataflow model is represented in Figure 13. The layout of the dataflow model representation is the same as in Figure 3.

Generated domain dataflow ontology is passed to the stage of code generation.

As it has been said to generate elements of domain computability and dataflow ontologies the rules are used. These rules are based on SPARQL-queries. Some basic principles of rule specification and functioning can be found in "Ontology Engineering" paragraph.

A set of ontological classes has been created by authors to organize the rules within SAS Ontology. These classes can be seen as a partial formalization of the approach stages: the rules used on a specific stage are linked to an appropriate class; the creation of an instance of such stage-class runs its rules. The following stages (sub-stages) are represented: the creation of computation units; the creation of computation nodes and levels; the activation of computation nodes.

Figure 14. SAS Framework architecture and main cycle

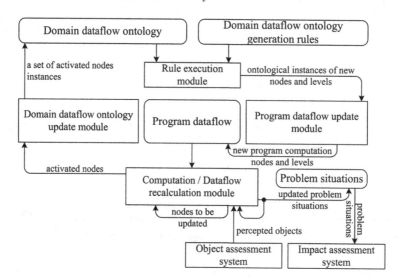

The rules for node activation play a specific role. The rules for the creation of computation nodes fully build nodes based on computation units except linking them to appropriate derivative elements (relation *hasDerivative*). This operation is implemented with the rules for node activation. Such separation allows using of the domain computability and dataflow ontologies not only on the design stage but also on the execution stage.

The goal of the design stage is to build the whole possible domain dataflow model that is used to generate all the necessary code. The code will be used for the computation of all known data within the given scenarios. That is why on this stage the rules for node activations are switched on and any generated node is immediately linked with its derivative elements making it possible to generate new nodes.

At the execution stage, the domain dataflow ontology is used to actualize a dataflow program structure within the SAS framework. It is possible (and in some case desirable) not to build the whole domain dataflow ontology but only the part that is supported with the actually calculated data. That is why the rules for the node activation stage are switched off on the execution. Instead, derivative elements are linked with computation node instances based on the information from the SAS Framework program dataflow. See paragraph "Domain-Independent SAS Framework".

The Domain Dataflow Ontology Construction Procedure

The described model transformations constitute the following procedure for the dataflow design and development process:

1. Build the domain ontology;
2. Inherit domain object properties from appropriate computability object properties (associative and generative relations);
3. Choose classes which instances will be received from the perception system or will be known a priori and inherit them from *Percepted* and *Known* classes respectively;

4. Launch SPARQL-based rules to generate calculation units that will fix calculation dependencies between domain elements in the form of computation units;
5. Launch SPARQL-based rules to generate levels and nodes of the dataflow process.

Domain-Independent SAS Framework

The generated code is integrated into the domain-independent framework implemented with Java language. The framework itself implements the domain-independent logic of the dataflow processes. The architecture and the main cycle of the framework are depicted in Figure 14.

At the execution stage, two representations of the dataflow model are supported: the domain dataflow ontology and the program dataflow. The first is the ontological "image" of the second. The idea of these structures cooperation is the following: the domain dataflow ontology determines what program nodes should be added to the program dataflow; at the same time, the knowledge of what elements have been computed by the program dataflow is used to determine what ontological computation nodes and levels can be generated by rules and added to the domain dataflow ontology.

Let's illustrate it with an example represented in Figure 13.

As it was mentioned in the previous paragraph rules for node activation are switched off on the execution stage. That is why nodes are not linked with derivative elements while rule execution. In this case, at the very beginning of the SAS execution stage, only a set of nodes belonging to the first level are generated as they do not depend on any derivative elements. In the considered example the set will include *node_cu_KnownGroup* and *node_cu_Participant* nodes.

The information about the current structure of the ontological domain dataflow is passed to the *Program dataflow update module*. The module initializes instances of corresponding program classes of nodes and updates the *Program dataflow*. Thus these nodes are fallen under the control of the *Computation module* which is responsible for starting user-specific functions associated with nodes.

Then program nodes get data from the *Object assessment system* that is used to compute user functions.

The *Dataflow recalculation module* tracks what kind of data is generated by the nodes. If a node only updates data generated on some previous iteration then only acceptor-nodes are notified. Otherwise, if the node generates data for the first time then apart from acceptor-nodes notification, the module also notifies the *Domain dataflow ontology update module*. It is said that the node has been activated.

Let's suppose that *node_cu_KnownGroup* and *node_cu_Participant* compute their first data. Then the *Domain dataflow ontology update module* will update the domain dataflow ontology as follows: the ontological computation nodes corresponding to the activated program nodes are linked (*hasDerivative*) with the derivative element (this information is taken from the corresponding computation unit) – *node_cu_KnownGroup* is linked with *KnownGroup* class and *node_cu_Participant* – with *Participant* class.

At the next iteration of the SAS Framework cycle, the *Rule execution module* reruns the rules that generate new nodes. In the considered example *node_cu_belongsTo* node will be generated, also without setting *hasDerivative* relation.

Information on the creation of the new node is passed to the *Program dataflow update model* which creates a program node corresponding to *node_cu_belongsTo* and links it with donor nodes *node_cu_KnownGroup* and *node_cu_Participant*. And so on.

Figure 15. Iteration of domain code generation cycle

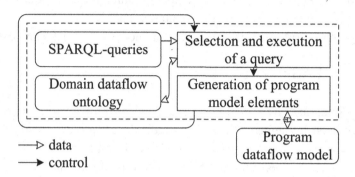

Domain Code Generation

The generated domain dataflow ontology is used to automatically build a domain-specific code. The code will include classes for domain model objects and relations, and classes for dataflow nodes. A class of a dataflow node contains a stub for a calculation function to be defined by the programmer. To make integration to the framework possible generated domain-specific classes are inherited from the framework's abstract classes.

A single iteration of a code generation algorithm includes the following steps, see Figure 15:

1. Get a fragment of the domain dataflow ontology with the help of SPARQL SELECT query;
2. Generate program components for the fragment (classes, field, method stubs). Generated components form a dataflow program structure that can be used in subsequent iterations.

The code generation algorithm is implemented in Java language with the help of CodeModel[13].

The order of iterations is defined by the program component dependencies. E.g. to generate classes for domain relations firstly classes for domain objects should be generated.

The following kinds of artifacts are generated. For each domain object, a Java class is generated that contains fields representing primitive properties. For each domain relation, a Java class is generated that contains fields representing the domain and the range of the relation. For each field setters and getters are generated.

For each node a Java class with the following elements is generated:

*   A constructor taking a level number as an input parameter;
*   Fields for node's derivative elements. Each field is a typed Java list. For each field a getter is generated;
*   A set of methods to initialize derivative elements. For example, if a node generates a relation a method will be generated which takes two objects (the domain and the range of the relation) and returns an initialized object of the relation. If an inverse relation is defined for this relation within the ontology then the method will also initialize the inverse relation. The method puts initialized elements into the appropriate derivative element list;

Table 1. The domain ontology fragment

OWL Concept	Domain Concept	Description
Class	massevent:KnownGroup	Class representing known social groups
Class	massevent:Participant	Class representing participants of known social groups
Object property	massevent:belongsTo	Property defining an affiliation with a group

Figure 16. An example of a rule

```
# # generates CU for percepted world entities
CONSTRUCT {
    ?cu a core2-1ed:GenerativeInitialCU .
    ?cu core2-1ed:hasDerivative ?percepted .
}
WHERE {
    ?percepted rdfs:subClassOf core2-1ed:Percepted .
    BIND (afn:namespace(?this) AS ?ns) .
    BIND (IRI(fn:concat(?ns, "cu_", afn:localname(?percepted))) AS ?cu) .
}
```

- A set of methods for linking a node with other nodes in the dataflow program structure. A double-dispatch technique is used (Ingalls, 1986). The first method is used to put this node as a donor for a node that passed as an argument. And other methods are used to set a node passed as an argument as a donor of some base elements. As a result, each node will have a list of acceptors which are notified if some derivative elements have been changed and a list of donors to pull base elements from;
- A method for user-defined implementation of situation model element calculation. The default implementation returns an indefinite result.

APPROACH EVALUATION

The goal of the approach is to automate labor-intensive stages of building SAS software for a wide variety of CPS applications. The approach is driven by a domain ontology and covers the main stages of the SAS software development process facilitating it by domain-independent components reuse.

Theoretical underpinnings of the approach including models and methods are represented above. The described set of instruments for the approach support includes the domain-independent SAS ontology, the domain-independent SAS framework, and the auxiliary software for code generation.

The approach was evaluated in prototyping SAS for CPS that is designed for mass event security maintenance. The SAS prototyping process in accordance with the technique described in "The Domain Dataflow Ontology Construction Procedure" is presented below.

In the first step, the domain ontology was built; see Table 1 where *massevent* is a namespace of the domain ontology. To work with ontologies TopBraid editor was used.

On the next step chosen properties should be inherited from appropriate computability object properties fixed in the domain-independent SAS ontology. For this purpose domain-independent SAS ontology

Table 2. Sets of rules for dataflow ontology generation

The Class Associated With Rules	Description
core2-1ed:LevelGeneration	Rules for generation of computation levels
core2-1ed:NDGeneration	Rules for generation of computation nodes
core2-1ed:NDActivation	Rules for activation of computation nodes

Table 3. Ontology-Java class correspondence

Ontology Class or Instance	Java Class or Interface
:KnownGroup	dd.massevent.sas.worldentity.KnownGroup dd.massevent.sas.worldentity.KnownGroupC
:Participant	dd.massevent.sas.worldentity.Participant dd.massevent.sas.worldentity.ParticipantC
:belongsTo	dd.massevent.sas.objectproperty.BelongsTo
:node_cu_Participant	dd.massevent.sas.computation.node.Node_cu_Participant dd.massevent.sas.computation.node.Node_cu_ParticipantOxidizing
:node_cu_KnownGroup	dd.massevent.sas.computation.node.Node_cu_KnownGroup dd.massevent.sas.computation.node.Node_cu_KnownGroupOxidizing
:node_cu_belongsTo	dd.massevent.sas.computation.node.Node_cu_belongsTo dd.massevent.sas.computation.node.Node_cu_belongsToOxidizing

was imported into the domain ontology and property *massevent:belongsTo* had been inherited from *core:associative*, see Figure 6.

Then it is necessary to fix classes whose instances will be received from the object assessment level or which are known a priori: *massevent:KnownGroup* class was inherited from *core:Known*, and *massevent:Participant* – from *core:Percepted*.

On the next step, the computability ontology was automatically generated for the given domain. It was done with the help of a set of rules implemented within Domain-Independent SAS Ontology. Each rule is a SPARQL-query linked with the class *core:CUWorldGeneration* of the domain-independent SAS ontology through SPIN primitive – *spin:rule*. To make the set of rules runnable it is necessary to create an instance of the class. TopBraid editor has an embedded engine to fulfill such rules and provides an appropriate user interface. An example of a rule is presented in Figure 16: the rule generates computability dependencies for perceived elements.

As a result, the following computability unities were received: *massevent:cu_Participant*, *massevent:cu_KnownGroup* and *massevent:cu_belongsTo* (see Figure 11).

Then sets of rules for the generation of levels and nodes comprising dataflow ontology were run. The sets are described in Table 2. The rules of these sets are implemented analogously to the previously mentioned set.

As a result, the dataflow ontology was built, see Figure 13.

The built dataflow ontology was used to automatically generate program code with the help of the auxiliary software (see "Domain Code Generation" paragraph). The correspondence between ontology classes and generated Java classes is represented in Table 3 (instead of *massevent* prefix a single semicolon is used). Classes that represent domain concepts and that do not end with "C" letter are interfaces that are used to implement multiple inheritance. Classes implementing nodes and ending with "Oxidizing" are used to implement the double-dispatch mechanism (see "Domain Code Generation" paragraph). The instances of computation level class are generated at runtime.

As any generated class of a computation node is a stub then the next step is to manually extend it with an appropriate function – the one implementing node-specific calculation. E.g. Node_cu_belongsTo node class should be extended with a function computing affiliation of a mass event participant with some known social group.

The process of generated code integration into the domain-independent framework is an incremental process: when the initial domain model is extended or modified then program classes should be generated once more. If node classes are extended with functions directly then a code transferring task will arise. It will be necessary to copy code from previously generated node classes to the new one. To solve this problem in the current version of the framework the following method is used: in parallel with the Java-package containing generated classes of computation nodes, a new package is created. The package will contain node classes overwriting the generated once. In such a way dd.massevent.sas.nodeimplementation.Node_cu_belongsTo class is created. This helps to separate a generated class and its implementation and allows updating generated classes with no transferring. If old implementations are not satisfying newly generated classes some compilation errors will arise.

Within the framework, a special code has been implemented that checks the overwriting at runtime. If a generated class has not been overwritten then a default implementation is used. This implementation does nothing and stops the propagation of data through the dataflow. So that it is possible to implement only a part of the dataflow, test it and if everything is good to go to the next iteration of the development process.

To interact with the object assessment level that provides SAS with perception data, an abstract class dd.massevent.sas.Perceptor2SASAdapter was generated. Thus on the next step, the abstract class Perceptor2SASAdapter was implemented. Within the approbation, the class implements a simulation of a perception process. The data is stored in a CSV-file where each line is a perception portion linked with a time tag, e.g: *1,10,12, Participant, Blue*. The first element (1) is the time tag, the second and third elements (10, 12) are coordinates of a participant, the fourth (Participant) – the class of the perceived object, the fifth (Blue) – a prevailing clothing color which is used compute the affiliation with some known social group (e.g. fans of Lazio football club).

In the last step, the main class was built. The class implements a SAS program entry point. Inside this class, two main calls are done: a call to the adapter Perceptor2SASAdapter to get initial data and a call to the SAS to build domain situation fragments such as the fact that some perceived participant belongs to some known group. SAS is represented with dd.sas.SAS class and implements the main framework cycle (see Figure 14).

So that SAS prototype software is built.

This evaluation has confirmed that the proposed approach and instruments are workable and helps to reduce design and development costs through automation and component reuse. A variant of numerical evaluation of the approach can be found in (Lebedev & Panteleyev, 2017).

DISCUSSION

The first question to be discussed is the value of code generation as the main way to increase software development efficiency. As can be seen from "Domain Code Generation" paragraph the generated program code is a kind of repetitive and boilerplate one. From this point of view, one would seem that the generated code is not of great value. But it is necessary to take into account the volume of code to be generated and the dynamism of SAS modification.

A domain model may include hundreds of elements with lots of relation and, hence, the dataflow process should also include the commensurate number of elements. All these elements should be generated. Further, the quick pace of change in ideas and concepts draw the fast evolution of domain models. All these changes should be reflected in the SAS software. Fully manual creation and maintenance of code become a tedious and error-prone task. So the purposes of the proposed approach are to ease dataflow structure modification and to let a developer implement the most complex parts of the code – functions of separate nodes.

The second question is the performance of SAS generated with the given instrument set. The importance of the question is due to the large volumes of data generated by sensors and their fast update rates. At this stage of development of the approach, performance and memory consumption issues were not considered. That is why the current version of instruments should be considered mostly as an instrument for prototyping. It is planned to address them in the next stages of the research. One of the possible solutions is to make the proposed framework compatible with some contemporary data-driven scalable framework so that the generated SAS data flow can be run on a cluster. One of the best candidates is Apache Beam that can be seen as a common API to a number of other widespread frameworks.

Also, it is necessary to mention works where ontologies are used on SAS execution stage to represent the current situation model and to enable a logical inference, e.g. (Baumgartner, Retschitzegger, & Schwinger, 2008; Matheus et al., 2005; Smart, Russell, Shadbolt, Carr, & others, 2007). The inference is used to calculate new elements of the situation model. In the approach proposed in the paper, ontologies are used to drive SAS design and development processes. The main goal is to simplify the usage of general programming language flexibility to implement arbitrary logic.

CONCLUSION

The evolution of CPS is on the stage of the creation of special platforms. The design and development of such platforms are complex tasks that should be supported by special means.

One of the central functions of CPS is SA that aimed at the fusion of data received from multiple sensors. Based on the data SA system (SAS) builds a problem situation model that is used for impact assessment and for decision making. To make processes of design and development of SAS effective it is necessary to isolate its domain-independent components that can be transferred among domains and reused. For this purpose, it is proposed to use the dataflow model that can be adapted to a particular domain. The SAS architecture based on this model is presented in the paper.

The manual configuration of the proposed architecture on a given domain can be a tedious and error-prone task. To make it more effective the ontology-based approach is proposed by authors. The idea of the approach is to simplify the transition from the domain ontology to the domain dataflow program structure. To make it possible the set of instruments is proposed and discussed including: 1) the domain-independent SAS ontology that is used on the design stage to construct the domain dataflow ontology; on the development stage to generate code; and on the execution, stage to construct the dataflow program structure. The ontology includes rules to automate transitions; 2) and the domain-independent SAS framework implementing the main domain-independent dataflow cycle; 3) the auxiliary software to generate program code. The proposed approach and the instrument set are illustrated in the mass event security scenario.

The directions for future work include the following: 1) extension and evolution of theoretical underpinning including the extension of types of OWL axioms interpreted by rules; 2) adaptation of SAS framework for running over a modern scalable high-performance dataflow framework (such as Apache Beam).

REFERENCES

Alcaraz, C., Cazorla, L., & Lopez, J. (2017). Cyber-physical systems for wide-area situational awareness. In *Cyber-Physical Systems* (pp. 305–317). Elsevier. doi:10.1016/B978-0-12-803801-7.00020-1

Alcaraz, C., & Lopez, J. (2013). Wide-Area Situational Awareness for Critical Infrastructure Protection. *Computer*, *46*(4), 30–37. doi:10.1109/MC.2013.72

Baumgartner, N., Mitsch, S., Müller, A., Retschitzegger, W., Salfinger, A., & Schwinger, W. (2014). A tour of BeAware--A situation awareness framework for control centers. *Information Fusion*, *20*, 155–173. doi:10.1016/j.inffus.2014.01.008

Baumgartner, N., Retschitzegger, W., & Schwinger, W. (2008). Application Scenarios of Ontology-Driven Situation Awareness SystemsExemplified for the Road Traffic Management Domain. In S. Borgo, & L. Lesno (Eds.), *Proceedings of the 2008 Conference on Formal Ontologies Meet Industry* (pp. 77–87). Amsterdam: IOS Press.

Blasch, E. (2017). JDL Model (III) Updates for an Information Management Enterprise. In H. Fourati (Ed.), *Multisensor Data Fusion: From Algorithms and Architectural Design to Applications* (pp. 55–73). Boca Raton, FL: CRC Press. doi:10.1201/b18851-4

Bonte, P., Ongenae, F., De Backere, F., Schaballie, J., Arndt, D., Verstichel, S., ... De Turck, F. (2017). The MASSIF platform: A modular and semantic platform for the development of flexible IoT services. *Knowledge and Information Systems*, *51*(1), 89–126. doi:10.100710115-016-0969-1

Endsley, M. R. (2016). *Designing for situation awareness: An approach to user-centered design* (2nd ed.). Boca Raton, FL: CRC Press. doi:10.1201/b11371

Foo, P. H., & Ng, G.-W. (2013). High-level information fusion: An overview. *Journal of Advances in Information Fusion*, *8*(1), 33–72.

Fujino, N., Ogawa, K., & Minowa, M. (2016). Wireless network technologies to support the age of IoT. *Fujitsu Scientific and Technical Journal*, *52*(4), 68–76.

Greer, C., Burns, M., Wollman, D., & Griffor, E. (2019). Cyber-Physical Systems & the Internet of Things. *NIST Special Publication*, *1900*, 202.

Guth, J., Breitenbücher, U., Falkenthal, M., Fremantle, P., Kopp, O., Leymann, F., & Reinfurt, L. (2018). A detailed analysis of IoT platform architectures: concepts, similarities, and differences. In *Internet of Everything* (pp. 81–101). Springer. doi:10.1007/978-981-10-5861-5_4

Hongfei, Y., Hongjian, W., Hongli, L., & Ying, W. (2016). Research on situation awareness based on ontology for UUV. In *2016 IEEE International Conference on Mechatronics and Automation* (pp. 2500–2506). Harbin: IEEE. 10.1109/ICMA.2016.7558959

Ingalls, D. H. H. (1986). A simple technique for handling multiple polymorphism. *ACM SIGPLAN Notices*, *21*(11), 347–349. doi:10.1145/960112.28732

Johnston, W. M., Hanna, J. R., & Millar, R. J. (2004). Advances in dataflow programming languages. *ACM Computing Surveys*, *36*(1), 1–34. doi:10.1145/1013208.1013209

Kocakulak, M., & Butun, I. (2017). An overview of Wireless Sensor Networks towards internet of things. In *2017 IEEE 7th Annual Computing and Communication Workshop and Conference (CCWC)* (pp. 1–6). Las Vegas, NV: IEEE. 10.1109/CCWC.2017.7868374

Kokar, M. M., Matheus, C. J., & Baclawski, K. (2009). Ontology-based situation awareness. *Information Fusion*, *10*(1), 83–98. doi:10.1016/j.inffus.2007.01.004

Lazarescu, M. T. (2017). Wireless sensor networks for the internet of things: Barriers and synergies. In *Components and Services for IoT Platforms* (pp. 155–186). Springer. doi:10.1007/978-3-319-42304-3_9

Lea, P. (2018). *Internet of Things for Architects: Architecting IoT solutions by implementing sensors, communication infrastructure, edge computing, analytics, and security*. Packt Publishing Ltd.

Lebedev, S., & Panteleyev, M. (2017). Ontology-Driven Situation Assessment System Design and Development in IoT Domains. *International Journal of Embedded and Real-Time Communication Systems*, *8*(1), 1–17. doi:10.4018/IJERTCS.2017010101

Lovas, R., Farkas, A., Marosi, A. C., Ács, S., Kovács, J., Szalóki, Á., & Kádár, B. (2018). Orchestrated platform for cyber-physical systems. *Complexity*.

Matheus, C. J., Kokar, M. M., Baclawski, K., Letkowski, J. A., Call, C., Hinman, M. L., … Boulware, D. M. (2005). SAWA: An assistant for higher-level fusion and situation awareness. In Multisensor, Multisource Information Fusion: Architectures, Algorithms, and Applications 2005 (Vol. 5813, pp. 75–86). International Society for Optics and Photonics.

Meiling, S., Purnomo, D., Shiraishi, J.-A., Fischer, M., & Schmid, T. C. (2018). MONICA in Hamburg: Towards Large-Scale IoT Deployments in a Smart City (18-21 June 2018, Ljubljana, Slovenia). In *2018 European Conference on Networks and Communications (EuCNC)* (pp. 224–229). IEEE. 10.1109/EuCNC.2018.8443213

Morrison, J. P. (2010). *Flow-Based Programming: A New Approach To Application Development* (2nd ed.). Charleston: Createspace Independent.

Pai, F.-P., Yang, L.-J., & Chung, Y.-C. (2017). Multi-layer ontology based information fusion for situation awareness. *Applied Intelligence*, *46*(2), 285–307. doi:10.100710489-016-0834-7

Petrov, V., Mikhaylov, K., Moltchanov, D., Andreev, S., Fodor, G., Torsner, J., ... Koucheryavy, Y. (2018). When IoT keeps people in the loop: A path towards a new global utility. *IEEE Communications Magazine*, *57*(1), 114–121. doi:10.1109/MCOM.2018.1700018

Seiger, R., Huber, S., Heisig, P., & Assmann, U. (2016). Enabling self-adaptive workflows for cyber-physical systems. In Enterprise, Business-Process and Information Systems Modeling (pp. 3–17). Springer. doi:10.1007/978-3-319-39429-9_1

Smart, P. R., Russell, A., Shadbolt, N. R., Carr, L. A., & ... (2007). Aktivesa: A technical demonstrator system for enhanced situation awareness. *The Computer Journal*, *50*(6), 703–716. doi:10.1093/comjnl/bxm067

Sun, Y., Yang, G., & Zhou, X. (2017). A survey on run-time supporting platforms for cyber physical systems. *Frontiers of Information Technology & Electronic Engineering*, *18*(10), 1458–1478. doi:10.1631/FITEE.1601579

Sztipanovits, J., Bapty, T., Koutsoukos, X., Lattmann, Z., Neema, S., & Jackson, E. (2018). Model and tool integration platforms for cyber-physical system design. *Proceedings of the IEEE*, (99), 1–26. 10.1109/JPROC.2018.2838530

Theodoropoulos, D., Mazumdar, S., Ayguade, E., Bettin, N., Bueno, J., Ermini, S., ... Giorgi, R. (2017). The AXIOM platform for next-generation cyber physical systems. *Microprocessors and Microsystems*, *52*, 540–555. doi:10.1016/j.micpro.2017.05.018

Tyugu, E., Matskin, M., & Penjam, J. (1999). Applications of structural synthesis of programs. In *International Symposium on Formal Methods* (pp. 551–569). Toulouse, France: Academic Press.

Wang, P., Yang, L. T., Li, J., Chen, J., & Hu, S. (2019). Data fusion in cyber-physical-social systems: State-of-the-art and perspectives. *Information Fusion*, *51*, 42–57. doi:10.1016/j.inffus.2018.11.002

Wang, Y., Tan, G., Wang, Y., & Yin, Y. (2012). Perceptual control architecture for cyber–physical systems in traffic incident management. *Journal of Systems Architecture*, *58*(10), 398–411. doi:10.1016/j.sysarc.2012.06.004

Yang, L., Yang, S.-H., & Plotnick, L. (2013). How the internet of things technology enhances emergency response operations. *Technological Forecasting and Social Change*, *80*(9), 1854–1867. doi:10.1016/j.techfore.2012.07.011

ENDNOTES

1   https://www.w3.org/Submission/spin-overview/
2   https://www.w3.org/TR/shacl/
3   http://protege.stanford.edu/
4   http://www.topquadrant.com
5   http://topbraid.org/spin/api/
6   https://data.world/
7   https://data.world/integrations/sputniq
8   https://jena.apache.org/
9   https://beam.apache.org/
10   https://spark.apache.org/
11   https://storm.apache.org/
12   https://flink.apache.org/
13   https://javaee.github.io/jaxb-codemodel/

Chapter 4
Embedded Networks Design and Simulation

Valentin Olenev

https://orcid.org/0000-0002-1817-2754

St. Petersburg State University of Aerospace Instrumentation, Russia

Yuriy Sheynin

St. Petersburg State University of Aerospace Instrumentation, Russia

Irina Lavrovskaya

St. Petersburg State University of Aerospace Instrumentation, Russia

Ilya Korobkov

https://orcid.org/0000-0003-3687-3033

St. Petersburg State University of Aerospace Instrumentation, Russia

Lev Kurbanov

St. Petersburg State University of Aerospace Instrumentation, Russia

Nadezhda Chumakova

St. Petersburg State University of Aerospace Instrumentation, Russia

Nikolay Sinyov

St. Petersburg State University of Aerospace Instrumentation, Russia

ABSTRACT

This chapter presents an approach for the design and simulation of embedded networks for spacecraft. The chapter provides an analysis of existing simulation tools for the on-board and local area networks. The authors overview the main abilities of the existing software and then propose the computer-aided design system for SpaceWire onboard networks design and simulation. This CAD system supports the full on-board network design and simulation flow, which begins from the network topology automated generation and finishes with getting the network structure, configuration and parameters setting, simulation results, and statistics – SpaceWire Automated Network Design and Simulation (SANDS). The authors describe formal theories, algorithms, methods, and approaches, which are used to solve general issues that appear in developing of onboard networks. The chapter covers topics of fault-tolerance in onboard networks, discusses routing problems, and approaches to organize deadlock-free routing. The authors propose schedule creation algorithms for STP ISS protocol and consider network simulation issues.

DOI: 10.4018/978-1-7998-1974-5.ch004

INTRODUCTION

Embedded systems became a big part of a modern life; you can face with them everywhere, in every area of human activities. Onboard networks for the spacecraft and aircraft is the area, where embedding and networking technologies are very popular. That is why the current chapter provides a good example for building of a software system for design and simulation of onboard networks. Described algorithms and methods could be applied to other embedded systems prototyping and implementation procedures.

Evolution of microelectronics has led to the growth of the on-board networks and systems sizes. Modern on-board networks consist of a huge number of computers, telemetry, radio transmitting and data transmitting devices, scientific instruments and sensors and devices for electricity, heating control, orientation and stabilization of a spacecraft. Interconnection of these systems is done via the on-board network with numerous devices that work at different frequencies and data transmission speeds, transmit different types of data with different intensity. Each data flow has different Quality of Service (QoS) requirements. If there are some errors in a channel, or a device is corrupted, important scientific information could be lost. All these situations need to be simulated and tested by networking models before the assembling and launching of a spacecraft.

NETWORK SIMULATION TOOLS OVERVIEW

Network simulators allow researchers to test the scenarios that are difficult or expensive to imitate in real world. It is particularly useful to test new communication protocols or to change the existing protocols in a controlled and reproducible environment. Simulators can be used to design different network topologies using various types of nodes. There are different types of network simulators and they can be compared based on the following features:

- **Range:** From very simple to very complex;
- Ability to specify nodes and links between those nodes and the traffic between the nodes;
- Ability to specify everything about protocols used to handle traffic in a network;
- **Graphical User Interface:** Allows users to easily visualize operation of their simulated environment;
- **Text-Based Applications:** Permit more advanced forms of customization;
- **Programming-Oriented Tools:** Providing a programming framework that customizes to create an application that simulates the networking environment to be tested (Siraj, Gupta, & Rinku-Badgujar, 2012).

Some of network simulators are commercial, which means that the source code of the software or the affiliated packages is not provided to users. All users have to pay to get a license to use this software or pay to order specific packages for their own specific usage requirements. On the other hand, open source network simulators and their interfaces are completely open for the developers.

Currently there is a number of tools and models that give an ability to simulate the operation of communication networks, but mostly these tools are intended for the Ethernet and Wi-Fi networks. Most popular network simulators are overviewed in the current chapter.

Figure 1. GloMoSim user interface

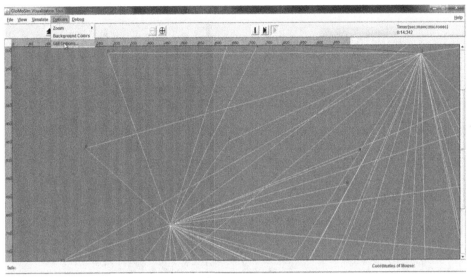

GloMoSim

Global Mobile Information System Simulator (GloMoSim) is a scalable simulation environment for large wireless and wireline communication networks. GloMoSim uses a parallel discrete-event simulation capability. It simulates networks with up to thousand nodes linked by a heterogeneous communications capability that includes multicast, asymmetric communications using direct satellite broadcasts, multi-hop wireless communications using ad-hoc networking, and traditional Internet protocols.

The node aggregation technique is introduced into GloMoSim to give significant benefits to the simulation performance. Initializing each node as a separate entity inherently limits the scalability because the memory requirements increase dramatically for a model with large number of nodes. With node aggregation, a single entity can simulate several network nodes in the system. Node aggregation technique implies that the number of nodes in the system can be increased while maintaining the same number of entities in the simulation. In GloMoSim the network nodes, which a particular entity represents, are determined by the physical position of the nodes (Nuevo, 2004). The GloMoSim user interface is shown in Figure 1.

It is built using a layered approach that is similar to the OSI seven layers network architecture. Standard APIs are used between the different simulation layers, to allow integration of models developed at different layers by different people. GloMoSim is thus perceived to be modular, easy to use and flexible, besides maintaining a high degree of detail (Siraj et al., 2012).

QualNet

QualNet is the commercial flavor of GloMoSim, and has additional implementations of layers/modules and features like GUI based analysis tools. It runs on all common platforms (Linux, Windows, Solaris, OS X) and is specialized in simulating all kind of wireless applications. It has a quite clear user interface

Figure 2. QualNet user interface

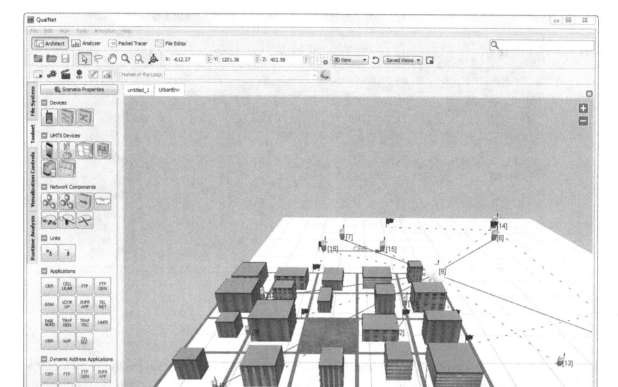

while also offering an easy to use command line interface (Doerffel, 2009). The QualNet user interface is shown in Figure 2.

QualNet is composed of the several main components. QualNet Architect is a graphical scenario design and visualization tool. QualNet Analyzer stands for a statistical graphing tool that displays hundreds of metrics collected during simulation of a network scenario. QualNet Packet Tracer is in order for providing of a graphical representation of packet trace files generated during the simulation of a network scenario. QualNet File Editor is a text editing tool and QualNet Command Line Interface – command line access to the simulator (SCALABLE Network Technologies, 2014).

Therefore, QualNet has a lot of benefits and useful components, but unfortunately, it is a very expensive solution.

Figure 3. OPNET user interface

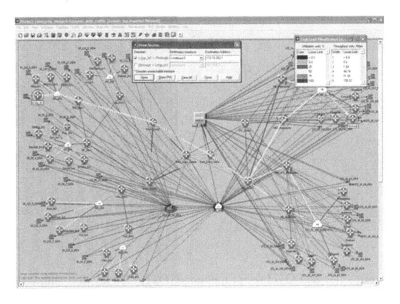

OPNET

OPNET is a registered commercial trademark and a name of product presented by OPNET Technologies incorporation. It became one of the most famous and popular commercial network simulators. OPNET claims to be the fastest simulation engine among leading industry solutions. It has a wide variety of niche simulators for the wired/wireless areas. It also has many of wired/wireless protocol and vendor device models with source code, and allows object-oriented modeling of components. Modeling environment is a hierarchical one and has a slightly more complex method of definition of nodes as finite state machines. They also have an optional System-in-the-Loop to interface simulations with live systems. The simulator is flexible and, therefore, allows integration with other libraries and simulators. The OPNET user interface is shown in Figure 3.

OPNET inherently has three main functions: modeling, simulating, and analysis. In modeling, it provides intuitive graphical environment to create all kinds of models of protocols for modeling. For simulating, it uses different advanced simulation technologies and can be used to address a wide range of studies. For analysis, the emulation results and data can be analyzed and displayed very easily for convince of its users. User friendly graphs, charts, statistics, and even animation can be generated by OPNET (Siraj et al., 2012; Jianru, Xiaomin, & Huixian, 2012).

NS-2

NS-2 is one of the most widely used network simulation tools in the research community and is available as freeware. Being an object-oriented discrete event simulator that follows the layered approach, NS-2 is accompanied by a rich set of protocols. Beside this NS-2 is also an emulator, and can talk to real networks. However, to its disadvantage, it has a large footprint, and is not very scalable. NS-2 also ranks low on the flexibility and ease of use fronts. In addition, the process of new protocols implemen-

Figure 4. NS-2 user interface

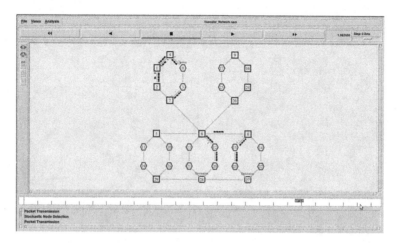

tation is complex. It uses C++ and OTcl script language (OTcl official web-site, 2019). The NS-2 user interface is shown in Figure 4.

NS-2 separates control path implementations from the data path implementation. The scenes can be changed easily by programming in the OTcl script. When a user wants to make a new network object, he can either create the new object or assemble a compound object from the existing object library, and plumb the data path through the object. This plumbing makes NS-2 very powerful. Another feature of NS-2 is the event scheduler. In NS-2, the event scheduler keeps track of simulation time and release all the events in the event queue by invoking appropriate network components (Issariyakul & Hossain, 2012).

NS-3

Similar to NS-2, NS-3 is also an open source discrete-event network simulator which targets primarily for research and educational use. NS-3 is licensed under the GNU, GPLv2 license, and is available for research and development. NS-3 is not backward-compatible with NS-2, it has different software core (C++ and Python), protocol entities are designed to be closer to real computers, lightweight virtual machines are used. NS-3 is developing a tracing and statistics gathering framework trying to enable customization of the output without rebuilding the simulation core (Siraj et al., 2012; NS-3 Manual, 2017). The NS-3 user interface is shown in Figure 5.

OMNet++

OMNeT++ is a C++-based discrete event simulator for modeling communication networks, multiprocessors and other distributed or parallel systems. OMNeT++ is public-source, and can be used under the Academic Public License that makes the software free for non-profit use. OMNET++ components are defined by nested hierarchical modules and simple text based language. It is easy to learn, while being very expressive. OMNet++ offers an easy to use GUI for graphical network editing, animation and configuring simulation runs; it has a basic output analyzer, which can display collected statistics in graphical formats. However, not many OSI-related models are implemented. The models or modules of

Figure 5. NS-3 user interface

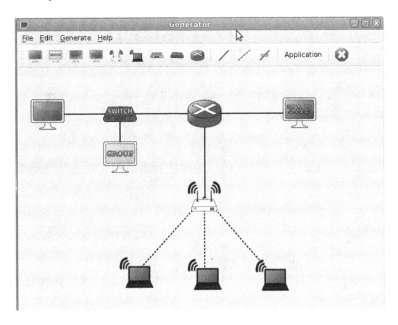

OMNeT++ are assembled from reusable components – modules, which can be combined in various ways, which is one of the main features of OMNeT++. The OMNeT++ user interface is shown in Figure 6.

The OMNeT++ approach significantly differs from that of NS-2, the most widely used network simulator in academic and research circles: while the NS-2 (and NS-3) project goal is to build a network simulator, OMNeT++ aims at providing a rich simulation platform, and leaves creating simulation models to independent research groups (Siraj, et al., 2012; Varga & Hornig, 2008).

SSFNet

SSFNet (Scalable Simulation Framework) is defined as a "public-domain standard for discrete-event simulation of large, complex systems in Java and C++". The SSFNet standard defines a minimalist API (which, however, was designed with parallel simulation in mind). The topology and configuration of SSFNet simulations are given in DML files. DML is a text-based format comparable to user-friendly graphs: OPNET XML can generate charts, statistics, and even animation, but it has own syntax. DML can be considered the SSFNet equivalent of NED, however it lacks expressing power and features to scale up to support large model frameworks built from reusable components. SSFNet also lacks OMNeT++'s INI files, all parameters need to be given in the DML. The SSFNet user interface is shown in Figure 7.

SSFNet has four implementations: DaSSF and CSSF in C++, and two Java implementations (Renesys Raceway and JSSF). There were significantly more simulation models developed for the Java versions than for DaSSF (SSFNet Official web-site, 2019).

Figure 6. OMNeT++ user interface

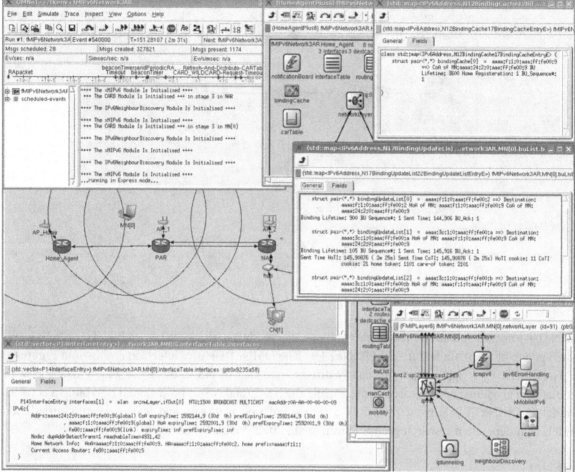

J-Sim

J-Sim (formerly known as JavaSim) is a component-based, compositional simulation environment, implemented in Java. J-Sim is similar to OMNeT++ in that simulation models are hierarchical and built from self-contained components, but the approach of assembling components into models is more like NS-2: J-Sim is also a dual-language simulation environment, in which classes are written in Java, and glued together using Tcl (or Java). The use of Tcl in J-Sim has the same drawback as with NS-2: it makes implementing graphical editors impossible. In fact, J-Sim does provide a graphical editor (gEditor), but its native format is XML. Although gEditor can export Tcl scripts, developers recommend that XML files are directly loaded into the simulator, bypassing Tcl. This way, XML becomes the equivalent of OMNeT++ NED. However, the problem with XML as native file format is that it is hard to read and write by humans. Simulation models are provided in the Inet package, which contains IPv4, TCP, MPLS and other protocol models.

Figure 7. SSFNet user interface

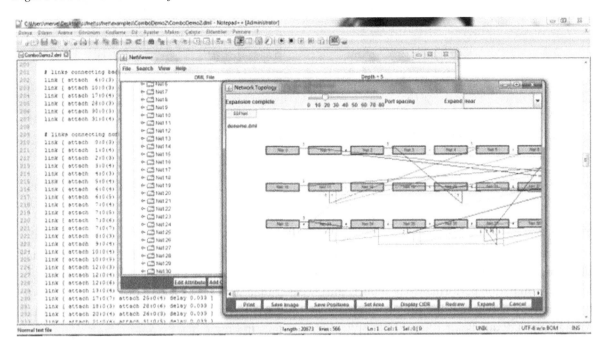

Figure 8. J-Sim gedit user interface

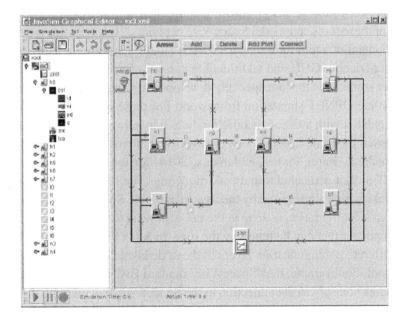

Figure 9. MOST user interface

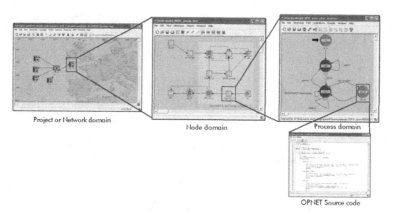

The fact that J-Sim is Java-based has some implications. On one hand, model development and debugging can be significantly faster than C++, due to existence of excellent Java development tools. However, simulation performance is significantly weaker than with C++, and, moreover, it is not possible to reuse existing real-life protocol implementations written in C as simulation models (Varga & Hornig, 2008). Example of J-Sim gedit application is shown in Figure 8.

SPACEWIRE NETWORK SIMULATION TOOLS

Most of considered network simulation tools are related to Ethernet and Wi-Fi networks simulation and unfortunately, none of these tools can model SpaceWire networks. However, this overview gives a good vision for the development of a tool for the SpaceWire simulation, because it shows the useful abilities and mechanisms, user-friendly GUIs and additional features for the network operation analysis. In addition, let us consider some tools that are specially developed for SpaceWire networks modeling. Most of them are based on the OPNET simulation framework. For these purposes OPNET was adapted for the SpaceWire and updated with a list of specific modules and network elements.

This way was chosen by Thales Alenia company, which implemented MOST (Modeling of Space-Wire Traffic) (Dellandrea, Gouin, Parkes, & Jameux, 2014) for the European Space Agency. MOST based on the OPNET toolkit dedicated to network modeling. The MOST library contains SpaceWire nodes, routers and links which are selected by the user to build the SpaceWire network topology thanks to drag & drop actions. Configuration is done at the network level thanks to a set of attributes attached to each network component that can be tuned by the user. In MOST the Building Block (BB) concept is used to identify different communication layers in the node layout and it is in order to offer to user a flexible simulation tool. For example, the "SpaceWire standard BB" (or CODEC) is a SpaceWire node interface, which ensures node physical connection to the SpaceWire network with the data transmission management. This "SpaceWire standard BB" is clearly separated from the protocol "RMAP BB". As a result, one BB can be enhanced anytime without impacting others BB. Example of MOST capabilities is shown in Figure 9.

Figure 10. VisualSIM user interface

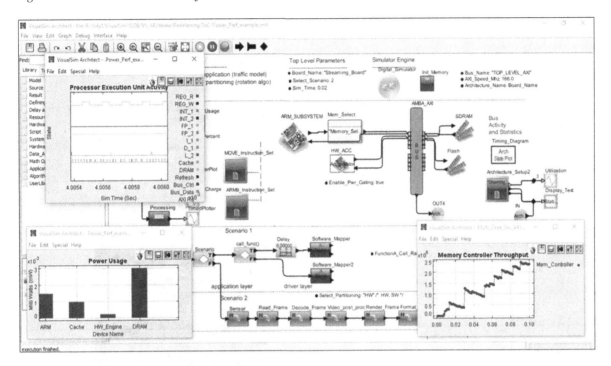

OPNET offers a tool to analyze simulation output. It provides various ways to display each type of data. SpaceWire traffic analysis is done based on observation of statistic parameters such as: the end-to-end delay, the bottleneck observation, packet size, packet latency or jitter, number of sent and received packets, evaluation of the sustained bandwidth and also buffers occupation. Observables are selected by the user and it can be chosen to observe the data at the node level (internally) or at the network level (Keshav, 1988). Latest MOST version is adapted and based on NS3 simulator.

Similar solution has been developed by Sandia National Laboratories (SNL) (Thales Alenia Space, 2011), but it gives less abilities than MOST, because it does not have an option to insert errors to the transmitted data, which is not good for testing and verification. The SNL team also used extension features within OPNET Modeler to create a set of general-purpose modules representing different network elements or basic building blocks for SpaceWire networks simulation. The modules include models of SpaceWire nodes, routers, broadcast servers, and links. These modules can be arranged to represent networks during the design stage. Then, these networks can be analyzed for the desired behavior.

The second ability of the tool is an in-depth analysis of the accurate distribution of system time across the SpaceWire network. To accomplish this task, the SNL team developed a packet broadcast mechanism that would lay upon the standard SpaceWire protocol. A representative SpaceWire network was constructed within the OPNET Modeler simulation environment. Based on this network representation, several simulations were executed to study the behavior of the network with respect to packet transmission time, jitter, and the accuracy of distributed system time.

SpaceWire models provide a generalized tool for examining network behavior and different network designs. The user interface is very similar to MOST because of the OPNET base.

Figure 11. DCNSimulator user interface

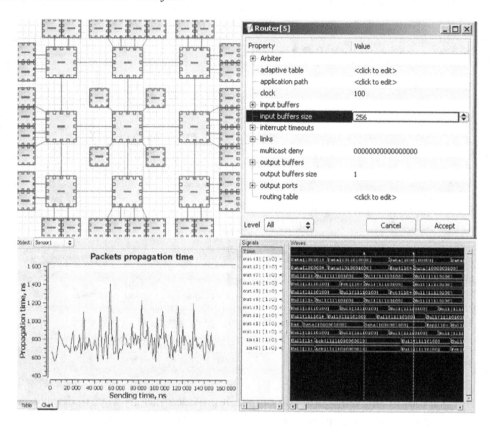

However, there is a tool that is not based on the OPNET. It is VisualSim SpaceWire modeling, developed by MIRABILIS Design Company (van Leeuwen, Eldridge, & Leemaster, 2011). VisualSim is intended for end-to-end system-level design. The graphical nature of the product and the availability of the parameterized library, SmartBlocks, make the tool easy to use, adopt and learn. VisualSim combines DSP, Analog, Protocols and Digital Architecture in a single simulation model. SmartBlocks are graphical representations of hardware, software and networking components at queuing, performance, transaction and cycle-accurate levels of abstraction. VisualSim can be used for performance trade-offs using metrics such as bandwidth utilization, application response time and buffer requirements. Architecture analysis of arbitration algorithms, component sizing, software instruction optimization, hardware-software trade-offs and system coverage. Therefore, VisualSim gives an ability to test the real hardware SpaceWire devices, but it is not applicable for prototyping of real onboard networks on early stages of the project. The VisualSim user interface is shown in Figure 10.

There is one non-commercial tool, which is able to simulate basic SpaceWire networks and transport-layer protocols – DCNSimulator (Eganyan, Suvorova, Sheynin, Khakhulin, & Orlovsky, 2013).

The Digital Communication Network Simulator (DCNSimulator) is a tool for design, system-level simulation and analysis of networks. DCNSimulator is based on Qt and SystemC. It consists of the simulation engine and libraries of network components. The simulation engine is a general part that could work for simulation of any network. Libraries of network components are specific for particular network standards and could represent network components at various details levels – from general virtual

Table 1. Comparison of SpaceWire network simulation tools

Feature	Software Name		
	DCNSimulator	**MOST**	**Visual SIM**
Purpose	Simulation of SpaceWire	Simulation of SpaceWire & SpaceFibre netwoks	Systems Design
Programming language	C (C++)	XML	Module-based
GUI quality	Poor	Good	Excellent
Dynamical construction of a network from typical blocks	No	Yes	Yes
Availability	Commercial, upon request	Commercial, upon request for ESA members	Commercial
Extendability	Not possible	Possible for experts	Not possible
Simulation speed	Low	Good	No information
Transport protocols support	Partly	Yes	No

components to cycle-accurate models of particular devices. Simulated device models are implemented in C++. Application software algorithms could run at end nodes thus generating realistic traffic for the simulated network. The simulator also allows users to design networks graphically in MS Visio. The DCNSimulator runs in Windows and does not require any other third party software for its operation. The DCNSimulator user interface is shown in Figure 11.

Comparison of SpaceWire Network Simulation Tools

Consequently, there are only three tools that give an ability to build SpaceWire networks and simulate their operation. To compare these tools we need to form the list of features that are needed for the CAD-system for the simulation of SpaceWire networks. The most important ones are availability for the end-users, GUI quality, network design parameters and simulation speed. But still the programming language, expendability and support for additional transport protocol and applications would be important parameters for the experts. Comparison of three simulators is represented in Table 1.

To conclude the comparison, VisualSIM is commercial and rather expensive tool. OPNET version of MOST tool is also expensive, but the latest version, based on NS3, is much cheaper, but it is available only for the list of European Space Agency users. DCNSimulator does not meet the requirements of usability and seems to be unfinished implementation of a SpaceWire simulator.

A NEW COMPUTER-AIDED DESIGN SYSTEM FOR THE SPACEWIRE NETWORKS SIMULATION

We gathered the requirements for simulation tool from industry. Analysis of these requirements showed that current versionы of the simulators does not meet all industry requirements. To be useful for the needs of the large industrial companies the following abilities should be provided by the network simulation tool:

Figure 12. Architecture of SpaceWire Automated network design and simulation toolset

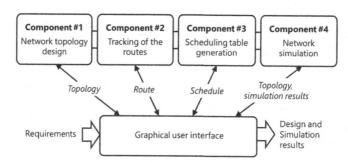

- Simulation of network models that are implemented according to the SpaceWire and SpaceWire-RUS standards. That means, it has to have GigaSpaceWire extension;
- Simulation of the protocols of transport and application levels in nodes (at least RMAP (ESA, 2010) and STP-ISS (Sheynin, Olenev, Lavrovskaya, Korobkov, & Dymov, 2014);
- Simulation of fault tolerance and redundancy;
- Simulation tool should be able to build a SpaceWire network consisting of network regions;
- Simulation tool should be able to save different designed objects (like nodes or switches) into a separate library that could be used for the other projects;
- Simulation tool should be able to build and model a network consisting of up to 1024 nodes.
- Simulation tool should give an ability to provide such simulation results like traffic between any two nodes, latencies, packet delivery time, transmission errors, channel bandwidth, etc.

Therefore, all these requirements should be implemented in a new software that would give an ability to use the simulation tool during the whole process of the spacecraft onboard network design. This simulation should be a part of a complex computer-aided design system and take the best from all the existing analogs. We called this new software SANDS.

SpaceWire Automated Network Design and Simulation (SANDS) is a computer-aided design system for SpaceWire networks, which supports full network design and simulation flow, which begins from the network topology automated generation and finishes with getting simulation results and statistics. SpaceWire is a common technology for onboard networks, which is easy to understand, it is compact and efficient in implementation ("SpaceWire Standard", 2008).

SANDS includes almost all of the functionality that is needed for the prototyping of a real on-board network. SANDS architecture is shown in Figure 12.

SANDS architecture includes four main components:

- **Component #1:** A component for onboard network topology design and evaluation of its structural characteristics;
- **Component #2:** A component for tracking of the deadlock-free routes for the data transmission in a network;
- **Component #3:** A component for generation of the scheduling table for the nodes with STP-ISS transport protocol for the transmission of the data with Scheduled quality of service;
- **Component #4:** A component for simulation of the network operation with all the data that component got from other three components and graphical user interface (Syschikov, Sheynin, Sedov, & Ivanova, 2014).

Each component of SANDS is based on formal algorithms and methods, which are the focus of the current chapter. We used graph theory, scheduling theory for development of our algorithms and methods.

APPLIED NOTATION AND TERMS

In this chapter, we use specific terms and notation, we present the math objects we use to describe proposed algorithms.

Let us consider the object of design – network. Network consists of three main elements: nodes, routers and links. Node is a functional device that can send/receive data to/from other nodes. Node can include up to three units. Unit is a part of device.

We consider a network as a graph $G = (V, E)$, where V is a set of network nodes and routers and E is a set of links between them. Note that graph $G = (V, E)$ is undirected.

The vertex connectivity ($k(G)$) of a graph is the minimum number of vertices that need to be removed to separate it into two pieces. The edge connectivity ($\lambda(G)$) of a graph is the minimum number of edges that need to be removed to separate it into two pieces (Sedgewick, 2002).

Graph $G = (V, A)$ is a directed acyclic graph of the network, where V is a set of network nodes and routers and A is a set of arcs between them. We use this graph in second component to make deadlock-free routes.

A directed graph, or digraph $D = (V, A')$, consists of a finite nonempty set V of points together with a prescribed collection A' of ordered pairs of distinct points. The elements of A' are directed lines, which are arcs (Harari, 1969).

A bridge in a graph is an edge that, if removed, would separate a connected graph into two disjoint subgraphs. An articulation point in a graph is a vertex that, if, removed, would separate a connected graph into at least two disjoint subgraphs.

We use directed graph $D = (V', A'')$ to describe channel dependencies in the graph D. Set V' consists of the vertices that correspond to each arc from A'. The elements of A'' are arcs between vertices of CDG and show the allowable sequence of used channels.

Figure 13. Transformation of network topology to a graph

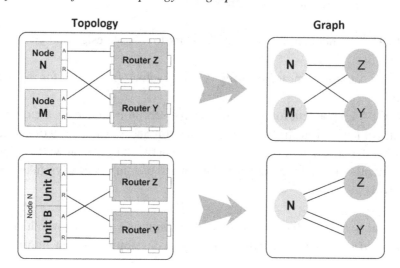

BUILDING OF A FAULT TOLERANT NETWORK

Fault Tolerance Evaluation

In designing or selecting a topological structure of onboard networks for a system, one of fundamental considerations is the fault-tolerance (Xu, 2001). In the context of this chapter we will assume that fault tolerance is a property that enables a system to continue operating properly in the event of the failure or one or more faults within some of its components. Basically, any system containing redundant components or functions has some of the properties of fault tolerance (Shooman, 2002).

Systems such as communication onboard networks have many nodes representing processors, sensors, control units, memory, etc. that desire to communicate and also have several links providing a number of interconnected pathways. These many interconnections increase reliability and topology complexity. As all these devices are connected to such a network, a failure or fault affect many people, thus the reliability goals must be set at a high level especially in the domain of spacecraft and avionics.

Generally, the onboard network is assembled from three main types of elements: terminal nodes, routers and links. Each of these elements can fail so that it cannot be repaired in any considerable time. However, a fault-tolerant system should continue its proper operation. This can be achieved by adding redundancy to the onboard network. For example, one terminal node can be represented by two or three redundant units. When one of redundant units fails another unit continues to operate properly, replacing the failed one.

Fault-tolerance can be usually characterized by connectivity and edge-connectivity of the topological structure of the network. Therefore, we consider a network as a graph $G = (V, E)$. The connectivity of a graph is a good estimate of the fault tolerance (f) of the network, since higher connectivity means more elements can fail without disrupting the communication among the rest of the onboard network (Cornejo & Lynch, 2010). It is necessary to have more than one route between each pair of vertices in a graph, so as to handle possible failures.

Figure 14. A digraph of a network topology

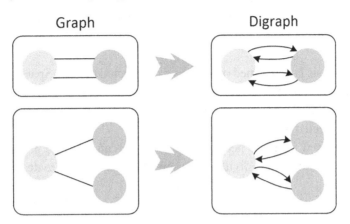

Figure 15. Splitting of vertex

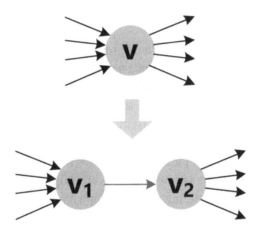

Fault tolerance analysis of onboard networks requires evaluation of vertex connectivity of the graph. This is due to failures of routers and nodes that can disable proper operation of the entire network. Moreover, there is a Whitney's inequality which relates edge connectivity, vertex-connectivity and minimum degree ($\delta(G)$) and states that for any graph G:

$$k(G) \leq \lambda(G) \leq \delta(G)$$

This means that vertex connectivity is less or equal to edge connectivity. Therefore, in this chapter we will evaluate vertex connectivity of a graph. Consequently, we will consider failures of nodes and routers, which correspond to vertices in a graph. Failures of links are not considered separately, because node or router failure leads to all adjacent links disconnection.

The input network topology should be transformed into a graph. The algorithm can analyze either full network topology or its part. We have set up a rule for graph construction (see Figure 13):

1. All redundant units of a node shall be associated with only one vertex of the graph.
2. All routers shall be represented by separate graph vertices.
3. All links shall be represented by graph edges.

The connectivity analysis is performed on the basis of directed graphs. SpaceWire standard provides bidirectional links, so each link shall be represented by a pair of edges with opposite orientations (see Figure 14). We use the digraph for the k-connectivity analysis because we should apply maxflow algorithms, which work in directed graphs.

Once the graph is created from the network topology we can start the general algorithm of fault-tolerance evaluation. The algorithm is divided into several steps, which are described below.

Step 1. Check the connectivity of a graph. If a graph is not connected, then there is no need to continue fault tolerance evaluation as it obviously does not tolerate any failure. Otherwise, if the graph is connected, move to Step 2.

Step 2. Evaluation of vertex connectivity of the graph. It is necessary to search through all pairs of graph vertices s and t, find the number of vertex disjoint paths from s to t and get the minimum, which corresponds to search value of the graph connectivity k.

The problem of finding vertex connectivity can be reduced to a problem of finding edge connectivity. For each pair of vertices s and t we should create new graph G' where each vertex v from the graph is split into two vertices v_1 and v_2. All incoming edges to the original vertex go to v_1 while all outgoing edges come from v_2 (see Figure 15). Moreover, we add an edge v_1-v_2 of the capacity equal to 1.

In theoretical computer science, graph connectivity has been well studied for more than forty years. It has a strong relationship with the problems of maximal network flow and minimal cut.

In order to find the number of disjoint paths from s to t we propose to use maxflow algorithms such as Ford-Fulkerson or Edmonds-Karp algorithms (Jungnickel, 2008). Let us assign each edge of the graph G' a capacity equal to 1. This allows applying maxflow algorithm to evaluate st-connectivity.

The minimal maxflow among all s-t pairs of the initial graph G yields the graph vertex connectivity value k. In order to decrease the number of iterations in the algorithm we propose to terminate the search once the connectivity value k becomes equal to 1. This means that the graph cannot be more than 1-connected, i.e. it cannot tolerate any failure. The connectivity search algorithm stops its execution and moves to Step 3.

Step 3. Calculate fault tolerance of the graph using the following formula:

$$f = k - 1$$

The upper bound of complexity of this algorithm is $O(|V|^{1/2}|E|^2)$ (Jungnickel, 2008).

If the value of fault tolerance is 0 then the algorithm starts a search of bottlenecks in a network. In the graph G bridges and articulation points represent bottlenecks. This can give an opportunity for the SANDS user to find out all bottlenecks of the designed network. Bridges in a graph correspond to links that are bottlenecks in the designed network. As for articulation point, it corresponds to a router, which failure can lead to breaking a network into two separate subnetworks with no means to communicate with each other.

Network Topology Transformation for Fault Tolerance

The more big and complex the onboard network is, the easier for a network topology designer to make a mistake in fault-tolerant structure. Therefore, SANDS implements another significant algorithm, which can be useful for building of fault-tolerant network – network topology transformation for increasing fault tolerance.

The problem can be described as follows. Given a network topology, place additional redundant units for terminal nodes, additional routers and communication links to achieve the required by user fault tolerance.

We propose to solve the stated problem in two stages, which are described below.

- Stage 1: Initialisation of a network topology with required fault tolerance f.
- Stage 2: Iterative improvement of the topology obtained on the stage 1.

Stage 1 consists of four steps, presented below.

- **Step 1:** *Fault tolerance analysis.* Firstly, it is necessary to evaluate fault tolerance of the initial network or its part. In case of fault, tolerance of the initial network is less than required fault tolerance, and then we move to the Step 2. Otherwise, there is no need to run the algorithm.
- **Step 2:** *Addition of redundant ports and units to terminal nodes.* This step checks the required number of ports and units in terminal nodes in order to provide required fault tolerance. If it is necessary, additional redundant ports or units should be added to terminal nodes (if the user allows to add units and ports). This step should be performed only when the initial network or its part contains terminal nodes.
- **Step 3:** *Addition of redundant communication links and routers.* This step checks the number of routers in the network or its part, adds new communication links and new routers to the network topology. This can be done in the following ways:
  - by connecting all routers in the initial network structure through additional links;
  - by replicating an initial network structure with all routers and links (except nodes) and then by connection of replicas into one network structure. Connection of replicas is performed by adding links between the routers' replicas.
- **Step 4:** *Fault tolerance analysis of the transformed network.* The final step of Stage 1 evaluates the fault tolerance of resulting network structure, which was obtained after previous steps. If the resulting fault tolerance is equal or even more than the required fault tolerance, then the algorithm moves to the Stage 2. If this is not the case, it means that the particular initial network topology cannot be transformed to obtain the required fault tolerance. This can occur when network routers have a very small number of ports.

This is the final step of Stage 1, which is followed by Stage 2.

Figure 16. Example of network topology

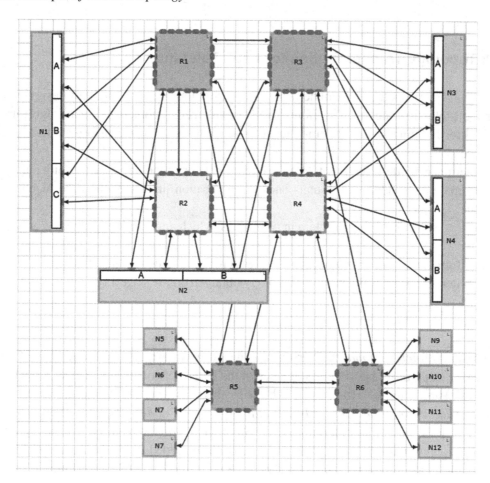

Stage 2 is intended for iterative improvement of the topology obtained on the Stage 1. Addition of new links and routers can cause excessive redundancy. This excessive redundancy can be unnecessary for achieving required fault tolerance. For reducing hardware costs, we need to remove extra routers and links.

Therefore, improvement consists in one by one removing added routers and links and then checking fault tolerance of the modified network. Otherwise, put the removed router with all corresponding links back to the network topology. Stop when all added routers have been considered.

SpaceWire network can consist of a large number of terminal nodes, so that it is better to divide the network is into a set of special network regions. Each region can consist of routers and nodes. The problem of network transformation for such a network is more complex than for a single region SpaceWire network. Providing that the initial network consist of several regions, network transformation shall be done in the following way:

Figure 17. Example of network transformation

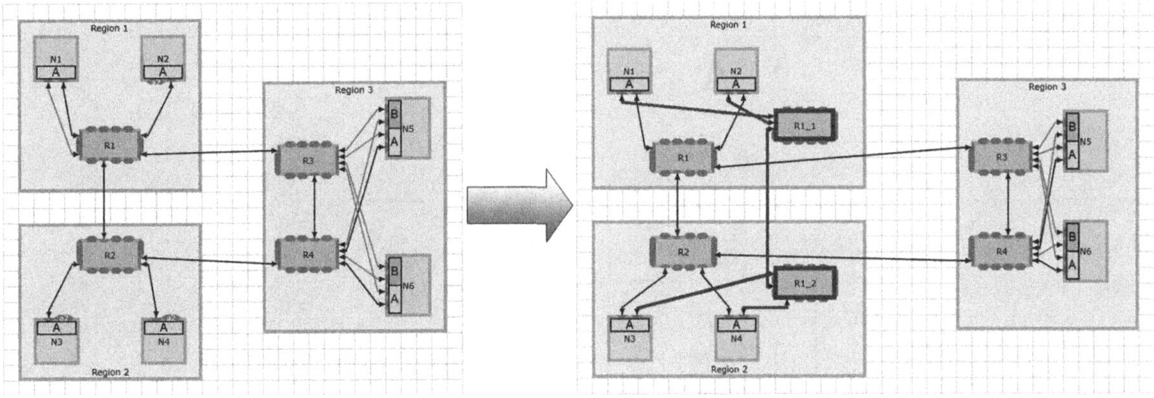

1. Perform transformation for each network region separately (Stage 1, Stage 2). Region transformation shall be done similarly to transformation of a network part.
2. Perform transformation for terminal nodes and routers, which are not included into regions (Stage 1, Stage 2).
3. Connect all routers by additional links. New links shall be added only for those pairs of routers, which are located in different regions or out of regions. Routers, which belong to one network region, shall not be connected by additional links. Then perform Stage 2 of the general algorithm.

All the described algorithms were successfully implemented in SANDS computer-aided design system for SpaceWire networks.

Network Topology Transformation and Fault Tolerance Analysis Use Case

We provide a use case of analysis features of SANDS. Figure 16 shows a network, which consist of 12 terminal nodes and 6 routers.

After performing analysis SANDS gives a detailed analysis report including mass parameters for routers and cables, power consumption estimation, minimal and maximal link rates. Moreover, it performs fault-tolerance analysis, which is one of the key features of this analysis (Lavrovskaya, Olenev, & Korobkov, 2017).

Fault-tolerance analysis for this network structure results in zero fault tolerance. There is a bottleneck in this network in its bottom part containing the following nodes and routers: N5 – N12, R5 and R6. This part of a network cannot tolerate any fault. The user is provided with all this information in the report and corresponding highlights in GUI.

Next use case is referred to the network topology transformation feature. Let us show an example of algorithm application to a network with regions (see Figure 17). The initial network topology consists of three regions. The whole network is not fault-tolerant, however, Region 3 is 1-fault-tolerant, because of cross-connections between nodes' units and routers R3 and R4.

In the discussed topology it can be observed that nodes N2, N3 and N4 have two ports, but only one port is connected to the router.

Figure 18. Example of deadlock

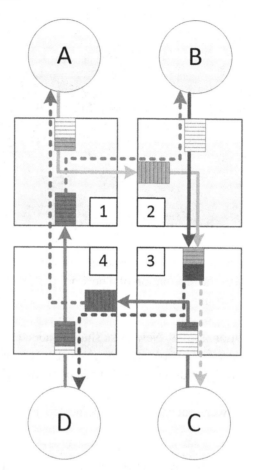

We ran SANDS software to obtain a network which is 1-fault-tolerant. The result of network transformation is shown in Figure 17. All new links are shown in heavy lines and new routers are shown with dark frames.

Our network transformation algorithm connected free ports of terminal nodes N1, N2, N3 and N4 for cross-connections. Each terminal node in Region 1 and Region 2 contains two SpaceWire ports which are connected to different routers in order to increase fault tolerance.

Moreover, we can observe two new routers R1_1 and R2_1, which were added to increase fault tolerance in Region 1 and Region 2. Topology transformation tool added 5 additional communication links. Region 3 was not transformed as it was originally 1-fault-tolerant. The resulting network topology is 1-fault-tolerant.

Figure 19. Channel Dependency Graph with cycles

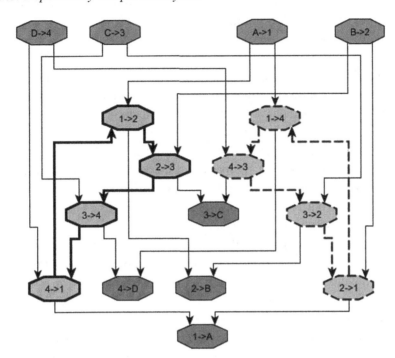

IMPLEMENTATION OF DEADLOCK-FREE ROUTING

Another key issue in onboard network design is routing. Routing implies the organization of data transmission routes through the network with required quality of service (QoS) criteria (data transmission delay, fault tolerance, etc.).

In this chapter, we talk about routing in the context of SpaceWire networks and their features. SpaceWire standard allows to use three types of addressing in the network: path addressing, logical addressing, regional-logical addressing. It means that data transmission routes can be stored in three different ways. SpaceWire standard obliges to use *static* and *wormhole* routing. It is very important to take these requirements into account for solving routing problem.

Static routing. There are two routing types: dynamic and static routing. Static routing differs from dynamic routing in that routing tables are configured in routers only once before network launch and cannot be automatically changed during network operation. Only manual changing the routing tables is possible, without special algorithms in contrast to dynamic routing. This is main disadvantage of static routing, but on the other hand static routing is more stable and does not require large hardware and software router resources for routing table service.

Wormhole routing. When a packet enters the input port in the router, the packet header is read, and according to the routing table the header is sent to the output port. Packet tail is transmitted through router "on the fly", taking up channel for transmission. Only one packet can be transmitted via the channel at a time.

The main problem that appears in solving of the routing problem is the packet blocking. There are three most popular types of packet blocking that may appear in the networks: starvation, livelock, and deadlock. Due to SpaceWire features starvation and livelock are solved and not actual for SpaceWire networks.

Deadlock. Deadlock is the situation when packets block each other and cannot be transmitted. The reason for this blocking is the incorrect routing scheme, that leads to the cyclic dependencies of resources (see Figure 18). Here resource is the physical channel. This blocking is actual for SpaceWire networks.

When a packet is transmitted over a network, it takes up a physical channel on each hop between routers. As the packet passes through the network, the tail of the packet releases previously occupied channels. If the required channel is busy, the packet is stored into the input buffer of the router and waits until the busy channel becomes free. If size of packet is larger than the buffer space, the rest of the packet is stored into input buffers of previous routers according to its route, occupying all channels between these routers. The packet cannot be separated and partially transmitted or transmitted through different routes. If the tail of blocked packet does not occupy full space in the buffer, the next incoming packet at this port will fill the rest of buffer space and will be blocked in same manner (Kurbanov, Rozhdestvenskaya, & Suvorova, 2018).

In Figure 18 deadlock includes all packet flows. A packet from node A is blocked in router 3 because of a packet from node B. A packet from node B is blocked in router 3 by a packet from node C. A packet from node C is waiting for free channel between router 4 and router 1, which is occupied by a packet from node D. A Packet from node D is blocked in router 1 because of a packet from node A.

Such a deadlock paralyzes the whole network, and data transmission is impossible.

To describe this situation, we create the channel dependency graph (CDG). An example you can see in Figure 19.

CDG describes dependency of channels, which are used by packets. Vertices represent channels of the network. Arcs correspond to a sequence of used channels by packets.

Dally W. J. and his colleagues in (Dally & Seitz, 1988) formulated the following theorem: *the routing function in the network is deadlock-free, if there are no cycles in the Channel Dependency Graph.* This theorem is fundamental in deadlock-free routing problem.

UP/Down routing. To solve deadlock-free routing problem we provide an approach that is based on Up/Down routing for regular and irregular topologies. The Up/Down routing is a popular solution for deadlock-free routing in the modern commercial networks.

The Up/Down rules can be formulated in following points that are consistent in their execution:

1. A route can be laid through zero or more channels in "up" (forward) direction;
2. A route can be laid through zero or more channels in "down" (backward) direction.

The sequence of applying of these rules is strictly regulated and requires consistent execution: *a* at first and then *b*. Applying *a* after *b* is forbidden. In this way, we can avoid channel dependencies, because of a packet cannot be transmitted through physical channel in "up" direction after transmitting through physical channel in "down" direction.

Figure 20. a) Source network graph with active part (black elements) and redundant part (gray elements); b) Oriented subgraph of the active network part

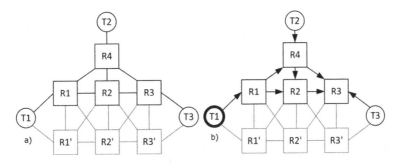

The classic Up/Down routing approach consists of the following steps:

1. Graph representation of the network.
2. Spanning tree construction with breadth-first-search algorithm (BFS).
3. Numbering of vertices in the spanning tree;
4. Direction assignment for the edges in spanning tree according to the numbering of vertices (direction from the vertex with lower number to the vertex with higher number). The resulting graph must be acyclic.
5. Applying Up/Down rules in the directed acyclic graph based on network structure.

In (Sancho, Robles, & Duato, 2000) authors in detail describe a method that creates the spanning tree based on depth-first-search algorithm (DFS). The provided algorithm is more flexible in criteria adjusting to create the route, than classic method with BFS-based spanning tree. Therefore, in our method we use DFS-based approach.

There are some reasons that cannot allow us to use existing DFS-based Up/Down approaches. We have to take into account that the network may contain redundant elements. So, set of routes for each data flow has to contain at least one route that uses only active elements. We should also understand that each router has to be able transmit data. Existing solutions (Sancho, Robles, & Duato, 2000; Sancho & Robles, 2000) may contain routers, in which data transmission is forbidden due to Up/Down rules.

An algorithm that we use does not require the vertices numbering to assign the edge direction. We assign the direction during the DFS-based graph traversing:

Step 1: Making an acyclic subgraph for an active part of the network using DFS-based approach.

In this step we choose a root vertex in the graph G = (V, E), that describes network topology. We do not consider router-vertices as a root, because in this case such router would not be able to transmit data due to the up/down routing rules. Therefore, we choose any terminal-vertex as the root. After that, we consider next vertices only among the active part network. The rule of choosing next vertex: next vertex is a vertex that has maximum number of connections with vertices from oriented subgraph. In case of tie, next vertex is a vertex that has maximum value of average topology distance (see *Figure 20*).

Figure 21. Conversion of the acyclic network graph to CDG

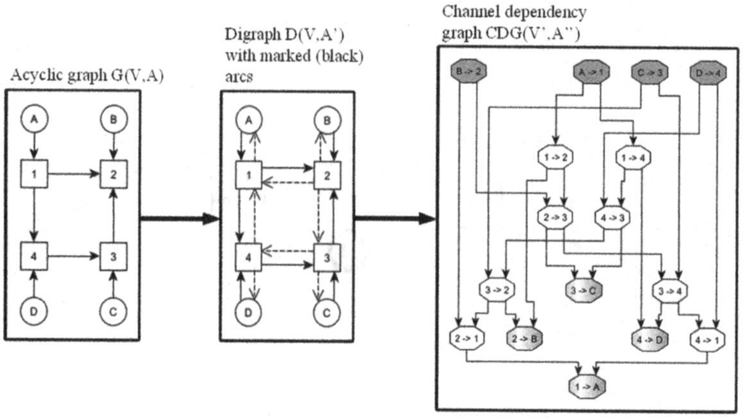

There are some rules for the edge direction assignment in the active part of the network:

- Between terminal- and router- vertices direction is always from terminal-vertex to router-vertex;
- In main branch (branch that is created until first recursive return) from current vertex to next vertex;
- In secondary branches (branches that are created after first recursive return) from next vertex to current vertex.

Step 2: Making an acyclic subgraph for a redundant part of the network basing on the active part structure.

When the active part is successfully built, we can assign edge directions in the redundant part. It is necessary to assign for each redundant router its active duplicate, because it influences the possibility to make a route over the redundant part.

There are some rules for edge direction assignment in the redundant part of the network:

- Between terminal- and router- vertices direction is always from terminal-vertex to router-vertex;
- Between redundant and its active duplicate direction is from the active duplicate to the redundant one;
- Between redundant vertices direction is the same like in the active part between their duplicates;
- Between redundant and active vertices. If it is possible to make direction path from the active duplicate to the active node, the direction from redundant to active node, otherwise direction is opposite.

Step 3: Conversion of the acyclic network graph to an acyclic channel dependency graph according to Up/down rules.

The aim of two previous steps is to get an acyclic graph of the network. If we have an acyclic network graph, we can make an acyclic CDG using Up/down rules. Conversion can be performed by two subtasks:

Figure 22. Topology for tracking of routes

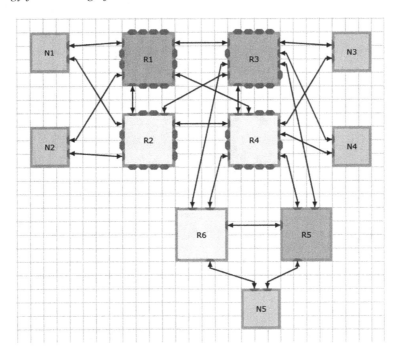

- Creating additional arcs in opposite direction. Since full-duplex channels are used in the network, we represent each channel as two arcs with opposite directions. As we work with directed graph at this stage, we create an arc with opposite direction for each arc in the graph, marking the original arc. Arc marking is necessary for connecting vertices in CDG. Graph with additional opposite arcs we call digraph D = (V, A'), where A' is a set of original and opposite arcs.
- Conversion of arcs to vertices of CDG and connecting them according to Up/Down rules. The vertices in CDG correspond to arcs in digraph D. The key moment in creating CDG is the connecting its vertices. Connections in CDG correspond to possible sequence of used channels by packet. We create CDG with respect to Up/Down rules and some sequences of used channels are forbidden. It means that arcs, which create cycles in the CDG, will be absent, therefore we avoid channel dependencies as well as deadlocks.

This step is represented in Figure 21.

Step 4: Applying BFS traversing algorithm from target nodes to mark reachable vertices among all vertices.

We use CDG to find deadlock-free routes. To decrease a set of vertices that can be considered as potential participant in the route, we mark the reachable ones using BFS traversing algorithm for CDG. We choose the target vertex as a start and using BFS algorithm move up to source nodes by the input arcs. Thus, we can set for each reachable vertex the distance to the target node to use it for route creation.

Step 5: Route creation with applying DFS algorithm from the source node using marked vertices from the previous step.

Since we have marked vertices in CDG, we can create all possible routes between source and target nodes. Using DFS algorithm allows us to make several routes and choose the most appropriate one.

Figure 23. Route from N1 to N4

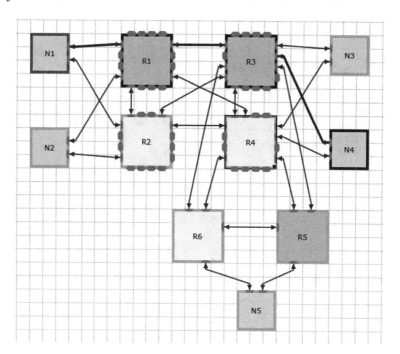

Table 2. Data transmission latencies for generated routes

Route	Number of Hops	Latency, ms
N1->R1->R3->N4	3	0,1666
N2->R1->R3->N3	3	0,1666
N5->R5->R3->R1->N1	4	1,2038
N3->R4->R5->N5	3	0,1413

Information about the distance to the target node on each vertex that we got in previous step allows us to make the shortest route. The main advantage is that all routes are deadlock-free, because CDG is an acyclic.

Deadlock-Free Routing Use Case

The following use case shows an example of tracking deadlock free routes in a network. Figure 22 shows a network which consist of 5 terminal nodes and 6 routers.

Let us assume the following communications in the network:

- Node N1 sends data to node N4;
- Node N2 sends data to node N3;
- Node N3 sends data to node N5;
- Node N5 sends data to node N1;

We run Component#2 software to get routes for data transmission. The resulting routes are given below:

- N1 - R1 - R3 - N4;
- N2 - R2 - R3 - N3;
- N3 - R3 - R5 - N5;
- N5 - R5 - R3 - R1 - N1.

Each route can be graphically highlighted for user's convenience (see Figure 23).

Dark frames for nodes show initiator and target nodes (N1 – initiator, N4 - target). Heavy lines for links and frames for routers show the transmission path.

Moreover, SANDS fills routing tables in accordance to the generated routes combination.

In addition, Component #2 calculates data transmission latencies for all defined by user information flows, see Table 2.

STP-ISS PROTOCOL SCHEDULE CREATION

The next significant issue in the general design flow is the problem of scheduling traffic in the onboard network. At this stage, using scheduling, you can regulate the information flows and avoid conflicts. Moreover, scheduling allows using the limited resources of the network and also provides guaranteed delays for packet transfer.

Nowadays there are transport layer protocols for SpaceWire that provide time division multiplexing mechanisms (e.g. STP-ISS, SpaceWire-D (Parkes, 2010)). Scheduling tables creation is a very complex problem which is difficult to solve for big networks with multiple data exchanges.

SANDS provides functionality for generation of scheduling tables for STP-ISS scheduling quality of service. These scheduling tables take into account the network structure and tracked routes.

The method of scheduling-table's design performs the construction of a STP-ISS schedule in which the delivery time of all packets for all traffics in the SpaceWire network would not exceed the maximum allowable latency, which was defined by the user. In case this is not possible, the user receives a corresponding message with recommendations (Olenev, Lavrovskaya, Korobkov, & Sheynin, 2019).

Input parameters for algorithm are:

- Parameters of traffics: route, packets size and bundle size, period of issue, guaranteed/non-guaranteed delivery (requires acknowledgement (ack) or not), acceptable latency of packets, acceptable latency of ack-packets; critical/non-critical traffic for spacecraft; order of packets issue.
- Max numbers of time-slots.
- Max duration of 1 epoch and 1 time-slot.
- Time to switch time-slots.
- Max channels bandwidth usage in percentage.
- Size of extra tail of packets.

This software provides the following functionality:

- Scheduling of information flows' transmission.
- Generation of scheduling tables for the STP-ISS transport protocol.
- Configuration should be done taking into account the network and structure tracked routes.

The scheduling table's design method can be represented in the following seven steps:

- **Step 1:** Getting and validation of input data:

  ○ Getting all input parameters.
  ○ Generation of a list of reply traffics. Examples: STP-ISS acknowledge packets, RMAP reply packets.
  ○ Generation of groups of traffics based on user-defined traffics order.
  ○ Adjustment of link speeds and packet sizes taking into account max channels bandwidth usage and extra tail size of packets.

  If there is an incorrect input data, go to step 7.

- **Step 2:** Checking the possibility of packet delivery with acceptable latencies:
  ○ Minimum delivery time is calculated for every packet.
  ○ Checking whether the rates of links are sufficient to transmit the packet with an acceptable latency – comparison of minimum delivery time and acceptable is performed. If the link rate is not enough, go to step 7.
- **Step 3:** Determining the epoch and time-slots duration:
  ○ Duration of one epoch with time between time-slots is calculated. Calculated epoch provides repetitiveness of packet issuing with corresponding periods for all traffics.
  ○ If there are some traffics which periods do not allow to calculate cyclic epoch not exceeding max duration of one epoch, go to step 7.
  ○ Duration of time-slots is updated taking into account the calculated epoch.
- **Step 4:** Check whether there is enough network bandwidth to transmit all packets of information flows within one epoch:
  ○ Intensity of incoming packets is computed for every port of all routers and nodes during one epoch.

Figure 24. Scheduling-table for all STP-ISS nodes

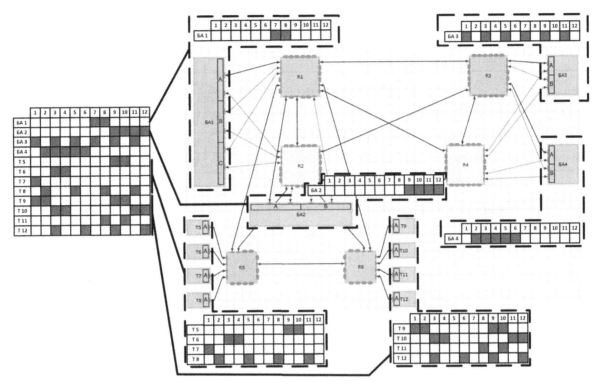

Figure 25. Topology for scheduling table generation

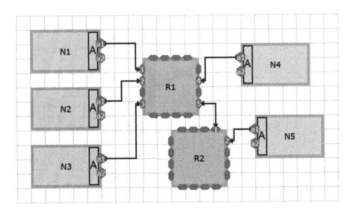

- ○ Maximum service intensity is also calculated taking into account operation cycles of device for every port.
- ○ Intensities of incoming packets and service are compared. If intensity of incoming packets is higher than service intensity, go to step 7.
- **Step 5:** Check the need for traffic scheduling:

Table 3. Network communications

Packet Type	Sender	Receiver
Regular Packets	N1	N3
	N3	N5
Express Packets	N2	N1
	N4	N3
Control Commands	N5	N1
	N5	N4
	N5	N2

Figure 26. Component #3 input parameters

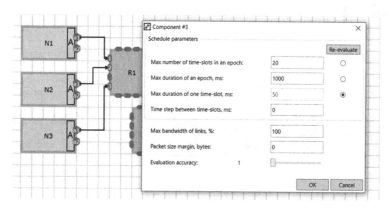

Figure 27. Component #3 schedule report

- All traffics are analysed to find conflicts of access to channel resources of a router or a node on the route.
- The worst packet delivery time is determined for all traffics.
- If there are conflicting traffics and packets of these traffics cannot be delivered with acceptable latencies, these traffics should be scheduled in time. As a result, all traffics will be filtered by those that need scheduling and do not need.
- **Step 6:** Scheduling – assignment of traffics to time-slots. Scheduling is based on the concept of Genetic Algorithm with backtracking search. It is an iterative process of resolving all previously found conflicts on the step 5. Placing of initial moments of the packets generation is determined,

Figure 28. Modeling of devices communication

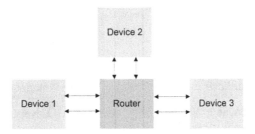

lower and upper bounds of the placing of traffics involved in the conflict or having an influence on it are calculated. The order of packets issue specified by the user is also taken into account. Transmission of all packets with replies on this placing is calculated and scheduled in time over the SpaceWire network. Packet priorities on the sender-node cause shifting send time of packets. For example: a regular packet will be sent after leaving of all high priority packets like acknowledges, control commands and express packets from the STP-ISS node. Packet priorities are also taken into consideration. Then, the resulting placement is estimated. If there are no improper conflicts, order of packet issue is fulfilled, packets' delivery time is within acceptable latencies, all packets are transmitted within early calculated epoch, then a solution is found – scheduling-table is generated for each node with enabled Scheduling QoS. Scheduling-table is based on the resulting placement. Otherwise, placement will be modified, then all calculations will be repeated. In the case there is no possibility to determine the placement that will lead to the solution, intermediate scheduling-table with recommendations how to improve input parameters – settings of traffics, nodes and routers – will be issued to user.

- **Step 7:** Output of operation results: recommendations, scheduling-table, duration of calculated epoch, etc.

STP-ISS Scheduling Table Creation Use Case

This use case shows an example of scheduling tables generation. *Figure 25* shows a network, which consist of 5 terminal nodes and 2 routers.

Communications in the network are presented in Table 3.

Component #3 requires also the following input parameters to generate schedule:

- Number of time-slots in an epoch. For the current use case we set this number to 20 time-slots.
- Epoch duration. For the current use case we set this duration to 1000 ms.
- Time step between time-slots. For the current use case we set time step to 0 ms.
- Bandwidth of links. For the current use case we set bandwidth to 100%.
- Packet size margin. For the current use case we set packet size margin to 0 bytes.
- Evaluations accuracy. For the current use case we set evaluations accuracy to 1.

Figure 26 show form for setting of input parameters.

Figure 29. Per layer modeling

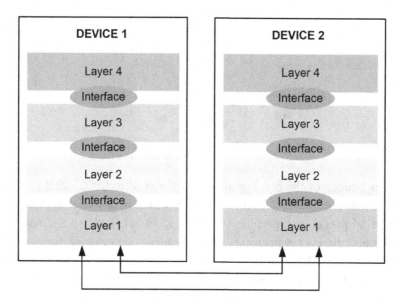

Figure 30. Two simulation modes in SANDS

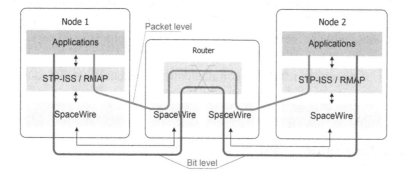

Component #3 report with scheduling-table creation results are show in Figure 27. In this use case scheduling-table successfully created.

HIERARCHICAL NETWORK SIMULATION

Besides all described above functionality, SANDS provides simulation features. Simulation of spacecraft's onboard networks covers many aspects of interactions within the network: transport, network, link interactions, inter-level interactions, etc. Depending on the problems, which should be solved during simulation and on the obtained results, there can be different approaches to the simulation of onboard networks. Consequently, at the design stage of the model, it is important to determine the tasks that the

Figure 31. SpaceWire network topology for the simulation

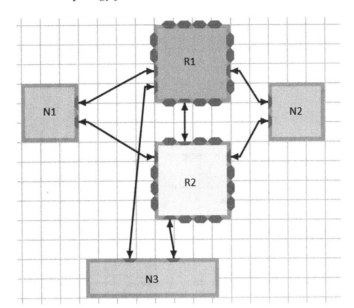

model shall solve and the results that the developer wants obtain. Based on this, you can determine the method that is convenient to use in a particular situation.

It is possible to distinguish two methods for software simulation of communication protocols:

- per layer modeling of the protocol stack;
- modeling of a system of devices.

The first method requires implementation of devices interaction model according to a particular protocol. In this case, interaction of components and processes inside the device (e.g. between layers of a stack) should not be considered (Olenev, 2009). Applications operation in the devices, packets formatting initialization procedures are not considered as well. The real interest represents here only the mechanism of devices' communications, such as transfer of packets, routing, delivery latencies, etc. Moreover, according to this method the implemented device model can be represented by several instances, i.e. it can be reused. This method is shown in Figure 28.

The advantage of this approach is that mechanisms of formation of packets, work of the device with the applications, some algorithms of checking the delivery and so forth simply are not considered, so it does not complicate model and does not make it more resource-intensive. Thus considering the work of one device here is not enough. For correct checking, it is necessary to model the bulk of devices to see all possible errors, which can occur during the transferring or routing.

The second method is per layer modeling of the protocol stack (see Figure 29). For this method, the decomposition of one task into a set of simple tasks or modules is used. Decomposition procedure includes accurate definition of functions of each module solving a separate problem and interfaces between them. The result is a logic simplification of a problem. Moreover, it gives a possibility of updating these separate modules without changing other parts of system.

Figure 32. Setting of traffic generator parameters

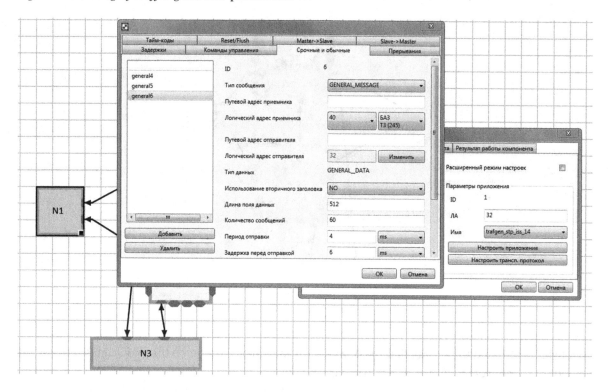

Figure 33. Setting of STP-ISS protocol parameters

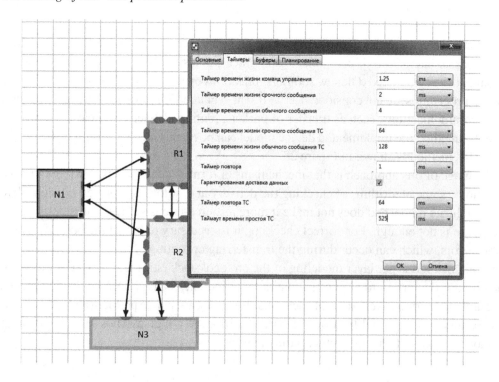

Figure 34. Starting of simulation

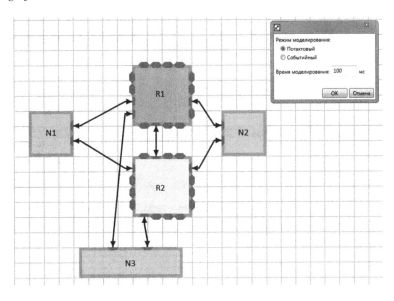

Figure 35. Simulation process

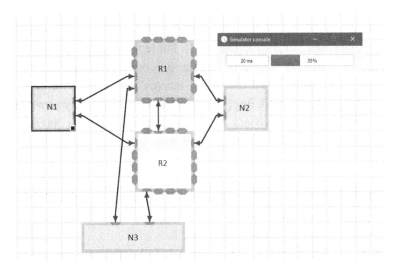

During the decomposition, the multilayer approach is often used. The set of modules is divided into layers forming a hierarchy. This set of modules in each layer is organized in such a manner that execution of tasks is performed by requesting only the modules of directly adjoining layers.

Such hierarchical decomposition assumes accurate definition of functions of each layer and interfaces between them. The interface defines a set of functions, which underlying layer provides to the overlying. Because of hierarchical decomposition, relative independence of layers and possibility of their easy replacement is reached (Olenev et al., 2014).

Figure 36. Onboard network model simulation results

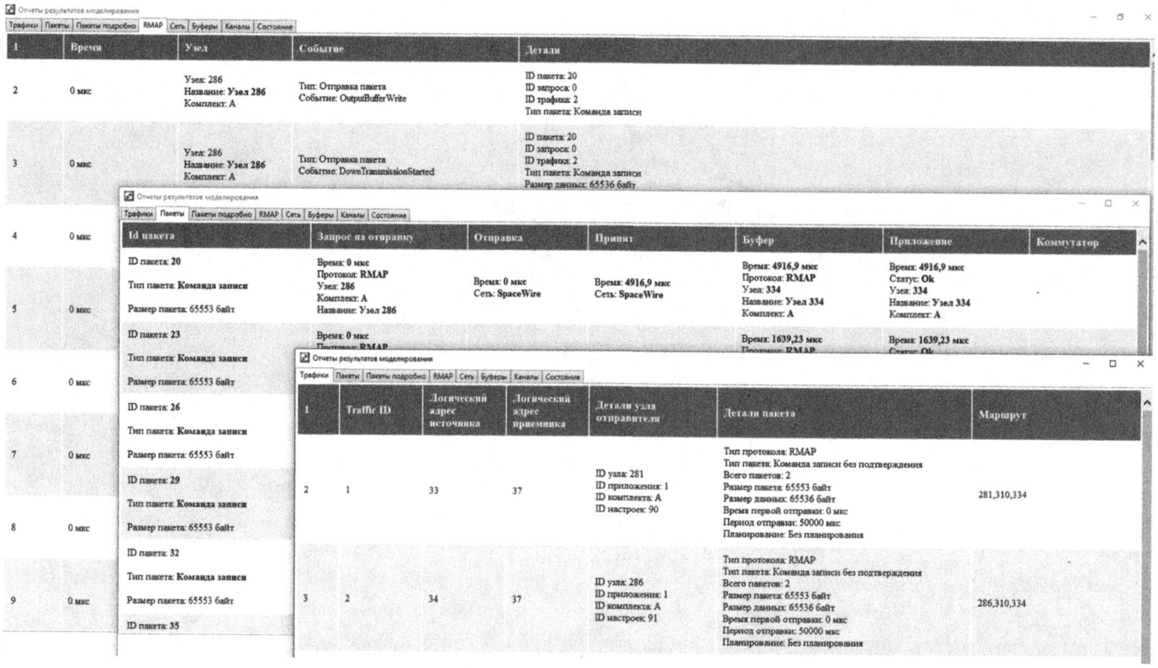

If we combine both methods in one simulation model, then it will give an opportunity to get simulation results for different purposes and abstraction levels. These two methods were used and implemented in simulation component of SANDS software. Simulation core is implemented in SystemC, which is a C++ library. SystemC is a set of C++ classes and macros that provide an event-driven simulation engine. It qualifies as a language for modeling, design and verification of systems, and it is specifically designed for modeling parallel systems (Black, Donovan, Bunton, & Keist, 2009).

There are two modes for simulation of network operation with different levels of details in SANDS (see Figure 30):

- Bit level – simulation of full SpaceWire stack and Transport protocol or Application.
- Packet level – simulation of upper layers only: Network, Transport, Application.

For bit level simulation SANDS uses SystemC clock based simulation option. This is done in order to achieve a more accurate comparison of the model with a hardware device. Nodes operation in a model closely corresponds to clock signals which impact data transmission latencies in links, ports and routers. However, bit level simulation gives significant difference between the real simulation time of the network and model time, since the model of each network component describes in detail all the internal mechanisms of the SpaceWire protocol.

Packet level simulation is implemented using event based mode in SystemC. Events, that appear while performing various functions, trigger other functions to be executed. In this simulation mode, the SpaceWire level operation is not considered, which greatly simplifies the model operation logic. Nodes operation in a model depends on various events while all data transmission delays in links, ports and routers are calculated basing on bit level simulation and are defined in correspondent network elements.

Such modeling significantly reduces the time for modeling the SpaceWire network, which makes it possible to simulate long periods of onboard network operation.

Hierarchical Modeling Use Case

This use case overviews simulation of the designed SpaceWire network. This is done by means of the Component #4. This Component takes as an input all the results, that user archived form Components #1-#3. Figure 31 shows the simple SpaceWire network that is planned to be simulated. Let us assume that this network has already been designed in Component #1, Component #2 tracked the routes in the network. For such a small network, we do not need to schedule the traffic, so we did not use Component #3.

To start the simulation firstly the user needs to configure the traffic generators in nodes: add different types of packets to be generated, set the generation periods and different fields of the SpaceWire packets. Then transport protocols in nodes also should be configured. Figure 32 and Figure 33 show different forms for setting of packet parameters and timers of STP-ISS transport protocol correspondingly.

When the network is fully configured at all levels of abstraction (application, transport and datalink), the user can start the simulation. To do this they need to choose the simulation type: bit-level simulation or packet-level simulation, then fill the simulation time field and then start the Component #4 (see Figure 34).

When simulation starts, the system shows a progress bar and the user needs to wait a bit to get the results (see Figure 35).

Simulation results are shown in Figure 36. Simulation log is represented in HTML form and gives full information for each event in the SpaceWire node, transport protocols, SpaceWire switches, channels and information on errors. All this information is presented in relation with the particular time of an event.

CONCLUSION

Nowadays, onboard networks are composed from a big number of elements with various functionality. All these elements are interconnected with each other via onboard network communication infrastructure. Onboard networks are now used in spacecraft and in avionics. A common technology for this kind of networking is SpaceWire, which is easy to understand, it is compact and efficient in implementation. As a network becomes larger, over some dozens of nodes, information streams becomes more dense, requirements and constraints stronger to design and operate SpaceWire network becomes tough tasks.

We overviewed existing simulation tools for on-board and local-area networks and proposed the solution of a new computer-aided design system SANDS for the SpaceWire onboard networks design and simulation. It supports full on-board network design and simulation flow, which begins from the network topology automated generation and finishes with getting simulation results, statistics and different diagrams. This software should solve important tasks, which spacecraft developers face with during implementation of satellites and other space vehicles. SANDS begins its workflow from the on-board network topology design and estimation of its physical characteristics. Then it gives an ability to track the routes for the data transmission in a network and generate the scheduling table for the STP-ISS transport protocol for data transmission with Guaranteed QoS. After the network design is finished – the last stage is the simulation of the network operation with real network characteristics. Graphical user interface provides possibilities to draw the network topology and set different parameters of nodes, switches and channels.

SANDS graphical user interface provides the visual network composition and management capabilities. It allows designing SpaceWire network topology in visual interactive way from components library, that is a replenish set of network nodes and switches relevant to physical devices that are available for network building. For all nodes, switches and channels the GUI provides the configuration interfaces to set up their parameters, configure transport protocols and application-level traffic generators. The designed network is exported to the intermediate XML representation format to be used in other CAD tools for simulator, routes tracking, scheduling calculation and other tools.

All the components of SANDS software are based on formal methods. All planned difficult tasks are successfully solved in this project. So in the current chapter we also discussed algorithms and methods used in SANDS: algorithms for building a fault-tolerant network, method for deadlock-free routing creation, building a schedule for the nodes in a network and, finally, a method for hierarchical network simulation. In addition, we provided use cases for each component of SANDS.

The proposed software system would be a good assistant during the spacecraft design, implementation and testing. SANDS is extensible system, it is possible to add new Transport and Link layer protocols and extend the functionality. Currently the software is fully implemented and in trial operation in industrial companies.

REFERENCES

Black, D., Donovan, J., Bunton, B., & Keist, A. (2009). *SystemC: From the ground up* (Vol. 71). Springer Science & Business Media.

Cornejo, A., & Lynch, N. (2010). Fault-Tolerance Through k-Connectivity. *Workshop on Network Science and Systems Issues in Multi-Robot Autonomy: ICRA.*

Dally W. J., & Seitz C. L. (1988). *Deadlock-free message routing in multiprocessor interconnection networks*. Academic Press.

Dellandrea, B., Gouin, B., Parkes, S., & Jameux, D. (2014). MOST: Modeling of SpaceWire & SpaceFiber Traffic-Applications and Operations: On-Board Segment. *Proceedings of the DASIA 2014 conference.*

Doerffel, T. (2009). Simulation of wireless ad-hoc sensor networks with QualNet. *Advanced Seminar on Embedded Systems, Technische Universitat Chemnitz, 16.*

Eganyan, A., Suvorova, E., Sheynin, Y., Khakhulin, A., & Orlovsky, I. (2013). DCNSimulator – Software Tool for SpaceWire Networks Simulation. *Proceedings of International SpaceWire Conference,* 216-221.

Harari, F. (1969). Graph Theory. Addison-Wesley Publishing Company.

Issariyakul, T., & Hossain, E. (2012). *Introduction to Network Simulator NS2*. Springer Science+Business Media.

Jianru, H., Xiaomin, C., & Huixian, S. (2012). An OPNET Model of SpaceWire and Validation. *Proceedings of the 2012 International Conference on Electronics, Communications and Control,* 792-795.

Jungnickel, D. (2008). *Graphs, Networks and Algorithms* (3rd ed.). Springer-Verlag Berlin Heidelberg. doi:10.1007/978-3-540-72780-4

Kurbanov, L., Rozhdestvenskaya, K., & Suvorova, E. (2018). Deadlock-Free Routing in SpaceWire Onboard Network. *2018 22nd Conference of Open Innovations Association (FRUCT),* 107-114.

Lavrovskaya, I., Olenev, V., & Korobkov, I. (2017). Fault-Tolerance Analysis Algorithm for SpaceWire Onboard Networks. In *Proceedings of the 21st Conference of Open Innovations Association FRUCT.* University of Helsinki.

NS-3 Manual. (2017). *NS-3 Network Simulator, 165.* doi:10.23919/FRUCT.2017.8250185

Nuevo, J. (2004). A Comprehensible GloMoSim Tutorial. *INRS, 34.*

Olenev, V. (2009). Different approaches for the stacks of protocols SystemC modelling analysis. *Proceedings of the Saint-Petersburg University of Aerospace Instrumentation scientific conference,* 112-113.

Olenev, V., Lavrovskaya, I., Korobkov, I., & Sheynin, Y. (2019). Design and Simulation of Onboard SpaceWire Networks. *2019 24th Conference of Open Innovations Association (FRUCT),* 291-299.

Olenev, V., Lavrovskaya, I., Morozkin, P., Rabin, A., Balandin, S., & Gillet, M. (2014). Co-Modeling of Embedded Networks Using SystemC and SDL: From theory to practice. Advancing Embedded systems and real-time communications with emerging technologies, 206-233.

OTcl Official website. (2019). *OTcl and TclCL.* Retrieved from https://sourceforge.net/projects/otcl-tclcl/

Parkes, S., & Ferrer-Florit, A. (2010). *SpaceWire-D – Deterministic Control and Data Delivery Over SpaceWire Networks.* Draft B.

Sancho, J., & Robles, A. (2000). Improving the up*/down* routing scheme for networks of workstations. *European Conference on Parallel Processing,* 882-889. 10.1007/3-540-44520-X_123

Sancho, J., Robles, A., & Duato, J. (2000). A new methodology to compute deadlock-free routing tables for irregular networks. *Network-Based Parallel Computing. Communication, Architecture, and Applications,* 45-60.

SCALABLE Network Technologies. (2014). Make Networks Work. Network modeling software for Development and Analysis. *QualNet Datasheet, 4.*

Sedgewick, R. (2002). *Algorithms in C++. Part 5 Graph Algorithms* (3rd ed.). Addison-Wesley.

Sheynin, Y., Olenev, V., Lavrovskaya, I., Korobkov, I., & Dymov, D. (2014). STP-ISS Transport Protocol for Spacecraft On-board Networks. *Proceedings of 6th International SpaceWire Conference 2014 Program,* 26-31. 10.1109/SpaceWire.2014.6936226

Shooman, M. L. (2002). *Reliability of Computer Systems and Networks. Fault Tolerance, Analysis, and Design.* New York: Wiley.

Siraj, S., Gupta, A. K., & Rinku-Badgujar. (2012). Network Simulation Tools Survey. *International Journal of Advanced Research in Computer and Communication Engineering, 1*(4), 201-210.

SpaceWire Standard. (2008). *ECSS – Space Engineering. SpaceWire – Links, Nodes, Routers and Networks*. ECSS-E-ST.

SSFNet Official website. (2019). *Scalable Simulation Network*. Retrieved from http://www.ssfnet.org/internetPage.html

ESA. Standard ECSS-E-ST-50-52C. (2010). *SpaceWire — Remote memory access protocol*. Noordwijk: Publications Division ESTEC.

Syschikov, A., Sheynin, Y., Sedov, B., & Ivanova, V. (2014). Domain-specific programming environment for heterogeneous multicore embedded systems. *International Journal of Embedded and Real-Time Communication Systems, 5*(4), 1–23. doi:10.4018/IJERTCS.2014100101

Thales Alenia Space. (2011). *Modeling Of SpaceWire Traffic*. Project Executive Summary & Final Report, 25. Author.

van Leeuwen, B., Eldridge, J., & Leemaster, J. (2011). SpaceWire Model Development Technology for Satellite Architecture. *Sandia Report. Sandia National Laboratories, 2011*, 30.

Varga, A., & Hornig, R. (2008). An overview of the OMNeT++ simulation environment. *Proceedings of the 1st international conference on Simulation tools and techniques for communications, networks and systems & workshops*. 10.4108/ICST.SIMUTOOLS2008.3027

Xu, J. (2001). *Topological Structure and Analysis of Interconnection Networks*. Kluwer Academic publishers. doi:10.1007/978-1-4757-3387-7

KEY TERMS AND DEFINITIONS

Deadlock-Free Routing: Creation of the routing tables for the routers that ensures that there would be no deadlocks during the data transmission in a network.

Embedded Network: A specific combination of computer hardware and software which is specifically designed to perform a particular function (or a range of functions) of a larger system.

Fault-Tolerance: Is the property that enables a system to continue operating properly in the event of the failure of (or one or more faults within) some of its components.

Modeling: A representation of an object by a model in order to obtain information about the object. This information is usually obtained through experiments with the object's model.

Onboard Network: Communication network, that is in order for transferring any kind of a data on a board of spacecraft, aircraft or any other kind of a vehicle.

Scheduling: A type of quality of service that makes the network operate in accordance to the single schedule, when each node has (or does not have) a permission to send data during the particular time interval.

Chapter 5
Model–Based Techniques and Tools for Programming Embedded Multicore Platforms

Konstantin Nedovodeev
St. Petersburg State University of Aerospace Instrumentation, Russia

Boris Sedov
St. Petersburg State University of Aerospace Instrumentation, Russia

Yuriy Sheynin
St. Petersburg State University of Aerospace Instrumentation, Russia

Vera Ivanova
St. Petersburg State University of Aerospace Instrumentation, Russia

Alexey Syschikov
St. Petersburg State University of Aerospace Instrumentation, Russia

Sergey Pakharev
St. Petersburg State University of Aerospace Instrumentation, Russia

ABSTRACT

The chapter considers VIPE development environment with the main emphasis on its formal ground. The detailed description of a formal VIPE model of computation (MoC) and the semantics of language constructs let the reader reason about the behavior of the constructs in question. The authors propose a rigorous description of program transformations applied to the program while it is compiled. The program after all the transformations is a correct one from the view of the host MoC. Its behavior meets the programmer's expectations even when it includes fragments, which belong to a guest MoC. Techniques for translation of the guest MoC (OpenVX) constructs into the host MoC (VIPE) constructs were proposed. The approach described here leads to the end program that is fully conformant to the host MoC. In addition, the whole toolset is at the programmer's disposal, namely visual editor, compiler, runtime, and analysis tools. They stay applicable to the program, some parts of which are now guest MoC constructs.

DOI: 10.4018/978-1-7998-1974-5.ch005

INTRODUCTION

Development of parallel programs, which should be efficiently executed on heterogeneous manycore platforms, is a hard challenge for embedded system developers. Such platforms are targeted to the domains like ADAS, cryptography, video surveillance, aerospace etc. Even today, there are many heterogeneous manycore platforms on the market from NVidia, Qualcomm, Imagination, AllWinner, Samsung, Mediatek, ELVEES and other vendors. Tomorrow most of embedded systems will be heterogeneous (Joshi, 2016).

Nowadays developer teams create complex computing embedded systems (Evans, 2004); (Balandin & Gillet, 2010). Teams often include many experts from various domains. For an efficient problem solving such teams desperately need a common language for their project. According to many researchers, a visual graph notation is a natural representation of an operations sequence (Mellor, Balcer, & Jacoboson, 2002). Each member of a developer team explicitly or implicitly uses some kind of a graphical flow chart in his project design. It is better to have a single "big picture" of the whole project, to which all the members have simultaneous access.

In addition, developers face extremely complex and contradictory requirements; for example, they need to produce a high-quality embedded solution for some task within a tight time frame. Meanwhile, the volume of code vastly increases. When companies describe existing situation they compare it to the shift from writing programs solely in an assembly language to writing them in a high-level language. It is more comprehensible and productive and let teams cope with large projects. Modern projects are so huge and sophisticated that the high-level text-based language fall into a state of an assembler. It is not a coincidence that source-to-source compilers are used there (Puschel, 2005); (Ayguadé, 2009).

The VIPE IDE (Syschikov, Sheynin, Sedov, & Ivanova, 2014) is the model-based visual integrated environment for software design – from parallel algorithms to portable parallel programs for multicore heterogeneous platforms. The chapter presents its adaptation to a specific domain (Syschikov, Sedov, Nedovodeev, & Pakharev, 2017) by integrating a DSL into VIPE, tacking OpenVX as an example.

BACKGROUND

A visual approach has a long history and has wide support by large players in software development tools, such as Mathworks (Simulink), National Instruments (LabVIEW), Esterel technologies (SCADE) etc. These systems are essentially similar in the main reason for using visual programming approach: make it easier for experts to develop high-quality software in limited time with reasonable resources.

However, these systems have key drawbacks for embedded software programming. Parallel programs which are not model-based ones lack quality and correctness. The aforementioned model-based development environments (MDE) are limited (Simulink) or unable (others) to provide software performance analysis, which is a significant part of embedded systems development. They are closed systems and give no convenient ways for creation of domain-specific languages or libraries. SCADE is the MDE most adapted to the embedded software design. The final stage of the development process is the generation of a C-code, which is not hardware-specific.

The next fundamental approach in visual and domain-specific development is UML. UML is a general-purpose modelling language. It lacks quantifiable notions of time, as well as an ability to express non-functional properties and constraints, take into consideration execution platforms features and characteristics that is vital in embedded software design. All these aspects are particular concerns for real-time and embedded system developers (Demathieu, Thomas, André, Gérard, & Terrier, 2008). There are known works to use UML for high-level design of embedded software (Ito & Matsuura, 2010), but a direct usage of UML for such tasks is not wide spread. To solve these problems, OMG consortium developed in 2007 the UML profile for the Modelling and Analysis of Real-Time and Embedded systems (MARTE). This profile simultaneously specializes and extends UML taking into account specifics of embedded systems. There are studies and researches regarding application of MARTE for embedded systems design (Mischkalla, He, & Mueller, 2010); (Cardoso, Barros, Prado, & Aziz, 2012). Finally, the Multicore Association has developed adaptable API, called the Multicore Communications API (MCAPI), which is trying to close the gap between the high-level models (UML/MARTE) and the final system implementations. There are some on-going researches of this approach (Nicolas, Posadas, Peñil, & Villar, 2014).

Development of embedded systems in academia and industry is shifting from code based development to model driven development (MDD) approach (Trombetti, et al., 2005), which is based on high-level modelling languages. Modelling languages could be not as generic as general-purpose programming languages, they provide more specialized language constructs, e.g. for the creation of dynamic systems (e.g. Simulink (Mosterman, 2007) or for the creation of system models (e.g. SysML (Rosenberg & Mancarella, 2010). These MDD approaches are supported by industrial tool chains; prominent examples of MDD tools that are applied in both academia and industry are Simulink, ASCET, SCADE, Rhapsody, Artisan, and MagicDraw. Model-driven or model-based approach in embedded systems development can bring significant benefits in estimation and proving various aspects of designed embedded software.

Thus, a technology for embedded software development should provide approaches, methods and tools for embedded software development that ensure:

- Programmability. Software development for various application domains with high involvement of domain experts in software development process.
- Predictability. Provides abilities to estimate program performance and other characteristics on different hardware platforms.
- Portability. Make solution portable for at least one hardware family (better - across several platform classes).

BIRD'S-EYE VIEW OF THE TECHNOLOGY

The technology presented here is a multi-layered interrelated system of formal approaches, methods and instruments. It covers full stack of the technology from the concept of computations and to the production of executable code. Figure 1 shows the structure of theoretical methods and implementing tools, which forms the basis of VIPE – VPL development technology.

Formal AGP-model defines the VPL language syntax, semantics of its elements and control structures. Program developer designs visual parallel schemas by using VPL language and supporting instruments of the VIPE IDE. The developed parallel program is exported to the Intermediate Representation (IR) that is used as a core component for integration of language backend tools. Optimizing schema compiler SputnikC produces supporting C code for the developed program schema. C code together with: runtime library SputnikRT, user libraries and guest libraries such as OpenVX are compiled to the executable code by platform compiler.

Figure 1. Theory and tools behind VIPE
(VPL technology)

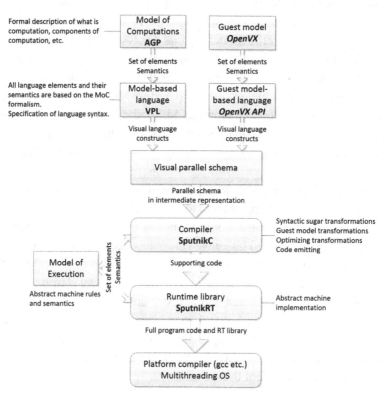

SputnikRT implements an asynchronous and (in general) parallel model of computation of the VPL language by providing a parallel execution environment for VPL-based programs on the platform, thus ensuring portability between different embedded multi-core platforms.

Key aspects of the VIPE technology, the formal basis and VPL compiling backend methods will be discussed next.

AGP-MODEL OF COMPUTATION

Parallel Computational Model: Goals and Requirements

In a parallel computation programming and implementation one deals with its functional behavior and its non-functional properties. Functional part is an algorithmic behavior, i.e. the target task algorithm representation. Timing of computations, scheduling and resource allocation are non-functional aspects. Though timing the computation and its implementation in limited resources environment could (and should!) influence the parallel computation unrolling and implementation, they should not influence correct parallel computation functionality.

In this approach specification of functional and non-functional features of parallel computations are separated in building the AGP-model, leaving in it only functional senses and leaving non-functional out of it, for another level of models and methods, for parallel computation implementation by its mapping. Non-functional constraints (time, resources) would affect the mapping but should not change the computation functionality. Functional and non-functional behavior of a parallel computation are not mixed in the AGP-model. The AGP-model is a purely computational model to represent parallel algorithms and make it in algorithmically complete way.

A Parallel Computational Model should give basic concepts of parallel computations in embedded platforms with heterogeneous parallel architecture and asynchronous operation of its components – processing cores and specific accelerators. Thus, a Computational Model should be an asynchronous parallel model with distributed control. Synchronous parallel computations with centralized control could be represented by the asynchronous model with distributed control; the converse is not true.

Nature of target multilayered parallel computations for a variety of applications will require static as well as dynamic parallel computations. Therefore, a Computational Model should give means to both dynamic and static parallel computations. Here it is good to remind the definition of dynamic parallel computations: *"dynamic computations are parallel computations which set of components and links between them depend on data values and change in the course of computation"*.

A parallel Computational Model provides a formal basis for development of a Parallel Programming Language, for specification of its semantics. Thus, the Computational Model provides a foundation for formal verification of parallel programs in this language, for parallel programs transformations to adapt to a platform and for optimization. Parallel program transformations for optimizations could be done and equivalence of the original and programs the optimized ones could be rigorously proved.

AGP-Models Hierarchy

In general, the Asynchronous Growing Processes Model of Parallel Computations (the "AGP-model") (Sheynin, 1998), is a family of parallel computational models, Figure 2.

The General AGP-model is specified in terms of uninterpreted parallel program schemes. The General AGP-model describes most general operation of dynamic parallel program schemes, which is irrespective to parallel program functionality. The General AGP-model introduces basic components of uninterpreted parallel program schemes and rules of their composition in a scheme. It establishes general rules of parallel program scheme construction and operation, of its dynamic transformation in the cause of computation. The General AGP-model sets up minimum restrictions on a parallel program schemes.

Next conventional step in the program scheme theory is defining an interpretation for some program scheme components while others remain uninterpreted. It gives so called partially interpreted program schemes. In the family of AGP-models, there are defined special AGP-models of parallel computations by introducing interpretations for some types of program scheme components and by setting up some constraints on parallel program scheme structure. Introduction of various sets of interpretation and constraints gives different special AGP-models. For instance, models for static parallel computations including pipeline and data-flow computations can be specified as rather simple specific AGP-models.

A family of Special AGP-models is scalable. Introduction of a specific model is ruled by objectives and targets of its application in parallel computations organization, optimization and analysis. Specific AGP-models inherit all the general properties and theoretical results, which are proved in the general AGP-model. However due to defined in a specific AGP-model particularities for same parallel program

Figure 2. Asynchronous growing processes models hierarchy

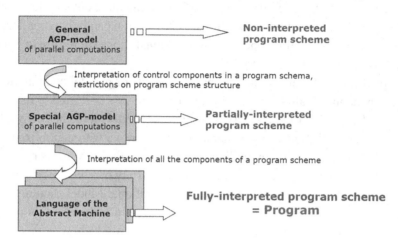

scheme structures and components behavior, it becomes possible to deduce new results, to prove new properties, which cannot be derived for more general class of parallel program scheme in the general AGP-model.

Finally, by specifying of interpretation for all the component types in parallel program schemes, here comes the programming language, with its syntax and semantics specified. A completely interpreted program scheme is a program. For a program in a language, which is specified by rigorous consistent interpretation for parallel program schemes under general and specific AGP-models, all the properties and formal analysis methodologies of these computational models will be valid.

AGP-Models Foundations, Informal Introduction

The general AGP-model is defined in terms of uninterpreted parallel program schemes. A parallel program scheme is represented by a directed graph. The graph vertexes (nodes) represent operators and data-objects.

Operators are an abstraction of program active components – functions, procedures, tasks (in respect to different parallelism granularity). Triggering of a corresponding operator node in a parallel program scheme is referred to as "firing" in traditions of asynchronous parallel models.

All interactions of processes are explicitly represented in the parallel program scheme. Thus, it can be controlled and verified at the level of parallel program scheme. Operators interact through data-objects (arcs in a data-flow graph can be considered as just a particular case of data-objects). Data accessed by several operators are explicitly represented in parallel program scheme as data-objects. Data objects are an abstraction for any types of storage and communication channels, which exist outside processes, launched by operators and can be used for operator interactions – from stored data in memory to physical or logical channels between computing modules in distributed computer architectures.

Operators share a data-object, which they have pointers to (be represented by arcs in the parallel program scheme graph). Many operators can access a shared data-object. However only linked to the data-object processes can access it. Other operators have no means neither to access the data-object nor to calculate its "address" and thus to get to it. Thus, there are shared data-objects in the model but not a shared memory.

The AGP-model sets formalism for most general type of parallel computations – for dynamic parallel computations. A parallel program scheme is transformed, in general, at every computation step – the graph itself is changing not only it's marking as was done in data-flow computations or Petri nets. A static parallel computation (e.g. data-flow computation) can be represented as a particular case of dynamic computations.

Alternative computations (if, case, etc.) can be implemented as generation of alternative parallel program scheme fragments instead of routing data to one of data-flow branches, which simultaneously occupy resources.

Control of computations in the AGP-model is defined in correspondence with ASP distributed architecture features. Control in the AGP-model is distributed, parallel and asynchronous. It is important that all these 3 key features are valid in regard to vertex readiness determination as well as to selection for firing. It is not so easy to ensure these properties in a general case in the context of asynchronous decentralized computations. For instance, such classical models as Petri nets are parallel and asynchronous in regard to transitions readiness determination but sequential, synchronous and centralized in regard to transitions firing. Special original formal methods are specified in the AGP-model to obtain the required qualities.

The general AGP-model is:

- A parallel model;
- An asynchronous model;
- A model with fully decentralised control.

It helps to fill parallel platform resources with computations as well as to pull high-parallel computations through limited platform resources.

The AGP-model forms an adequate basis for structured parallel programming. It provides all necessary means for hierarchical parallel program representation and its dynamic unrolling in the course of computation (static unrolling also, as a static computation is just a particular case of dynamic computation in the model).

Parallel Program Schemes Structure and Properties

A parallel program schemes is defined as a marked bi-partied directed graph.

$$S = \{Vp, Vd, F, W, M\},$$

where:

$v \in Vp$ – operator vertex (*Op*), $v \in Vd$ – data-object vertex (*DO*),
F – incidence relation $F \subseteq Vp \times Vd$
W – marking of edges;
M – marking of vertexes of the graph S.
$W = (W_A, W_B, W_C)$;
$W_A \in A = \{\alpha_s, \alpha_n\}$;
$W_B \in B = \{\beta_I, \beta_n\}$;
$W_C \in C = \{\sigma_w, \sigma_r, \sigma_{re}, \sigma_{rew}\}$;
$M: A = \{\zeta, \psi\}$
$\zeta = (\xi n, \xi r)$
$\psi = (\varphi e, \varphi f)$.

The arc marking W represents access types of arcs (sub-alphabet *C*), the influence of an arc on the operator readiness for firing (sub-alphabet *A*), actual reference on operator firing (sub-alphabet *B*).

$C = \{\sigma_w, \sigma_r, \sigma_{re}, \sigma_{rew}\}$

σ_w – write access; σ_r – read access, σ_{re} – read-erase access;, σ_{rew} – read-erase-write access.

$A = \{\alpha_s, \alpha_n\}$

α_s – "influence on readiness" marking; α_n – "no influence on readiness" marking.

$B = \{\beta_I, \beta_n\}$

β_I – marking "reference to data-object through the arc on the operator firing";
β_n - marking "no reference to data-object through the arc on the operator firing".

Thus in general case not all the arcs that outcome from the operator can be used in the operator readiness condition or can be used for data transfer to/from the operator on its firing.

The M represents state markings of the graph nodes.

$\psi = (\varphi e, \varphi f)$,

where φe – "data object is empty", φf – "data-object is full"

$\zeta = (\xi n, \xi r)$,

where ξn – "operator node is not ready"; $\xi r - \xi n$ – "operator node is ready".

The set of all the nodes of S is:

$Y = Vp \cup Vd$

For some formal considerations, it is convenient to correlate an information link graph G with the parallel program scheme representation – the graph S.

$G = \{Vp, Vd, H, W_H, M\}$

vertex linkage graph;

$H = \{xHy \mid (x \in Vd, y \in Vp, yFx \wedge W(yFx) \in \{\sigma_r, \sigma_{re}, \sigma_{rew}\}) \vee (x \in Vp, y \in Vd, xFy \wedge W(xFy) = \sigma_w, \sigma_{rew}) \}$,

$^\circ x = \{y \mid yHx\}$ – set of *input* vertexes for x,
$x^\circ = \{y \mid xHy\}$ – set of *ouput* vertexes for x.

The c(v) designates a set of data nodes that are adjacent to the operator node v in the parallel program scheme S.

$c(x) = {}^\circ x \cup x^\circ, x \in Y$

set of *adjacent* vertexes for x.

A parallel program schemes is called "*finite scheme*" if its sets Vp and Vd are finite sets.

The *empty scheme* Ω is defined, $Vp^\Omega = \varnothing$, $Vd^\Omega = \varnothing$, $F^\Omega = \varnothing$.

For parallel program schemes in the General AGP-model the following properties are postulated:

A0. $Vp \cap Vd = \varnothing$;

A1. $\forall x \in Vp, c(x) \subseteq Vd$;

A2. $(F\varnothing \neq) \wedge (\forall x \in Vd, \exists y \in Vp, yFx) \vee ((F=\varnothing) \wedge (Vd=\varnothing))$;

A2a. (*consequence from A2*) At least one operator vertex exists in a coherent constituent:

$\forall Sc \subseteq S, \exists z \in Yc, z \in Vp_c$;

where Sc – a coherent constituent.

A3. $\forall v \in Vp, \Gamma(S,v): S \to S', v \notin S'$;

Single firing rule (single execution) of an operator vertex.

A4. $\forall v,w \in Vp, v \neq w$,

$$\left(Vp_v^{Fr} \cup Vd_v^{Fr}\right) \cap \left(Vp_w^{Fr} \cup Vd_w^{Fr}\right) = \phi,$$
$$F_v^{Fr} \cap F_w^{Fr} = \phi, F_v^{link} \cap F_w^{link} = \phi$$

Generated scheme fragments *do not intersect*.

A5. $\forall v \in Vp$,

$$\left(Vp_v^{Fr} \cup Vd_v^{Fr}\right) \cap \left(Vp \cup Vd\right) = \phi,$$
$$F_v^{Fr} \cap F = \phi, F_v^{link} \cap F = \phi.$$

Generated scheme fragments do not intersect with the original program scheme.

Operator Nodes Readiness

The set of ready operator nodes, R, is constituted from all operator nodes $v \in Vp$ for which readiness predicate is true $\Phi(v)$=true.

A general condition of operator node readiness is that a node is ready when it has ready for read input data (input data nodes are not empty) and it has space to put its output data in (output data nodes exist and are empty). The $\Phi(v)$ predicate is defined in terms of the input and output data nodes marking for the operator node v.

A sensibility list sen is defined for an operator node v. The sen includes all data nodes which are adjacent to the v node in the graph S and that influence at the v readiness. In general, sen $\subseteq c(v)$. If all the adjacent to v data nodes influence at the v readiness then sen=$c(v)$. This particular case is called the "strict readiness condition"; the readiness predicate for this case is labeled as $\Phi s(v)$. If for all the $v \in Vp$ the $\Phi s(v)$ is specified we say that we have a strict readiness condition parallel program scheme.

Scheme Transformation

A parallel program scheme operation is in firing its operator nodes and is caused by them transformations of the program scheme.

Let us designate by Γ a transformations of the scheme S into a scheme S' as the result of the v node firing. Transformation of the scheme S by firing operator vertex $v \in Vp$,

$\Gamma(S,v): S \rightarrow S'$

Firing of an operator node v in a program scheme S causes, in general, the deletion of the v node from the graph and generation of some new fragment SFr in the parallel scheme graph.

The transformation $\Gamma(S,v)$ is defined as superposition of the graph structure transformation, $\mathfrak{I}1$, and the graph marking transformation, $\mathfrak{I}2$:

$\Gamma(S,v) = \mathfrak{I}2(\mathfrak{I}1(S,v)).$

In the General AGP-model minimal constraints are imposed on the SFr (axioms A4 and A5). The parallel scheme graph transformation is followed by subsequent transformation of the S graph marking.

The $\mathfrak{I}1$ and $\mathfrak{I}2$, in term, are defined as superposition of correspondent partial transformations.

I1 – Scheme Structure Transformation

$\mathfrak{I}1(S,v) = \mathfrak{I}1c\,(\mathfrak{I}1b\,(\mathfrak{I}1a\,(S,v)))$

($\Im$1a) Vp'=Vp\v ∪ V^{Fr}p.

($\Im$1b) F'=F\{vFx | x∈Vd} ∪F^{Fr} ∪ F_v^{link}

($\Im$1c) Vd'=Vd\<u>Vers</u> ∪V^{Fr}d,

where:

Vers(v)={z | z∈c(v), ∀y∈Vp' {yF'z}=∅},

S^{Fr} – a generated scheme fragment.

I2 - Scheme Marking Transformation

$\Im$2(S,v) = $\Im$2c($\Im$2b($\Im$2a(S,v))),

$$
(\Im 20): For\ x \in Vp', y \in Vd', W'\left(xF'y\right) = \begin{cases} W(xFy), if\ x \in Vp, y \in Vd, \\ W(xF^{Fr}y), if\ x \in V^{Fr}p, y \in V^{Fr}d, \\ \sigma' \in \{\underline{Inh}(W(vFy))\}, if\ x \in V^{Fr}p, y \in Vd, y \in c(v) \end{cases}
$$

$$
(\Im 2b): M'\left(x\right) = \begin{cases} \phi e, if\ (x \in \underline{Inf}(v)) \wedge (x \in *v) \wedge (W(vFx) = \sigma_{re}), \\ M(x), if\ (x \in \underline{Inf}(v)) \wedge (x \in *v) \wedge (W(vFx) = \sigma_r), \\ \phi f, if\ (x \in \underline{Inf}(v)) \wedge (x \in v*), \\ M^{Fr}(x), if\ x \in V^{Fr}d, \\ M(x), if\ x \notin \underline{Inf}(v). \end{cases}
$$

$$
(\Im 2c): M'(u) = \begin{cases} \xi n, if\ (u \in U \wedge \Phi(u) = false), \\ \xi r, if\ (u \in U \wedge \Phi(u) = true), \\ M(u), if\ u \notin U, \end{cases}
$$

Where:

U= c(c(v)) ∪ V^{Fr}p.

<u>Inf</u>(v) = {x | x∈c(v), W$_B$(vFx) = β$_1$}; the set of nodes that are adjacent to the v and on which marking the v firing can influence.

Inh(σ) – marking inheritance rule;

$$Inh(\sigma) = \begin{cases} \{\sigma_w\}, if\ \sigma \in \sigma_w, \\ \{\sigma_r, \sigma_{re}\}, if\ \sigma = \sigma_{re}, \\ \{\sigma_r\}, if\ \sigma = \sigma_r, \\ \{\sigma_r, \sigma_{re}, \sigma_w, \sigma_{rew}\}, if\ \sigma = \sigma_{rew} \end{cases}$$

Thus, we can unroll this nested superposition into the:

$\Gamma(S,v) = \Im 2c\ (\Im 2b\ (\Im 2a\ (\Im 1c\ (\Im 1b\ (\Im 1a\ (S,v))))))$.

This notation precisely reflects also the sequence of applying partial transformation to a parallel scheme S, from $\Im 1a$ up to $\Im 2c$.

Operator Nodes Firing

At any moment, there is an **R** set of ready operator nodes in the parallel program scheme S. In asynchronous computational models, it is typical to claim that any subset $\mathbf{R'} \subseteq \mathbf{R}$ of ready nodes can be fired. Just such a claim we see in data-flow computational models – Data Flow Graphs by Jack Dennis (Dennis, Fosseen, & Linderman, 1974), Data Driven Nets by Alan Davis (Davis, 1978), etc.

Unlike data-flow models, in the AGP-model a parallel program scheme can have data nodes, which shared by operator nodes. Thus firing of a node can influence the readiness predicate of another operator node. It can cause an ambiguity in parallel program scheme operation.

To avoid an ambiguity without sacrificing the model parallelism the *incompatibility relation* is defined for operator nodes in the AGP-model. Operator nodes v and w, v, w$\in$Vp, v$\neq$w, are considered to have incompatible readiness conditions if firing of one of the nodes and caused by it program scheme S transformation make the other one node not ready. The incompatibility relation is designated as v¬w,

$$v¬w:\ M(v){=}\xi r\ \xrightarrow{\ \Gamma(S,v)\ }\ M'(w){=}\xi n\ .$$

An *incompatibility cluster* $Cl(v)$ for a v operator node in a parallel program scheme S is defined as a set of all the operator nodes that are in pair wise incompatibility relation with the v node:

$\underline{Cl}(v) = \{x \mid x \in Vp, (x¬v) \vee (v¬x)\}$.

Parallel Transformation

At a current moment, any subset **Fi** of ready operator nodes can be fired, but not more than one operator node from every incompatibility cluster can be fired.

$\mathbf{Fi} = \{x_k \mid x_k \in \mathbf{R^*};\ \mathbf{R^*} \subseteq \mathbf{R},\ \forall x_m \in \mathbf{Fi},\ x_k \notin \underline{Cl}(x_m)\}$.

With a set **Fi** of simultaneously fired operator, nodes we define caused by them summery transformation of the program schemes – *parallel transformation* $\wp(S, \textbf{Fi})$:

$$\wp(S, \textbf{Fi}) = \bigcup_{v \in Fi} \Gamma(S, v).$$

The result of a parallel transformation $\wp(S, \textbf{Fi})$ of the parallel program scheme S will be a parallel program scheme S′ with a new structure and a new marking,

$$S \xrightarrow[\wp(S, Fi)]{} S'$$

It is proved that a parallel transformation holds valid the axiomatic properties of parallel program schemes in the AGP-model.

Computations in the General AGP-Model

Computations in the General AGP-model are defined as operation of an interpreted parallel program scheme. A computation is represented by a sequence of program schemes. A step of the computation is the transition from a program scheme S to a program scheme S' as the result of a parallel transformation. The Initial program scheme is designated by S_0. A parallel program scheme Sb *immediately follows* a program scheme S_a, $S_a \rightarrow S_b$, in a computation P if S_b is the result of a parallel transformation of S_a.

$$S_0 \rightarrow S_1 \rightarrow S_2 \rightarrow S_3 \ldots \rightarrow S_k \rightarrow \ldots .$$

An ordered set T of program schemes corresponds to a computation P;

$$T = \{S_0, S_1, \ldots, S_N, \ldots\}.$$

Any S_i and S_{i-1} in T are related by the relation "immediately follows", for any $i > 0$. The set T is called the "trace" of the computation P; the #T – the "trace length", designates a number of schemes in the set T.

The set T can be finite. It means that the computation P "stops"; and its "final scheme" $\hat{S}$ can be determined. The set T can be infinite; it corresponds to the situation, which is called "computation cycling"; #T=∞; no final scheme can be determined for a cycling computation P.

For dynamic computations that are defined by the AGP-model a normal completion of a computation process is considered to be the completion with an empty final program scheme, $\hat{S}=\Omega$. If a computation stops with not empty final program scheme, it is considered as a deadlock. A deadlock program scheme is a scheme S, $S \neq \Omega$ for which the R is empty, R=$\varnothing$.

By the "full set" $^-F(R)$ we designate such a subset of F(R), $^-F(R) \subseteq F(R)$, that not one F_i^j element of $^-F(R)$ is an internal subset of another element F_i^k of the $^-F(R)$.

$$^-F(\textbf{R}) \subseteq F(\textbf{R}), \forall \textbf{Fi}^J, \textbf{Fi}^B \in {}^-F(\textbf{R}), \textbf{Fi}^J \not\subset \textbf{Fi}^B.$$

Figure 3. Parallel program in VPL

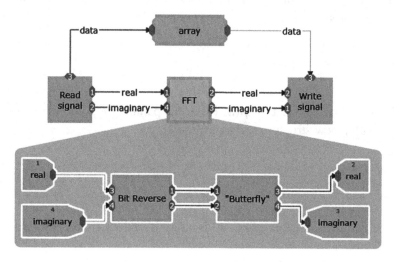

The set $\overline{\ }F(R)$ is ordered in correspondence with the number of operator nodes in a set F_i^j:
The maximal element F_i^{max} of the set $\overline{\ }F(R)$ is defined as:

$$\forall \mathbf{Fi^j} \in \overline{\ }F(R), \ \left\| \mathbf{Fi^j} \right\| \leq \left\| \mathbf{Fi^{max}} \right\|.$$

With these notions some useful classes of parallel program schemes and generated by them computations are defined. A parallel program scheme is called "conclusive" if $\| \overline{\ }F(R) \|=1$. A process, for which every program scheme in the trace is conclusive, is called "*scheme conclusive*" computation. The "*persistent*" computation is a computation, in which any operator node that becomes ready will stay in the ready state until it will be fired.

A parallel transformation $P(S, F_i)$ is called to be "*stable*" if the formed by it scheme S' will be equal to a scheme S", which can be formed by any superposition of single node transformation $\Gamma(S,v)$ for all the $v \in F_i$. The "*stable computation*" is a computation in which every parallel transformation is stable. The "*finite-scheme*" computation is a computation in which the initial scheme is finite and firing of any operator node generates a finite scheme fragment. The "*sequential computation*" is a computation in which at every step only one operator node is fired, $\| Fi \|=1$. The "*parallel computation*" is defined as a computation in which at least at one step i more than one operator node are fired, $\| Fi \| >1$. The "*maximum parallel computation*" is a computation in which at every step i a maximal element Fi_{max} of the $\overline{\ }F(R)$ is selected for firing.

VPL LANGUAGE

Parallel program in VPL is a hierarchical network (graph) of terminal operators, control operators and data-objects (Figure 3).

"Terminal" operators are the instrument for functional transformation (for example, "Bit Reverse", "Butterfly" objects in the Figure 3). During its operation, a "terminal" operator gets source data form input ports, performs data processing and puts resulting data to output ports. "Terminal" operator has two layers of description: external graphical and internal textual. The operator internals are described with a textual programming language. It allows describing local data processing with a mainstream programming language and in familiar terms. A "terminal" operator is a "black box" for the VPL language: its specification is out of the VPL formalism. However, according to the model semantics, such terminal operator implementation is compliant, because it could not change the behavior of the VPL program.

Structural operators are essential to express dynamic parallel computations. During the operation, structural operator generates the VPL program sub-scheme, defined in its body description. Structural operator body could contain any VPL language objects. Complex operator is the simplest operator used to add a hierarchy to a parallel program (for example, the "FFT" object on Figure 3). Control nodes provide algorithmic completeness of the VPL language. They allow expressing computations, which are dependent on data values at the VPL scheme level. VPL specifies the necessary and sufficient set of control operators: "if" / "switch" for conditional computations / "while" for loop processing.

Data-objects (for example, "array" in Figure 3) are used to store and share data between operators. Data-objects have types at the level of the VPL language, which include simple (for single data) and structural (queue, array). The single datum in VPL has no type. Special virtual data objects are used in a body of a structural operator to provide access to the data located outside of this body (on some of the upper levels of hierarchy).

Virtual data-object is a special object, which could be placed only in a body of a structural operator (for example, "real", "imaginary" on Figure 3). It is used to transmit data into/from structural operator body and is similar to formal parameter of function/procedure in conventional languages. Recursive virtual data-objects are used to transmit data between consecutive iterations of a loop operator.

The reader may find a detailed description of VIPE tools in another article (Syschikov, Sedov, & Sheynin, 2016).

VIPE TOOLSET

In Figure 4 the VIPE tool flow is presented. Tool flow provides three stages of embedded software design process:

1. Development of algorithms and programs
2. Performance evaluation
3. Deploying onto target platform

Authors omit the description of first and second stages to conserve space. The reader may find a detailed description of VIPE tools in another article (Syschikov, Sedov, & Sheynin, 2016).

Part of the VPL language backend (SputnikC in "Deploying onto target platforms" stage) and the theory behind it is as important as the formal specification. This theory is considered next.

Figure 4. VIPE toolflow

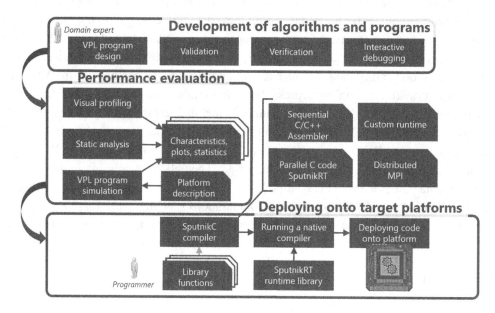

VPL SCHEME TRANSFORMATIONS

VIPE (Syschikov, Sedov, Nedovodeev, & Pakharev, 2017) has a compiler for VPL (see SputnikC in *Figure 4*). Any schema is compiled in multiple passes. There are four kinds of passes:

- Validation;
- Analysis;
- Transformation;
- Code generation.

Various passes aim at different goals, namely:

- Remove some syntax sugar (Van-Roy & Harid, 2004);
- Gather some information into a local window for subsequent transformation and code generation;
- Validate semantics of various constructs;
- Translate domain specific language (Fowler, 2010) constructs to the native VPL (described later);
- Build some auxiliary data structures that support a guest model of computation (described later).

Any schema is a tree of subschemas. All the passes build upon one driving principle – traverse the tree one subschema at a time and build some **local windows**. For each window, we consider only the elements inside it.

In the following, we give a description of two passes, which illustrates how the properties of a pass are established through a rigorous process of proof construction. One is a validation pass, while another one is a mixture of two passes: analysis and transformation.

Figure 5. A window to check a forbidden pair of links (NonREWToREWWindow)

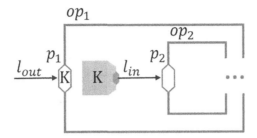

Ensure Consistency of Access for a Link Chain with No Read-Erase-Write Links

There could exist a direct transfer of data between a port of a parent composite operator and a port of a child operator and vice versa. We call a sequence of links that take part in such transfers in which a previous port is "linked" to the next port through a link, plugged to some virtual data a **link chain**.

To simplify the data exchange protocol for ports of those operators that either consume or produce data we need to add some constraints to link chains. Both properties we introduce here concern a link access type. The first one follows the intuition.

Proposition 1: The link chains with both write and read(-erase) links are prohibited.

This property is maintained by the editor, which simply does not permit adding a write link to an input port, adding a read(-erase) link to an output port as well as for a virtual datum.

As an example of a validation pass, we introduce the one that checks the second property we need to transform the schema later in such a way that for any of the data consuming (producing) ports it is of one of the following types: input, output or inout.

Validate Link Chains with Read-Erase-Write Links

The pass proceeds by traversing the tree of subschemas using a depth-first search (DFS) algorithm. For each subschema we try to build the NonREWToREWWindow window (Figure 5). Note that l_{out} is a link that has read(-erase) or write access type, but l_{in} has read-erase-write access type. Each time the window is created an error message is emitted and compilation of the schema terminates. op_1 denotes a parent composite operator, op_2 denotes a child operator. p_1, p_2 are some ports.

When a link chain has a link l such that its parent subschema has minimum depth among all the links of the link chain we say the link chain **starts from** l. The following property let us use local checks to ensure that no schema with a link chain that starts with non-read-erase-write link and has a read-erase-write one compiles successfully.

Lemma 1: The access type checking pass ensures there is no link chain which starts with a read(-erase) or write link and also has a read-erase-write link in a schema.

Proof. Every link chain has a finite number of links. Hence, according to the condition of the lemma there is a NonREWToREWWindow (Figure 5) such that both links are parts of the link chain in question. Hence, the result follows trivially.

Figure 6. A window to branch subtrees (REWWindow)

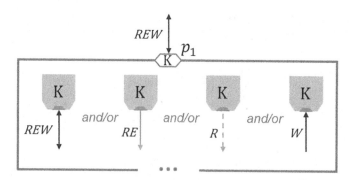

Obviously, the editor could maintain the aforementioned property as well. Nevertheless, in the current version of a toolchain it is a compiler responsibility to validate a schema and find a violation.

For the material that follows, we may summarize what links may constitute a chain in a schema that pass the validation.

Corollary 1: A valid link chain may:

- Contain only read(-erase) links;
- Contain only write links;
- Contain only read-erase-write links;
- Start from a read-erase-write link and have a postfix of read(-erase) links;
- Start from a read-erase-write link and have a postfix of write links.

By a postfix, we mean there is a link l with minimum depth such that all the links in a chain deeper than l has the same access type as l. It is easy to see that the "direction" of every data consuming (producing) port becomes permanent for the first three kinds of link chains. The last couple of link chain types are processed in a pass we introduce next.

Link Chain Separation Pass

There are actually two passes involved. The first one is an analysis pass that establishes the following property:

Lemma 2: Let c be a link chain that starts from a read-erase-write link connecting a data object to the port p. For each port p' that is a part of c the attribute ancestor_port(p') = port_id(p). For any port p'' that is not part of such a chain ancestor_port(p'') = 0.

We omit the description of this pass to conserve space. It simply traverses the tree of subschemas using DFS and each time we "enter" a subschema we either set the attribute or transfer its value to the next port in a chain. Initially, for each port we have a zero value of the attribute.

The second pass makes the actual separation for the last two types of chains in Corollary 1. It traverses the tree of subschemas using DFS and builds windows each time it "leaves" a subschema, i.e. in a bottom-up way.

Figure 7. (a) A window to remove a port on a child operator (RemovePortChildWindow). (b) A window to remove a port on an ancestor operator (RemovePortWindow)

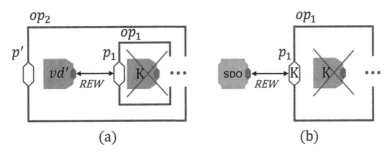

Figure 8. (a) A window to merge read(-erase) subtrees (MergeRSubtreeWindow). (b) A window to connect new subtrees (ConnectNewSubtreeWindow)

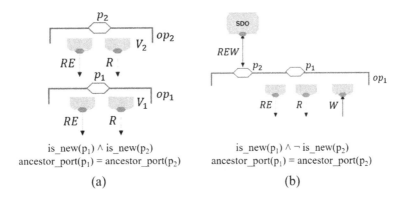

Table 1. Algorithm BranchSubtreesc

1	**if** has_virtual(p_1) $\wedge$ has_child_non_rew_links(p_1) **then**
2	**if** child_r_re_links(p_1) $\neq \varnothing$ **then**
3	add(p')
4	**for all** vd $\in$ r_re_virts(p_1) **then**
5	connect(vd, p')
6	**end for**
7	is_new(p') $\leftarrow$ True
8	ancestor_port(p') $\leftarrow$ ancestor_port(p_1)
9	**end if**
10	**if** child_w_links(p_1) $\neq \varnothing$ **then**
11	// The same steps but for write // links
12	**end if**
13	**end if**

Table 2. Algorithm RemoveChildPort

1	remove(l)
2	**if** safe_to_remove(vd) **then**
3	remove(vd)
4	**end if**
5	remove(p_1)

Table 3. Algorithm RemoveAncestorPort

1	remove(l)
2	remove(p_1)

Table 4. Algorithm MergeReadSubtree

1	**if** ¬exists(p_2: is_new(p_2) ∧ has_child_r_re_links(p_2) ∧ ancestor_port(p_2) = ancestor_port(p_1)) **then**
2	create(p_2)
3	is_new(p_2) ← True
4	ancestor_port(p_2) ← ancestor_port(p_1)
5	**end if**
6	create(vd')
7	connect(vd', p_2)
8	create(l: is_re(l))
9	connect(l, vd')
10	connect(l, p_1)

Table 5. Algorithm ConnectNewSubtree

1	**if** has_child_w_link(p_1) **then**
2	create(l: is_w(l))
3	**else**
4	create(l: is_re(l))
5	**end if**
6	connect(l, p_1)
7	connect(l, sdo)

First, we should make some remarks. In case we cannot add a link to a link chain, we call it **complete**. According to syntactical rules, initial schema may not contain dangling links, i.e. both ends of a link should be plugged. There is no dangling virtual data in an initial schema, i.e. each one has at least one link plugged to it and refers to a port of a parent operator (output recursive virtual datum refers to a couple of ports: input one and output one (after every occurrence of syntactic sugar (n,x) is removed)). There could be some ports of conditional operators (If and Switch) that have no virtual data that refer to them. Operators of other types may not contain such ports according to the VPL syntax.

In algorithms Table 1 through Table 5 has_virtual(p) is true if there is a virtual datum that refers to the p port. has_child_non_rew_links(p) is true if there is at least one non-read-erase-write link plugged to a virtual datum that refers to the p port. has_child_r_re_links(p) and has_child_w_links(p) mean the same for read(-erase) and write links accordingly. safe_to_remove(vd) is true in case there is no link plugged to the virtual datum vd. child_r_re_links(p) is a set (possibly, an empty one) of read(-erase) links that are plugged to some virtual data referring to the p port. child_w_links(p) has the same meaning, but for write links. r_re_virts(p) is a set of virtual data that refer to the p port and have some read(-erase) links plugged to them. is_re(l), is_w(l) are true when the link l has corresponding access type. connect(vd, p) action make the vd virtual datum refer to the p port, other variations of this action should be self-evident. p: condition notation means the port p satisfies the condition, l: condition means the same for the link l.

There is a one-to-one correspondence between the algorithms and the windows in this pass. Branch-Subtrees (Table 1) corresponds to REWWindow (Figure 6), RemoveChildPort (Table 2) corresponds to RemovePortChildWindow (Figure 7), RemoveAncestorPort (Table 3) corresponds to RemovePortWindow (Figure 7), MergeReadSubtree (Table 4) corresponds to MergeRSubtreeWindow (Figure 8) and ConnectNewSubtree (Table 5) corresponds to ConnectNewSubtreeWindow (Figure 8). Note that the algorithms of this pass respect the following call sequence:

- BranchSubtrees;
- MergeRead(Write)Subtree;
- ConnectNewSubtree;
- RemoveChildPort;
- RemoveAncestorPort.

MergeWriteSubtree is a variation of MergeReadSubtree, but for the write links, so the lines 1 and 8 should be changed accordingly. Changes are trivial, so we skip the full description of this algorithm.

Before we establish this pass is correct, we should check that some elementary properties hold.

Proposition 2: After the link chain separation pass there is no dangling link.

Proof. Initially it is true due to the VPL syntax. Each time we add a link (lines 8-10 in MergeRead-Subtree and ConnectNewSubtree) we plug both ends of it. Each time we remove port we remove the link plugged (RemoveChildPort and RemoveAncestorPort), each time we remove virtual data there is no link plugged (line 2 in RemoveChildPort). □

Proposition 3: After the link chain separation pass each input virtual datum refers to exactly one port of a parent operator.

Proof: Initially it is true due to the VPL syntax. Each time we remove port (RemoveChildPort and RemoveAncestorPort), there is no virtual datum that refers to it. Hence, the result follows trivially. □

Proposition 4: After the link chain separation pass each virtual datum has at least one link plugged.

Proof: Initially it is true due to the VPL syntax. Each time we add a virtual datum we plug a link to it (lines 6 and 9 in MergeReadSubtree). Each time we remove the last link plugged to a virtual datum we remove the virtual datum also (lines 1-4 in RemoveChildPort). We do not change a connection between a link and a virtual datum after it is established, hence the result follows. □

Proposition 5: After the link chain separation pass each new port is a port of some composite operator, and it is not a control port and it has some virtual data that refer to it.

Proof. We do not create composite operators, hence each port we create is not a control one. We add ports for composite operators only (line 3 in BranchSubtrees, line 2 in MergeReadSubtree and Merge-WriteSubtree). Each time we add a port we make some virtual data refer to it (line 5 in BranchSubtrees, line 7 in MergeReadSubtree and MergeWriteSubtree). □

Proposition 6: After the link chain separation pass each port has exactly one link plugged.

Proof: Initially it is true due to the VPL syntax. Each time we remove a link we remove a port it was plugged to (lines 1,5 in RemoveChildPort and RemoveAncestorPort). Each time we add a port we mark it with an is_new attribute (lines 3,7 in BranchSubtrees, lines 2,3 in MergeReadSubtree and MergeWrite-Subtree). For each port marked with an is_new attribute we plug a link (line 10 in MergeReadSubtree and MergeWriteSubtree, line 6 in ConnectNewSubtree). We do it once per one port on a child operator in MergeRSubtreeWindow (Figure 8). □

Corollary 2: After the link chain separation pass any complete link chain may not end on:

- A new port of a composite operator;
- A new port of a terminal operator;
- A dangling link;
- A virtual datum.

Corollary 3: After the link chain separation pass any complete link chain may not start on:

- A virtual datum;
- A dangling link;
- A dangling port of a composite operator.

Theorem 1: After the link chain separation pass any complete link chain starts on either a data object or a port of some operator and ends on a port of some operator (possibly a control port or a port with no virtual data referring to it). Moreover, there was a chain between this couple of ports before the transformation.

Proof: The first part trivially derives from Corollary 2 and 3. A port the complete input link chain ends on is not a created one. Given there is a complete link chain that connects two ports or a data object with a port, which were not connected before the transformation. Then we should have done one of the following: one of the existing virtual datum reference to a port is changed, an existing link is now plugged to another virtual datum, port or data object.

The latter never happens, only the former (line 5 in BranchSubtrees), but a new port p' is created. By Lemma 2 ancestor_port(p') is equal to the id of a port (line 8 in BranchSubtrees) linked with the data object through a read-erase-write link, which could be reached from p_1 (see Figure 6).

Applying MergeReadSubtree or MergeWriteSubtree and finally applying ConnectNewSubtree we get the complete chain that includes p' and starts on a data object one expects (line 3,4 in MergeReadSubtree and a condition in Figure 8b). That concludes the proof. □

Theorem 2: After the link chain separation pass any complete link chain satisfy one and only one of the following:

- Contains only read(-erase) links;
- Contains only write links;
- Contains only read-erase-write links.

Proof: By Corollary 1 it is sufficient to cover only those link chains that start with a read-erase-write link and finishes with a postfix either of read(-erase) or write links.

It is easy to see, that each link chain we consider has a port, which takes part in some REWWindow (Figure 6). Repeat the last part of a proof of Theorem 1, note that we add read-erase links in case child links are read(-erase) and write links in case they are write ones (line 8 in MergeReadSubtree and MergeWriteSubtree, lines 1-5 in ConnectNewSubtree).

Consider REWWindow (Figure 6). Any postfix that contains read(-erase) or write links and starts on p_1 is "branched" into a chain that satisfies the theorem. The same way the first part of Theorem 1 is established, we can guarantee that for any read-erase-write link that exists in a schema after the transformation the link connects the same elements of the schema. That concludes the proof. $\square$

We gave an overview of the VPL compiler that has four kinds of passes: validation, analysis, transformation and code generation. One example of a validation pass and one example of a transformation pass were presented. They were rigorously examined so that the reader be acquainted with the process of establishing compiler correctness one pass at a time.

From a purely practical standpoint, integration of such a portable parallel programming model as OpenVX into VIPE (Syschikov, Sedov, Nedovodeev, & Pakharev, 2017) is of a particular interest in a highly diverse domain of embedded computing. The main goal is not only to close the gap between a representation a programmer sees on a screen and a mental model it uses, but also to make it feasible to reason about visual schema when it includes some "guest" elements. The next part describes the solid ground, which such an integration is based on.

OPENVX DSL INTEGRATION

Computer vision experts, involved in many of the aforementioned application domains, most frequently require performance for their tasks, so effective use of platform resources is crucial for the success. Responding to the industry demand, Khronos Group developed the OpenVX standard. OpenVX (Khronos Vision Working Group, 2017) is a low-level programming framework for efficient access to computer vision hardware acceleration with both functional and performance portability. OpenVX was designed for diverse hardware platforms, providing a computer vision framework that efficiently addresses current and future hardware architectures with minimal impact on applications.

The OpenVX standard describes a model of computation (MoC) for an entity called graph. Each graph may be comprised of some nodes, which perform data transformation, and data objects which vx_delay is a specific kind of. Conceptually, this is a ring buffer (Khronos Vision Working Group, 2017), which could be explicitly shifted using a special kind of function – ageDelay.

For each of the OpenVX MoC components there is a corresponding visual component in VIPE. There are also two kind of operators, namely, DRead and DWrite, whose sole purpose is to link an operator to a specific element of a vx_delay. It may seem, that a set of these components constitute only a visual library, but actually it comprises a vocabulary of a domain-specific language (DSL) (Fowler, 2010) (sometimes, a DSL is also called a "small language", see (Raymond, 2003), for example). Each of the

OpenVX visual components has its own semantics, which is distinct from the semantics of any of the VPL language operators and data objects that is why it is a VPL language extension, not a syntax sugar (Van-Roy & Harid, 2004).

Verification of a vx_graph is an expensive operation. To increase program performance it makes sense to reuse those graphs that were already verified. When a graph is created those vx_delay that it uses are bound to it. In general case a program may contain a pair of graphs both using the same vx_delay for data exchange. Hence, which vx_graph to use for a vxGraph operator reading from a vxDelay data object depends on a vx_graph chosen for a vxGraph operator writing to the same vxDelay data object, thus the choice of a graph is not arbitrary. This fact complicates SputnikC compiler, working on a schema, containing OpenVX DSL constructs.

The VIPE scheme, which contains any of the OpenVX DSL constructs, is translated to a pure VPL scheme in multiple passes. There are two kinds of compiler passes: analysis and transformation.

While analyzing a scheme the compiler:

- Spreads information about which data objects (vx_delays included) does an operator have access to down the scheme to the corresponding ports of the operator (e.g., vxGraph),
- Builds the descriptor tree (described later);
- Finds out which operators may access a descriptor instance.

Scheme transformation includes passes, which:

- Change each link in a chain to a read link for those chains that access vxDelay;
- Aggregate all the vxDelay on a single subscheme into a single token queue (described later);
- Transform every vxData object into a VPL queue;
- Eliminate every redundant link chain, which connects an operator with a token queue;
- Create token emitters (described later) and connect them with link chains.

Code generator passes are not described here, because the main emphasis is on models of computation. Nonetheless, a description of OpenVX graph construction could not be omitted and will be described later.

The overall VPL scheme that corresponds to an input scheme with DSL constructs contains the following core components, which substitute DSL elements: token queues, token emitters and data queues. Before we could state what every of the aforementioned components is for the notion of a descriptor tree needs to be introduced.

A **descriptor** is an abstract (in a model of computation sense) data structure, that contains information about those data objects (vx_delay and vx_data), which are "visible outside" of an operator, that has access to an instance of this descriptor. Instance of an operator reads a **token** (a reference to a descriptor instance) and accesses those fields that contain references to the OpenVX data objects needed.

In general, multiple instances of a single vxGraph may be created while the scheme fires. There could be two independent instances (their firing order is not prescribed) among them, which should access different instances of a vxDelay according to the semantics of a scheme. As an example consider a schema, in which a loop body contains a vxDelay and vxGraph. A couple of instances of a vxGraph is an example of a pair of operators that need different instances of a vxDelay object. As long as those operators may fire in any order, we could not use a single vxDelay. Otherwise, either read or write operation may happen at an inappropriate moment.

Figure 9. Example of a descriptor tree for a schema with some vxDelay objects

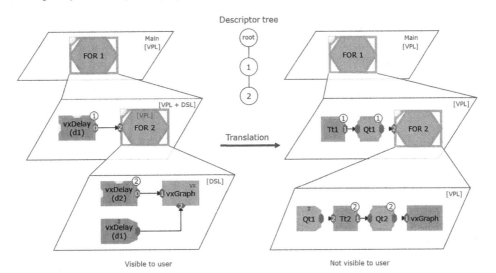

We say that a descriptor *d* owns a vxDelay in case it contains a reference to this data object and there is no other descriptor with the reference that is an ancestor for the descriptor *d*. We need a child descriptor each time there could be multiple instances of a vxDelay per parent descriptor instance. Interestingly enough, the root descriptor might even own no vxDelay at all. The **branch point** is a body, in which there is at least a single vxDelay and we need to "branch" the parent descriptor due to a single vxDelay – single descriptor (owner) rule. As long as each descriptor (except the root one) has a single parent, all of them may be built in a single **descriptor tree**.

The following components, mentioned earlier, may now be described: token queues and token emitters. After an aggregation phase has been finished, every vxDelay in a single body is transformed into a single queue (**token queue**), which may hold a single token, pointing to a descriptor instance. This descriptor instance contains references to each of the vxDelay objects, aggregated into the queue. The token has to be produced and be written into a token queue by a special kind of a terminal operator, which we call a **token emitter**. An instance of this terminal operator creates the aforementioned vxDelay instances and put references to them into the descriptor instance. A token emitter whose parent body is a branch point creates an instance of a child descriptor when fires. Each time a token queue in a branch point dies, an instance of a corresponding descriptor also dies and all the vxDelay instances it owns have to be released.

In Figure 9 each body of a loop is a branch point, so the corresponding token emitters (T_t^1 and T_t^2) will create one descriptor instance per each iteration of a loop. That is why each instance of the vxGraph operator will access it's own instance of a vxDelay d_2 and share the vxDelay d_1 with other vxGraph instances that are descendants of the same iteration of an "outer" For loop.

Descriptor Tree Construction

A parent-child relation could be established for subschemas. As long as the main body is an ancestor of all the other bodies, there is a tree of subschemas for any schema. The following algorithms are used in order to build a descriptor tree. A tree of subschemas is traversed with a depth-first search (DFS) algorithm. Both of the described algorithms are called each time we "enter" a subschemes.

Table 6. Algorithm ComputeForkDescriptor

1	**if** exist(parent(s)) **then**
2	ForkDescriptor(s) ← is_loop(op) V (¬HasTokenQueue(parent(s))
3	∧ ForkDescriptor(parent(s)))
4	**end if**

Table 7. Algorithm AddDescriptor

1	**if** BranchingPoint(s) **then**
2	V ← V ∪ {d$_i$} // d$_i$ – a new descriptor
3	E ← E ∪ {d$_{curr}$, d$_i$}
4	push(S, d$_{curr}$)
5	d$_{curr}$ ← d$_i$
6	**end if**

We need a function ForkDescriptor that indicates the subschema is a branch point. We build it using the algorithm presented below (Table 6).

Here, s is a current subschema. The value of a parent(s) is a subschema of which the parent operator of a subschema s is a child. The value of an is_loop(op) is true if the op is a For or While operator. HasTokenQueue(s) is true if there is a child token queue in s. An operator op is the parent of s.

We call a subschema s_1 a parent of a subschema s_2 in case there is a child operator op in s_1, which is a parent of s_2. We call s_2 a child of an s_1. We establish an ancestor and descendant relations for a pair of subschemas in a standard way. In the same way, an ancestor and descendant relations between an operator and subschema follow one's intuition hence we will not describe it here.

Definition 1: Let op_1 be the closest ancestor loop operator to a subschema s. The subschema s is a **branch point** if there is a child token queue in it and s is the closest one to the op_1 among descendant subschemas of op_1 with a child token queue.

The algorithm building a descriptor tree uses the following lemma.

Proposition 7: The value of a function ForkDescriptor(s) is true if and only if a subschema s is a branch point.

Proof: First, we show that ForkDescriptor(s) = true implies s is a branch point. There are two cases to consider (consider the assignment in lines 2,3 of Algorithm 6). Either the parent of s is a loop operator, or there exists a closest ancestor loop operator, such that any of its descendant subschemas, which are also ancestors of s, contain no token queue. Hence, by definition s is a branch point.

Next, we show that in case s is a branch point, ForkDescriptor(s) = true. By definition, there are two cases to consider. First, there is a parent loop operator for s, in this case ForkDescriptor(s) is obviously true. Second, there is a closest ancestor loop operator, for its child subschema ForkDescriptor(s) = true. By definition, each descendant subschema s' that is also an ancestor of s contains no token queue. Therefore, ForkDescriptor(s') = true. It's easy to see that ForkDescriptor(s) = true. □

Table 8. Algorithm ChangeAttachPoint

1	**if** BranchingPoint(s) **then**
2	$d_{curr} \leftarrow$ pop(S)
3	**end if**

A tree of descriptors is built using AddDescriptor algorithm (Table 7). We denote S a stack with conventional push and pop operations. Let d_{curr} be the current descriptor, initially set to d_0 – the root descriptor of the tree. Let T = <V, E> be the tree of descriptors, initially V = $\{d_0\}$, E = ø.

Each time we leave the subschema s we call ChangeAttachPoint (Table 8). This way we maintain a node (d_{curr}) to connect a new descriptor to.

We must ensure that T is correct. In order to do so we establish the following three properties of T.

Proposition 8: (from (Christofides, 1975)). Let a graph G = <V, E> has a single connected component and |V| = |E| + 1. Then G is a tree.

Proposition 9 (T is a Tree): After DFS over all subschemas is finished, T is a tree.

Proof: T is obviously a single connected component, because each node we link with one of the existing ones. Initially, there is the root node. The condition of Proposition 8 is satisfied, hence the result follows.

Proposition 10 (One-To-One Correspondence): Let D be a set of descriptors in a descriptor tree, B – a set of branch points in the scheme. There exists a total function f: B → D that is a bijection.

Proof. This derives trivially from the fact that we enter each branch point once in a BFS and add exactly one descriptor into a tree.

Proposition 11 (Closest Ancestor Branch Point Maps to Parent): Let bp_1 and bp_2 are branch points. bp_1 is the closest ancestor of bp_2. d_1 corresponds to bp_1, d_2 corresponds to bp_2. Then d_1 is a parent of d_2 in a descriptor tree.

Proof: Two cases must be considered. Either bp_2 is the first visited descendant branch point of bp_1, or there are other descendant branch points of bp_1 visited earlier than bp_2 (let C be the set of such branch points). In the first case, the proposition holds by construction.

BFS implies we visit each branch point exactly once (one enter and one exit). Thus, the state of the stack S at the moment immediately before entering bp_2 matches the one immediately after entering bp_1, because all of the branch points in C has been pushed and popped out of the stack. Hence, the proposition holds. □

An example of a descriptor tree is presented in Figure 9. The first descriptor corresponds to Q_t^1, the second one corresponds to Q_t^2.

The pass building a descriptor tree is an example of an analysis pass. The material presented earlier demonstrate how we ensure this pass is correct with respect to the definition of a central data structure called the tree of descriptors. Now we introduce yet another pass, which is an example of a schema transformation.

Adding Token Emitters, Token Queues and Link Them

The main goal of this pass is to create terminal operators of a special kind, so called, token emitters and connect them. These terminal operators create instances of vxDelays (aggregated into the corresponding token queues) in such a way, that an instance of an operator, that has to have access to a vxDelay

Figure 10. A window for a token terminal to be inserted (HasTokenQueueWindow)

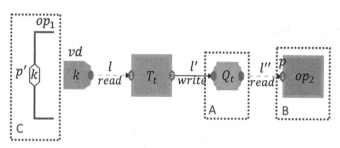

Figure 11. A window for additional links to be inserted (NoTokenQueueWindow)

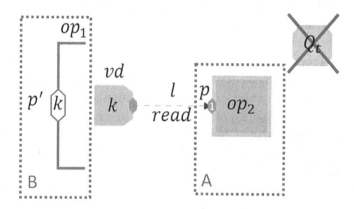

according to the schema before all the transformations take place, has access to an instance of a vxDelay which is alive when the operator fires. The structure of a descriptor tree and this pass ensure that all the operator instances access vxDelay objects in a consistent way.

The basic driving principle of the pass stays the same. We try to build a window for each subschema. In case of success, we transform the subschema according to some rules. There are two kinds of windows, shown in Figure 10 and Figure 11. Some parts of the window are surrounded with a dashed box with a letter, we call them components. In order to describe the contents of a window, we use (Kleene) star, a plus and question mark operator (Hopcroft, Motwani, & Ullman, 2001) just like in a regular expression syntax. The '*' means zero or more components, '+' means one or more components, '?' means zero or one component. We denote the structure of the window HasTokenQueueWindow (Figure 10) as AB*C?, while the structure of the window NoTokenQueueWindow (Figure 11) may be described as A+B.

In Figure 10 we denote op_1 and op_2 as composite operators, T_t a token emitter to be added, Q_t a token queue. In Figure 11 we denote op_1 and op_2 as composite operators. There should be no token queue in the op_1 operator body, which is a part of this window that is why Q_t is crossed.

An algorithm CreateTokenEmitter (Table 9) is called when HasTokenQueueWindow is constructed. It links every chain inside a composite operator op_2 to the token queue Q_t in case it needs to. It creates a token emitter T_t that will write a token into Q_t. Links Tt with Qt and creates the finishing part of a chain, ending with T_t. The latter happens only in case there exists another token queue in an ancestor of

Table 9. Algorithm CreateTokenEmitter

```
1    add( Tₜ )
2    add( l' ) // l' connects Tₜ to Qₜ
3    for all p: need_token( p ) do
4            add( l'' ) // l'' connects Qₜ to op₂
5    end for
6    if ¬root_queue( Qₜ ) then
7            if ¬exist( p': need_token( p' ) ) then
8                    add( p' )
9                    need_token(p') ← True
10           end if
11           add( vd ) // vd refers to p'
12           add( l ) // l connects vd to Tₜ
13   end if
```

Table 10. Algorithm ConnectTokenEmitters

```
1    if ¬exist( p': need_token( p' ) ) then
2    add( p' )
3    need_token( p' ) ← True
4    end if
5    for all p: need_token( p ) do
6    add( vd ) // vd refers to p'
7    add( l ) // l connects vd to p
8    end for
```

the body of op₁ which is a part of this window (root_queue(Qₜ) indicates there is no such a token queue). The notation p: need_token(p) literally means p such that need_token(p) is true.

An algorithm ConnectTokenEmitters (Table 10) is called when NoTokenQueueWindow is constructed. This algorithm builds the chain one level up the scheme to connect descendant token emitters to the token queue in the end.

Now we introduce basic properties of this pass, which help us establish the correctness theorem. The latter states that a descriptor instance to be used by an operator (e.g., vxGraph) contains information about instances of all the vxDelay data objects to be accessed by the operator when it fires. Notice that due to syntactical rules of the VPL two connected data objects is a prohibited construct. OpenVX data objects are treated as data objects in this regard, thus could not be connected to a virtual datum on a scheme.

Lemma 3: For each token emitter T_t there is a chain of read links connecting it to the token queue Q_t that is the closest one to T_t in case Q_t exists.

Proof: To prove this we use induction on subschemas. Notice that we add the final link in a chain connected to a token terminal T_t only in case there is a token queue Q_t' in an ancestor body of T_t. Hence, there is a token queue Q_t in the closest ancestor body. Notice we create at most one port for each composite operator (line 7 of CreateTokenEmitter and line 1 of ConnectTokenEmitters).

Base case is a chain, starting from p' to the T_t in HasTokenQueueWindow. Let us assume there is op_2 that has some chain from its own port p to the T_t, which is a descendant of op_2 in NoTokenQueueWindow. Then there obviously exists a chain from p' to T_t.

Recall that there exists Q_t and notice, that we connect the first port p in a chain leading to T_t to Q_t. Hence, there is a link chain between Q_t and T_t. □

Proposition 12: There is exactly one chain of read links connecting a token emitter to the closest token queue in case the latter exists.

Proof: Trivially derives from the fact that for each port p of a composite operator with need_token(p) and the port of a token emitter we add exactly one link that plug to a virtual datum that refers exactly one port of a parent operator. Moreover, each token emitter has at most one input port. □

Proposition 13: Each port, virtual datum and link (except l' in HasTokenQueueWindow) we add is part of a chain of links connecting some token emitter to the closest token queue.

Proof: We proceed gradually one syntax element at a time. First, let us establish the property for a virtual datum. We use induction on subschemas.

First, we need to prove there is a chain starting from a virtual datum whose end is some token emitter. Base case is a virtual datum in HasTokenQueueWindow, connected to a T_t. Notice p' has need_token(p') and is the starting point of a chain leading to T_t. Let us assume there exists op_2 that has need_token(p) (see NoTokenQueueWindow), then obviously vd is part of a chain to a token emitter.

Because there is p' which is part of a chain to some token emitter there is a token queue Q_t in the closest ancestor body. We could prove there is a chain from token queue to the virtual datum the same way Lemma 3 is proved. Hence, there is a link chain between some token queue and some token emitter that goes through the virtual datum.

It is easy to see the property holds for any port we add.

Each link we add (except l') may connect a virtual datum to some token emitter (line 12 in Create-TokenEmitter), some virtual datum to a port p of composite operator having need_token(p) (line 7 in ConnectTokenEmitters), or some token queue to a port p of a composite operator that has need_token(p). Note that need_token(p) means there is link chain from p to a token emitter. Each virtual datum and port we refer to previously are added, hence the result follows trivially. □

Lemma 4: Given an operator (e.g., vxGraph) op that has access to some vxDelay in an initial schema. Let d be a vxDelay with maximum depth that op has access to. After all the transformations, op has access to exactly one token queue that corresponds to d.

Proof is skipped.

Theorem 3 (Token Emitters are Ordered): In case, a consumer of a descriptor instance fires all the token emitters that create or access any ancestor descriptor instances or the descriptor instance that is consumed have already fired.

Let T_n be a token emitter that does not create an instance of a descriptor. Let T_u, T_d be token emitters in closest ancestor and descendant branch points for T_n. Then T_u fires before T_n that fires before T_d.

Each token emitter reads information form a token that points to a descriptor instance, which either has been written to a token queue in the closest ancestor branch point or is an instance of the root descriptor.

Proof: According to Lemma 3 each token emitter in an ancestor subschema of the consumer operator is linked to the closest token queue in its ancestor subschema. Lemma 4 tells that the consumer operator reads a token from the closest token queue. Each token queue has a token written by some token emitter (line 2 in CreateTokenEmitter). Hence, the first property is straightforward.

Likewise, the second property holds.

Recall that the token emitter creates new descriptor instance only if it is a child of a branch point. The emitter that has no ancestor subschema with a token queue touches the only one root descriptor instance. By Lemma 3 the third property holds. □

An example schema before and after transformation is shown in Figure 9. It is easy to see that the token emitters T_t^1 and T_t^2 are ordered. The former writes a token into Q_t^1, while the latter one reads it from Q_t^1 through the chain of "read" links.

For the sake of completeness, we need to consider how a vxGraph operator works. In general case in an initial schema this operator may have access to some vxData and vxDelay objects. Each vxData object is transformed into a VPL queue, so that an instance of a vxData object could be stored in it. Despite the fact that initially vxGraph operator is a composite one, it is transformed into a terminal operator that performs the same logic. When the graph operator fires it preforms the following steps:

- Read the input vx_data instances;
- Create a vx_graph instance;
- Patch (Khronos Vision Working Group, 2017) every input vx_data;
- Run it, waits for it to complete;
- Create and patch the output vx_data instances;
- Write the output vx_data instances.

By Lemma 4 the graph operator reads single descriptor instance. It has information about which vx_delay instances it uses and which vx_data instances correspond to vxData objects on a schema to perform patch operations correctly.

The main emphasis of all the passes of the compiler is on ensuring the following properties.

Theorem 4 (Delay Liveness): Let op be an operator that has a link chain to a vxDelay in an initial schema. Let there is an instance op_1 of the operator op that reads a descriptor instance di. Then all the vxDelay instances that the di refers to are alive when op_1 fires.

Proof: Without loss of generality, we may assume di is not the root descriptor instance. Recall that OpenVX data objects could not be linked with virtual data directly. Hence, if an operator has access to vxDelay it is a descendant one.

A descriptor instance dies when the corresponding token queue in a branch point dies. Hence, if op_1 is alive, the closest token queue is also alive.

Notice that all the references to ancestor vxDelay instances are copied when an instance of a child descriptor is created. Hence, the result derives from Lemma 4, Theorem 3 and Lemma 3. □

Theorem 5 (Consistency Of Delay Access): Given a pair of operators op_1, op_2 each of which has a link chain to the same vxDelay d in an initial schema S. Given S' the schema after all the transformations. Then each pair of instances of op_1, op_2 that access the same instance of d in S use the same instance of d when they fire in S'.

Proof is skipped.

In the last part of this chapter, we have presented additional passes needed to compile a schema, which contains some DSL constructs. OpenVX MoC is an example of a guest MoC, which has been successfully integrated into the VPL MoC. The notion of a descriptor tree is the central element that makes vxDelay objects work properly according to user expectations. Special kind of terminal operators and queues are added to manage the lifecycle of a dynamic tree of instances of descriptors. The proofs of theorems and propositions illustrate how the correctness of each of the analysis and transformation stages has been established. We believe the material presented here convince the reader that the end schema is conformant to the VPL MoC and is syntactically correct, despite some details are omitted due to the lack of space.

CONCLUSION

In this chapter, theory and tools behind the VIPE IDE were presented.

The key elements of the technology are AGP-models of computation, namely: general, special, language of parallel abstract machine. Computations in the abstract machine are defined as operation of an interpreted parallel program schema. A computation is represented by a sequence of program schemas.

The SputnikC compiler (part of the VIPE toolset) performs some analysis and program transformations. A rigorous description of some of the passes is presented, namely:

- Validation pass performing access type checking for a link chain.
- Link chain separation pass which removes syntax sugar.

To establish correctness of each pass considered some properties were rigorously examined.

The OpenVX MoC is an example of a guest model of computation successfully integrated into VIPE. To increase performance we need to reuse OpenVX graphs. In general case we cannot choose an OpenVX graph reading data from OpenVX delay arbitrarily. This leads to the complex compiler transformations for a schema with OpenVX DSL constructs. The proofs of theorems and propositions presented in the chapter have shown how the correctness of each of the analysis and transformation passes has been established.

REFERENCES

Ayguadé, E. B.-O. (2009). An extension of the StarSs programming model for platforms with multiple GPUs. *European Conference on Parallel Processing*, 851-862. 10.1007/978-3-642-03869-3_79

Balandin, S., & Gillet, M. (2010). Embedded Network in Mobile Devices. *International Journal of Embedded and Real-Time Communication Systems*, *1*(1), 22–36. doi:10.4018/jertcs.2010103002

Cardoso, T., Barros, E., Prado, B., & Aziz, A. (2012). Communication software synthesis from UML-ESL models. In *25th Symposium on Integrated Circuits and Systems Design (SBCCI)* (pp. 1-6). Brasilia: IEEE.

Christofides, N. (1975). *Graph theory: An algorithmic approach (Computer science and applied mathematics)*. Academic Press, Inc.

Davis, A. L. (1978). *Data Driven Nets: A Maximally Concurrent, Procedural, Parallel Process Representation for Distributed Control Systems. Computer Science Dept*. Salt Lake City, UT: University of Utah.

Demathieu, S., Thomas, F., André, C., Gérard, S., & Terrier, F. (2008). First Experiments Using the UML Profile for MARTE. In *2008 11th IEEE International Symposium on Object and Component-Oriented Real-Time Distributed Computing (ISORC)* (pp. 50-57). Orlando, FL: IEEE.

Dennis, J. B., Fosseen, J. B., & Linderman, J. P. (1974). *Data flow schemas*. Springer-Verlag Berlin Heidelberg. doi:10.1007/3-540-06720-5_15

Evans, E. (2004). *Domain-driven design: tackling complexity in the heart of software*. Addison-Wesley Professional.

Fowler, M. (2010). *Domain-Specific Languages*. Pearson Education.

Hopcroft, J. E., Motwani, R., & Ullman, J. D. (2001, March). Introduction to automata theory, languages, and computation. *ACM SIGACT News*.

Ito, K., & Matsuura, S. (2010). Model driven development for embedded systems. In *Proceedings of the 9th WSEAS international conference on Software engineering, parallel and distributed systems* (pp. 102-108). World Scientific and Engineering Academy and Society (WSEAS).

Joshi, A. (2016). *Embedded Systems: Technologies and Markets*. BCC Research.

Karsai, G., Sztipanovits, J., Lédeczi, Á., & Bapty, T. (2003, January 29). Model-integrated development of embedded software. *Proceedings of the IEEE, 91*(1), 145–164. doi:10.1109/JPROC.2002.805824

Khronos Vision Working Group. (2017, March 10). *The OpenVX™ Specification v1.1*. Retrieved from https://www.khronos.org/registry/OpenVX/specs/1.1/OpenVX_Specification_1_1.pdf

Mellor, S., Balcer, M., & Jacoboson, I. (2002). *Executable UML: A foundation for model-driven architectures*. Addison-Wesley Professional.

Mischkalla, F., He, D., & Mueller, W. (2010). Closing the gap between UML-based modeling, simulation and synthesis of combined HW/SW systems. In *Proceedings of the Conference on Design, Automation and Test in Europe* (pp. 1201-1206). Dresden: European Design and Automation Association. 10.1109/DATE.2010.5456990

Mosterman, P. J. (2007). *MATLAB and Simulink for Embedded System Design*. The MathWorks.

Nicolas, A., Posadas, H., Peñil, P., & Villar, E. (2014). Automatic deployment of component-based embedded systems from UML/MARTE models using MCAPI. In *Design of Circuits and Integrated Systems* (pp. 1-6). Madrid: IEEE.

Peñil, P., Posadas, H., Nicolás, A., & Villar, E. (2012). Automatic synthesis from UML/MARTE models using channel semantics. In *Proceedings of the 5th International Workshop on Model Based Architecting and Construction of Embedded Systems* (pp. 49-54). Innsbruck: Association for Computing Machinery.

Puschel, M. M., Moura, J. M. F., Johnson, J. R., Padua, D., Veloso, M. M., Singer, B. W., ... Rizzolo, N. (2005). SPIRAL: Code Generation for DSP Transforms. *SPIRAL: Code generation for DSP transforms. Proceedings of the IEEE, 93*(2), 232–275. doi:10.1109/JPROC.2004.840306

Raymond, E. S. (2003). *The art of Unix programming*. Addison-Wesley.

Rosenberg, D., & Mancarella, S. (2010). *Embedded system development using SysML*. Academic Press.

Sheynin, Y. (1998). Asynchronous Growing Processes - the formal model of parallel computations in distributed computing structures (in Russian). In *Proceedings of the International Conference "Distributed information processing" (DIP-98)* (pp. 111-115). Novosibirsk: ISP SO RAN.

Syschikov, A., Sedov, B., Nedovodeev, K., & Pakharev, S. (2017). Visual Development Environment for OpenVX. *Proceedings of the 20th Conference of Open Innovations Association FRUCT.*

Syschikov, A., Sedov, B., & Sheynin, Y. (2016). Domain-Specific Programming Technology for Heterogeneous Manycore Platforms. In *Proceedings of the 12th Central and Eastern European Software Engineering Conference in Russia* (p. 15). ACM. 10.1145/3022211.3022224

Syschikov, A., Sheynin, Y., Sedov, B., & Ivanova, V. (2014). Domain-Specific Programming Environment for Heterogeneous Multicore Embedded Systems. *International Journal of Embedded and Real-Time Communication Systems, 5*(4), 1–23. doi:10.4018/IJERTCS.2014100101

Trombetti, G., Gokhale, A., Schmidt, D. C., Greenwald, J., Hatcliff, J., Jung, G., & Singh, G. (2005). An Integrated Model-Driven Development Environment for Composing and Validating Distributed Real-Time and Embedded Systems. In S. Beydeda, M. Book, & V. Gruhn (Eds.), Model-Driven Software Development (pp. 329-361). Springer-Verlag Berlin Heidelberg. doi:10.1007/3-540-28554-7_15

Van-Roy, P., & Harid, S. (2004). *Concepts, Techniques, and Models of Computer Programming.* MIT Press.

Chapter 6
Mobile Heart Monitoring System Prototype

Andrey Kuzmin
Penza State University, Russia

Maxim Safronov
Penza State University, Russia

Oleg Bodin
Penza State University, Russia

Victor Baranov
Penza State University, Russia

ABSTRACT

This chapter describes a design of prototype of mobile heart monitoring system based on the Texas Instruments ADS1298R ECG front end and NRF52832 wireless data transmission chip. The described design and technical details allow developing a new mobile heart monitoring system consisting of ECG recording device, mobile computer (smartphone or tablet). The algorithm for ECG recovery using a reverse filter, whose parameters are determined by means of bioimpedance measurement, is described. The new algorithm of J-point detection is described and examined on the test ECG database. The detection rate is from 88% to 93%. It will allow mobile monitoring system to inform the user about any signs of dangerous heart condition in ECG. The chapter also describes experimental results of wireless protocol bandwidth and contact break detection. The results confirm the efficiency of the proposed technical solutions to mobile heart monitoring for wide range of applications from sports and fitness to monitoring for medical reasons.

DOI: 10.4018/978-1-7998-1974-5.ch006

INTRODUCTION

Nowadays heart disease is an important medical and social problem, the leading reason of human death and physical dysfunction. Modern trends in the heart diagnostics are mobility, wearable devices, ease of use and user-friendly interface.

Currently, portable systems for disease diagnosis and monitoring of human functional state are becoming more common. The market is growing due to increasing demand for information technologies in medicine and the policy of many countries of strengthening the health of their population.

Wearable devices of control and diagnostics of cardiovascular system are the leaders among popular medical devices. "This technology for improving public awareness of health metrics and for the early diagnosis of cardiac symptoms is quite promising" (Bruining, Caiani, Chronaki, Guzik, & van der Velde, 2014, p. 12). Modern technologies allow to design and develop a miniature wearable device for recording of functional state parameters of the person. For their work it is necessary to improve the classical tools and the algorithms for registration and processing of ECG, because work in free movement conditions is characterized by high noise level and smaller number of measurement channels, therefore it requires more energy efficiency.

One of the unsolved problems of modern health care is the risk of sudden cardiac death. This risk affects both the elderly people with known heart disease, and young people who have no idea about their health problems. To reduce the risk of sudden cardiac death it is necessary to improve portable systems recording and processing of ECG, both in hardware and software by improving the methods and means of processing, applying them in free movement conditions. Portable computing devices, such as smartphones or tablets, could increase the effectiveness of heart monitoring (Reyss & Balandin, 2010). The fundamentals of proposed solutions are given in (Kuzmin, Safronov, Bodin, Petrovsky, & Sergeenkov, 2016a) and (Safronov, Kuzmin, Bodin, Baranov, Trofimov, & Tychkov, 2019).

The improvement of portable systems for ECG monitoring is an actual scientific task. This task is complex and it involves hardware engineering, software development, algorithms, experimental studies etc. Two basic aspects that are chosen for current research are:

- Bioimpedance measurement as the ability to restore a real ECG signal in ECG monitoring;
- Cardiac cycle analysis – the ability to detect dangerous heart conditions autonomously using mobile software.

STATE OF THE ART

A lot of modern solutions for mobile heart monitoring could be used under free movement conditions. Some of them are described below.

AliveCor's Kardia Mobile is a modern device used to measure the heart rate and cardiac rhythm (AliveCor, 2016). It is used for recording, storing and transmitting data. The device connects to any portable computer with iOS or Android. It is automatically turned on and connected with AliveCor's application via wireless connection. It informs the user with valuable information of the heart rate that could be used for the early detection of arrhythmia.

With all the advantages – ease of use and accessibility for users, the device has significant drawbacks. First of all, this a short time of ECG records, which does not allow a full diagnosis of the heart condition. ECG analysis is available in clinical version only. It checks only one standard allocation that imposes restrictions on the use of the device in free movement conditions.

AliveCor monitor is also used as a platform for some third-party projects. For example, CardiaCare is an application for visualizing a cardiogram on the screen of the smartphone and detecting arrhythmias (CardiaCare, 2012).

eMotion Faros ECG is a remote ECG monitoring system (eMotion mobile FAROS sensor for ECG, HRV, 2019) The solution contains ECG sensor and eMotion ECG Mobile software for real-time ECG monitoring. Continuous monitoring in real time is possible at home and at work. This solution is mostly focused on remote ECG analysis by the specialist. Report can be obtained after the analysis is done. The alarming system for reporting problems with patients or device is also provided. Additional functionality is available with HRV Scanner software.

A review of the current state of the problem (Grier, 2014) allows us to conclude that recording and analyzing the ECG in terms of free movement conditions has a certain specificity, due to the increased level of noise and signal artifacts, instability of contacts, etc.

Common functions of the systems that are described above are heart rate monitoring, ECG recording and transmitting to the server. Main focus of the modern heart monitoring systems is given on HRV analysis, but one of the main risk factors remains signs of dangerous heart condition suddenly appeared in ECG and it requires analysis of ECG signals in the domain of single cardiac cycle for example detection of signs of ischemia (Sato, Tanabe, Chinushi, Hayashi, Yoshida, Ito, Izumi, Iijima, Yagihara, Watanabe, Furushima, & Aizawa, 2012). Detection of these signs is particularly important and effective in terms of free movement conditions when the person may not feel the acute symptoms of the disease and maintain normal or even increased physical activity.

However, most of existing portable systems allow to record heart activity parameters in terms of free movement conditions, but most of them do not provide the ability to detect dangerous heart conditions in offline mode (without connection to the server) (Svennberg, Engdahl, Al-Khalili, Friberg, Frykman, & Rosenqvist, 2015). It is worth mentioning that these systems cannot perform an ECG signal correction with the help of measured bioimpedance of tissues, which is necessary in terms of free movement conditions.

These tasks can be resolved by the tools amplitude-time analysis and corresponding systems. Most of automated ECG analysis software tools for clinical (AcqKnowledge ECG Analysis, 2017; LabChartECG Analysis Add-On, 2017) or research (Draisma, Swenne, van de Vooren, Maan, van Huysduynen, van der Wall, & Schalij, 2005; Vicente, Johannesen, Galeotti, & Strauss, 2013) usage are intended for stationary conditions and 12 lead ECG. This gap between possibilities of portable heart monitoring systems and effective ECG analysis tools is the field of the current research.

Besides the problems with J-point detection even by the clinical grade ECG analyzing systems, there is a problem with noisiness of ECG recorded by an ambulatory monitoring systems in terms of patient free movement conditions. Nowadays, there are some modern means for ECG digital filtration embedded into modern ambulatory ECG monitoring systems. However, there are no such systems on the mobile devices market right now that can correct an ECG signal changes caused by bioimpedance issues. This may lead to a slight error, only a few tens of microvolts, but even this error may result in a misdiagnosis. The proposed system prototype has a built-in bioimpedance measuring channel to prevent such errors in the ECG recording.

Solution Vision

Authors use common architecture of mobile heart monitoring system (Borodin, Zavyalova, Zaharov, &Yamushev, 2015) that consists of ECG recording device, mobile computing device, and remote server, and state following common requirements to mobile heart monitoring system:

- Automated detection of signs of dangerous heart condition in ECG (offline mode without connection to medical data server);
- Usability for target users (minimum requirements for the qualification of the users in the field of medical knowledge and special skills);
- Creation of common information space that provides centralized maintenance, storage, adjustment and analysis of information;
- High performance;
- High reliability;
- Scalability.

The system scheme is given in Figure1. It consists of: multiple ECG devices (with portable computers); remote medical data server (Internet available) to which the physicians have remote access; terminals providing access to the medical data server.

Special requirements to the ECG device are small size and ergonomics, low current consumption, sufficient accuracy of ECG recording and safety.

Generally, free movement conditions in itself are concerned with such difficulties and limitations as reduced number of ECG leads, high level of noise and artifacts and limited time of autonomous device operation. All of these features should be taken into account while designing a new mobile heart monitoring system.

Each mobile ECG device implements pre-processing, storage and transfer to the server for further storage and analysis. Pre-processing performs signal filtering with a digital low-pass filters. Each channel portable ECG device has its own low-pass filter, which has a positive effect on performance of the mobile ECG device. To implement the interaction of each individual portable device and medical data server secure connection protocol SOAP is used.

The aim of the current work is to propose the design of the modern ECG monitoring system that can be implemented on the base of available hardware solutions. In modern portable ECG recording systems, self-adhesive electrodes with a diameter of up to 50 mm are used. Such electrodes with a connector coated with Ag/AgCl provide an acceptable quality of the recorded signal in a stationary position; however they are also shifted from their places in the process of free motor activity. In addition to the patient's movements, the state of the skin integument on which the electrodes are located has a significant effect on the ECG form. Changes in the electrical parameters of the skin integument are usually not taken into account during stationary ECG recording, since the surface of the skin is pre-defatting with alcohol-containing compounds. In ambulatory ECG monitoring systems, skin defatting is either very rare (1 time per day) or is not performed at all, which inevitably leads to distortions of the recorded signal due to perspiration, pollution, etc. (Steinberg, Varma, Cygankiewicz, & Aziz, 2017)

One of the tasks of the current work is to develop an offline ECG analyzing system that can detect dangerous heart conditions on the fly without any extended internet connections. One the most important parts of the proposed system is ECG Segment module that can divide one cardiac cycle into components,

Figure 1. Heart monitoring system scheme

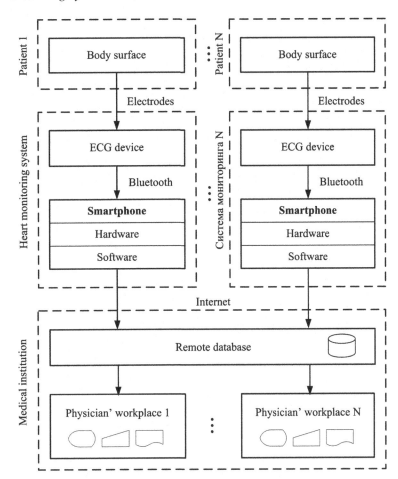

such as J-point, ST-wave, etc. for further analysis. This module consists of many algorithms, but in the current work it is J-point detection algorithm that is considered.

J-point detection algorithm should also be experimentally tested taking into account the above-mentioned features of ECG registered by portable device in free movement conditions like noise and artifacts and reduced number of leads, etc. It is important because an absolute value of J-point to isoelectric line offset, greater than 2 mm (or 200 μV) is a diagnostic sign of myocardial infraction (Antzelevitch et al., 2010). Portability also presumes electrode contact breaks and it should be experimentally investigated what the optimal parameters of contact break detections are and how these parameters affect the energy efficiency. Finally the proposed design should be tested for data bandwidth that verify the ability of chosen configuration to transmit ECG signal in real time. This is a minimal set of tasks resolving which will allow to implement working prototype of ECG monitoring system with offline ECG analysis.

Figure 2. ECG device scheme

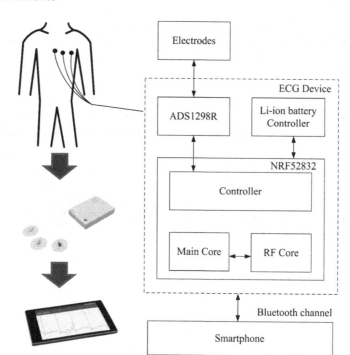

PROTOTYPE IMPLEMENTATION

Hardware

The main part of heart monitoring system is a mobile ECG device that implements functions of amplifying, data transmitting and self-diagnosis (Svennberg, Engdahl, Al-Khalili, Friberg, Frykman, & Rosenqvist, 2015). Another mobile part of the system is portable computer (smartphone or tablet) that implements functions of temporary data storage, ECS analysis and interaction with the user (Walsh, Topol, & Steinhubl, 2014; Haberman, Jahn, Bose, Tun, Shinbane, & Doshi, 2015).

As shown in Figure 2, ECG device includes ECG recording unit (sensor, amplifier and ADC), control unit (detection of electrodes breaks and contact loss), preprocessing unit, wireless data transmission unit.

Smartphone with installed software is used as mobile data processing device (Le Page, MacLachlan, Anderson, Penn, Moss, & Mitchell, 2015).

ECG device is implemented on the base of ADS1298R ECG front end (ADS129x Low-Power, 8-Channel, 24-Bit Analog Front-End for Biopotential Measurements, 2016). Choice of the ADS1298R ECG front end is motivated by a large number of channels and low power consumption. It allows recording a relatively large number of ECG leads for a long period of time.

A number of analog front end solutions for ECG/EEG devices are available on the market. Two biggest manufacturers are Texas Instruments and Analog devices. They propose two alternative solutions: ADAS1000 and ADS129X correspondingly. Parameters and capabilities of these chips are approximately equal. Most important of them is low power consumption. However Texas Instruments was the first who proposed wide support from the manufacturer, evaluation kits for its ADS chips, etc. The variant for 1

Table 1. ADS1298R settings

Parameter Description	Value	Bit name	Code
CONFIG1 (01h)			
Energy efficiency mode	low power mode (LP)	HR	0
Multiple readback mode	activated	DAISY_EN	0
Sampling rate	500 sPS	DR2 DR1 DR0	1 0 1
CONFIG2 (02h)			
Test signals generation by the ADC	enabled	AINT_TEST	1
Test signal amplitude	-	TEST_AMP	0
Test signal frequency	-	TEST_FREQ	01
CONFIG3 (03h)			
Galvanic separation	enabled	PD_REFBUF	1
reference voltage of ADC	2.4 V	VREF_4V	0
Processing of data from Right Leg Drive (RLD)	turned on	RLD_MEAS	1
Reference signal for RLD is generated by ADC	enabled	RLDREF_INT	1
CONFIG4 (17h)			
Continuous Mode	activated	SINGLE_SHOT	0
Lead–off comparator	activated	PD_LOFF_COMP	1

or 2 leads is also possible. It allows to decrease the size of the components, power consumption and a price for target user.

ADS1298R configuring is done to meet the requirements of mobile ECG recording by sending serially the values for 4 configuration registers *CONFIG 1-4* and for 8 *CH1-8SET* in from high to low mode. Configuration parameters description is given in Table 1.

After preliminary setup of ADS1298R final setup should be completed. It includes the disabling of unused channels (PDm = 1) and configuring of the used channels by setting the type of the input signal – standard signal from electrodes MUXn = 000 and setting the gain of the amplifier, initial value is 4, i.e. GAINn = 100.

After the above setup ADS1298R chip is in continuous read data mode at sampling rate of 500 Hz. The output data contains 96 bit of information: 24 bit for status register information and 72 bits for 3–Channel ECG Data. This set of information is available via SPI.

ECG device and the smartphone are connected by widely used communication protocols (otherwise, the implementation of interaction of mobile devices becomes difficult). One of the main requirements for wireless devices is low power consumption for battery life improvement. It causes using data Bluetooth 4.2 wireless protocol (Bluetooth Low Energy). The group of developers SIG (Bluetooth Special Interest Group) officially presents the latest version of Bluetooth 4.2. The speed remained at the level of Bluetooth 4.2 LE with the value of 1 Mbps, but the range increased to 100 meters (in direct visibility). It is exactly that which, with the simultaneous decrease of power consumption, allows to use the technology in autonomous devices.

To implement this Bluetooth Low Energy (BLE) protocol a turnkey solution from Nordic Semiconductor – AGX-832 on the chip NRF52832 (nRF52832, 2018) was chosen. There are some alternative Bluetooth 4.2 solutions on the market: from Texas Instruments, Nordic Semiconductor, etc. The choice is imposed by availability and ease of use. Chip from Texas Instruments meets the requirements for low power consumption, which positively affects the battery life and has relatively low cost.

Software for portative ECG device is a program for a microcontroller. This microcontroller is a master device in SPI connection with ADS1298R ECG front end and at the same time it is a slave device in wireless connection with mobile computer, where the mobile application runs.

For connection with ADS1298R via SPI pins P1_0–5 are used. The data that is obtained via SPI is recorded in XREG registers as in a buffer.

Interaction of NRF52832 microcontroller and mobile computer is implemented with ECG Signal Transmission Profile/Service profile and service that are developed on the base of Bluetooth - Heart Rate Profile/Service profile and service. These profile and service are implemented for effective packing of ECG data of 1-3 ECG leads into standard Bluetooth Low Energy 4.2. Packet size is 20 bytes, where 16 bytes is useful information.

The special experimental prototype is developed for wireless ECG data transmission tests. This ECG data is a result of analog-digital conversion of the ECG signal. The experimental prototype is shown in Fig 3. It consists of signal level matching scheme, ADS1298R chip, Atmega328 microcontroller and AGX-832 from ARGENOX. Analog ECG signal is emulated by the audio signal from soundcard of the PC. This audio signal comes from the line output to signal level matching scheme where its amplitude is decreased by 500. After it the amplitude corresponds to ECG signal amplitude. Then this signal comes to corresponding inputs of the first ADC channel (other channels are previously turned off as well as RLD). After analog-digital conversation the signal is transmitted to the PC by NRF52832 chip (part of BLE 112) via wireless data transmission channel.

Software

The recording device acts as Slave and the smartphone takes the role of Master. At the same Bluetooth module of the ECG device acts as a server that provides access to the attributes, and the client role is given to the smartphone.

Interaction between devices is performed as follows. Bluetooth module located in the ECG device goes into Advertisement mode. After that it becomes available for other devices to detect ECG device. The Bluetooth module of the smartphone detects the ECG device and stores information about it.

At the start of the analysis of ECG the user connects with the ECG device, if it has already been detected, or before connecting it searches for devices and connects after the detection. During the ECG recording application on the smartphone periodically polls the server and if it detects any new information that is available, it submits the request and reads the new data from the table of server attributes. These operations, as well as providing data security, are carried out through a set of special services, or services that underpin the implementation of the Protocol Bluetooth 4.2.

The software of the ECG device that controls wireless data transmission directly uses only the upper levels of protocol stack the Bluetooth 4.2. It is a SPI-bridge which allows to connect ECG device with smartphone directly, as if they were connected by wires.

Figure 3. Experimental prototype

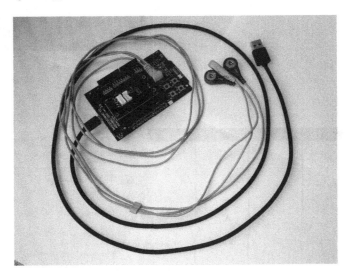

Application execution consists of the following steps:

- Selection an ECG device from the list of existing pairs;
- Connection to the ECG device;
- Data exchange with the ECG device;
- ECG data recording;
- Data visualization;
- Data transmission to the server.

Selecting an ECG device from the list of existing pairs. It should be mentioned that application does not offer to create a pair with the ECG device. It is done by the android Bluetooth API, therefore connection with ECG device should exist prior to communication. Steps of pairing and bonding should be done.

Connection to the ECG device. After ECG device is selected connection to the device is opened with the use of MAC – address of the client device and UUID ECG Signal Transmission Service. It allows to start communication.

Data exchange with the ECG device. Since for communication between mobile application and ECG device modified version of standard BLE Heartrate Profile/Service is used, interaction between application and ECG device is occurred synchronously in "request/response" manner, i.e. every new packet from ECG device is transmitted to the smartphone on demand from the application.

ECG data recording. While receiving data from the ECG device mobile application buffer of one packet length is filled. It is initial buffer of data exchange. If data transmission request is numbered with i then ECG device response relative to received and transmitted data is numbered with $i+1$. It means that data set $i+1$ from initial data exchange buffer is actual for i data packet transmitted by the application only. Correspondingly for $i+2$ packet transmitted by the application $i+3$ packet is actual and so on. Dynamic array of unsigned int16 is used for cyclic data extension from initial data exchange buffer. Recording the data from aforesaid array to the text file named by the timestamp is intermediate result of application execution.

Figure 4. Mobile application: (a) ECG window; (b) main screen

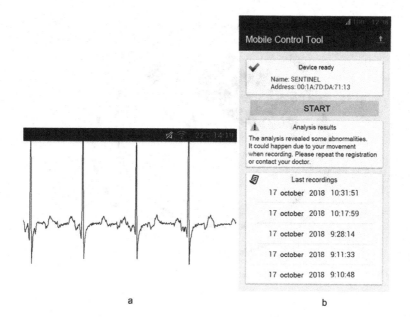

a   b

Data visualization is implemented in two modes of ECG signal drawing:

- Real-time visualization;
- Visualization of previously recorded data.

In case of real-time visualization it is done by cyclic rewriting of *A* and *B* buffers. Their size is enough to store of 1 second long ECG signal of 3 leads with 500 Hz sampling rate and 24 bit resolution, i.e. 4 500 byte. Data from buffer A is drawn while buffer B is filled with ECG signal data. After this they are swapped – buffer A is cleared and filled with ECG signal data and data from buffer B is drawn.

In case of visualization of previously recorded data the data from text file is recorded to the array. After this the array is centered and scaled. Then the data is used by canvas painter in static manner. Results of ECG signal visualization are shown in the Figure 4a.

Data transmission to the server suspects appropriate TCP connection.

Software is currently implemented as a standalone constantly running application using the Android Studio environment and Java programming language and is intended for use with Android version 4.4.2. A general view of this application is shown in Figure 4b. The next step is to run application as a service that periodically requests, gets and analyses data from ECG device.

Application interface is divided into 3 parts (see Figure 4b):

- ECG device connection information panel, where user can see the status of the Bluetooth connection, status of the device, ECG device name and its address;
- ECG analysis information panel, where user can see the results of the last analysis (it is also visualized with a pictogram) and its short description;

Figure 5. Electrical schemes: (a) source model of the heart electrical signal; (b) bioimpedance measurement channel.

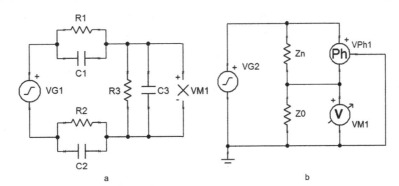

- ECG recordings list, where user can see the list of last ECG records, marker with date and time; user can tap on every record from the list and view the recorded ECG signal in another window (see Figure 4a).

ECG analysis software tools are included into Android application. If ECG contains the signs of dangerous heart condition it needs more in-depth analysis that may be performed by qualified medical personnel (e.g., cardiologist). This requires the transfer of the ECG to the medical data server (where the information is transmitted to the stationary terminal, which is a workplace of a cardiologist or other physician).These Stationary terminals are PCs with third-party software to work with a medical data server and to analyze ECG professionally.

ALGORITHMS

Bioimpedance Measurement

An ideal voltage source (*VG1*) is a model of the heart during the formation and registration of the ECG. This voltage source is connected to two electrodes of an ECG device via four-pole network formed by three two-pole networks (*RC1- 3*). Each two-pole network is composed of a resistor (*R1-3*) and a capacitor (*C1-3*). Two-pole networks (*RC1-2*), whose complex resistances are considered to be equal (*Z1=Z2*), simulate the complex resistance of organs and tissues between the heart and the electrode. A two-pole network (*RC3*) models the complex resistance between the electrodes attached to the body. A source model of the heart electrical signal connected to the input of the ECG device is shown in Fig. 5.

A source model of the heart electrical signal Thus, it is not the voltage (*VG1*) but the voltage (*VM1*) that is supplied to the ECG device input:

$$VM1 = \frac{Z3}{Z1 + Z2 + Z3} \cdot VG1 = K \cdot VG1 \tag{1}$$

where Zn is a parallel-connected resistor Rn and a capacitor Cn according to Fig. 2 ($n = 1, 2, 3$). The complex coefficient (K) can be considered as a transfer characteristic of a parasitic electric filter that distorts the voltage form ($VG1$). Bioimpedance distortions of the form of the electrical signal of the heart adversely affect the detectability of diagnostic signs of cardiovascular diseases. For example, a diagnostic sign of myocardial infarction is a displacement of J-point, etc. [7].

The process of measuring bioimpedance is carried out using the measuring circuit shown in Fig. 5a. A harmonic signal with amplitude of 1 V and a frequency of 1 kHz is fed via certain electrodes from a functional generator $VG2$, which is a digital-to-analog converter (DAC), to the patient's skin Zn. This signal is then recorded by the remaining electrodes in accordance with the table of leads preset in the device. After that, the above process is repeated at a frequency of 500 Hz. Then, the recorded signals are digitally subtracted from the modulated signal, whose parameters are known in advance. The resulting values of the difference function for both frequencies are laid out in the spectra, thereby determining the parameters of rejection of the useful signal by the patient's skin. Bioimpedance measurement is carried out on the base exponential form of a complex number. Generator ($VG1$, see Fig. 5a) is designed on the base of DAC controlled by microprocessor. It generates harmonic voltage with effective value $Us=1$ V and frequency of 1 kHz. Measurement scheme is a voltage divider which consists of measurable impedance and reference resistive element ($Z0$). During bioimpedance measurement digital voltmeter measures effective voltage value $U0$ on reference element $Z0$. The result of voltage measurement ($U0$) is used by microprocessor for the estimation of the effective voltage value (Un) on measurable impedance (Zn) and for estimation of impedance (Zn):

$$Zn = \frac{(Us - U0)Z0}{U0} \tag{2}$$

Simultaneously digital phase meter measures a phase shift (PH) between the output of voltage generator ($VG1$) and the voltage on reference element ($Z0$) that is the voltage on the middle point of measuring circuit. On the base of measured effective voltage on the object (that is in direct proportion to modulus of measurable impedance zn) and voltage phase shift exponential impedance form is synthesized:

$$Zn = zne^{jPH} \tag{3}$$

where $e = 2,718...$, j – imaginary unit. The algorithm of the portable ECG recording system excluding bioimpedance influence of its form is shown in Fig. 5.

An impedance ($Z1$) is related to the components of the parasitic filter by the dependence:

$$Zn = \frac{2Z1Z2}{2Z1 + Z2} = 2Z1K \tag{4}$$

Consequently, the transfer characteristic S of the reconstruction filter can be defined as:

$$S = 1 / K = 2Z1 / Zn \tag{5}$$

Figure 6. Algorithm of the portable ECG recording with bioimpedance measurement

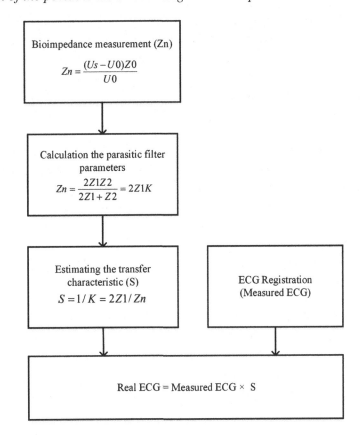

The reconstruction of the form of the heart electrical signal is carried out by the microprocessor by multiplying the recorded signal values by the transfer characteristic S. The corrected numerical sequence describing the undistorted signal form of the patient's body by bioimpedance is transmitted to the workstation of a cardiologist for presentation in the ECG form.

J-Point Detection

Detection of the J-point of the cardiac cycle is important when analyzing heart electrical activity. J-point is located next after R – wave in ST – segment. The aim is to detect the area next to R – wave, where the absolute difference of amplitudes is lower than threshold. This area is the part of ST – segment and its left border is J – point.

A number of J-point detection algorithms are used, for example implemented in LEADS (Draisma, Swenne, van de Vooren, Maan, van Huysduynen, van der Wall, & Schalij, 2005), Std-12 algorithm (Melgaard, Struijk, Hansen, Kanters, Jensen, Schmidt, & Graff, 2014), Modified triangle morphology algorithm (Li, Jin, Jiang,& Park, (Eds.), 2014). The accuracy of the J-point detection algorithms is an open issue (Man, ter Haar, de Jongh, Maan, Schalij, & Swenne, 2017) due to the number of reasons. Accuracy of some algorithms is questioned (Li, Jin, Jiang,& Park, (Eds.), 2014). The majority of J-point detection algorithms are intended for work with 12 lead ECG signals and they are hardly applicable to portable heart monitoring systems. At the same time accuracy of the detected J-point position is extremely important for automated diagnostics (Man, ter Haar, de Jongh, Maan, Schalij, & Swenne, 2017).

These reasons force the authors to implement a new algorithm for J-point detection, that is intended to work with reduced number of ECG leads in free movement conditions. The algorithm of J–point detection (Kuzmin, Safronov, Bodin, Petrovsky, & Sergeenkov, 2016b) consists of the following steps.

The first step is R – wave detection with calculation of derivative of ECG signal for all ECG leads.

The second step is detection of J - point:

- Location the begin point for J - point detection: $t_{begin} = R_i + 0.3$ sec. This time offset is based on the standard amplitude – time parameters of ECG (Clifford, Azuaje, & McSharry (Eds.), 2006);
- Location the end point for J - point detection: $t_{end} = R_i + 0.8$ sec. This time offset is based on the standard amplitude – time parameters of ECG (Clifford, Azuaje, & McSharry (Eds.), 2006);
- Selection two sets of samples inside the bounds X_1 and X_2 next after X_1, number of samples of each set corresponds to time window of 0.2 sec size;
- Calculation of simple average of amplitudes M_1 for samples of X_1 set;
- Calculation of simple average of amplitudes M_2 for samples of X_2 set;
- Calculation of absolute average amplitudes difference between M_1 and M_2;
- Detection of J-point position for j ECG lead. It is first sample of X1 set, where D is lower the threshold 15 µV. Detected positions of J-point can slightly vary from lead to lead;
- Location the final position of J - point at the latest of detected J - point positions of all ECG leads.

This algorithm was implemented in Matlab. The general scheme is given in Fig.7.

EXPERIMENTAL RESULTS AND DISCUSSION

Bioimpedance Measurments

A. Investigation scheme Experimental study of the effect of the parasitic impedance on the detected ECG signals from the electrodes is carried out in the Texas Instruments TINA environment (TINA Circuit Simulator for Analog, RF, Digital, MCU, HDL, Symbolic & Mixed Circuit Simulation with Integrated PCB Design, 2019). The experimental scheme is shown in Fig. 8. The VM2 node was added to simultaneously display the reference and filtered signals.

The authors suppose that the parasitic impedance of the skin leads to change in the shape of the recorded ECG signal. For testing purposes, computer simulation of the processes of the equivalent scheme of skin bioimpedance was carried out. The record 100.dat from the open database of physiological signals PhysioNet (section MIT-BH Arrhythmia Database) was adopted as a reference signal (Goldberger, Amaral, Glass, Hausdorff, Ivanov, Mark, Mietus, Moody, Peng, & Stanley, 2000). This record was then converted to WAV format using the MATLAB environment, the resulting WAV file was used to generate signal via *VG1* DAC (see Fig. 5). This signal was passed through an equivalent bioimpedance scheme of the skin with average values of permissible ranges of all elements and registered using the *VM1* node. Fig. 9 represents the curves of the reference and filtered signals.

Figure 7. J-point detection algorithm scheme

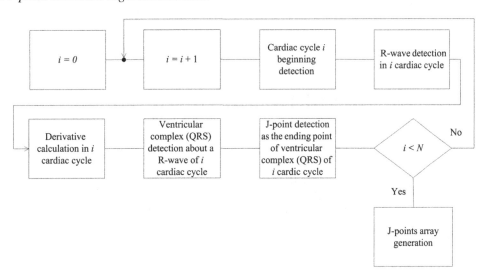

Figure 8. Diagram of a simulation model in TINA environment

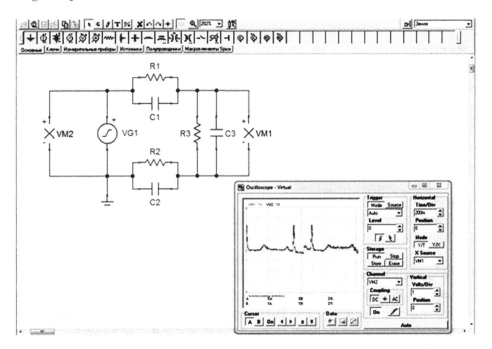

As shown in Fig. 7, there are two sharp distinctions between reference and filtered curves marked by the letters «A» and «B»: x «A», a decrease in the R-wave amplitude was found, which can lead to a wrong diagnosis of such diseases as exudative pericarditis, myocardiofibrosis, myxedema and cachexia (Shin, Wee, Song, & Lee, 2014); x «B», a change (in this case, a rise) of J-point, which is the beginning of the ST-segment, is detected. The displacement of the J-point relative to the isoelectric line more than

Figure 9. Reference and filtered ECG curves

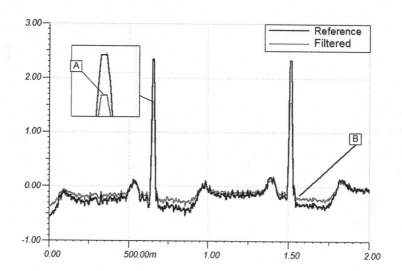

2 mm is one of the signs of myocardial infarction (Kuzmin, Safronov, Bodin, Petrovsky, & Sergeenkov, 2016a). So, from the simulation results it can be seen that the parasitic bioimpedance of the skin can be the reason of a wrong diagnosis.

J-Point Detection

Current experiment is focused on the analysis of the proposed algorithm of allocating the beginning of ventricular repolarization (J - point). To estimate the results of the J - point detection expert evaluation method was chosen, because expert method is considered to be the most reliable, algorithm results are compared with expert results (Li, Jin, Jiang, & Park, (Eds.), 2014).

The experimental investigation includes the following stages:

- Formation of database of ECG records;
- J - point allocation by means of developed program;
- Expert verification of the results.

Set of 200 30-seconds ECG records from different people was taken for this test. Nehb leads ECG records were used. The sample set includes ECG records from people of different age groups and with various conditions of cardiovascular system. To import the signals from the PhysioNet library extension wfdb-app-toolbox-0-9-9 was used. It allows to import various signals and processes it.

Test ECG records are divided into two groups: signals with low level of noise and artifacts and signals with relatively high one. It allows to investigate how signal quality impacts the effectiveness of the algorithm.

All test ECG signals were previously smoothed. Result of the ECG record processing is a set of J-points detected for every heart beat.

Example of the result is given in Figure 10.

Figure 10. J-point detection results: (a) - normal ECG record; (b) - ECG record with artifacts

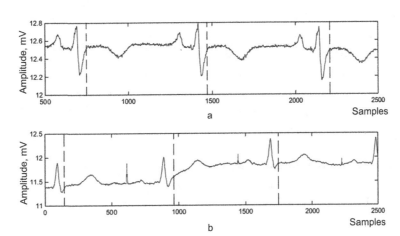

Table 2. J - point detection results

Lead	Beats Number	Right J-Point Detection (True Positive)	Right J-Point Detection,%	Right J-point detection Confidence interval	Missed J-Points (False Negative)	Missed J-Points, %	Number of False J-Points (False Positive)	False J-Points, %
ECG Areas With Low Noise Level								
I	1026	954	93%	+/- 1,56%	72	7%	0	0%
D	1536	1398	91%	+/- 1,43%	138	9%	0	0%
A	1536	1390	90,5%	+/- 1,47%	146	9,5%	0	0%
In	1536	1391	90,6%	+/- 1,46%	145	9,4%	2	0,001%
ECG Areas With Abnormalities and Artifacts								
I	1009	898	89%	+/- 1,93%	111	11%	6	0,006%
D	1067	949	88,9%	+/- 1,88%	118	11,1%	8	0,007%
A	1066	938	88%	+/- 1,95%	128	12%	12	0,011%
In	1066	939	88%	+/- 1,94%	127	12%	11	0,01%

The obtained results of the experiment are given in Table 2. The results are given in absolute numbers of true positive, false negative and false positive detections that is used for detection algorithms (Saini, Singh,& Khosla, 2013; Man, ter Haar, de Jongh, Maan, Schalij, & Swenne, 2017) as well as in percents of these detection results. J-point detection is right (true positive) if the algorithm correctly detects the J-point, false negative if J-point is missed, and false positive if the algorithm detects J-point falsely.

The reliability of the results is estimated statistically. Confidence probability value for right J – point detections is 0.95 and statistically based confidence intervals of right J – point detections are calculated (less than +/- 2% in all experiments).

These results are estimated by the expert cardiologist. Average difference between J-points detected by expert and by the program was 0.1 – 0.15 mV for ECG areas with low noise level and from 0.13 mV to 0.16 mV for ECG areas with abnormalities and artifacts. The accuracy of the algorithm depends on the actual ECG lead and quality of current signal.

The best results of J – point detection is for D lead (Dorsalis, Nehb) – statistically based reliability is from 89.57% to 92.43%. Missed and false J – points belong mostly to ECG signals with artifacts and noise (especially high – frequency noise). Therefore, the accuracy of the algorithm can be increased by applying the appropriate preprocessing methods and filtering.

Experimental results allow to make a conclusion about the practical applicability of this automated method to select the beginning of ventricular repolarization in free movement conditions. The application of this method allows determining some valuable parameters of electrical heart activity which allows diagnosing dangerous heart condition in real time, for example, the deviation of the ST segment (Man, ter Haar, Maan, Schalij, & Swenne, 2015).

Foregoing experimental results allow to make preliminary conclusions only. The algorithm needs more experimental studies to approve its reliability for example separate tests for healthy people and people with different heart pathologies, lead to lead J-point position difference and error distribution estimation.

Wireless Protocols Tests

ECG device is used for a long-time autonomous work, therefore, energy-saving protocols are considered. Among them: ANT/ANT+; ZigBee; Bluetooth 4.2-5.0.

All existing data transfer protocols with low power consumption are suitable for the transmission of medical information. For a more detailed verification of the feasibility of ECG transmission of information through energy-saving wireless protocols experiment was planned. It consists of measuring real bandwidth of the wireless channel by transferring the data that simulate real ECG data. Chip NRF52832 from Texas Instruments is used as wireless module. This module is a microcontroller with integrated Bluetooth 4.2 stack. The experimental setup is as follows.

The module with program simulating the transmission of data from three ECG channels in 24-bit resolution and a sampling rate of 500 Hz is used as a data source. This configuration was selected as the most frequently used in modern portable devices.

The same module is used as a receiver with connection to a PC. The data is transmitted by packets of 5 bytes size. The bandwidth is tested by means of Matlab. The obtained results are shown in Figure 11.

The measured data transfer rate is about 48 kbit/s, which is fully consistent with the real-time transmission of test ECG data

The obtained results allow concluding that the chosen wireless protocol with low energy consumption fully corresponds to the development of mobile heart monitoring system.

Figure 11. Wireless protocol bandwidth test results

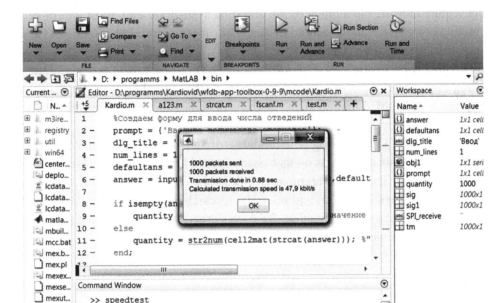

FUTURE WORK

The project is on the prototype level now. Future work consists of the following steps.

First and most important is changing the wireless protocol to Bluetooth 4.2. This new protocol, according to the specifications, allows:

- To optimize data transfer process by adaptation of ECG Signal Transmission Profile/Service to the new packet structure and size;
- To decrease the transmitter power (TX-power) that leads to increasing the time of autonomous work and overall energy efficiency of the system.

Another step is new supplied software mobile platforms, especially iOS and Tizen. Mobile devices based on iOS are about 30% of the market in the USA and about 17% in Europe. Tizen is a relatively new operation system that is supplied by Samsung. Now it is widely spread in Asia. It is decided to use native development solutions (XCODE with Swift for iOS, Tizen SDK) to create the application for new platforms. Cross-platform frameworks like Xamarin, Titanium and Kony Platform make the development process easier, but they are not appropriate for complex system applications. Moreover no cross-platform framework allows developer to work with Bluetooth Low Energy.

Changing the type of mobile application from Stand-Alone application to Mobile Service and configurable graphical application (GUI-application). It allows to run application in flexible manner.

Start remote server in test mode. This server will be used for storage of user's ECG data. ECG data is enabled for remote access. Physicians can view and analyze this data.

One more step is optimizing the interaction with wireless Internet connection. Permanent TCP connection is not required for the functioning of the proposed system, because most part of ECG analysis is done by mobile computer without remote means. Thus it is proposed to establish TCP-connection only if it is needed.

The mobile application requires more algorithms of ECG analysis that are appropriate for mobile usage (Borodin, Pogorelov, & Zavyalova, 2013). Basically they are algorithms for detection of some types of arrhythmia, myocardial infarction and analysis of some other parameters of electrical activity of the heart.

Final goal is an open ECG monitoring with module structure that allows to implement and to investigate different ECG analysis algorithms on its base and could be connected to eHealth infrastructural projects (Korzun, Borodin, Timofeev, Paramonov, & Balandin, 2015), healthy life applications (Laure, Medvedev, Balandin, & Lagutina, 2015) and scientific research projects (Meigal, Gerasimova-Meigal, Borodin, A., Voronova, Yelaeva, & Kuzmina, 2016)concerned with collecting ECG data while daily life by means of portable devices.

CONCLUSION

This work shows the technical implementation of mobile heart monitoring system prototype. Hardware part is based on the Texas Instruments ECG front-end and Bluetooth chip. Software part is Android mobile application with minimal necessary functions. The main tasks of the research were resolved. Experimental tests show that proposed J - point detection implemented especially for portable usage confirmed its ability to work with reduced number of leads in free movement conditions. Bioimpedance measurement allows retrieving real ECG signal while continuous heart monitoring with changing parameters of bioimpedance. The proposed prototype could be a base for implementation of ECG analysis, physical activity monitoring and electrical activity of the heart analysis algorithms, and could play a role of ECG data collecting element in other projects concerned with mobile ECG data analysis.

ACKNOWLEDGMENT

The work is supported by the Russian Science Foundation (project N° 17-71-20029). Authors are grateful to the Scientific Research Institute of fundamental and applied researches of Penza state university for the possibility of using the area and equipment of Biomedical and cognitive technologies laboratory, and to Internal diseases sub department of Medical institute of Penza state university for the medical expertise of the research.

REFERENCES

AcqKnowledge ECG Analysis. (2017). *BIOPAC Systems Inc. official website*. Retrieved June 25, 2019 from https://www.biopac.com/knowledge-base/ecg-analysis/

ADS129x Low-Power, 8-Channel, 24-Bit Analog Front-End for Biopotential Measurements. (2016). *Texas Instruments Official Website*. Retrieved June 25, 2019 from http://www.ti.com/lit/ds/symlink/ads1298.pdf

Adafruit Bluefruit, L. E. SPI Friend – Bluetooth Low Energy (BLE). (2016). *Adafruit Official Website*. Retrieved October 27, 2016 from https://www.adafruit.com/product/2633

AliveCor. (2016). *AliveCor Official Website*. Retrieved June 25, 2019 from https://www.alivecor.com/

Antzelevitch, C., Yan, G. X., Ackerman, M. J., Borggrefe, M., Corrado, D., Guo, J., … Wilde, A.A. (2016). J-Wave syndromes expert consensus conference report: Emerging concepts and gaps in knowledge. *Journal of Arrhythmia*, 32(5), 315–339.

Borodin, A., Pogorelov, A., & Zavyalova, Y. (2013) Overview of Algorithms for Electrocardiograms Analysis. In *13th Conference of Open Innovations Association FRUCT and 2nd Seminar on e-Tourism for Karelia and Oulu Region* (pp 14-19). Helsinki, Finland: FRUCT Oy.

Borodin, A., Zavyalova, Y., Zaharov, A., & Yamushev, I. (2015). Architectural Approach to the Multisource Health Monitoring Application Design. In *17th Conference of Open Innovations Association FRUCT* (pp. 16-21). Helsinki, Finland: FRUCT Oy. 10.1109/FRUCT.2015.7117965

Bruining, N., Caiani, E., Chronaki, C., Guzik, P., & van der Velde, E. (2014). Task Force of the E-cardiology Working Group. Acquisition and Analysis of Cardiovascular Signals on Smartphones: Potential, Pitfalls and Perspectives. *European Journal of Preventive Cardiology*, 21(2_suppl), 4–13. doi:10.1177/2047487314552604 PMID:25354948

CardiaCare. (2012). *CardiaCare project Official Page*. Retrieved June 25, 2019 from http://oss.fruct.org/projects/cardiacare/

Clifford, G., Azuaje, F., & McSharry, P. (Eds.). (2006). *Advanced Methods and Tools for ECG Data Analysis*. Norwood, MA: Artech House.

Draisma, H., Swenne, C., van de Vooren, H., Maan, A., van Huysduynen, B., van der Wall, E., & Schalij, M. (2005). LEADS: An Interactive Research Oriented ECG/VCG Analysis System. *Computers in Cardiology*, 32, 515–518.

eMotion mobile FAROS sensor for ECG, HRV. (2019). *Biomation official website*. Retrieved June 25, 2019 from http://ecg.biomation.com/faros.htm

Goldberger, A., Amaral, L., Glass, L., Hausdorff, J., Ivanov, P., Mark, R., … Stanley, H. (2000). PhysioBank, PhysioToolkit, and PhysioNet: Components of a New Research Resource for Complex Physiologic Signals. *Circulation*, 101(23), 215–220. doi:10.1161/01.CIR.101.23.e215 PMID:10851218

Grier, J. W. (2014). Comparison and Review of Portable, Handheld, 1-lead/channel ECG / EKG Recorders. *North Dakota State University Official Website*. Retrieved October 27, 2016 from https://www.ndsu.edu/pubweb/~grier/Comparison-handheld-ECG-EKG.html

Haberman, Z. C., Jahn, R. T., Bose, R., Tun, H., Shinbane, J. S., Doshi, R. N., ... Saxon, L. A. (2015). Wireless Smartphone ECG Enables Large-Scale Screening in Diverse Populations. *Journal of Cardiovascular Electrophysiology*, *26*(5), 520–526. doi:10.1111/jce.12634 PMID:25651872

Korzun, D. G., Borodin, A. V., Timofeev, I. A., Paramonov, I. V., & Balandin, S. I. (2015). Digital Assistance Services for Emergency Situations in Personalized Mobile Healthcare: Smart Space Based Approach. *2015 International Conference on Biomedical Engineering and Computational Technologies (SIBIRCON)*, 1-6. 10.1109/SIBIRCON.2015.7361852

Kuzmin, A., Safronov, M., Bodin, O., Petrovsky, M., & Sergeenkov, A. (2016a). Device and Software for Mobile Heart Monitoring. In S. Balandin (Ed.), *19th Conference of Open Innovations Association FRUCT* (pp. 121-127). Helsinki, Finland: FRUCT Oy. 10.23919/FRUCT.2016.7892191

Kuzmin, A., Safronov, M., Bodin, O., Petrovsky, M., & Sergeenkov, A. (2016b). Mobile Heart Monitoring System Prototype Based on the Texas Instruments Hardware: Energy Efficiency and J-point Detection. *International Journal of Embedded and Real-Time Communication Systems*, *7*(1), 64–84. doi:10.4018/IJERTCS.2016010104

LabChartECG Analysis Add-On. (2017). *ADInstruments official website*. Retrieved June 25, 2019 from https://www.adinstruments.com/products/ecg-analysis

Laure, D., Medvedev, O., Balandin, S., & Lagutina, K. (2015). Mobile Apps for Stimulating Healthy Life: Walky Doggy Reference Example. In *17th Conference of Open Innovations Association FRUCT*. Helsinki, Finland: FRUCT Oy.

Le Page, P., MacLachlan, H., Anderson, L., Penn, L., Moss, A., & Mitchell, A. (2015). The efficacy of a Smartphone ECG Application for Cardiac Screening in an Unselected Island Population. *Britain Journal Cardiology*, *22*, 31–33.

Li, S., Jin, Q., Jiang, X., & Park, J. (Eds.). (2014). *Frontier and Future Development of Information Technology in Medicine and Education. Lecture Notes in Electrical Engineering 269*. Springer Science and Business Media Dordrecht. doi:10.1007/978-94-007-7618-0

Man, S., ter Haar, C., de Jongh, M., Maan, A., Schalij, M., & Swenne, C. (2017). Position of ST-Deviation Measurements Relative to the J-point: Impact for Ischemia Detection. *Journal of Electrocardiology*, *50*(1), 82–8981. doi:10.1016/j.jelectrocard.2016.10.012 PMID:27914634

Man, S., ter Haar, C., Maan, A., Schalij, M., & Swenne, C. (2015). The Dependence of the STEMI Classification on the Position of ST-deviation Measurement Instant Relative to the J point. *Computers in Cardiology*, *42*, 837–840.

Meigal, A., Gerasimova-Meigal, L., Borodin, A., Voronova, N., Yelaeva, L., & Kuzmina, G. (2016). Mobile Health Service is Promising to Detect the Blood Pressure and HRV Fluctuations Across the Menstrual and the Lunar Cycle. In *19th Conference of Open Innovations Association FRUCT* (pp. 167-172). Helsinki, Finland: FRUCT Oy.

Melgaard, J., Struijk, J. J., Hansen, J., Kanters, J. K., Jensen, A. S., Schmidt, S., & Graff, C. (2014). Automatic J-point Location in Subjects with Electrocardiographic Early Repolarization. *Computers in Cardiology*, *41*, 585–588.

nRF52832. (2018). *Nordic Semiconductor Official Website*. Retrieved June 25, 2019 from https://www.nordicsemi.com/Products/Low-power-short-range-wireless/nRF52832

Reyss, A., & Balandin, S. (2010). Healthcare, Medical Support and Consultancy Applications and Services for Mobile Devices. *IEEE Region 8 International Conference on Computational Technologies in Electrical and Electronics Engineering (SIBIRCON)*, 300–305.

Safronov, M., Kuzmin, A., Bodin, O., Baranov, V., Trofimov, A., & Tychkov, A. (2019). Mobile ECG Monitoring Device with Bioimpedance Measurement and Analysis. In S. Balandin (Ed.), *24th Conference of Open Innovations Association FRUCT* (pp. 375-380). Helsinki, Finland: FRUCT Oy. 10.23919/FRUCT.2019.8711944

Saini, I., Singh, D., & Khosla, A. (2013). QRS Detection Using K-Nearest Neighbor Algorithm (KNN) and Evaluation on Standard ECG Databases. *Journal of Advanced Research*, *4*(4), 331–344. doi:10.1016/j.jare.2012.05.007 PMID:25685438

Sato, A., Tanabe, Y., Chinushi, M., Hayashi, Y., Yoshida, T., Ito, E., ... Aizawa, Y. (2012). Analysis of J Waves During Myocardial Ischaemia. *Europace*, *14*(5), 715–723. doi:10.1093/europace/eur323 PMID:22037542

Shin, Y.-S., Wee, J.-K., Song, I., & Lee, S. (2014). Small-area low-power heart condition monitoring system using dual-mode SAR-ADC for low-cost wearable healthcare systems. In *3rd International Conference on Biomedical Engineering and Technology (iCBEB 2014)* (pp. S277-S284). Beijing, China: Metapress.

Steinberg, J. S., Varma, N., Cygankiewicz, I., Aziz, P., Balsam, P., Baranchuk, A., ... Piotrowicz, R. (2017). ISHNE-HRS Expert Consensus Statement on Ambulatory ECG and External Cardiac Monitoring/Telemetry. *Annals of Noninvasive Electrocardiology*, *22*(3), 1–40. doi:10.1111/anec.12447 PMID:28480632

Svennberg, E., Engdahl, J., Al-Khalili, F., Friberg, L., Frykman, V., & Rosenqvist, M. (2015). Mass Screening for Untreated Atrial Fibrillation: The STROKESTOP Study. *Circulation*, *131*(25), 2176–2184. doi:10.1161/CIRCULATIONAHA.114.014343 PMID:25910800

TINA Circuit Simulator for Analog RF, Digital, MCU, HDL, Symbolic & Mixed Circuit Simulation with Integrated PCB Design. (2019) *Designsoft official website*. Retrieved June 25, 2019 from https://www.tina.com

Vicente, J., Johannesen, L., Galeotti, L., & Strauss, D. (2013). ECGlab: User Friendly ECG/VCG Analysis Tool for Research Environments. *Computers in Cardiology*, *40*, 775–778.

Walsh, J. A. III, Topol, E. J., & Steinhubl, S. R. (2014). Novel Wireless Devices for Cardiac Monitoring. *Circulation*, *130*(7), 573–575. doi:10.1161/CIRCULATIONAHA.114.009024 PMID:25114186

Chapter 7
Ambient Assisted Living At–Home Laboratory for Motor Status Diagnostics in Parkinson's Disease Patients and Aged People

Alexander Yu. Meigal
https://orcid.org/0000-0003-2088-5101
Petrozavodsk State University, Russia

Dmitry G. Korzun
https://orcid.org/0000-0003-1723-5247
Petrozavodsk State University, Russia

Alex P. Moschevikin
Nanoseti LTD, Petrozavodsk State University, Russia

Sergey Reginya
https://orcid.org/0000-0002-9508-2525
Petrozavodsk State University, Nanoseti LTD, Russia

Liudmila I. Gerasimova-Meigal
https://orcid.org/0000-0002-3677-3764
Petrozavodsk State University, Russia

ABSTRACT

The chapter summarizes the authors' development on the concept of "at-home lab" (AHL). The concept employs the methods of artificial intelligence (AI), smart internet of things (IoT) technologies, and data mining techniques. The aim is at support for patients with Parkinson's disease and aged people to continuously monitor and evaluate their motor and cognitive status using own smartphone (in particular, IMU as wearable sensor, apps for testing cognitive status, camera for motor tracking). In addition, other devices in the IoT environment can participate in creating the information assistance support for people. This chapter presents and discuss the AHL concept as a further development step of AI in respect with human evolution (NeoNeoCortex). The focus is on evolutionary, environmental, and biological aspects of AI.

DOI: 10.4018/978-1-7998-1974-5.ch007

INTRODUCTION

In the past decade, several global problems have emerged: 1) acceleration of mankind's aging, 2) "silver economy" phenomenon, and 3) swift development in the sphere of the artificial intelligence (AI), both technologies and economy. Very much likely, these three phenomena do not just correlate or coincide, but rather have causal interlinks. We posit that emergence of AI may well have been provoked by the global aging of population for the sake of compensation for natural intelligence decrease, which happens with aging. Within this paradigm, varied modern technologies suggested to help older people, such as Ambient Assisted Living (AAL), Internet of Things (IoT) environments, and Ambient Intelligence (AmI), can be regarded as a kind of evolutionary response to the challenges raised by the environment in a form of global aging.

This chapter considers our study on evolutionary aspects of AI in respect to the information and communication technology (ICT) progress (Korzun, Nikolaevskiy, & Gurtov, 2016; Meigal, Prokhorov, Gerasimova-Meigal, Bazhenov, & Korzun 2017; Zavyalova, Korzun, Meigal, & Borodin, 2017; Meigal, Korzun, Gerasimova-Meigal, Borodin, & Zavialova, 2019; Reginya, Meigal, Gerasimova-Meigal, Prokhorov, & Moschevikin, 2019). We argue that biological aspects of environment, e.g., aging and neurodegenerative disease, do play critical role for AI emergence and development. This is in good line with the work of (Augusto, Nakashima, & Aghajan, 2009) who regarded the environment and the intelligent system as equal parts of the AI. Therefore, in this chapter we focus on evolutionary, environmental and biological aspects of AI, AmI and AAL.

Parkinson's disease (PD), as one of the neurodegenerative diseases, exerts profound multi-domain impact on either individual human's life or whole mankind living. In PD patients, such symptoms as tremor, akinesia, rigidity, balance disorder, depression, cognitive and autonomic dysfunction appear as major disabling factors. Even without PD, aged people often share these symptoms. Early detection of these symptoms and, hence diagnosis of PD, would have provided retardation of the PD progression. Existing methods of instrumented study of motor function (e.g., video capture, power tracks) are technically expensive and require specialized equipment and performance in professional (laboratory/hospital) conditions. These methods are not personalized, i.e. not adapted to the characteristics of the patient and to the conditions of his daily life, and are not used at home conditions by the patient or his relatives.

In this regard, accessible, informative and reliable methods for movement and cognition evaluation in PD patients have to be elaborated. In this paper we propose to address this problem with help of inertial measuring units (IMU) of a smartphone attached to the body of a human, either during standard neurological tests or free moving. Further, information collected with smartphones and other gadgets can be analyzed and conceived with help of Smart Space and Big Data technologies (Bazhenov, Korzun, & Balandin, 2018). In several studies, the idea of a kind of at-hand laboratory which provides values of numerous parameters of gait and postural reactions is already proposed (Mancini et al., 2011). Also, varied batteries of instrumented tests and clinical scales are used to better extract data on motion and cognition during neurological pathologies (Muller & Muhlack, 2010). To the moment, the mobile-based batteries of motor-cognitive tests are under development and testing (Arora et al., 2015).

We discuss our own concept of NeoNeoCortex or the Fourth Brain, which opens additional layer for human brain (Meigal, Korzun, Gerasimova-Meigal, Borodin, & Zavialova, 2019). We consider the concept of At-Home Laboratory (AHL) as a step towards implementation of the NeoNeoCortex. The concepts support building AAL systems for comfortable assistance in patient's daily life conditions. Socio-cyber-medicine, which altogether would have allowed Additionally, besides pure technological and methodological aspects, the AHL would have provided novel opportunities in designing physiological experiments of higher power, what leads to bigger data sets in shorter time periods, non-stop experiments, and better semantic extraction from heterogeneous data.

BACKGROUND

One cannot regard PD as merely a disease. It is the second most common neurodegenerative disease after Alzheimer's disease, and the number of patients with PD is constantly growing because of the aging of the population. Few neurological diseases, such as the spinal cord injury, stroke, PD, and Alzheimer's disease exert stressful discomfort on daily life of patients. Among them, PD looks the most interesting in respect with rehabilitation. First, PD appears as one the most well-known in public. Even people naive in medicine readily recall that PD is associated with tremor and slowness. Next, in PD one can find unique medical issues to be addressed. Then, PD can be considered as a kind of research instrument, market pain, model disease, and technology driver. Finally, PD is very similar with aging, sharing the above issues.

First, from the medical point of view, PD appears as unique disease. Indeed, PD is comprised of few specific motion deficits, which include "classic" motor triad (rest tremor, muscle rigidity, akinesia), and postural instability. Additionally, PD patients suffer of cognitive (depression, apathy, slowed reaction time and decision-making), behavioral (REM-sleep disorder), sensory (impaired olfaction and color vision) and autonomic (constipation, drooling) disorders. The etiology and pathogenesis of PD remain not well understood. Yet, PD is known to be provoked by both genetic and environmental factors (Tysnes, & Storstein, 2017). From the medical point of view, PD 1) PD develops slowly, 2) it lasts long, and 3) patients with PD potentially can live a full life. Due to that, PD looks as the best ever candidate to elaborate rehabilitation interventions and assisting technologies. Studying PD would also have contributed to understanding such critical concept as "disease management".

Then, besides its pure medical issues, PD can be imagined as a kind of "research instrument", or a "window" into human brain, because such basic neural mechanisms and concepts as muscle tone, gait, motor commands, motion execution, programming, and posture are deteriorated or disordered at PD. Understanding of mechanisms of rest tremor at PD would have contributed to the whole theory of tremor. The ability of PD patients to move surprisingly fast and coordinative in urgent situations (at fire, or being lost in the forest) prompts that motor commands are still preserved and active, though there are problems with their retrieving and coordination. Muscle rigidity at PD represents a very specific type of muscle hypertonus ("viscous" hypertonus) understanding of which would have help elucidating the neurophysiological mechanisms of muscle tone. Finally, PD presents typical "parkinsonian" gait with small shuffling steps, imperative walking forth (propulsion), postural instability, and "freezing" (inability to start motion). In a way, PD serves as a kind of "clinical laboratory" for neural science.

Third, PD appears as the "Market Pain". Globally, the number of patients with PD is estimated nowadays as 5 million with further projected growth up to 10 million by the year 2030 (Wirdefeldt, Adami, Cole, Trichopoulos, & Mandel, 2011). This is inevitably translated in the notably high economic burden on family and society due to direct medication costs, indirect economical losses from inability to work, and rehabilitation costs. As such, PD appears as a typical "market pain" that must be addressed.

Fourth, due to its relatively high incidence in economically developed societies and growing interest to its neuropathological mechanisms, PD becomes a kind of "model" pathology (Pasluosta, Gassner, Winkler, Klucken, & Eskofier, 2015), similar with such "model" biological objects as *Esherichia coli* in bacteriology, or *Arabidopsis thaliana* and *Drosophyla* fly in genetics. As such, there is a strong urge to standardize methods of examination, investigation and interpretation of clinical signs of PD.

Finally, PD comes up as "Technology Driver". Besides pure economic burden, PD provokes also substantial problems for patients in respect with quality of life. Due to motion and cognition deficits, the ability to keep self-service, to provide security, to navigate outdoors and to stay informed and informing that means communication is deteriorated in PD patients. Very often people with PD find themselves in confusing environment, for example alone and helpless, day-after-day without a day-off.

PD is rare in 40-50 years old people, but approximately 1% people over 60 years have PD or parkinsonism (Wirdefeldt, Adami, Cole, Trichopoulos, & Mandel, 2011). The number of patients with PD is constantly growing because of the aging of the population. Older people and patients at late stages of PD share similar motor and cognitive problems in daily life activities, working abilities, decreased personal capital, and lowered quality of life. Unlike to patients with more robust neural pathology (post-stroke spasticity, tetraplegia, Alzheimer's disease, dementia, etc) patients with PD under anti-PD therapy can lead normal daily life. Altogether, the above-mentioned issues put PD in a privileged position among other pathologies in respect with its technology-driving potential, and PD patients seem perfect candidates to test varied technical innovations.

Many of clinical symptoms of PD are readily visible in a form of disordered gait, posture, voice, articulation, tremor, and slowness. Such explicit "external" projection of PD symptoms prompts invention of sensing and classifying technologies for the use in diagnostics of PD and control of anti-PD therapy. Therefore, the early instrumented detection of PD and the slowing down of the PD progression appear as critical problems of nowadays neurology.

The existing methods of instrumented study of the motor function are technically sound, while they are expensive, require specialized equipment, and perform in laboratory conditions. These methods are not yet personalized and are not prepared for the use at every-day home conditions. Additionally, these methods often exist in a form of a single one equipment elaborated and applied in one particular scientific laboratory. Some of existing edge-cutting technologies, for example, robotic-assisted therapy or virtual reality (Asakawa et al., 2019) have already been tested for the use of rehabilitation of patients with PD. In older people, the emerging concepts of IoT, AI for Big Data, AmI, AAL become widely applied with ultimate goal to increase their quality of life, e.g., see (Blackman et al., 2016).

Our experience on socio-cyber-medicine systems in respect to AAL for PD patients and aged people is presented in our previous work (Korzun, 2017; Zavyalova, Korzun, Meigal, & Borodin, 2017; Meigal, Prokhorov, Gerasimova-Meigal, Bazhenov, & Korzun 2017; Korzun, Meigal, Borodin, & Gerasimova-Meigal, 2017; Zavyalova, Kuznetsova, Korzun, Borodin, Meigal, 2018; Reginya, Meigal, Gerasimova-Meigal, Prokhorov, & Moschevikin, 2019). In this chapter, the authors summarizes this previous study.

BIOLOGICAL ANALOGUES FOR AMBIENT ASSISTED LIVING

Before starting considering the problem of AI-based AAL intelligent systems for patients with PD, it would be essential to overview the biological/neurological mechanisms which help individuals to cope with the problems raised by PD. We presume that such "biological" start point would be helpful to find parallels between biology- and AI-based approaches to invent AAL technologies. Work (Augusto, Nakashima, & Aghajan, 2009) discussed the idea of integrating the environment into the intelligent system. According to this idea, the environment progressively becomes a natural part of the intelligent system, rather than its distinct counterpart. In a way, the intelligent system would eventually expand to the environment, either physical, biological or social, losing its original input-output relations. The latter idea was formalized in the "disappearing computer" concept (Streitz, Kameas, & Mavromatti, 2007). The idea that "The best computer is a quiet, invisible servant" was discussed earlier in (Weiser, 1991) in the context of ubiquitous computing and calm technology (Weiser & Brown, 1995).

Therefore, any computer-based intelligent system, as a kind of entity, likely progresses to the environment, including its biological aspect. This is indirectly aligned with our earlier idea that nowadays the human brain evolves towards the computer, what was formalized in our concept of the "Fourth Brain" or the "NeoNeoCortex (Meigal, Korzun, Gerasimova-Meigal, Borodin, & Zavialova, 2019). This looks like the "disappearing computer" concept turned inside out. We would nominate it as "expanding brain". The major focus of this chapter is on discussion of creating an intelligent system that acts closely to the human brain. Let us start with presenting examples how aging brain copes with shrinking functionality in the domains of neurobiology and behavior.

Endogenous Neural Rehabilitation of the Brain: The Mechanism of Self-Scaffolding

From neurology it is known that the human brain efficiently copes with its aging, and, to some extent, with PD, what is seen from the long pre-clinic period of compensated pathology in PD. For example, through the last decade the concept of "successful cognitive aging" becomes increasingly popular. It is provided by the neural mechanisms of 1) maintenance, 2) compensation, and 3) selection (Lindenberger, 2014). These mechanisms are capable of supporting functioning of the brain on a desired level for long time by redirecting decision-making to both hemispheres (bilateralization) and frontal cortex. Similarly, according to the "scaffolding theory of aging and cognition" (STAC) the human brain is capable of reorganizing its connectivity and repairing its impairments (Park, & Reuter-Lorenz, 2009).

Indeed, while the memory capacity and data processing speed are gradually reduced, the vocabulary and world knowledge keep growing along aging (Park, Reuter-Lorenz, 2009). In a way, the discussed mechanisms can be considered as the self-rehabilitation of the central nervous system (CNS). "Scaffolding" of the cognitive functionality can be promoted by physical training and cognitive activity (Park, Reuter-Lorenz, 2009). Altogether, some aged people can keep good cognitive condition while ageing by better using of their brain space and reorganizing the connectivity.

Exogenous Behavioral Rehabilitation of the Brain: The Mechanism of Adaptive Scaffolding Based on the Environment

In aged people, decreased motor or cognitive functionality is often caused by lacking self-initiation and motivation. In patients with PD, lowered initiative is seen as the "freezing" phenomenon that holds for a condition when patient is not able to start motion. Younger people rely on external cues only in 15-20% trials when are charged with task, while elder people are in 80% (Loh, & Kanai, 2016). In a way, elder people intuitively look for information support from the environment thus forming a kind of "external scaffolding", analogous to the above mentioned internal neural scaffolding. Therefore, the environment presents big potential in supporting cognitive and, hence, motor health of aging human in a form of "environmental outsourcing" (Lindenberger, 2014).

Figure 1. Degrading functionality of the motor system and cognition is compensated (to some extend and limited time period) by neural and behavioral mechanisms of self-rehabilitation

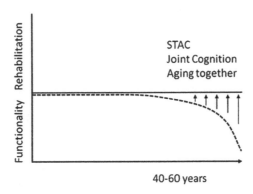

The search for suchlike environment "outsourcing" is conducted in varied forms. Primarily, aging and/or gradually disabling human can receive support from her/his family. The family provides a kind of "supplementary collective" brain for an individual which provides reminding, cues, alarming, motivation, and also physical assistance. This was formalized in the concept of "Ageing Together" of two (or more) people in a family (Maehara, Saito, & Towse, 2019). Ageing together leads to notably lesser social de-adaptation due to "exogenous" motivational, emotional, and social stimulation. Such external support may have also helped mediating endogenous (internal) brain plasticity. The "Ageing Together" concept is close to the concept of "Joint Cognition" based on task-sharing (Maehara, Saito, & Towse, 2019). From the neuroscience point of view, these concepts/strategies can be regarded as behavioral because they clearly modify individual's behavior and learning.

The above considerations are summarized in a simple visual scheme (Figure 1). It depicts that with age human cognitive, motion and other capabilities decline, most evident over the age 60 years. Neural self-rehabilitation and joint cognition allow partly compensating this degradation. The human intelligence (HI) keeps struggling to survive and strive. Nonetheless, people lose their cognitive and motion capacities with age, because they still need more information about themselves and more support from the environment, either social and biological. The question is how to proceed when the person stays alone? More support should come from the digital environment and technology achievements. People become using digital scaffolding.

Exogenous Non-Biological Rehabilitation: The Mechanisms of Digital Scaffolding

The "Joint Cognition" concept seems congruent with our "Fourth Brain" concept (Meigal, Korzun, Gerasimova-Meigal, Borodin, & Zavialova, 2019). The Fourth Brain stems from a such extremely simplified model of the human brain as the "Triune Brain" (MacLean, 1990). It is still popular in public and even among some scientists. The Triune Brain model speculatively admits that brain of higher mammals consists of three layers. Each of these three layers can be imagined as a result of lengthy brain evolution, and corresponds to 1) the most ancient and aggressive "reptile" brain, which has emerged to protect territory and provide reproduction, 2) the "limbic" brain of early mammalians, which has allegedly evolved to conduct emotions, nursing and parenting behavior, and 3) the "neocortex", or new brain

Figure 2. The Fourth Brain Concept. On the left side: the Triune Brain according to McLean. On the right side: the additional 4th (digital) layer surrounds human brain.

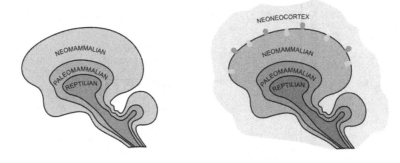

cortex, which was attributed to so-called "neo-mammalians", including humans, who finally elaborated cognition and intelligence.

Due to lengthy and slow evolution within millions of years these layers are finely interlinked and balanced to each other, thus forming the above said "triunity". The essence of the Fourth Brain is the idea that AI appears (or still have to get appeared) as mere evolutionary expansion (or continuation) of natural human intelligence into the digital environment. Consequently, the Fourth Brain can be imagined as a novel emerging layer of the brain, or NeoNeoCortex (Figure 2).

As the result, aging (as a new environmental factor) possibly drives the evolution towards novel, digital continuation of the human brain. In future, such "augmented", but still largely human intelligence will help to keep desired level of motor and cognition functionality.

POSSIBLE ORIGINS OF ARTIFICIAL INTELLIGENSE

The authors expect that the At-Home Lab (AHL) is a possible step towards implementation of the NeoNeoCortex (Meigal, Prokhorov, Gerasimova-Meigal, Bazhenov, & Korzun, 2017; Meigal, Korzun, Gerasimova-Meigal, Borodin, & Zavialova, 2019). The Fourth Brain along with its AHL implementation forms an additional (or reserve) self-developing portion of human brain. A multitude of augmented data sources are used (Korzun & Meigal, 2019). In particular, various sensors monitor individual bioparameters based on advances of wearable and implantable devices for human body.

From the practical point of view, the best "additional" brain is still a brain of another human, especially when that brain is smart and behaves empathically. Likewise, the best augmented intelligence is made by some other, friendly human. Nonetheless, most humans still have to cope with their cognition and motion problems on their own, which is especially common for PD patients and many elderlies. The major idea of AHL is to augment the human's CNS and, respectively, human intelligence. The AHL creates a kind of "parallel" AI such that AAL employs the opportunity of digital (visual, audio) communication between human and AI system in joint decision making (task-sharing).

There are two biologically inspired approaches for the AI augmentation of the human brain. The first is the evolutionary one. It assumes that the human brain has emerged and evolved from very simple systems (cells, molecules) to complex tissues (brain) and complex behavior. That evolution could go forth, including expansion to cyber space, forming very complicated socio-cyber-medicine systems

(Korzun, 2017). The second approach is the ontogenetic (developmental) one, when the human brain develops along the human's life span. Therefore, the idea of implementing AI in the form of AHL for AAL functions has the firm biological basis on which we focus in this section.

The Evolutionary Aspect of AI: Co-Evolution With Human Intelligence

The human brain is considered as the result of long term and strict natural selection for the purpose of efficient operating in complex natural and social environment (Wilson, 2012). Eventually, the human brain has accommodated to the following actions: 1) aggression, 2) altruism, 3) empathy, 4) planning of social interaction, 5) emotion interpreting, and 6) lifelong strategies. That is, the human brain is primarily preoccupied with what other people think about her/him and how she/he is presented in their minds. Indeed, people talk a lot about each other and take much effort to cultivate good opinion in others' minds. In a way, people build in an on-going manner own individual in-mind presentation and relentlessly modify it.

The human brain evolved as highly intellectual instrument for understanding other people's minds, and was aimed at personal and population survival. The human brain evolution was (and most likely is) highly pro-social. People frequently make paradoxical or unpredictable deeds driven not only by virtue. For that reason, people did not evolve and behave as "angelic robots" (Douglas, 2012). There are no signs that further evolution of the human brain would proceed according to another evolutionary paradigm. Our hypothesis is that AI has emerged as the pre-programmed result of HI evolution (Meigal, Korzun, Gerasimova-Meigal, Borodin, & Zavialova, 2019). Earlier, evolutionary and philosophic aspects of AI were discussed in (Spector, 2006). The idea and practice of AI can be regarded as an intrinsic (innate) for the HI. As such, many studies in the AI domain can be accounted as inevitable or pre-programmed continuation of the human evolution.

Human language, as one of aspects of HI, diminishes social tension and helps acting together, what keeps people together in big groups. The estimation is that a human language emerges when group number has reached approximately 150 members (Zimmer, 2006). Modern Internet-enabled social networks and Web-based collaborative work systems have crucially modified the very idea of communication by multiplication of the number of virtual mates by tens. Modern young people born after the Internet and smartphone invention ("digital natives"), roughly after the year 2000, stay in principally different information environment in comparison with their historical coevals born after the Urban or the Industrial revolutions. The human brain (and intelligence) has to react on this novel influential environment. Probably, it tries to cope with such ever growing avalanche of information exactly by building augmented intelligence. Thus, search for the AI might appeared as mere reaction of HI on modifications in communication. In that respect, the very theory and practice of AI, and its further connection to or interaction with HI may have proved as a mere act of evolution. The alternative opinion poses the AI as a by-product of the human evolution (Ganapathy, Abdul, & Nursetyo, 2018). The general concept of the evolution-mediated emergence of AI is shown in Figure 3.

The Ontogenetic Aspect of AI: Life-Long Development of the Brain

Human's life span is relatively not lengthy (typical period is 70-80 years long). However, within one's life span the human brain and, hence HI, undergoes substantial modification. At the beginning of life, this modification appears as development and maturing, then as ageing. Between development and aging,

Figure 3. Possible way of connecting AI and HI. The AI and HI emerged and further develop in cooperation.

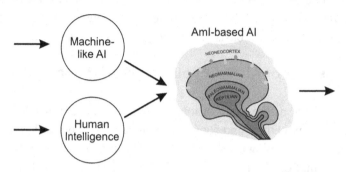

many functions stay stable until the age of 40-60 years, but in senior age some functions (e.g., cognitive ones) increasingly degrade (Lindenberger, 2014). Various kinds of memory (momentary, working) and speed of information processing become degrading even earlier, from 20-30 years old (Park, Reuter-Lorenz, 2009). In contrast, the so-called "crystallized" cognitive abilities, which express accumulated personal knowledge about the world (e.g., vocabulary and individual life experience such as wisdom, philosophy), remain unimpaired along life span and even increase and become sophisticated.

There is no doubt (Harper, 2014) that (a) the mankind becomes more aged and (b) aged people by their retirement are well skilled and experienced. Two further influential sequences are: 1) more people will have to work in their late age, and 2) the global economy will produce more goods and services precisely for the elderly customers. That phenomenon is referred as the "silver economy". Many of the aged and experienced people due to growing deficit of qualified specialists would stay employed as long as possible. Accordingly, that demands keeping their physical and mental performance on the level required for work.

The observed tendencies (mankind aging and digital revolution) are currently synchronized. In practical daily life, it is seen as the situation when more and more aged people have to interfere with information communication technologies (ICT), including on-line banking, personal on-line office, and modern Internet telephone applications (Viber, Skype, WhatsApp, etc.). Additionally, the global aging of population provokes expansion of age-associated diseases, such as arterial hypertension, PD, and Alzheimer's disease, through the global population. Also, the ongoing digital revolution and ICT development progress inevitably and profoundly transform human thoughts and behavior (Loh, Kanai, 2016). Altogether, these factors present ever growing requirements to the human brain, especially of the elderly and more especially of PD patients. As a result, many aged people and PD patients find themselves in unfriendly and stressful environment, which is characterized by the following properties:

- Constantly decreasing physiological functionality;
- Lowered cognitive and intellectual status;
- Need to work (some people);
- Need to learn novel ICT.

Ultimately, that can interfere the social adaptation, leading to loneliness, abandonment, non-inclusiveness. A concept of human's social adaptation can be measured by scaling the individual physical and mental capabilities, including 1) personal security, 2) self-service, 3) possibility to communicate with environment and remote people, and 4) free mobility. Accordingly, losing or diminishing of these capabilities leads to emergence and increasing the social de-adaptation and, therefore, impaired quality of life. The aging human brain appears as a fair model of gradually losing the intelligence function. As such, ageing, especially in combination with PD, could serve as a reliable model for application of AI methods aimed at restoration of human brain capabilities or rehabilitation.

How to Connect Artificial Intelligence to Human Intelligence?

The Neocortex (third layer of human brain) and the digital Fourth Brain (Neoneocortex) seem rather heterogeneous in respect to each other. That makes connection between HI and AI a non-trivial scientific and practical problem. Rapid converging, connection and integration of such closely related areas as machine learning algorithms, deep learning, neurolinguistic programming, semantic networks, generative adversarial networks, mechanotronics, and robotics (Bini, 2018) prompts that AI has fair chances to be created as a computer-like system. Thus, AI is widely assumed as a kind of a machine-like system, primarily computer-like, that mimics human-like behavior and provides functionality attributable to human intelligence. Also, AI is often imagined as embodied in a human-like body with human-morphed brain, thus looking like a kind of a smart humanoid machine. This kind of AI can be regarded as totally exogenous (or alien) to HI. That autonomous machine (produced exogenously to the people) would be capable of making fast computations and adequate decisions, learning with help of algorithms, assisting, supporting, reminding, advising, and providing many other useful functions, just like "angelic robots" (Douglas, 2012; Wilson, 2012). The connection of such AI to HI can be imagined only as "chimerical" or, syncretic, "switching" with slots, alike two electromechanical machines (personal computers).

The Fourth Brain concept overcomes this profound discrepancy between the AI and HI by proposing more natural combination of endogenous (human-like) AI with a concrete person (with her/his HI). As we already mentioned, AI could be rather a natural continuation HI than its replacement or reserve. In other words, the AI must emerge from a sequence of events: 1) conception, 2) cultivation, and 3) growing up like a fetus (baby), with "personal-like" abilities to empathize to its host, to interpret emotions, and, probably, to elaborate own ideas. This digital scaffolding is supposed to be continuously build up by users of the Internet by projecting/delegating some part of their cognitive domains (memory, attention, will, learning, decision making, communicating, navigating, locating, etc.) to the cyber space.

More specifically, the Internet provides the opportunity to enhance learning and memory with Wikipedia and alike, communication with social networks, Internet stores, etc. Nowadays this opportunity is regarded as cognition extends (Zavyalova, Korzun, Meigal, & Borodin, 2017), i.e., AI appears as "gadgets" for HI. Interestingly, the persons' profiles and user community networks are growing and developing all the time presenting an example of evolving entity in the Internet with strong personalization attitude. Based on smartphones and other smart IoT devices (mobile or embedded) these digital extends are customized to the person, her/his current environment, and needs (Korzun, 2017). It would not be exaggeration to say that the growing share (or expansion) of our brain to the environment is already nested in the Internet.

Presumably, this permanent digital scaffolding and extending by Internet gadgets of the human brain (alike "natural" scaffolding), would allow sustained recovery of the decay in the natural HI function. Therefore, a result is sustained social adaptation in PD patients and the elderly people. Nonetheless, the digital extends require active volitional efforts from the aging people while many of them have problems with the self-initiation. Therefore, a proactive AAL system based on surrounding mobile, embedded, and multimedia devices seems more appropriate. That is, AI should appear as AmI, where various context services surround the users and proactively assist them.

AT-HOME LABORATORY FOR PARKINSON'S DISEASE PATIENTS AND AGED PEOPLE

We believe that even at present time assembling a kind of digital scaffolding to create the Fourth Brain is technically feasible. It could be embodied in a form of "at-hand" personalized, non-costly smart system to support and assist a given PD patient in her/his daily life. As such, this idea finds itself generally within the smart space paradigm for IoT (Korzun, 2017). Several authors have already reviewed existing smart space-based applications (Augusto, Nakashima, & Aghajan, 2009; Sadri, 2011). Our vision on such a system is formulated as At-Home Laboratory (AHL), where wearable sensors, home embedded equipment, and smartphones play the crucial role (Meigal, Prokhorov, Gerasimova-Meigal, Bazhenov, & Korzun, 2017).

Embodied intelligence and Physiologist's Novel Instrument

The PD patients, as well as their families, older people, physicians, and medical administrators need an accessible, informative, and reliable method for continuous monitoring, evaluation and classifying of their functional deficits:

1. Motion deficits during daily living activity indoors and outdoors;
2. Cognitive deterioration (depression, slowed reaction time, memory problems);
3. Hemodynamic problems (arterial hypertension, arrhythmia attributed to older age).

These three functional domains are essential for motility and, hence, social adaptation of PD patients as well as aged people (Korzun, Meigal, Borodin, & Gerasimova-Meigal, 2017).

The AHL aims at assisting the patients in their daily life conditions (Meigal, Prokhorov, Gerasimova-Meigal, Bazhenov, & Korzun, 2017; Meigal, Korzun, Gerasimova-Meigal, Borodin, & Zavialova, 2019). Such a laboratory for everyday use should be:

1. Comfortable in use,
2. Easy in operation (in ideal - subtle and imperceptible for the user),
3. Efficient what means to accurately measure bioparameters.

Primary AHL ability is correctly identifying, interpreting, and classifying abnormal patterns and features based on continuous (online) measurements. The AHL is connected to a telemedicine or mobile healthcare system to keep users posted with current raw information and provide them with reminders and advises. The AHL can also operate as an additional artificial layer of the CNS, so provides assistance in decision making and, hence to modify behavior to prevent potentially dangerous events, e.g. falling, "freezing", diskinesia, cardiac arrhythmia, etc. The AHL could operate as a parallel CNS with the advantage of connecting to it and getting timely advises from it. In ideal, it must also be proactive, i.e., to anticipate threatening conditions.

As such, the AHL would require technological and ideological rationale from the AI, AmI, smart spaces, and IoT methods. Personal mobile computers (tablets, smartphones) are promising candidates to implement technological solutions since they have effective prerequisites for sensing signals, transferring information and connecting/communicating with other devices. They are always "at-hand" and are highly personalized. We expect that they make the AHL as easy-for-use, comfortable for users (patients, family members, physicians, medical administrators), as most of them are not necessarily familiar with ever sophisticated health devices. Also, the AHL presents clear comprehensible information based on feature extraction, classifying, and diagnostics. The rapid progress in microelectronics technology with ever more superior sensors inside (e.g., inertial measuring units - IMU) makes a smartphone a very universal tool for implementing AI methods.

The idea to employ many devices in a smart space to implement health data monitoring, collecting, and analysis for PD patients is not new (Pasluosta, Gassner, Winkler, Klucken, & Eskofier, 2015; D'Antrassi et al., 2019; Asakawa et al., 2019). However, these systems are mostly interactive, they are based on protocols to be followed, and request compliance from patients. So, these systems still resemble a kind of clinical examination (self-examination) or a kind of experiment.

The general AHL concept is shown in Figure 4. Various cheap IoT devices (tablets, smartphones, surveillance cameras, wearable sensors, etc.) form an additional data sensing and processing system that surrounds the person in the everyday or home environment. In particular, the system augments the peripheral nervous system. The data are collected and transformed to assistance services to deliver to the user in visual or audio digital form. The services inform about the bodily functions (heart rate, blood pressure and glucose, stride length and variability, walking speed, calories expended, reaction time, coordination, etc.). The services can provide recommendations in the form of recognized patterns, features, symptoms.

The audio form of communication with AHL seems preferable because during cognition/thinking a human uses the so-called "internal" speech. One would agree that it is much more comfortable to receive information on the bodily functions in a comprehensible constant on-line form (to be posted) and to react to these posts by comprehensible behavioral modifications (slowing down during walking, modifying food intake, having a rest during work, etc.). It would be nice to keep a kind of "conversation" with AHL.

The AHL is much more psychologically reliable than operation in a professional medical laboratory. For example, measurements of physiological parameters (e.g., blood pressure) are usually compromised due to agitation and familiarization to procedure in professional laboratory settings. Similarly, in PD patients tremor often emerges or become enhanced during clinical examination. Likewise, under relaxing conditions (alone, in the nature) PD patients move surprisingly well. Thus, the AHL integrates non-professional devices in a personalized self-developing smart system.

Powerful Physiological Laboratory

Besides purely medical, technological, and methodological aspects, the AHL provides exciting novel opportunities for physiologists in designing "large-scale" experiments with faster and more valued outcome. The methods of crowd sourced science allow extracting the semantics from heterogenous physiological data and patient's context. An additional nervous system becomes opened for continuous data acquisition. That is the key reason to call AHL as a laboratory. Similarly, a scientifically close personalized data collection system is presented in (D'Antrassi et al., 2019).

Figure 4. General AHL concept. On the left side (real human being): the CNS receives and analyses signals from varied neural sensors (receptors). On the right side (wearable or environment-embedded sensors): AHL collects data on the most informative parameters of the human bodily systems and constructs assistance services based on collected data. Vis - visual, Vest - vestibular, Visc - visceral, proprio - proprioceptive signal

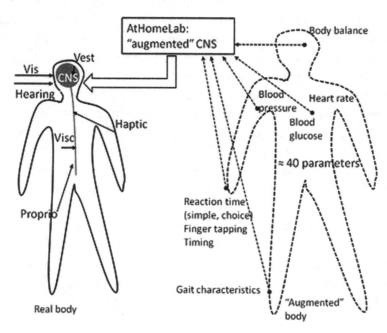

Requirements for AmI-Based Self-Monitoring

The AmI concept has the following widely accepted properties creating an intelligent, embedded, digital environment that is sensitive and responsive to the presence of people (Gaggioli, 2005; Sadri, 2011). The AmI environment aims at freeing people from tedious regular routine tasks by providing assistance in many circumstances (Sadri, 2011). Thus, AmI-based self-monitoring for obtaining reliable longitudinal information about everyday functioning from PD patients in their natural environment is critical for clinical care and research" (Espay et al., 2019). To keep the elderly people or PD patients within their zone of social adaptation, the AmI environment must be capable of the following functions (Korzun, 2017): 1) monitoring, 2) assessment, and 3) management of physiological status of a human (primarily, cognitive, motor, and cardiovascular).

The following requirements are essential for AmI-based self-monitoring of users.

1. The system must be accurate (presenting realistic wellness information), with the option of manipulability (interface optimized for elder people and family members' daily use), and minimal data complexity (senior adult should not have difficulty in understanding what information is requested), see (Huh, Le, Reeder, Thompson, & Demiris, 2013, Demiris, 2016; Elers, Hunter, Whiddett, Lockhart, Guesgen, & Singh, 2018).

2. It must support memory issues, because elder people usually have diminished memory capacity, must have simple attractive interface (not repulsive for elder or disabled people), see (Joe, 2017).

3.   It must be adaptive (modifiable for user's habits), anticipatory (predicting user's needs is based on long-term monitoring of medical and non-medical indicators), personalized (individual human norms are taken into account in the analysis), ubiquitous (embedded among the environment services organize data collection without user intervention), transparent (most actions are without direct action or knowledge by the user), context aware (here-and-now situation complements medical information for more comprehensive analysis), see (Triberti, Barello, 2016; Sadri, 2011).

The above requirements have been already actuated in Consumer-Health Informatics (Demiris, 2016). The patient can participate not only in evaluation (self-quantification) of her/his health status, but even in decision-making on the health-care actions to be taken. The enlisted requirements match well those of the HI. The most challenging issue is the AmI opportunity to proper compensate the declining capability of own user's intelligence. The human CNS functioning comprises signal sensing and transmission, evaluation (comparison with normal standard values), and decision-making (taking action). The AmI-based AHL can act in the same manner: the AmI environment needs monitoring of predefined critical parameters, sensors to record the parameters, diagnostic system (evaluation, in the context of observed situation), and the outcome (such as reminding, alarming, informing, recommending).

Let us discuss some biomarkers that can be chosen to assess human physiological functions. In that respect, AmI actually represents the emerging and growing Fourth Brain layer surrounding the human brain.

Biomarkers for AmI Environments

AmI must be sensitive and reactive to human motion and cognition state (performance, capabilities). Several studies provide list of parameters (biomarkers, or predictors) which supply information on vitally important physiological processes (Lara et al., 2013). The core list is very similar in all these studies and includes several domains, e.g. metabolic health, physical capability, cognitive function, social and psychological wellbeing. These domains further consist of sub-domains. For example, cardiovascular function includes blood pressure and blood lipids. Physical capability includes hand grip strength, gait speed, dexterity and body standing balance, chair standing test. The cognitive function is comprised, primarily, of reaction time (RT), memory tests, tapping test.

Altogether, currently around 40 biomarkers are used as predictive measures for health status (Lara et al., 2015). These biomarkers can accurately assess healthy ageing and predict ageing-related phenotypes, morbidity, mortality, quality of life and health span are searched (Vervoort, Vuillerme, Kosse, Hortobágyi, & Lamoth, 2016). These biomarkers can keep the individual posted with digital values and inform on the meaning of these values. In a way, they play role of sensors and may be regarded as augmented peripheral nervous system. We figure out that far less than 40 parameters are needed to start elaborating an intelligent system to support PD patients.

Specific Biomarkers for PD

Locomotion, which is active transport on the distance larger than the body itself, is critical for individual independent living. Also, locomotion is essential for communication, access to services, and employment of a person. Therefore, prediction and prevention of locomotion disorders in PD patients and aged people would contribute to cope with the problem of social de-adaptation. Precise description (accurate data) of human locomotion and extraction of its crucial features is likely to be helpful to point on a specific motor disorder, while less-precise characterization (big data) of locomotion would be more reliable for AmI environments and the AHL needs.

It has been already established that PD locomotion is characterized by several activity patterns, gait signatures and parameters that can be observed by physician, assessed by clinical scales and instrumentally measured. For example, shuffling of gait, short and slow steps, impaired turning, irregular gait are the symptoms (signatures) can be observed. While such parameters as gait variability, foot angles, stride length, foot clearance, cadence (Eskofier et al., 2017), turn velocity, foot strike angle (Hasegawa et al., 2019), upper body accelerations (Buckley, Galna, Rochester, & Mazzà, 2019) must be measured and carefully analyzed.

Earlier Reginya et al. supposed that spectral analysis of gyroscope signals might be very informative to determine early stages of PD (Reginya, Meigal, Gerasimova-Meigal, Prokhorov, & Moschevikin, 2019). In PD patients, the significant excess of power spectral density at frequencies in range of 4-8 Hz was observed what means presence of powerful rotation of the head in all directions with the frequency characteristic for PD. This prompts that gyroscope sensor could provide valuable information on PD at early stages of the disease.

Nonetheless, even knowing these biomarkers, PD remains mostly a clinically-defined disease subjectively influenced by physician (Schlachetzki et al., 2017). Biomarkers of PD in the domain of cognition are largely the same with those applied to monitor aging (timing, reaction time, memory, and motor execution tests).

EXPERIMENTS WITH BIOMARKER DATA

The AHL needs to collect data on specific parameters (biomarkers) from the target physiological systems. Then, it is needed to transfer the signal to analyzing system for feature extraction, to compare it with normal values, and to find semantics after adding the context information. Finally, the user must conceive and reasonably use the information. Sensors appear as important, if not critical, part of the AtHomeLab design. They must be unobtrusive, sensitive, informative, and compatible with ICT (IoT, AAL) methods. As we already mentioned, physical capacity is best predicted by human gait (turning velocity, step variability), balance at easy stance (stabilometry, posturography), hand grip strength, chair rising time, hand dexterity. Cognitive function is evaluated by reaction time, timing, and finger tapping test. We regard that even such rather short list is essential to keep PD patients and older people posted of their motion and cognition.

AHL for Gait Analysis

Currently, two methods are regarded as the "gold standard" to assess physical performance: 1) video motion capture, 2) walkway force platforms. The methods provide high precision for objective kinematic and force metrics such that the gait is characterized in detail (Schlachetzki et al., 2017; Brito, Fong, Song, Cho, Bhatt, & Korzun, 2018). Dut to this precision property, the methods are complex for use on common everyday devices (e.g., smartphone or camera). Powerful digital equipment and sophisticated algorithms are required to implement the video data analysis (Schlachetzki et al., 2017). To our experience, such a motion video capture system may take some hours to produce the analytics. The corresponding digital instruments require a trained technician (engineer, not medical personnel) to conduct the measurement.

This professional type of video motion capture is restricted to limited space and cannot be used in home setting due to optical obstacles (furniture, wall corners, other people). The motion video capture is vulnerable to illumination change (Fukui, Ifuku, Watanabe, Shimosaka, & Sato, 2015). Instrumented walkways are even less practical for home and everyday use. Therefore, the video motion capture and instrumented walkways are inappropriate for implementing AHL within an AmI environment.

We (as well as other researchers) experimented with surveillance cameras and smartphone-embedded cameras for motion video capture with light returning spheres to trace human motion (Meigal, Prokhorov, Gerasimova-Meigal, Bazhenov, & Korzun, 2017, Kim, Kim, Rietdyk, & Ziaie, 2015). The results showed the potential for constructing valuable analytics although the video data are of low quality. However, the methods still need more elaboration to reduce data processing time.

Another group of methods leads to such technologies as smart shoes or other clothes with foot pressure sensors, wearable inertial 3-axial accelerometers, gyroscopes, magnetometers, electrogoniometers, and inclinometers (Vienne, Barrois, Buffat, Ricard, & Vidal, 2017; Anwary, Yu, & Vassallo 2018). Smartphones are usually equipped with IMU, which includes an accelerometer, so applicable to evaluate tremor and gait characteristics in humans (Barrantes S. et al., 2017; Silsupadol, Teja, & Lugade, 2017; Bastas, Fleck, Peters, & Zelik, 2018; Proessl, Swanson, Rudroff, Fling, & Tracy, 2018). The gyroscope may provide valuable novel information on angular rotations during walking in addition to accelerometer (Proessl, Swanson, Rudroff, Fling, & Tracy, 2018). Due to that, gyro-sensors (embedded in smartphone IMU) are becoming popular for gait analysis (Anwary, Yu, & Vassallo; Zago et al., 2018).

The wearable sensors are usually mounted on major segments or joints of a human body (Silsupadol, Teja, & Lugade, 2017). However, Prateek et al. (2017) proposed to use only one sensor fixed on the top of a head. Indeed, reliable 3D-tracking of the head can be obtained with the help of single light returning sphere mounted on head (Meigal, Prokhorov, Gerasimova-Meigal, Bazhenov, & Korzun, 2017), probably because the head undergoes the largest displacements in the vertical axis during walking. In our recent pilot study, we managed to characterize gait with IMU of a smartphone attached to head of healthy young subjects and PD patients (Reginya, Meigal, Gerasimova-Meigal, Prokhorov, & Moschevikin, 2019).

Wearable sensors provide several dozens of parameters during each gait test. However, only few of them are highly informative to make correct diagnostics in PD (Hasegawa et al., 2019). Among these are vertical acceleration at the second step, range of anterior-posterior velocity at the pre-last step (Micó-Amigo et al., 2017), stride length, gait velocity (Schlachetzki et al., 2017), cadence, foot clearance, foot angles, gait variability (Kluge et al., 2017), stride timing variability (Hubble et al., 2015, and, especially, turning velocity (Hasegawa et al., 2019). Direct comparison of validity of the video-based methods of gait assessment with the inertial sensor systems showed a good agreement between these techniques during the walk phase (Beyea, McGibbon, Sexton, Noble, & O'Connell, 2017). However, that was not the case for the transitional phases (sit-to-stand, turn, turn-to-sit) (Beyea et al., 2017, Meigal, Reginya, Gerasimova-Meigal, Prokhorov, & Moschevikin, 2018). The smartphone-based techniques reportedly outmatch conventional video motion capture systems in detecting episodes of freezing of gate in PD patients (Capecci, Pepa, Verdini, & Ceravolo, 2016).

In sum, we can conclude that moble devices equipped with IMU (smartphone) can used for assessment of walk with promising outcome (Reginya, Meigal, Gerasimova-Meigal, Prokhorov, & Moschevikin, 2019).

AHL for Body Balance and Posture Analysis

Body balance either during easy stance or during walking (dynamic balance) provide valuable information on the condition of the motor system. Additionally, it has great prognostic values for traumas, falling etc. (Riva et al., 2019). The stabilometry and varied clinical tests are widely used to detect postural instability in elderly and PD patients (Hasegawa et al., 2019). These tests are clearly set for laboratory or hospital conditions. However, accelerometers have already been successfully used to trace travels of the center of gravity (Mancini et al., 2012). Additionally, special mHealth apps for personal body balance assessment are now available in the Internet, and they are already evaluated for functionality (Moral-Munoz, Esteban-Moreno, Herrera-Viedma, Cobo, & Pérez, 2018).

At-Home Laboratory for Cognition Tasks

As for the cognitive biomarkers for PD and aging, the most informative and easy-to-do methods to assess cognitive functions are the simple (SRT) and the choice reaction time (CRT), see (Lindenberger, 2014). The SRT estimates the time to detect the signal by measuring time between visual (or auditory) stimulus and the motor respond by pressing as fast as possible (or releasing) a panel button or key on computer keyboard (Vlagsma et al., 2016). The CRT method measures the signal detection time and time to discriminate between two different stimuli, e.g., between green and red light (Wyma, Woods, Yund, Herron, & Reed, 2015). The reaction-based method has well-defined neurophysiological basement (Criaud et al., 2016; Dunovan, Vich, Clapp, Verstynen, & Rubin, 2019) and applied to such domains of cognition as attention, motivation, memory, timing, decision making. The so-called digitomotography can be used to measure the motor function (e.g., to assess bradykinesia in PD patients). The finger tapping test is typically performed using a contact board and electronic tapper. However, even a simple smartphone application can be used for tapping test as well (Lee et al., 2016). Specific interaction with computer keyboard may serve as an indicator of early PD (Giancardo et al., 2016).

Several single (only motion) and dual (motion plus cognition) tasks are used to make gait features more explicit. Among these, the Timed-Up and Go (TUG) test gains most attention, because it is easy in comprehension and performance by a subject (especially by a patient with neurodegeneration), and it requires no special instrumental settings to conduct. The TUG test comprises of the chain of motor executions which correspond with human's daily living activity: 1) sit-to-stand, 2) stand-to-go motion, 3) short (3 m) straight walk, 4) U-turn, 5) back walk, and 6) stand-to-sit motion (Vervoort, Vuillerme, Kosse, Hortobágyi, & Lamoth, 2016; Coelho-Junior et al., 2018). In its classic (3 m long) form, the TUG test allows analyzing only few (3-4) steps in one direction. Besides that, each of these steps appears as mechanically unique because it is linked to specific task within the test: 1) to initiation of the walk (the first step after standing up), 2) to preparation to turn, 3) to the turn, 4) to the stop (the last step). Thus, only as much as 1-2 steps in the middle of walk can be adopted as "standard" ones, what is not enough for accurate statistical analysis. To address this, longer (7-10 m) versions of the TUG test were introduced (Haas et al., 2017), which allow obtaining more (up to 20) standard steps (Reginya, Meigal, Gerasimova-Meigal, Prokhorov, & Moschevikin, 2019).

Usually TUG is conducted as a single task test, but it can also be performed along with a mental task in a form of the Dual Task TUG (DT-TUG). During DT-TUG the subject has to subtract number "1" or "3" from number "100" (Tamura, Kocher, Finer, Murata, & Stickley, 2018). This test, alike the CRT, allows combined assessment of the motor and cognitive functionality.

Figure 5. Smart space to surround the patient with assistance services

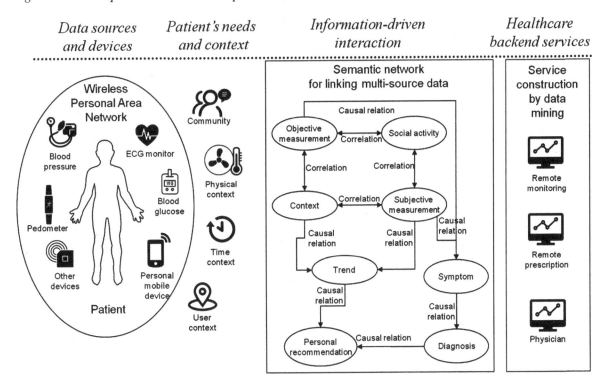

All the discussed tests can be implemented using mobile technologies, similarly as now they use desktop and personal computers. Consequently, the tests provide important data sources within the AmI environment for AHL.

AT-HOME LABORATORY AS A SERVICE-ORIENTED INFORMATION SYSTEM

As we have shown in our previous work (Zavyalova, Korzun, Meigal, & Borodin, 2017; Korzun, Meigal, Borodin, & Gerasimova-Meigal, 2017; Korzun & Meigal, 2019) semantic data mining can be implemented using smart spaces. The smart space system model is shown in Figure 5.

The system needs to interrelate large, heterogeneous, and fragmented data from the physical, cyber, and social worlds, where the medical and physiological biomarkers are not the only sensed parameters. For mobile personalized healthcare services, the semantics from the following classes of data sources are important for collecting.

- **Subjective Measurements:** The patient provides information about her/himself. A typical way is using surveys or questionnaires. In the active form, the medical personnel can make such a survey when directly communicating with the patient. In the passive form, the patient provides information without explicit coupling in space or time with medical personnel. Although the data come from a single person the multi-source property still exists. Such measurements are separated by topics (about a particular health component) and by time (initiated in a particular situation).

- **Objective Measurements:** Medical sensors provide physiological data for evaluation of patient's health parameters, either vital or supplementary ones. For instance, an electrocardiography (ECG) sensor provides 150…300 values per second continuously during 12…28 hours. Another example of personal medical sensors is blood glucose sensors and blood pressure sensors. The patient motion can be monitored using accelerometers, e.g., embedded into such personal mobile devices as smartphones.
- **Context Information:** Recent situation around the patient is characterized based on various IoT devices in the surrounding environment. The following context is considered in respect to healthcare services.
  - **User Context:** User profile, geo-location, social status.
  - **Physical Context:** Parameters of the surrounding environment.
  - **Time Context:** Time of a day, week, month, season, etc.

Social resources: The patient can be supported with resources from other people, in addition to the professional medical support from physicians. First, it improves the motivation for the patient to follow the treatment and other healthcare or wellbeing recommendations. In particular, activity within a group of patients allows sharing experience between the patients. Second, the patient lives in a community, and its members (e.g., relatives, friends, volunteers) can provide essential help for personalized healthcare.

Much information can be extracted from the above data sources. For the integrative representation the semantic network model can be used. The semantic network is defined as directed graph $G=(V, L)$. Nodes v in V represent patient-related objects (e.g., data source, disease, health status). Links l in L represent relations between objects (e.g., data source confirms the disease).

The graph G is multi-weighted using a set of functions F such that for f in F some weight value $f(x)$ is associated with a given node or link x. Subgraphs in G (typically connected structures) correspond to particular knowledge by interpreting as facts or events (e.g., occurrence of the disease and its progress level).

The valued information can be extracted from the semantic network in the form of assistance services. In particular, the system implements the following service-oriented actions.

1. Assisting the patient with mobile personalized services based on devices in the surrounding environments.
2. Providing the access to resources in remote parts of the physical, cyber, and social worlds, e.g., to healthcare backend services located in hospital.
3. Supporting the human intelligence functioning based on semantic linking together numerous physical, social, and virtual objects and data mining over this semantic network.

Services support personalization—the service providers and users interact to create a value such that the service construction and delivery continuously adjust to user's individual and constantly changing needs. The following classes of mobile personalized healthcare services can be constructed within the proposed concept model of smart space.

1. Individual health monitoring: based on continuous mobile sensing and assessment of patient's data.
2. Group health monitoring: when several patients are clustered based on a certain criterion (e.g., geospatial proximity).
3. Survey-driven assessment: when health questionnaires provide information for making decisions.
4. Advanced detection of patient status deviations based on multisource data analytics.

The assistance is typically implemented as information recommendations. That is, the service provides the user (patient, volunteer, doctor) the most relevant information about the current situation. Then, the user makes the final decision based on the provided information. Basically, it means that AI does not substitute HI; AI just extends the HI functions, as we discussed from the beginning of this chapter.

CONCLUSION

This chapter analyzed the relation of human intelligence and artificial intelligence. We presented a theoretical basement for a biology and evolution-centered concept of AI. According to this concept, named either as the Fourth Brain or NeoNeoCortex, the human brain (co-operatively and globally) builds its additional (augmented) layer using which the AI surrounds and extends the HI based on co-working of technology and biology. The implementation of this connection of AI and HI is the At-Home Laboratory that makes Ambient Assisted Living for PD patients and aged people. We expect that AHL is less stressful for people because its AmI properties can be elaborated gradually, preferably from younger age, personally, with the opportunity to choose options. The Fourth Brain will pass through its own ontogenetic development over the life span of an individual. The cognition functionality, including such popular functions as reaction time, timing, decision-making, can well be assessed by tablets or smartphones. Current mobile technologies allow measuring and evaluating such important parameters as blood pressure, heart rate variability, oxyhemoglobin saturation, with glucose and other biochemical parameters ahead. Our study complements well the concept of "disappearing" computer because both of them investigate the convergence of AI and environment, AI and human brain. We presume that finally the human brain and AI will feel comfortable with each other.

ACKNOWLEDGMENT

The work of A. Meigal is supported by the Ministry of Education and Science of Russia within project #17.7302.2017/6.7 of the state research assignment for 2017–2019. The work of D. Korzun is supported by the Ministry of Education and Science of Russia within project # 2.5124.2017/8.9 of the basic part of state research assignment for 2017–2019. The research is implemented within the Government Program of Flagship University Development for Petrozavodsk State University in 2017–2021.

REFERENCES

Anwary, A. R., Yu, H., & Vassallo, M. (2018). An automatic gait feature extraction method for identifying gait asymmetry using wearable sensors. *Sensors (Basel)*, *18*(2), 676. doi:10.339018020676 PMID:29495299

Arora, S., Venkataraman, V., Zhan, A., Donohue, S., Biglan, K. M., Dorsey, E. R., & Little, M. A. (2015). Detecting and monitoring the symptoms of Parkinson's disease using smartphones: A pilot study. *Parkinsonism & Related Disorders*, *21*(6), 650–553. doi:10.1016/j.parkreldis.2015.02.026 PMID:25819808

Asakawa, T., Sugiyama, K., Nozaki, T., Sameshima, T., Kobayashi, S., Wang, L., ... Namba, H. (2019). Can the latest computerized technologies revolutionize conventional assessment tools and therapies for a neurological disease? The example of Parkinson's disease. *Neurologia Medico-Chirurgica*, *59*(3), 69–78. doi:10.2176/nmc.ra.2018-0045 PMID:30760657

Barrantes, S., Egea, A. J. S., Rojas, H. A. G., & Martí, M. J. (2017). Differential diagnosis between Parkinson's disease and essential tremor using the smartphone's accelerometer. *PLoS One*, *12*(8), e0183843. doi:10.1371/journal.pone.0183843 PMID:28841694

Bastas, G., Fleck, J. J., Peters, R. A., & Zelik, K. E. (2018). IMU-based gait analysis in lower limb prosthesis users: Comparison of step demarcation algorithms. *Gait & Posture*, *64*, 30–37. doi:10.1016/j.gaitpost.2018.05.025 PMID:29807270

Bazhenov, N., Korzun, D., & Balandin, S. (2018). Smartphone-Oriented Development of Video Data Based Services. In *Proceedings of the 23rd conference of FRUCT Association* (pp. 62-68). IEEE. 10.23919/FRUCT.2018.8588068

Beyea, J., McGibbon, C. A., Sexton, A., Noble, J., & O'Connell, C. (2017). Convergent validity of a wearable sensor system for measuring sub-task performance during the timed up-and-go test. *Sensors (Basel)*, *17*(4), 934. doi:10.339017040934 PMID:28441748

Bini, S. A. (2018). Artificial intelligence, machine learning, deep learning, and cognitive computing: What do these terms mean and how will they impact health care? *The Journal of Arthroplasty*, *33*(8), 2358–2361. doi:10.1016/j.arth.2018.02.067 PMID:29656964

Blackman, S., Matlo, C., Bobrovitskiy, A., Fang, M. L., Jackson, P., Mihailidis, L., ... Sixsmith, A. (2016). Ambient assisted living technologies for aging well. *Journal of Intelligent Systems*, *25*(1), 55–69. doi:10.1515/jisys-2014-0136

Brito, R., Fong, S., Song, W., Cho, K., Bhatt, C., & Korzun, D. (2018). Detecting Unusual Human Activities Using GPU-Enabled Neural Network and Kinect Sensors. In Internet of Things and Big Data Technologies for Next Generation Healthcare. Series: Studies in Big Data (Vol. 23, pp. 290-296). Springer.

Buckley, C., Galna, B., Rochester, L., & Mazzà, C. (2019). Upper body accelerations as a biomarker of gait impairment in the early stages of Parkinson's disease. *Gait & Posture*, *71*, 289–295. doi:10.1016/j.gaitpost.2018.06.166 PMID:30139646

Coelho-Junior, H. J., Rodrigues, B., de Oliveira Gonзalves, I., Asano, R. Y., Uchida, M. C., & Marzetti, E. (2018). The physical capabilities underlying timed "Up and Go" test are time-dependent in community-dwelling older women. *Experimental Gerontology*, *104*, 138–146. doi:10.1016/j.exger.2018.01.025 PMID:29410234

Criaud, M., Poisson, A., Thobois, S., Metereau, E., Redouté, J., Ibarrola, D., … Boulinguez, P. (2016). Slowness in movement initiation is associated with proactive inhibitory network dysfunction in Parkinson's disease. *Journal of Parkinson's Disease*, *6*(2), 433–440. doi:10.3233/JPD-150750 PMID:27061065

D'Antrassi, P., Prenassi, M., Rossi, L., Ferrucci, R., Barbieri, S., Priori, A., & Marceglia, S. (2019). Personally collected health data for precision medicine and longitudinal research. *Frontiers in Medicine.*, *6*, 125. doi:10.3389/fmed.2019.00125 PMID:31231653

Del Din, S., Godfrey, A., Mazzà, C., Lord, S., & Rochester, L. (2016). Free-living monitoring of Parkinson's disease: Lessons from the field. *Movement Disorders*, *31*(9), 1293–1313. doi:10.1002/mds.26718 PMID:27452964

Demiris, G. (2016). Consumer health informatics: Past, present, and future of a rapidly evolving domain. *Yearbook of Medical Informatics*, *25*(Suppl 1), S42–S47. doi:10.15265/IYS-2016-s005 PMID:27199196

Douglas, K. (2012). Homo virtuous: The evolution of good and evil. *New Scientist*, *216*(2890), 42–45. doi:10.1016/S0262-4079(12)62895-4

Dunovan, K., Vich, C., Clapp, M., Verstynen, T., & Rubin, J. (2019). Reward-driven changes in striatal pathway competition shape evidence evaluation in decision-making. *PLoS Computational Biology*, *15*(5), 1–32. doi:10.1371/journal.pcbi.1006998 PMID:31060045

Elers, P., Hunter, I., Whiddett, D., Lockhart, C., Guesgen, H., & Singh, A. (2018). User requirements for technology to assist aging in place: Qualitative study of older people and their informal support networks. *JMIR mHealth and uHealth*, *6*(6), e10741. doi:10.2196/10741 PMID:29875083

Eskofier, B. M., Lee, S. I., Baron, M., Simon, A., Martindale, C. F., Gabner, H., & Klucken, J. (2017). An overview of smart shoes in the internet of health things: Gait and mobility assessment in health promotion and disease monitoring. *Applied Sciences*, *7*(10), 986. doi:10.3390/app7100986

Espay, A. J., Hausdorff, J. M., Sánchez-Ferro, Á., Klucken, J., Merola, A., Bonato, P., … Maetzler, W. (2019). Movement Disorder Society Task Force on Technology. A roadmap for implementation of patient-centered digital outcome measures in Parkinson's disease obtained using mobile health technologies. *Movement Disorders*, *34*(5), 657–663. doi:10.1002/mds.27671 PMID:30901495

Ganapathy, K., Abdul, S. S., & Nursetyo, A. A. (2018). Artificial intelligence in neurosciences: A clinician's perspective. *Neurology India*, *66*(4), 934–939. doi:10.4103/0028-3886.236971 PMID:30038071

Giancardo, L., Sánchez-Ferro, A., Arroyo-Gallego, T., Butterworth, I., Mendoza, C. S., Montero, P., … Estépar, R. S. (2016). Computer keyboard interaction as an indicator of early Parkinson's disease. *Scientific Reports*, *6*(1), 34468. doi:10.1038rep34468 PMID:27703257

Haas, B., Clarke, E., Elver, L., Gowman, E., Mortimer, E., & Byrd, E. (2017). The reliability and validity of the L-test in people with Parkinson's disease. *Physiotherapy*, *105*(1), 84–89. doi:10.1016/j.physio.2017.11.218 PMID:29395266

Harper, S. (2014). Economic and social implications of aging societies. *Science*, *346*(6209), 587–591. doi:10.1126cience.1254405 PMID:25359967

Hasegawa, N., Shah, V. V., Carlson-Kuhta, P., Nutt, J. G., Horak, F. B., & Mancini, M. (2019). How to select balance measures sensitive to Parkinson's disease from body-worn inertial sensors-separating the trees from the forest. *Sensors (Basel)*, *19*(15), 3320. doi:10.339019153320 PMID:31357742

Hubble, R. P., Naughton, G. A., Silburn, P. A., & Cole, M. H. (2015). Wearable sensor use for assessing standing balance and walking stability in people with Parkinson's disease: A systematic review. *PLoS One*, *10*(4), e0123705. doi:10.1371/journal.pone.0123705 PMID:25894561

Huh, J., Le, T., Reeder, B., Thompson, H. J., & Demiris, G. (2013). Perspectives on wellness self-monitoring tools for older adults. *International Journal of Medical Informatics*, *82*(11), 1092–1103. doi:10.1016/j.ijmedinf.2013.08.009 PMID:24041452

Joe, J., Hall, A., Chi, N. C., Thompson, H., & Demiris, G. (2018). IT-based wellness tools for older adults: Design concepts and feedback. *Informatics for Health & Social Care*, *43*(2), 142–158. doi:10.1080/17538157.2017.1290637 PMID:28350186

Kim, A., Kim, J., Rietdyk, S., & Ziaie, B. (2015). A wearable smartphone-enabled camera-based system for gait assessment. *Gait & Posture*, *42*(2), 138–144. doi:10.1016/j.gaitpost.2015.05.001 PMID:26059484

Kluge, F., Gaßner, H., Hannink, J., Pasluosta, C., Klucken, J., & Eskofier, B. M. (2017). Towards mobile gait analysis: Concurrent validity and test-retest reliability of an inertial measurement system for the assessment of spatio-temporal gait parameters. *Sensors (Basel)*, *17*(7), 1522. doi:10.339017071522 PMID:28657587

Korzun, D. (2017). Internet of things meets mobile health systems in smart spaces: An overview. In Internet of Things and Big Data Technologies for Next Generation Healthcare. Studies in Big Data (vol. 23, pp. 111-129). Springer.

Korzun, D., & Meigal, A. (2019). Multi-Source Data Sensing in Mobile Personalized Healthcare Systems: Semantic Linking and Data Mining. In *Proceedings of the 24th conference of FRUCT Association* (pp. 187-192). IEEE. 10.23919/FRUCT.2019.8711950

Korzun, D., Meigal, A., Borodin, A., & Gerasimova-Meigal, L. (2017). On mobile personalized healthcare services for human involvement into prevention, therapy, mutual support, and social rehabilitation. In *Proceedings of the 2017 International Multi-Conference on Engineering, Computer and Information Sciences* (pp. 276-281). IEEE. 10.1109/SIBIRCON.2017.8109888

Korzun, D., Nikolaevskiy, I., & Gurtov, A. (2016). Service Intelligence and Communication Security for Ambient Assisted Living. *International Journal of Embedded and Real-Time Communication Systems*, *6*(1), 75–100.

Lara, J., Cooper, R., Nissan, J., Ginty, A. T., Khaw, K. T., Deary, I. J., ... Mathers, J. C. (2015). A proposed panel of biomarkers of healthy ageing. *BMC Medicine*, *13*(1), 222. doi:10.118612916-015-0470-9 PMID:26373927

Lara, J., Godfrey, A., Evans, E., Heaven, B., Brown, L. J., Barron, E., ... Mathers, J. C. (2013). Towards measurement of the Healthy Ageing Phenotype in lifestyle-based intervention studies. *Maturitas*, *76*(2), 189–199. doi:10.1016/j.maturitas.2013.07.007 PMID:23932426

Lee, C. Y., Kang, S. J., Hong, S. K., Ma, H. I., Lee, U., & Kim, Y. J. (2016). A validation study of a smartphonebased finger tapping application for quantitative assessment of bradykinesia in Parkinson's disease. *PLoS One*, *11*(7), 1–11. doi:10.1371/journal.pone.0158852

Lindenberger, U. (2014). Human cognitive aging: Corriger la fortune? *Science*, *346*(6209), 572–578. doi:10.1126cience.1254403 PMID:25359964

Loh, K. K., & Kanai, R. (2016). How has the Internet reshaped human cognition? *The Neuroscientist*, *22*(5), 506–520. doi:10.1177/1073858415595005 PMID:26170005

MacLean, P. D. (1990). *The triune brain in evolution: role in paleocerebral functions*. Springer.

Maehara, Y., Saito, S., & Towse, J. N. (2019). Joint cognition and the role of human agency in random number choices. *Psychological Research*, *83*(3), 574–589. doi:10.100700426-017-0944-9 PMID:29110078

Mancini, M., Carlson-Kuhta, P., Zampieri, C., Nutt, G., Chiari, L., & Horak, F. B. (2012). Postural sway as a marker of progression in Parkinson's disease: A pilot longitudinal study. *Gait & Posture*, *36*(3), 471–476. doi:10.1016/j.gaitpost.2012.04.010 PMID:22750016

Mancini, M., King, L., Salarian, A., Holmstrom, L., McNames, J., Horak, F.B. (2011). Mobility Lab to Assess Balance and Gait with Synchronized Body-worn Sensors. *Journal of Bioengineering & Biomedical Science, S1*.

Meigal, A., Korzun, D., Gerasimova-Meigal, L., Borodin, A., & Zavialova, Y. (2019). Ambient intelligence At-Home Laboratory for human everyday life. *International Journal of Embedded and Real-Time Communication Systems*, *10*(2), 117–134. doi:10.4018/IJERTCS.2019040108

Meigal, A., Prokhorov, K., Gerasimova-Meigal, L., Bazhenov, N., & Korzun, D. (2017). Towards a Personal At-Home Lab for Motion Video Tracking in Patients with Parkinson's Disease. In *Proceedings of the 21st conference of FRUCT Association* (pp. 231-237). IEEE. 10.23919/FRUCT.2017.8250187

Meigal, A., Reginya, S., Gerasimova-Meigal, L., Prochorov, K., & Moschevikin, A. (2018). Analysis of human gait based on smartphone inertial measurement unit: a feasibility study. In *Proceedings of the 22nd conference of FRUCT Association* (pp. 151-158). IEEE. 10.23919/FRUCT.2018.8468264

Micó-Amigo, M. E., Kingma, I., Faber, G. S., Kunikoshi, A., van Uem, J. M. T., van Lummel, R. C., ... van Dieлn, J. H. (2017). Is the Assessment of 5 Meters of Gait with a Single Body-Fixed-Sensor Enough to Recognize Idiopathic Parkinson's Disease-Associated Gait? *Annals of Biomedical Engineering*, *45*(5), 1266–1278. doi:10.100710439-017-1794-8 PMID:28108943

Moral-Munoz, J. A., Esteban-Moreno, B., Herrera-Viedma, E., Cobo, M. J., & Pérez, I. J. (2018). Smartphone Applications to Perform Body Balance Assessment: A Standardized Review. *Journal of Medical Systems*, *42*(7), 119. doi:10.100710916-018-0970-1 PMID:29845455

Park, D. C., & Reuter-Lorenz, P. (2009). The adaptive brain: Aging and neurocognitive scaffolding. *Annual Review of Psychology*, *60*(1), 173–196. doi:10.1146/annurev.psych.59.103006.093656 PMID:19035823

Pasluosta, C. F., Gassner, H., Winkler, J., Klucken, J., & Eskofier, B. (2015). Parkinson's disease as a working model for global healthcare restructuration. In *Proceedings of the 5th EAI International Conference on Wireless Mobile Communication and Healthcare* (pp. 162-165). ACM.

Pasluosta, C. F., Gassner, H., Winkler, J., Klucken, J., & Eskofier, B. M. (2015). An emerging era in the management of Parkinson's disease: Wearable technologies and the internet of things. *IEEE Journal of Biomedical and Health Informatics*, *19*(6), 1873–1881. doi:10.1109/JBHI.2015.2461555 PMID:26241979

Prateek, G. V., Skog, I., McNeely, M. E., Duncan, R. P., Earhart, G. M., & Nehorai, A. (2017). Modeling, detecting, and tracking freezing of gait in Parkinson disease using inertial sensors. *IEEE Transactions on Biomedical Engineering*. doi:10.1109/TBME.2017.2785625 PMID:29989948

Proessl, F., Swanson, C. W., Rudroff, T., Fling, B. W., & Tracy, B. L. (2018). Good agreement between smart device and inertial sensor-based gait parameters during a 6-min walk. *Gait & Posture*, *64*, 63–67. doi:10.1016/j.gaitpost.2018.05.030 PMID:29859414

Reginya, S., Meigal, A., Gerasimova-Meigal, L., Prokhorov, K., & Moschevikin, A. (2019). Using Smartphone Inertial Measurement Unit for Analysis of Human Gait. *International Journal of Embedded and Real-Time Communication Systems*, *10*(3), 101–117. doi:10.4018/IJERTCS.2019070107

Riva, D., Fani, M., Benedetti, M. G., Scarsini, A., Rocca, F., & Mamo, C. (2019). Effects of high-frequency proprioceptive training on single stance stability in older adults: Implications for fall prevention. *BioMed Research International*, *2019*(2382747), 1–11. doi:10.1155/2019/2382747 PMID:31240206

Sadri, F. (2011). Ambient intelligence: A survey. *ACM Computing Surveys*, *43*(4), 36:1-36:66.

Schlachetzki, J. C., Barth, J., Marxreiter, F., Gossler, J., Kohl, Z., Reinfelder, S., ... Klucken, J. (2017). Wearable sensors objectively measure gait parameters in Parkinson's disease. *PLoS One*, *12*(10), e0183989. doi:10.1371/journal.pone.0183989 PMID:29020012

Shull, P. B., Jirattigalachote, W., Hunt, M. A., Cutkosky, M. R., & Delp, S. L. (2014). Quantified self and human movement: A review on the clinical impact of wearable sensing and feedback for gait analysis and intervention. *Gait & Posture*, *40*(1), 11–19. doi:10.1016/j.gaitpost.2014.03.189 PMID:24768525

Silsupadol, P., Teja, K., & Lugade, V. (2017). Reliability and validity of a smartphone-based assessment of gait parameters across walking speed and smartphone locations: Body, bag, belt, hand, and pocket. *Gait & Posture*, *58*, 516–522. doi:10.1016/j.gaitpost.2017.09.030 PMID:28961548

Spector, L. (2006). Evolution of artificial intelligence. *Artificial Intelligence*, *170*(18), 1251–1253. doi:10.1016/j.artint.2006.10.009

Tamura, K., Kocher, M., Finer, L., Murata, N., & Stickley, C. (2018). Reliability of clinically feasible dual-task tests: Expanded timed get up and go test as a motor task on young healthy individuals. *Gait & Posture*, *60*, 22–27. doi:10.1016/j.gaitpost.2017.11.002 PMID:29132071

Triberti, S., & Barello, S. (2016). The quest for engaging AmI: Patient engagement and experience design tools to promote effective assisted living. *Journal of Biomedical Informatics*, *63*, 150–156. doi:10.1016/j.jbi.2016.08.010 PMID:27515924

Tysnes, O. B., & Storstein, A. (2017). Epidemiology of Parkinson's disease. *Journal of Neural Transmission (Vienna, Austria)*, *124*(8), 901–905. doi:10.100700702-017-1686-y PMID:28150045

Vervoort, D., Vuillerme, N., Kosse, N., Hortobágyi, T., & Lamoth, C. J. (2016). Multivariate analyses and classification of inertial sensor data to identify aging effects on the Timed-Up-and-Go test. *PLoS One*, *11*(6), e0155984. doi:10.1371/journal.pone.0155984 PMID:27271994

Vienne, A., Barrois, R. P., Buffat, S., Ricard, D., & Vidal, P. P. (2017). Inertial sensors to assess gait quality in patients with neurological disorders: A systematic review of technical and analytical challenges. *Frontiers in Psychology*, *8*, 817. doi:10.3389/fpsyg.2017.00817 PMID:28572784

Vlagsma, T. T., Koerts, J., Tucha, O., Dijkstra, H. T., Duits, A. A., van Laar, T., & Spikman, J. M. (2016). Mental slowness in patients with Parkinson's disease: Associations with cognitive functions? *Journal of Clinical and Experimental Neuropsychology*, *38*(8), 844–852. doi:10.1080/13803395.2016.1167840 PMID:27132647

Weiser, M. (1991). The Computer for the Twenty-First Century. *Scientific American*, *256*(3), 94–104. doi:10.1038cientificamerican0991-94 PMID:1675486

Weiser, M., & Brown, J. S. (1995). Designing Calm Technology. *Powergrid Journal*, *1*, 1–5.

Wilson, E. O. (2012). *The Social Conquest of Earth*. New York: Live right Publishing Corporation.

Wirdefeldt, K., Adami, H. O., Cole, P., Trichopoulos, D., & Mandel, J. (2011). Epidemiology and etiology of Parkinson's disease: A review of the evidence. *European Journal of Epidemiology*, *26*(S1Suppl. 1), S1–S58. doi:10.100710654-011-9581-6 PMID:21626386

Wyma, J. M., Woods, D. L., Yund, E. W., Herron, T. J., & Reed, B. (2015). Age-related slowing of response selection and production in a visual choice reaction time task. *Frontiers in Human Neuroscience*, *9*, 193:1-193:12.

Zago, M., Sforza, C., Pacifici, I., Cimolin, V., Camerota, F., Celletti, C., ... Galli, M. (2018). Gait evaluation using Inertial Measurement Units in subjects with Parkinson's disease. *Journal of Electromyography and Kinesiology*, *42*, 44–48. doi:10.1016/j.jelekin.2018.06.009 PMID:29940494

Zavyalova, Y., Korzun, D., Meigal, A., & Borodin, A. (2017). Towards the development of smart spaces-based socio-cyber-medicine systems. *International Journal of Embedded and Real-Time Communication Systems*, *8*(1), 45–63. doi:10.4018/IJERTCS.2017010104

Zavyalova, Y., Kuznetsova, T., Korzun, D., Borodin, A., & Meigal, A. (2018). Designing a Mobile Recommender System for Treatment Adherence Improvement among Hypertensives. In *Proceedings of the 22nd conference of FRUCT Association* (pp. 290-296). IEEE. 10.23919/FRUCT.2018.8468269

Zimmer, C. (2006). *Evolution: The Triumph of an Idea*. Harper Perennial.

Chapter 8
Human–Computer Cloud and Its Applications in E–Tourism

Andrew Ponomarev

St. Petersburg Institute for Informatics and Automation of Russian Academy of Sciences (SPIIRAS),
Russia

Nikolay Shilov

St. Petersburg Institute for Informatics and Automation of Russian Academy of Sciences (SPIIRAS),
Russia

ABSTRACT

The chapter addresses two problems that typically arise during the creation of decision support systems that include humans in the information processing workflow, namely, resource management and complexity of decision support in dynamic environments, where it is impossible (or impractical) to implement all possible information processing workflows that can be useful for a decision-maker. The chapter proposes the concept of human-computer cloud, providing typical cloud features (elasticity, on demand resource provisioning) to the applications that require human input (so-called human-based applications) and, on top of resource management functionality, a facility for building information processing workflows for ad hoc tasks in an automated way. The chapter discusses main concepts lying behind the proposed cloud environment, as well as its architecture and some implementation details. It is also shown how the proposed human-computer cloud environment solves information and decision support demands in the dynamic and actively developing area of e-tourism.

INTRODUCTION

Vast majority of cyber-physical systems rely on some kind of human involvement. They are built for human benefit (it is natural), besides, they usually operate alongside with humans, or are supported by them. The exploration of possible interactions of humans and cyber-physical systems have recently led to widening the traditional scope of research in cyber-physical systems and to the emergence of the area of socio-cyber-physical systems (e.g., Hozdic, 2019; Calinescu, Camara & 2019), or cyber-physical-social systems (e.g., Wang et al., 2019). This new area not only explores cyber-physical systems in a

DOI: 10.4018/978-1-7998-1974-5.ch008

wider scope, but also offers new approaches on building systems of heterogeneous components. This trend also goes well with the fact that the development of the Internet and communication technologies (allowing to access the Internet from virtually any place on the Earth) has led to the emergence of a new kind of hybrid human-machine systems, where distributed group (crowd) of people becomes involved in the process of information provision and processing. Particular examples of such systems include microtask markets (with the most prominent Amazon Mechanical Turk), various citizen science projects (Franzoni & Sauermann, 2014; Shamir, Diamond & Wallin, 2016), community sense and response systems (e.g., Faulkner et al., 2014), general collaborative mapping (e.g., OpenStreetMap, Google Map Maker, WikiMapia), crisis mapping (e.g., Ushahidi; Meier, 2017) and many others.

The approach described in this chapter addresses two particular problems that typically arise during the construction of human-machine computational systems. The first problem is resource management: all systems that require human attention and human input require a large number of contributors and collecting this number of contributors may require significant time and effort. This problem is typically addressed with a help of specialized platforms (e.g., Amazon Mechanical Turk), but these platforms (unlike modern cloud systems) do not usually provide any guarantees about resources available to particular applications making it virtually impossible to employ them for human-based applications that require operative output. The second problem has a bit wider scope, it is the complexity of decision support in dynamic environments, where it is impossible (or impractical) to implement all possible information processing workflows that can be useful for a decision-maker.

This chapter discusses a human-computer cloud architecture that addresses both of these problems. The environment includes two parts: the first one (platform), provides a unified resource management environment, that can serve as a basis on which any human-based application could be deployed decoupling computing resource management issues from application software. Leveraging this platform can significantly streamline the development of human-based applications and services that are important and inevitable in some application areas. The second part (decision support software, running on top of the platform) allows to automatically decompose tasks to subtasks and distribute them among human participants, making it possible to automatically compose a workflow for an ad hoc decision support problem without explicit programming. One of the core mechanisms of the cloud environment is ontological representation of cloud resources, which simplifies the problem of human resource description and discovery. Ontological representations and mechanisms are also used on top of the unified resource management to implement an ad hoc decision support environment, where ontology-driven human-computer service composition allows to perform decision support tasks that don't have specialized services.

One of the important areas for human-computer decision support systems is e-Tourism, where human input and human involvement is essential due to the subjective nature the domain. Therefore, to motivate the development of the human-computer cloud, decision support in tourism is discussed and projected on the generic architecture of the cloud environment.

The paper is organized as follows. Background section clarifies the topic and the goal of the paper by providing more details on how modern human-powered and cloud systems are interrelated. It also shows the importance of human-driven information processing in eTourism domain. The Architecture section contains the description of the proposed architecture, including principal actors, service layers and interactions needed to implement some typical cloud environment operations. Implementation section describes main foundational technologies used for implementation of the system. Applications in Tourism section discusses how the proposed human-computer cloud environment can be used to implement several important scenarios in the area of tourism. Finally, Evaluation section describes some outcomes of the practical evaluation of the environment. The results achieved are summarized in the Conclusion.

BACKGROUND

Cloud computing technology has become a de facto standard in elastic hardware and software resources provisioning, as it has established a convenient way to abstract computational resources needed by an application and to dynamically adjust the needed amount of resource. National Institute of Standards and Technology (NIST) recommendations document (Mell & Grance, 2011) describes three service models that have formed in the area of cloud computing: Infrastructure as a Service (IaaS), Platform as a Service (Paas), Software as a Service (SaaS). In other words, typical capabilities provided by cloud environments are processing, storage, network and software. However, the cloud concept is now perceived as something more fundamental and pervasive. Therefore, there are recent developments applying the cloud principles of elastic resource provisioning to a wider spectrum of resources. The authors are also extending the spectrum of resources managed by the cloud to human resources. The rationale is that currently each system that relies on human in the loop (recommendation systems, review aggregators, participatory sensing systems, etc.) needs to form its own pool of users, which can take long time and require some advertising effort, and that is one of the factors that hampers the use of human computation technologies. Cloud computing technology allows to abstract computational resources and decouple them from application services in a system, allowing, in turn, to dynamically use the required amount of the resource, on the pay-per-use basis. Treating human effort as a special kind of resource would obviate the need to collect the significant number of users/contributors for human-in-the-loop applications and streamline the process of developing and deploying this kind of applications.

However, elastic resources provisioning is only a tool, or a foundation, on which decision support tools integrating software services and human efforts can be built. So, the more elaborate goal is to create a stack of technologies to compose flexible decision support systems based on human-computer cloud.

The e-tourism was chosen as an example application area for three main reasons:

- it is one of the largest and fastest-growing economic sectors. According to the World Tourism Organization (UNWTO) report, international tourist arrivals doubled in the last two decades (from 527 million in 1995 to 1186 million in 2015). International tourism receipts earned by destinations worldwide have surged from US\$ 415 billion in 1995 to US\$ 1260 billion in 2015. Moreover, UNWTO expects that the number of international tourist arrivals worldwide would increase by an average of 3.3% a year over the period 2010 to 2030, reaching approximately 1.8 billion in 2030 (UNWTO, 2016).
- it requires decision support. Not only because of large number of aspects that need to be paid attention to: tourist mobility, high risk and uncertainty in unfamiliar environment, distributed nature of information sources and several other factors (Gretzel, 2011), but also because the increasing use of ICTs in tourism services allows tourists to take a more active role in the production of tourism products, being no longer satisfied with standardized products (Berka & Plößnig, 2004). Moreover, not only tourists travelling in an unfamiliar environment need support, but also destination management organizations (DMOs) need a tool (or a suite of tools) that would help to make

decisions about what should be done to make destination more attractive for tourists, to develop a sustainable and profitable tourist economy.

- finally, tourist information (and decision) support systems today use a wide spectrum of technologies, including GIS, knowledge-based inference, information retrieval, social network processing and various recommendation systems. This spectrum includes both machine-driven (solely computational) technologies like GIS or knowledge-based inference and also human-driven ones like recommendation systems. However, this variety lacks standardization that can be achieved via proper cloud abstraction mechanisms.

The proposed approach and architecture are based on the synergy of the following areas: cloud computing (especially the *extended* cloud paradigm, where human services and human effort is regarded as another special type of resources) and ontological modeling (especially, ontological modeling of cloud services). The proposed architecture is applied to decision support in tourism. Therefore, this section contains brief description of the recent and competing developments in each of these areas and is structured accordingly.

Cloud Computing

Relevant developments in applying cloud principles of elastic resource provisioning to a wider spectrum of resources can be classified into two groups: 1) cloud sensing and actuation environments and 2) cloud-managed human resource environments.

One of the examples of cloud sensing and actuation environment is (Distefano, Merlino & Puliafito, 2012), where sensing resource is regarded as a service that can be allocated and used in some unified way independently of the application that needs access to the resource. Later, based on this work Merlino et al. (2016) designed a cloud architecture for mobile crowdsensing MCSaaS (Mobile CrowdSensing as a Service), which defines a unified interface allowing any smartphone user to become a part of a cloud and allow to use his/her smartphone sensors in some way that he/she finds acceptable in exchange for some monetary reward or even voluntary.

ClouT (Cloud+IoT) project (Formisano et al., 2015) falls in the same category and is aimed on providing enhanced solutions for smart cities by using cloud computing in the IoT domain. It proposes multi-layer cloud architecture where lower (infrastructure) layer manages both sensing and computing resources. Both ClouT and MCSaaS approaches are highly relevant to the system being designed, because, as it was noted earlier, smart tourism requires "smartness" of tourist destination, and these projects develop the idea of cloud architecture for smart cities (or a part of it). However, they are focused mostly on sensing resources and consider human resources only due to the fact, that human provides the access to his/her smartphone and can control it to make some operations (i.e. point camera lens to some object and make a picture) requested by the application working on top of the infrastructure layer, or a specific kind of virtual sensor. A human, however, may be not only a supplier of information (like sensor), but a processor of it.

The second group, namely cloud-managed human resource environments, has another perspective aiming on managing member's skills and competencies in a standardized flexible way (e.g. Dustdar, Bhattacharya, 2011; Sengupta et al., 2013), regarding human as a specific resource that can be allocated from a pool for performing some tasks. For example, in (Dustdar & Bhattacharya, 2011) the cloud consisting of human-based services and software-based services is considered. On the infrastructure layer, they define a human-computing unit, which is a resource capable of providing human-based services. Like hardware infrastructure is described in terms of some characteristics (CPU, memory, network bandwidth), human-computing unit in this model is described by the set of skills. The authors do not list the exact skills, leaving it to the application domain.

This paper adopts the idea of sensor virtualization and cloud implementation of IoT from (Merlino et al., 2016) and (Formisano et al., 2015), but also extends this idea by directly managing human resources by infrastructure layer (Dustdar & Bhattacharya, 2011).

There are also numerous relevant research papers on crowdsourcing/crowd computing (including crowdsensing), e.g. (Kochhar et al., 2010; Ahmad et al., 2011; Kamar et al., 2012; Ra et al., 2012) where crowd computing platforms are proposed. While using some of the ideas of the existing crowd computing platforms (e.g., typical workflows ensuring quality control, elements of skill management), human-computer cloud is aimed on a standardization of human effort and seamless integration of it into a cloud stack.

Ontology-Based Cloud Modeling

Decision support system usually relies on some representation of the problem. There are several approaches for the representation, but one of the most popular (especially when it comes to intelligent decision support) is the use of ontologies (Sheth & Ranabahu, 2010a; Sheth & Ranabahu, 2010b). There are several definitions of an ontology, and the most widely accepted is from (Gruber, 1993): *An ontology is an explicit specification of a conceptualization.* The use of ontologies not only allows to solve semantic interoperability problems by defining the domain dictionary and relations between dictionary terms (concepts), but also to streamline formalization by means of ontology reuse.

There are several attempts to apply ontologies in the domain of cloud computing. The authors of (Androcec, Vrcek & Seva, 2012) define several directions of applying ontologies to the cloud computing field: a) cloud resources and service description; b) cloud security; c) cloud interoperability; d) cloud services discovery and selection.

Some of the concrete ontologies that are successfully applied to model various aspects of a cloud system are (Bellini, Cenni & Nesi, 2016): SKOS, mOSAIC, Linked USDL, CoCoOn, UFO-S. UFO-S (Livieri, 2015), for example, being a core reference ontology for services, is able to explain a number of perspectives on services, including those that emphasize services as value co-creation, as capabilities and as application of competences. As a core ontology, UFO-S refines concepts of a foundational ontology (the Unified Foundational Ontology (UFO), proposed in (Guizzardi, 2005), by providing a conceptualization for services that is independent of a particular application domain.

The modeling of SLA in cloud is another problem that attracts much attention (Bellini, Cenni & Nesti, 2016); there are approaches based on WSLA for the definition of SLAs of WebServices (Ludwig et al., 2003), WS-Agreement was developed from the Grid Resource Allocation Agreement Protocol Working Group (GRAAP-WG), SLAng (Lamanna, Skene & Emmerich, 2003), LinkedUSDL-SLA (in the context of FI-WARE project) etc.

Although, these developments are important in the domain of cloud computing, they have to be adapted to the human-computer cloud, as they do not consider human part, besides, the eventual goal of the cloud environment is to mitigate the creation of hybrid (human-machine) decision support systems, and these ontologies are not related to decision support.

eTourism

The main point and primary goal of this paper is not to build just a decision support system in tourism. It is about building the ontology-based cloud environment, where ontological models and ontology-based mechanisms are used to support typical cloud environment scenarios (independently of the application domain of the services deployed in this environment). However, this environment provides tools for building domain-oriented decision support systems that heavily use ontology-based representations and inference. Therefore, domain ontologies are also relevant (but only for applying the cloud environment, building a decision support system for particular domain). The difficulty of creating ontology of tourism domain is discussed in detail, for example, in (Barta et al., 2009). The idea is that during a tourist trip a person can do almost anything he/she can do in an everyday life: go shopping, eat out, go sightseeing etc. Therefore, an ontology of tourism can include almost entire ontology of customer services coupled with cultural one. On the other hand, this ontology should somehow deal with dates, time intervals, geography and other common concepts that are best dealt with by some upper-level ontology. Several specialized tourism ontologies were proposed in the literature, e.g. (Fodor & Werthner, 2005; Park, Yoon, & Kwon, 2012; Choi et al., 2009). There are also several ontologies that do not deal with tourist domain but may be useful, as they describe either broader part of world than tourism or cover in detail some subset of information usually relevant for tourists: (Shema.org; GoodRelations). Besides, several papers discuss the list of tasks that should be implemented in a decision support in tourism: e.g., (Yu, 2005; Kulakov et al., 2016; Masron, Ismail & Marzuki, 2016; Korzun et al., 2016; Baggio & Caporarello, 2008). However, thorough analysis of these ontologies and typical decision support tasks is not a part of this paper, they were performed in the previous work of the authors (Ponomarev & Parfenov, 2015) and (Smirnov et al., 2016a).

ARCHITECTURE OVERVIEW

This section discusses the general architecture of the proposed cloud environment, including the set of principal actors interacting with the environment, services and service layers, as well as interaction scenarios that implement some typical operations provided by cloud environment (e.g., service deployment scenario).

Actors

The proposed human-computer cloud adopts two most important types of actors out of five identified in the NIST recommendation document (Mell & Grance, 2011), namely Cloud Consumer and Cloud Provider. Besides, one specific actor type is added, which corresponds to humans who provide their resources via cloud environment. Therefore, following actors are identified:

Cloud consumers, who use the applications and services deployed in the cloud environment (and provided by Cloud Provider). Further, this category of actors can be divided into *End users* and *Service developers*. This division is mostly determined by the kind (and a level) of services a consumer deals with. For example, when using the cloud in tourism domain, possible *end users* are tourists (e.g., getting support in trip planning) and destination management organizations (e.g., getting information support in making decisions about tourism destination), because they use cloud services (mostly, on the SaaS layer) to solve domain specific tasks. *Service developers* use the services of the platform layer to create application services for end users. These services can rely not only on physical infrastructure and software, but also on human effort, which is accessed via standardized protocols. Therefore, services, that are mostly accessed by Service developers are deployment service, data processing, information storage, workflow and other services of the platform layer.

Contributors, i.e., citizens, who are available to serve as human resources in a human-computer cloud environment.

Cloud providers, individuals or organization who own and maintain the required hardware and software infrastructure provided to Cloud Consumers. This includes, for example, system administrators.

Cloud Layers and Services

The proposed human-computer cloud concepts mainly touches two cloud models: PaaS and SaaS. Though, elastic "low-level" resource provisioning is also necessary (e.g., to run the services and applications deployed as a part of PaaS), the proposed concept do not offer a specific IaaS level solution, reusing existing ones.

Platform Layer

Platform layer contains services that allow to develop and execute human-based applications. To achieve that, one specific type of resources is added to the cloud environment, which is human-provided resource, associated with some contributor. Contributors can join human-computer cloud and define the resources they can provide, time and load restrictions, a type of tasks they may participate. For example, a user may define that he/she is available after 20 p.m. to provide some local information/advices assuming that that activity will not take more than 10 minutes, or that he/she is available during typical working hours to perform Russian-English translation. A contributor may also define the expected compensation for his/her efforts. It is important, that resources (including human resources, or contributors) are not locked to some particular domain. Instead, they describe their competencies and possible kinds of activities using some of the available ontologies to leverage the resource identification phase that happens when some service that require human participation is deployed in the cloud environment. Ontology-based resource discovery service performs ontology search involving ontology matching techniques as necessary. The reason why ontological representation is used here to describe human skills and capabilities is that there are many different skills and capabilities that humans can have. Cloud environment, of course, cannot fix the list of possible capabilities, as they may be application specific. Therefore, to describe skills and capabilities of humans the environment defines a very generic model that can be filled with whatever application specific skills a human is wishing to advertise. Due to mechanisms of direct mapping between ontologies and even the possibility of automated matching (Euzenat & Shvaiko, 2013), the resources can be discovered even if resource requirements (provided by service developers) are written in different terms than resource descriptions (provided by contributors).

Resource management service monitors contributor connections and disconnections and collects information about effectiveness of each contributor (separately for each skill a contributor is allocated by) and uses it in further allocation requests. Specifically, virtualized resources of each contributor are described with the historically determined effectiveness, thus, it allows to allocate, for example, a "local expertise in Paris" contributor with estimated performance "expert" to ask him/her a question.

Contributor's profile consists of the explicit part filled in by the contributor him-/herself, and an implicit part that is filled and adjusted during the interaction of the contributor with the platform.

On the other hand, platform layer provides a set of tools for HBA developers, making resource allocation transparent for them. For example, imagine a tourist itinerary planning application that involves correction of the itinerary by people familiar with the area of planned trip. If this application is developed from scratch the developers would need to promote it to collect a rather big number of participants. However, if built on the base of human-computer cloud infrastructure, a developer can rely on allocation of human resources from the cloud. Moreover, platform layer may provide, for example, an Iterative-Improvement (Little, Chilton, Goldman & Miller, 2010) human computation pattern that is implemented as an allocation of several human members (meeting some requirements), and redirecting a task to them in sequence. An application developer could then just use this service, sending to it an initial itinerary received from the user and general requirements to members who can take part in itinerary planning.

Development tools of the platform layer allow to deploy services in cloud environment and to monitor them. Each service being deployed includes an ontology-based descriptor, specifying:

- Building/configuration instructions;
- Hardware and software requirements of the service (what platform services it relies on, e.g., database service, human workflow service, etc.);
- Human resource requirements (if any), specifying what human skills and competencies this service need to function. These requirements are also resolved during the service deployment, but as (1) resolving these requirements employs ontology matching which may result in some tradeoffs, (2) human resources are much more limited than hardware/software, the status and details of the requirements resolution are available to the developer and can be browsed via the management console;
- Description of the service functions and entry points to be published in the application domain service repository and used by the ad hoc dynamic workflow service.

Typical interoperability scenario that is initiated in the platform layer during deployment is the following: the human resources connected to the cloud environment describe their capabilities using some problem-specific dictionaries. Each application/service that is deployed in this cloud environment contains a description of its requirements (including the requirements to the resources), which is expressed in terms of the most appropriate ontology selected (or even designed) by the application developers. It is very unlikely that human resources have used this exact ontology to describe their capabilities when connecting to the system. However, the advantage in using ontologies here is that due to the formal semantics inherent to them different ontologies can be matched. Hence, in the process of service deployment, human resources that are potentially able to fulfill the human requirements of the service are identified (despite the fact that they are not described initially in terms of the application ontology). Later, during the functioning of the service, the participants' description can evolve, because his/her performance in the capabilities required by the service (and expressed in terms of service's ontology) is recorded and processed. For each further service that is deployed in this environment, the process of aligning requirements with the capabilities of human resources becomes easier, as human resources definition becomes more and more detailed.

Software Layer

This layer consists of a suite of services and applications designed for a particular problem area.

The core feature of this layer is an ad hoc knowledge-based decision support that is implemented via ontology-driven dynamic workflow service. The goal of this service is to automatically build workflows to solve problems, for which there are no existing services. To make it possible, simple services developed by third-party organizations and deployed in the cloud environment register in the service registry providing ontological description of their functions (based on some problem domain ontology). End user of the decision support service, in his/her turn, provides a formal definition on the problem which is also formalized and represented in terms of problem domain ontology. The dynamic workflow service, decomposes the formalized problem description into tasks that may be assigned to registered resources and services. The problem result is then composed from the task results. If the process of decomposition and assignment fails, the unstructured problem definition is assigned to the community of contributors.

Aside from decision support service dealing with ad hoc problems via their ontology-driven decomposition, which is the major aim of the authors on the software layer, there are also other services that solve particular tasks actual for the application domain. Currently, the authors focus on smart tourism applications (Teslya & Ponomarev, 2016; Smirnov, Ponomarev, Levashova & Teslya, 2016b), that serve as a good example of a domain where human input and information processing abilities are very valuable. The example services in the SaaS layer for tourism domain are provided in the respective section. Other domains that may significantly benefit from the unified human-machine infrastructure and platform management are Smart Cities and emergency decision support.

PLATFORM LAYER

The specifics of using humans as one of the types of resources dictate additional requirements to the PaaS platform. Say, significant difference in productivity and huge number of possible skills and knowledge a human may possibly possess (unlike hardware or software resources typical for current cloud environments) requires extensive (and dynamic) description of each human resource and intelligent discovery and allocation mechanisms. Limited nature of human resources requires that the amount of resources available for the particular human-based application deployed in the cloud has to be estimated and made available for the application developer. It is essential, because each application, in its turn, provides some services and their capacity is effectively limited by the amount of human resources; particular value of this limitation may influence QoS policies of the application, its pricing and so on.

Distinguishing features of the proposed human-computer cloud platform are ontologies and digital contracts. Ontological mechanisms (ability to precisely define semantics and use inference to find related terms) are used to find and allocate human resources required by software services. While digital contracts are used to achieve predictability required by cloud users (application developers). These digital contracts specify terms on which a contributor agrees to provide his/her competencies to the cloud application developer, rewarding and possible penalties. Cloud environment uses these contracts both to allocate service's task and to inform users about possible capacity.

Primary requirements from the side of *End users* considered in the platform design are following:

- The platform must provide tools to deploy, run, and monitor applications that require human information processing.
- The platform must allow to specify what kind of human information processing is required for an application (as some human-based services, like, e.g., image tagging, require very common skills, while others, like tourism decision support, require at least local expertise in certain location).
- The platform must allow to estimate and monitor human resources available for the application. This requirement contrasts to conventional cloud applications, where overall amount of resources possessed by cloud provider is considered to be inexhaustible, and the capacity consumed by an application is in theory limited only by the available budget. However, human resources are always limited, especially when it comes to people with some specialized competencies and knowledge. Besides, the particular rewarding scheme designed by the application developer may be not appealing and not able to collect the required number of contributors. Therefore, application developer should be able to have information to know what capacity is available to the application. Based on this information he/she may change the rewarding scheme, set up his/her own SLA (for his/her consumers) etc.
- The platform must account for temporal dimension of resource availability. Like in the previous requirement, this is specific mostly for human resources. For example, some contributors are ready to participate in information processing activities controlled by the cloud platform in their spare time (non-working hours) only. It means that resource capacity during non-working hours will be larger than during working hours. However, for some applications (e.g., online tourist support) reaction time is important. Therefore, tourist decision support service developers should have temporal perspective of the resource availability.

Application Description

The aim of any cloud environment providing the PaaS service model is to streamline the development and deployment of the applications by providing specialized software libraries and tools that help developers to write code abstracting from many details of resource management. Instead, those resource management operations are performed automatically by PaaS environment usually according to some description (declarative configuration) provided by the developer of the service being executed. The human-computer cloud environment being developed supports similar approach, however, with inevitable extensions caused by the necessity of working with human resources. To streamline the development of applications that require human actions, the platform allows both a developer to describe what kind of human resources are required for this particular application, and a contributor to describe what kind of activities he/she can be involved in and what competencies he/she possesses. Declarative specification of service requirements is quite typical for cloud environments. They are used, for example, in cloud orchestration definition language TOSCA, that allows, for example, to specify how many virtual machines and with what services should be created for a particular application running in cloud. However, these definitions turn out to be insufficient for the purpose of human-computer cloud. One of the reasons is multifarious nature of possible human skills and competencies. While virtual machine can be described with a very limited number of features (e.g. cpu, ram, i/o capacity), human contributor's skills and abilities are highly multidimensional, they can be described in different levels of detail and be connected to wide

Figure 1. Application descriptor's general structure

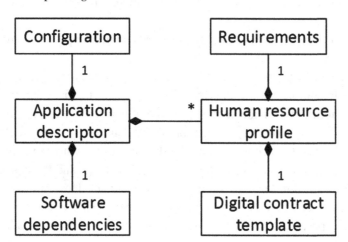

range of particular application areas. Besides, the same skills can be described in different ways, and, finally, most of the skill descriptions in real world are incomplete (however, there might be a possibility to infer some skills that a human might possess from those that he/she explicitly declared).

Application that is to be deployed in the proposed human-computer cloud beside the source code must contain a descriptor that includes following components (here we list all the components, but focus on those, relevant to human part):

- Configuration parameters (e.g. environment variables controlling the behavior of the compiled code);
- Software dependencies of the application (what platform services and/or other applications it relies on, e.g., database service, messaging service, etc.);
- Human resource requirements, specifying what human skills and competencies the application needs to function. These requirements are also (as software requirements) are resolved during the service deployment, but as (1) resolving these requirements employs ontology matching which may result in some tradeoffs, (2) human resources are much more limited than hardware/software, the status and details of the requirements resolution are available to the developer and can be browsed via the management console;
- Digital contract template for each type of human resources. By the type of human resource we mean each specific profile of requirements. For example, an itinerary planning application may require people with significant local expertise as well as people with shallow local expertise but good language skills. The application defines these two requirements profiles and may associate different digital contracts for them (in terms of reaction time and/or payment).

More formally, the general structure of an application descriptor can be drawn as a UML diagram (Fig. 1).

One of the distinguishing features of the proposed platform is the way to formally describe requirements addressing the different ways of describing the same human capabilities. First of all, the three-way (knowledge, skill, and attitude) understanding of human competencies common in current literature is adopted. Then (and the most important) the environment allows to use arbitrary ontology concepts as specific skills or knowledge areas.

Therefore, the application requirements definition is equivalent to *SELECT* pattern of a SPARQL (SPARQL) query. E.g.:

```
?contributor hcc:knows gno:660129.
```

Here hcc:knows is a property defined in the platform ontology, gno is a namespace for geographical objects described with Geonames ontology (Geonames Geographical Database), and 660129 is the identifier of an object in Geonames ontology (Espoo). In other words, this pattern is to match all contributors who specified that they have knowledge of Espoo. The major benefit of using ontologies is that it is possible to discover resources defined with related, similar but not exact terms. This is done either by using existing public mappings between ontologies (stating equivalence between concepts of different ontologies), or by ontology inference (e.g., local knowledge of Espoo concept implies to some degree local knowledge of Helsinki concept and Uusimaa concept), or potentially even by ontology matching (Euzenat, Shvaiko, 2013). So, the pattern above will also match those contributors who described their knowledge not using Geonames ontology but other geographical ontologies.

However, human resource requirement of the form above is quite rare (it only usable as a requirement for local applications for Espoo). Application that need local knowledge in any region are more widespread. To account for this, more general, case requirement definition may contain placeholders, e.g.:

```
?contributor hcc:knows
 [?p a gn:A;
 ?p gn:countryCode "FI"].
```

Here ?p is a placeholder, and its value has to be an administrative boundary (due to Geonames A concept) and be located in Finland (due to Geonames countryCode property). Therefore, this requirement will be fulfilled for any contributor that has local experience in some region in Finland (and the respective contributor will be attributed the value of placeholder).

It is important that we do not fix any particular set of ontologies, but support ontology-based resource discovery. It allows tourist applications deployed on the platform to use public cultural, historical, and geographical ontologies, whereas, e.g., applications, that employ human-based information processing in the area of medicine or biology use the ontologies of the respective domain. The only restriction is that these ontologies have to be expressed in OWL 2 (OWL 2). Moreover, to guarantee computational efficiency, they have to conform to OWL 2 EL profile.

Another distinguishing feature of the approach is the concept of *digital contract*. It is an agreement between contributor and platform about terms of work, quality management principles and rewarding. This contract may be as lightweight as commonly accepted in modern microtask markets (like Amazon Mechanical Turk), specifying that a contributor may pick tasks from common service pools when he/she is comfortable and as many as he/she can. However, this contract may also be rather strict, requiring that a contributor should be available during the specified time and be able to process not less than specified number of tasks per time interval. Terms of this *digital contract* are essential for estimating the amount of resources available for a service and its capacity (including time perspective of the capacity). The necessity of this *digital contract* is caused by the fact that human resources are limited. In

Figure 2. Contributor's description structure

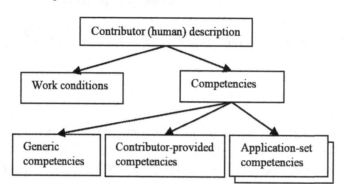

case of ordinary hardware managing cloud the cloud infrastructure provider can buy as many computers as needed, human participation is less controllable due to free will, therefore, attracting and retaining contributors can be a complex task. As a result, the abstraction of inexhaustible resource pool that is exploited in the provider-consumer relationship of current cloud environments turns out to be inadequate for human-computer cloud. A consumer should be informed about the human capacity available for his/ her application to make an informed decision about revising *digital contracts* (making contribution to this application more appealing), or providing changes to their own service level agreements. This creates a competition between consumers for the available resources and finally will create a kind of job market where different digital contract statements will have its own price.

Important platform feature that is also provided by *digital contracts* is the support of different types of contributor allocation for a service. Namely, per task allocation and per time allocation. In the former case, the contract usually sets per task rewards and can optionally require that certain number of tasks be processed over some relatively large time span (e.g., 20 requests per day). While in the latter case, the contract enforces particular time spans of availability and therefore quick reaction of a contributor in the respective time span which is crucial for some applications.

Contributor Description

When a contributor joins the cloud platform he/she provides two main types of information, that are very similar to pieces of application descriptor. Namely, competencies definition, and work conditions (Fig. 2). Competencies definition is made in terms of any ontology the contributor is aware of. For those contributors who cannot use ontologies there is another option, the definition of competencies is made iteratively via contributors' text description analysis followed by ontology-based term disambiguation. In any case, internally, each contributor is described by skills, knowledge and attitude, linked to shared ontology concepts.

Contributor's competency definition is multi-layered. The first layer is provided by the contributor him-/herself, but additional layers are added by applications in which a contributor takes part. For this purpose, human resource management API available for application code can manage application-specific skills and qualifications, which also can be described in some ontology (application-specific or not).

Therefore, despite initial description of competencies may be rather terse, during the contributor's participation in different applications run over the platform it becomes more and more rich. And that alleviates further human resource discovery. Note, however, that each application can access its own contributor description layer, all the layers are visible only for deployment and resource discovery services of the platform.

Work conditions include preferred skills, as well as payment threshold, reactivity and availability limitations. This parameters are also similar to those included in *digital contract* template in the application descriptor. During application enquiry and application deployment its contract template is matched against contributors' work conditions. Moreover, this matching touches not only contributor's declared work conditions and one application contract (of the deployed application) but also other applications which contracts this contributor has already accepted, controlling overall responsibilities that are taken by the contributor and resolving possible conflicts.

Use Cases

Use case diagram showing actors and main use cases of the platform is presented in Fig. 3. This diagram connects platform functions involving core concepts introduced earlier and user categories.

Application/service developers can deploy application (which initiates advertisement process to identify human resources available to this application), edit digital contracts, monitor, and delete application (this releases all resources allocated for the application, including human resources). Editing digital contracts is necessary, for example, when application developer is trying to compete for resources with other applications by offering higher rewards. This effectively changes the descriptor of the deployed application (producing a new version of it) and leads to a new wave of advertisements. Monitor application use case generalizes various functions that are necessary for application developer and are common to many current PaaS, like reading usage statistics, logs and other. This also includes monitoring of the available human resources by each requirement type as well its prediction. Inner scenario of application advertising includes identifying compatible resources based on matching of resource definition (competence profile) and requirement specification.

Contributor can edit competence profile, providing the initial version of it or reflecting further changes, browse application advertisements routed to him/her (compatible with his/her competence profile and work conditions) with an option to accept some of them by signing digital contract and attaching to the respective application. Further, contributor can perform application-specific tasks and detach from application.

System administrator, besides monitoring the status of the platform (usage of hardware/human resources, communication channels throughput, platform services' health) can also do some activities in tuning the platform parameters. The diagram highlights only one kind of tuning which is editing ontology mappings. These mappings are used by the platform during identification of compatible resources (contributors) for advertising applications. The explicit mappings represent one of the ways for the platform to match competencies expressed in different ontologies.

Service Deployment Scenario

This section describes the mechanism of human-based service deployment. When a contributor registers at the human-computer platform he/she is not immediately available for requests of all human-based applications that may run on this environment. However, he/she starts to receive *advertisements* of applications, which are being deployed (or are already deployed) based on the similarity of a declared

Figure 3. Simplified use case diagram of the platform

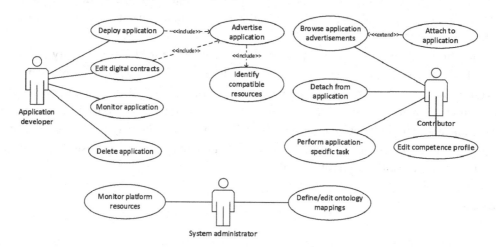

competence profile (including additional layers created by applications a contributor participates) and applications' competence requests and correspondence of digital contract templates of the application and working conditions of contributor. These advertisements include description of service (its end-user functionality), type of human-based activities that are required for this service, the proposed rewarding scheme, specific performance evaluation techniques and so on. Based on the information contained in the *advertisement,* a contributor makes a decision if he/she will receive tasks from this application in future and what is acceptable schedule and maximum load. In other words, if a registered contributor agrees to contribute to the particular service a *digital contract* is signed specifying intensity of task flow, the rewarding and penalty details and quality measurement strategy. In general, there is many-to-many relation between applications and platform contributors, i.e, one contributor may sign *digital contracts* with several applications.

After a contributor and the platform (on behalf of particular application) signed a *digital contract,* application's requests for human operations are made available to the contributor. A contributor also can detach from an application (however, the mechanism and terms of this detaching can also be a part of *digital contract* to ensure the application provider can react to it accordingly).

As it was already noted, the process of service advertising is based on ontological representation of service requirements and human competencies and their matching.

RENE: THE DECISION SUPPORT SERVICE

The *René* decision support service is an application, running on top of the human-computer cloud infrastructure exposed as a SaaS and leveraging some features of the platform (e.g., resource management and provisioning). Expected user of *René* is a decision-maker who passes some task specification to the service to build an on-the-fly network capable of performing the task. It should be noted, that *René* exposes an API, by which ontology-based structured representation of the task specification is passed. The problem of creating such specification (for example, as a result of text analysis) is out of the scope both of this paper and of *René* functions.

To decompose a task specification into a smaller tasks *René* uses a problem-specific task ontology, where domain tasks and their input and output parameters are described. After performing the decomposition *René* tries to distribute the elementary subtasks among the available resources. The list of available resources is retrieved via an API from underlying layers of the environment, which monitor all the contributor's connections and disconnections and software resource registrations. The resource management service under the hood treats human and software resources a bit differently. Human resources (contributors) describe their competencies with a help of ontology and receive *advertisements* to join human-based applications if their requirements are compatible to the declared competencies of the user. In this sense, *René* is one of these human-based applications and may only distribute subtasks to those contributors who agreed to work with it. Software services are made available to *René* by their developers and maintainers by placing a special section into the deployment descriptor of the application. Practical assignment is also done via interfaces of underlying resource management layer, aware of the status and load of the resources and terms of their digital contracts.

Finally, *René* monitors the availability of the resources (via the underlying layer) during execution of the subtasks and rebuilds the assignment if some of the resources fail or become unavailable.

Task Decomposition

Task decomposition is the first step for building the resource network. Main operation that drives the decomposition is actually task composition, i.e. deriving networks of tasks connected by input/output parameters. Furthermore, task decomposition in this approach can be viewed as finding such composition of basic tasks defined in the ontology that is equivalent to the task given by the user.

For the purposes of decision support system, a structure of the task ontology is proposed. According to the proposed structure, the task ontology should consist of a set of tasks and subtasks, sets of input and output parameters of task, sets of valid values of parameters, as well as the set of restrictions describing the relations between tasks/subtasks and parameters and parameters and valid values of the parameters:

$$O = (T, IP, OP, I, E) \tag{1}$$

where *T* is set of tasks and subtasks, *IP* – set of input task parameters, *OP* – set of output task parameters, *I* – set of valid parameter values, *E* – restrictions on the parameters of the task and parameter domain.

Unlike task decomposition ontology containing relationships between task and their subtasks in explicit form (Ko, Lee & Lee, 2012), task composition ontology is implemented so that the relationships are implicit. Such principle of ontology structure allows, on the one hand, to specify tasks and subtasks in the same axiomatic form and, on the other hand, to derive task composition structure by reasoning tools. Thus, the proposed ontology opens the possibility to describe a number of different tasks in the same form and after that to construct a number of their compositions using appropriate criteria.

For the purpose of task composition ontology development the ontology language OWL 2 is used. The ontology is expressed by *ALC* description logic, which is decidable and has PSpace-complete complexity of concept satisfiability and ABox consistency (Baader et al., 2005) in the case when TBox is acyclic. In addition, SWRL-rules are specified for composition chain deriving. The main concepts of the ontology are *Task* and *Parameter*. The concept *Parameter* is used to describe a task semantically. The main requirement for TBox definition is that it shouldn't contain cyclic and multiple definitions, and must contain only concept definitions specified by class equivalence.

Figure 4. Task composition structure

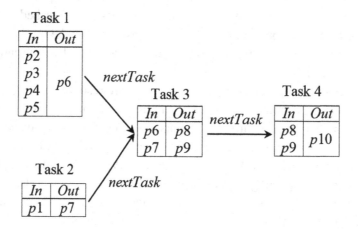

The task should have at least one input and one output parameter. The parameter taxonomy in the OWL 2 ontology is presented by a number of subclasses of the class *Parameter*. The type of parameters related to their input or output role are defined by appropriate role construct. The corresponding OWL 2 syntax expression is the Object Property. In the ontology, the appropriate object properties are *hasInputParameter* and *hasOutputParameter*. The domain of the properties is *Task* and the range – *Parameter*. Thereby the parameter could be input parameter of one task and output parameter of another. The task definition is expressed formally as follows:

$$T \equiv (\exists R.IP1 \sqcap \exists R.IP2 \ldots \sqcap \exists R.IPN)_{\sqcap}$$

$$(\exists R.OP1 \sqcap \exists R.OP2 \ldots {}_{\sqcap} \exists R.OPN) \tag{2}$$

where T is the task, IP_i – the input parameter subclass, OP_i – the input parameter subclass, R – the appropriate role. In other words, the task is defined solely by its input and output parameters.

The proposed task definition (2) is used for task composition process because in composition output parameters of one task are input for another. This relationship is used to construct task composition by the SWRL rule. The corresponding SWRL rule specifies input and output parameter match condition in the antecedent and if the antecedent condition is satisfied, infers the relationship *nextTask* between the respective tasks. This relationship essentially means that one task should be done after another. To encode this relationship in the ontology an object property has been created binding two tasks, where the domain is the predecessor task and range is the accessor one. Neither two tasks are connected by the property explicitly. The rule of task composition can be expressed as follows:

$$has InputParameter(?ta, ?p) \wedge has OutputParameter(?tb, ?p) \rightarrow nextTask(?tb, ?ta) \tag{3}$$

where h*asInputParameter*, h*asOutputParameter*, n*extTask* are the mentioned object properties, t*a* – the next task, t*b* – the previous task, p – the parameter.

The proposed rule (3) allows to deriving all task connections by the object property *nextTask*. The example of task composition is presented in Fig. 4. E.g., relationship *nextTask* is inferred between Task 1 and Task 3 because parameter *p*6 is input for Task 3 and output for Task 1, meaning that Task 3 can only be executed after Task 1.

The advantages of the described approach is that it allows to simplify task description (in comparison to the approaches where task/subtask relations are explicit) and to derive task compositions dynamically. The shortcomings are the possible deriving complexity and the lack of the support of alternative task compositions.

Subtask Distribution

The specifics of the distribution of tasks in cloud computing systems lies in the fact that the presence of a very large number of available computing resources, which are usually interchangeable (alternative) (Ergu et al., 2013; Kong, Zhang, Ye, 2017). The research is focused on the solution of specialized tasks (subtasks) that require certain competencies, which on the one hand narrows the range of resources capable of solving these subtasks, and on the other hand requires taking into account these competencies. Therefore, the algorithms used in this field cannot be used directly.

In the areas of distribution of tasks among the robots or agents that are most similar to those under consideration, the most common approach of instant distribution of tasks (instantaneous task allocation) (Sujit, George, Beard, 2008; Kim, Baik, Lee, 2015) focused on the dynamic uncertain environment. This approach involves tying tasks to resources that currently provide the maximum "benefit" according to the given priorities. This approach does not take into account that at some point all resources with the required competencies may be occupied. Thus, it is usually supplemented by some heuristics specific to a particular application area.

Let, A – is a task, which contains several subtasks a_i:

$$A = \{a_i\}, i \in \{1, ..., n\} \tag{4}$$

Let, O – is the vocabulary of competencies:

$$O = \{o_1, o_2, ..., o_m\} \tag{5}$$

Thus, the matrix of competencies required to accomplish subtasks can be defined as:

$$(ao_{i,j} \in \{0, 1, ..., 100\}), i \in \{1,..., n\}, j \in \{1,..., m\} \tag{6}$$

The set of human-computer cloud resources R is defined as:

$$R = \{r_1, r_2, ..., r_k\} \tag{7}$$

The set of resource characteristics (speed, cost, etc) C is defined as:

$$C = \{c_1, c_2, ..., c_l\} \tag{8}$$

Thus, each resource r_i is described by the following pair of competencies and characteristics vectors:

$$r_i = ((ro_{i,1}, ..., ro_{i,m}), (rc_{i,1}, ..., rc_{i,l})) \qquad (9)$$

where $i \in \{1, ..., n\}$, $ro_{i,j} \in \{0, ..., 100\}$ – is the value of competency j of the resource i, and $rc_{i,j}$ is the value of the characteristic j of the resource i.

The solution of the task A describes the distribution of work among system resources and is defined as:

$$S_A = (s_{i,j}), i \in \{1, ..., n\}, j \in \{1, ..., k\} \qquad (10)$$

where $s_{i,j} = 1$, if the resource j is used for solving subtask i, and $s_{i,j} = 0$ otherwise.

The objective function, which also performs normalization of various characteristics, is defined as follows:

$$F(S_A) = f(F_1(s_{1,1}, s_{2,1}, ..., s_{n,1}),$$

$$F_2(s_{1,2}, s_{2,2}, ..., s_{n,2}), ...,$$

$$F_k(s_{1,k}, s_{2,k}, ..., s_{n,k})) \to \min \qquad (11)$$

Specific formulas for calculating partial assignment efficiency (F_i) can use values of resource characteristics (e.g., speed or cost) $rc_{i,j}$, as well as competence values of both resources ($ro_{i,j}$) and subtasks ($ao_{i,j}$).

The minimization must be performed with respect to the following constraints. First, each subtask must be assigned to some resource:

$$\forall i: \sum_{j=1}^{k} s_{i,j} \geq 1 \qquad (12)$$

Second, assignment can only be done if the competency values of the resource are not less than the required competency values of the subtask:

$$\forall i,j,q: ((s_{i,j} = 1) \to (ro_{j,q} \geq ao_{i,q})) \qquad (13)$$

Instantaneous Distribution of Tasks Algorithm

Since the problem is NP-complete, it is not possible to solve it by an exhaustive search method in a reasonable time (provided that a real-world problem is solved). As a result of the analysis of existing methods it is proposed to use the approach of instantaneous task allocation.

With regard to the problem, the algorithm based on the approach of instantaneous distribution of tasks is as follows:

1. Take the first subtask from the existing ai, and exclude it from the set of subtasks A;
2. Select such resource *j* from the available resources to satisfy all conditions and $F(S_A) \rightarrow$ min, where $S_A = (s_{1,1} = 0, ..., s_{1,j} = 1, ..., s_{1,k} = 0)$;
3. If a suitable resource is not found, assume that the problem is unsolvable (the system does not have a resource that meets the required competencies);
4. Repeat steps starting from step 4 until set A is empty (i.e. all tasks are assigned to resources).

Multi-Agent Distribution of Tasks

There are two types of agents that are used to perform multi-agent modeling: the customer agent that is responsible for generating jobs and making the final decision, and the execution agents that represent the resources of the cloud environment and perform on-premises optimization for each resource. In the optimization process, agents form coalitions that change from step to step to improve the values of the objective function.

In the process of negotiations, agents of 3 roles are singled out: a member of the coalition (an agent belonging to the coalition), a leader of the coalition (an agent negotiating on behalf of the coalition) and an applicant (an agent who can become a member of the coalition).

At the beginning of the negotiations, each agent forms a separate coalition (SC, which has the structure of the *SA* solution), and becomes its leader. Suggestions of agents (tabular representation $F(s_{1,1}, s_{2,1}, ..., s_{n,1})$ are published in all available agents repository of information on the blackboard. At each stage of the negotiations, the agents analyze the proposals of other agents, and choose those whose proposals can improve the coalition: to solve a larger number of subtasks or the same number of subtasks but with a better value of the objective function ($F(SC) > F(SC')$, where SC is the current coalition, SC' – possible coalition). Coalition leaders make appropriate proposals to agents, and the latter decide whether to stay in the current coalition or move to the proposed one. The transition to the proposed coalition is considered if one of the above conditions is met: the proposed coalition can solve more subtasks than the current one, or the same number of subtasks, but with a better value of the objective function.

The process is terminated if at the next stage there is no changes in the composition of coalitions, after a specified time, when the permissible value of the objective function is reached.

APPLICATIONS IN TOURISM

Decision Support in Tourism

There are two different perspectives in the analysis of decision tasks (and, therefore, their support) in tourism: tourist's perspective, and DMO's perspective. Tourist usually deals with decisions about where to stay, how to travel, what points-of-interest (POIs) and in what sequence to attend and the like. The aim of a DMO is to be responsible for the planning and marketing of the tourist destination and to have the power and resources to organize infrastructures, local stakeholders and their relationships. There are many definitions of a tourist destination, but informally, every place to visit may be considered as a destination. Hence, as a result of DMO's activity, destination offers a combination of tourism products and services under a brand of the destination (Ritchie & Crouch, 2003).

Usually, these perspectives are discussed separately. There are papers focused on tourist decision support (Yu, 2005; Kulakov et al., 2016; Masron, Ismail & Marzuki, 2016; Korzun et al., 2016), and there are papers focused on decision support for DMO (Baggio & Caporarello, 2008). That makes sense, because types of decisions taken by these groups are completely different. However, the information that is taken into account by these groups of users largely intersects. For example, both groups are interested in visiting statistics – but the kinds of decisions taken based on this statistics are different: tourists find the most popular places that are "must see", but DMOs use this information to identify places that need promotion and some marketing actions. Another example of information used by both groups is visitor opinions. Therefore, there are some low level functions (such as data collection and processing, opinion monitoring) that are useful for both groups.

In the previous work (Smirnov et al., 2016), the authors have analyzed the list of typical functional requirements for both tourists and destination management organizations. One of the outcomes of the analysis of the main decision support functions from the both perspectives is that human-based services play an important role in both of them. The most obvious, is that humans are a valuable source of information about current situation, thus making a solid contribution to situation awareness required for decision-making. Not that obvious is the fact that human contributors may also participate in the provisioning of some services other than simple feedback, for example, there are some experimental systems, where itinerary planning is performed with the help of human contributors either in the form of user-generated content (as in Mygola, Tripoto, TripHobo services), or in the form of online real-time crowd activity (Zhang, 2012). However, these human-based services require different characteristics from a contributor (a human, providing a service). For various kinds of feedback and evaluation, a human should be a tourist, who recently interacted with an object, because that is the entire idea of collaborative recommendation – complex evaluation of an object by a person who is similar to you. From the point of DMOs it is also interesting how the destination (and its attractions and services) are evaluated by the consumers. For planning services or on-line help service local expertise is a primary requirement. It can be found either among local citizens, or among some experienced tourists. There also are services that do not require neither complex evaluation from the consumer perspective, nor local expertise – usually it is provisioning of some factual information of performing context-free information processing operations.

Another outcome of the use case analysis is that several functions of the two perspectives actually are quite close. For example, measuring tourist satisfaction is performed by DMOs, but is also performed by tourists during selection of the destination to visit or specific tourist attractions. That supports the original idea of putting both kinds of decision support on one platform, leveraging reuse of some core services.

Situation Awareness

It can be noticed, both from the analysis of the decision support tasks provided, as well as from decision support literature, that one of the core functions in most decision support systems is the collecting data about the state of the system and its dynamics. These data then may be processed to form convenient and informative visual representations (in "reporting" and data-driven decision support systems), used to build and verify models of different parts of the problem domain (in model-based decision support systems), provided as an input for inference engines of knowledge-based decision support systems to obtain some cues about what can be done. In some sense, decision support is about collecting relevant data about the problem domain, structuring it, and then employing various techniques to make use of these data.

In the domain, where man is the measure of all things, both for tourists who are interested in the behavior of likeminded tourists, and for DMOs whose aim is to change the destination to make it more appealing for visitors, an important source of input data is the data provided by humans. That makes participatory sensing and crowdsensing scenarios highly relevant for the human-computer cloud being developed. Specifically, a human-computer cloud that is aimed on decision support in tourism must (in some sense) support participatory sensing and crowdsensing scenarios.

Support of Business Travelers

For organizations whose business processes significantly rely on business trips of their employees, business trip resilience and business trip risk management are important parts of a holistic approach to business process resilience (Dolan, 2018). It means that an organization should be able to react to any changes in the environment (possibly in countries/regions where there even no regular offices of that organization) that may influence well-being of the employees and their effectiveness in performing business responsibilities.

Increasing importance of this problem is supported by various analytical reports. E.g., according to Ipsos MORI Global Business Resilience Trends Watch 2018, 63% of business decision-makers perceive travel risks to have increased in 2017. At the same time, only 9% of organizations updated their sustainability program to include travel risk policy (Ipsos, 2018).

The key of reaching resilience is identification of influences and quickly adapting to them. In the technological sense, one important perspective of changes is availability of computing infrastructure and variation of computing resource utilization (that can be caused by different external factors). These changes can be addressed with a help of conventional cloud computing technology, which provides means to elastically manage the computing capacity consumed by business processes (Mell, Grance, 2011) and various redundancy schemes allowing to minimize negative effects of hardware outage. However, there is much more in business resilience than flexible computational resource scaling in response to the environment. Another significant aspect of adaptability and resilience is human resource capacity limitations, which may in some situations restrict the possible profit (e.g., may simply lack required human resources to quickly react to some change in the environment and make profit of it).

Taking into account limitations of crowdsourcing applicability (e.g., requirement of some specific expertise, sensitive data processing) and factors influencing the possibility of crowdsourcing, first, a set of particular tasks of travel risk management that were implemented as human-based applications was mostly limited to information-collection tasks, second, the private-public human-computer cloud approach was proposed.

The proposed approach touches Risk monitoring (RMON) and Risk assessment (RA) process areas of Travel Risk Management Maturity Model (TRM3) (TRM3, 2012) developed by Global Business Travel Association (GBTA) partnered with iJET Intelligent Risk Systems. Specifically, the proposed solution will help to reach Level 3 according to this maturity model in the process area of Risk monitoring.

GBTA Europe Risk Committee has recently identified five pillars of travel risk management (GBTA, 2017):

1. A business travel health, safety and security policy. Most companies already have a safety and security policy in place, but every company needs a specific set of policies around business travel.
2. Travel safety and security information. Companies must base their advice off of reliable travel information, both of which should be relayed to travelers before they embark on a trip.
3. Restrictions on travel to higher risk countries. You must have a plan for controlling travel to high-risk countries. Companies may define high-risk differently based on their corporate risk appetite.
4. Knowing where your people are. In the case of a safety, security or health incident, you must be able to reach out to your travelers to ensure their safety and offer support.
5. An incident and crisis management plan for when things go wrong.

The Ipsos Report (Ipsos, 2018) also confirms that many companies have recently undertaken some steps that go well with the activity areas above:

- Introduced pre-trip and during trip advisory emails (39%).
- Included travel risk assessment in travel approval process (37%).
- Implemented travel safety training and security training (33%).
- Provided annual health check-up's (32%).
- Updated travel risk policy (excluding diversity related issues) (31%).

To build effective policies around business travel (task 1), prepare safety and security instructions (task 2) as well as an incident and crisis management plans (task 5) the organization (represented by a responsible role) has to have reliable, complete and up-to-date information about possible threats. The proposed roles of HCC-based applications are primarily concentrated around collecting such information from local experts and recent travelers to the destination. On the other hand, Travel Risk Management Maturity Model specifies several activities and processes (e.g. Risk monitoring) that must be done in the recurring basis and require access to actual information about business trip destination.

Besides, in case something unexpected happens while an employee is on the trip, he/she might need information support accounting for the new situation. And that may also be simpler for persons with local knowledge. Therefore, there are basically two scenarios human-based information collection applications are used in business trip management: pre-trip risk assessment and on-trip support.

Architecture Adaptations

This subsection briefly describes the adaptations of the general architecture presented in the previous section to the tourism application domain. These adaptations touch the list of actors and the list of application services provided by the cloud environment.

The generic list of actors described earlier is concretized with the specific actors and roles typical to the tourist domain. The relationship between generic actor types and domain-specific actors are presented in Fig. 5.

DMO representatives play two roles, first, they are involved in tourist service development, second, they use application services to monitor and control the status of local tourism.

Figure 5. Tourism-specific actors

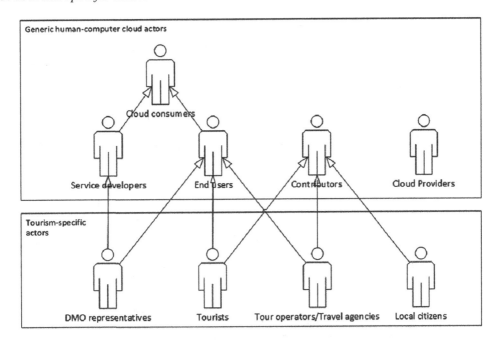

Tourists are mostly consumers of various applications and services provided by the cloud (its SaaS level), but they also can participate as contributors, especially in various evaluation scenarios initiated by the DMO representatives or provide subjective evaluation of various locations/facilities and events to other tourists.

Tour operators/travel agencies access various end user services and applications (acting on behalf of a tourist), but can also provide various services. For example, a tourist can choose whether he/she will use an automated trip planning service, or a trip planning service provided by some travel agency.

Finally, local citizens mostly act as contributors, sharing their local and language expertise.

It can be seen, that the generic role of Cloud providers was not matched to any domain specific roles. Main reason is that the human-computer cloud being developed is not problem-specific itself. Therefore, cloud provider doesn't have to be connected to a specific domain. Its role is to provide infrastructure, management services, maintenance and the service level according to agreement with consumers.

The list of application services relevant to the domain of tourism can be divided into two groups: core services, that implement some general operations, and specific services, exposed to end users.

Core services include the profile management service representing a centralized storage of user's history and preferences, and the local context service. A user may define what information of his/her profile can be accessed by other services in different queries (personalized or anonymized). Local context service provides various information about current situation in the selected area.

Application services include attraction information and recommendation services, itinerary planning, local transport information, etc.

Due to privacy issues and possible presence of sensitive information, usage of external human resources (i.e., crowdsourcing as one of the cloud resources) may be limited. However, it doesn't apply to the internal human resources of the organization. Therefore, for such scenarios the so-called hybrid

Figure 6. Illustration of the human-computer cloud-based decision support in a business process

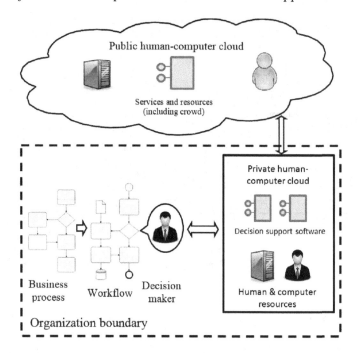

cloud model becomes reasonable, where all the resources are divided into private (on-premise) cloud and public (external) cloud. In case of traditional computing resources, directly accessible private cloud reduces time and latency compared to access to public resources, besides, private cloud may cover average workload, retaining the ability to use public resources, when it is needed. Hybrid HCC inherits all those features, but has one more. Private cloud contains a pool of unique human resources that can be used with much less restrictions then those from the outside. Uniqueness of these resources is due to the fact that members of the private cloud are actually employees of the organization with all legal and practical consequences, e.g., they are enforced to obey non-disclosure agreement, and they may be more familiar with the context of each particular task. It puts human resource scheduler of the private cloud very close to the workflow engine (e.g., BPEL- or BPMN-based), but modelling all the human resources (private and public) as cloud resources allows to build a unified scheduler. I.e., a single scheduler 'faced' with some request that contains a sensitive data may allocate resources from the private cloud, but 'faced' with some request that doesn't contain sensitive data may automatically allocate resources from public cloud, automatically resorting to 'crowdsourcing'. This is only possible if resources of the both clouds are described in the same form and provide aligned APIs.

The decision support assumes delegation of tasks to a cloud consisting of both (a) IT tools, which can provide information for decision support (decision support systems), provide recommendations (recommendation systems) or even do some decision making (expert systems); and (b) company (and outer) experts, who can either assist in decision making or make the required decisions. Therefore, all the three cloud layers are present in the architecture. Infrastructure-as-a-Service (IaaS) layer is formed by computing, storage and human resources, that can be used in the process of decision support. Platform-as-a-Service (PaaS) layer is not explicitly depicted in Fig. 6, but it is formed by the intermediary services allowing to build end-user applications. Finally, the Software-as-a-Service (SaaS) layer that is represented by different forms of decision support software.

Scenarios

Itinerary Planning

Creating an itinerary is a typical task performed by tourists or by travel agencies. As this is an end user functionality, it is to be implemented in a SaaS layer, moreover, there might be several concurrent implementations of itinerary planning services, provided by various vendors, with different characteristics (price, time etc.). There may be different implementations of this task. This paper focuses on the demonstration of an itinerary planning service that makes full use of human part of human-computer cloud environment. Input for this service includes:

- tourist destination, where local itinerary is to be built;
- time constraints, specified as absolute timestamps of the time frame that should contain the itinerary. Absolute time stamps may be useful to consider inclusion in the itinerary of some unique events that might occur in the specified destination;
- tourist preferences (shared portions of the information contained in tourist information profile and additional requirements) including places a tourist would like to see, those he/she already seen, general interests etc.

The itinerary service is built using database service and human workflow services provided by the cloud platform. The database service is used to store accepted (and probably high quality) itineraries made for different users in the past, and the human workflow service is used to define an Iterative-Improvement scheme for itineraries being composed. Besides, the itinerary planning service uses some of the core application services, e.g. local context service (providing current and predicted information about weather, traffic situation etc.).

Itinerary service first enriches the incoming request with local context, supplied by local context service, then looks up in the database past accepted itineraries for users with similar preferences and in similar contexts, and finally via human workflow service allocates several contributors (both among past tourists and local citizens) to review and possibly improve candidate itineraries.

Surveys

This simplified scenario corresponds to measuring travel motivators activity typically performed by DMOs. The idea is that DMOs may want to ask some questions to tourists recently visited destination or some particular attractions (and therefore, this activity is also related to the last phase of a tourist's trip). To do this, an opinion monitoring in the application layer can be used. Opinion monitoring service also uses human workflow service provided by the cloud platform, but workflow here is quite simplistic – just collect the required number feedbacks from contributors without any processing. The selection of contributors is performed by resource management service, based on survey query and extensive information about contributors (which includes areas of expertise and, most important for this scenario, travel history).

IMPLEMENTATION

A research prototype of a cloud environment based on the proposed models and methods has been developed. In particular, two cloud computing models were implemented: platform-as-a-service (PaaS) and software-as-a-service (SaaS). The platform provides the developers of applications that require human knowledge and skills with a set of tools for designing, deploying, executing and monitoring such applications. The SaaS model is represented by an intelligent decision support service (referred to as René) that organizes (human-computer) resource networks for on-the-fly tasks through ontology-based task decomposition and subtasks distribution among the resources (human participants and software services).

The prototype environment comprises several components: 1) a server-side code that performs all the resource management activities and provides a set of application program interfaces (APIs), 2) a set of command line utilities that run on the computers of appropriate categories of users (platform administrator, developer, administrator of IDSS) and by accessing the API, enable to implement the main scenarios necessary for these users, 3) Web-applications for participants and decision makers. Also, it is possible to implement the interface of the participant for an Android-based mobile device.

The prototype environment interacts with social networks (ResearchGate, LinkedIn) to build and refine a participant competence profile. Also, the environment interacts with the applications deployed on it, providing them certain services (for instance, request human-participants, data warehouses, etc.).

Because at the heart of each application that uses human resources (HBA, human-based application), there is software code that provides a specific interface to the end users of this application, the open source platform Flynn (Flynn) is chosen to support deployment and execution of this code. The capabilities of the platform are extended with special functions (registration of participants, an ontological-oriented search for participants, a mechanism for supporting digital contracts).

The intelligent decision support service (IDSS) is an application deployed in the human-computer cloud environment and using the functions provided by the environment (for instance, to organize interactions with participants). Main functions of the IDSS are: 1) decomposition of the task that the decision maker deals with into subtasks using the task ontology and inference engine that supports OWL ontology language and SWRL-rules (for instance, Pellet, HermiT, etc.); 2) allocation of the subtasks to participants based on coalition games. The IDSS provides REST API to interact with the platform.

The architecture of IDSS (Fig. 7), in its turn, can be divided into several logical layers:

- The Data Access Layer is a series of DAO abstractions that use the JPA standard for object-relational mapping of data model classes (Domain model) that perform the simplest CRUD operations using ORM Hibernate and implemented using Spring Data.
- The Business Logic Layer of the application is represented by two main services: the task decomposition service and the workflow distribution service. The task decomposition service operates with an ontology, described using the ontology description language OWL 2, which includes rules in SWRL and SQWRL. Knowledge output (task decomposition) is carried out using inference engines (Pellet, HermiT, and others). To extract data from ontology, Jena APIs are used for ontologies recorded using OWL/RDF syntax using the SPARQL query language and OWL API for other ontology scenarios (changing ontology structure, managing individuals, logical inference). The workflow building service provides support for the coalition game of agents of the human-machine computing platform agents.

Figure 7. IDSS implementation

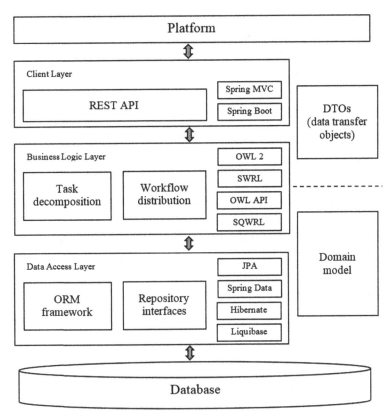

- At the Client Layer, REST API services are implemented for interacting with the platform, providing an interface for interacting with the platform and indirect user interaction.

EVALUATION

An experimental evaluation of the research prototype has been carried out. As the functionality of the application of the problem-oriented IDSS built according to the proposed approach is determined by the task ontology (namely, the basic tasks represented in this ontology and their input and output parameters), a task ontology for the e-tourism domain has been developed (specifically, for building tourist itineraries). In the experiments, dynamic task networks (for building tourist itineraries) did actually organize, and their execution resulted in valid lists of itineraries.

To evaluate the performance, the developed software was deployed at the computing nodes of the local network of the research laboratory (an access to the server components from the Internet was also provided). 34 people were registered as participants available for task assignment. An ontology to describe the competences of resources (and the requirements for competences of deployable applications requiring human participation) representing 46 basic competences was used. With the experimental parameters (performance of hardware resources, number of participants, size of the competence ontology), the application deployment time differed from the application deployment time in the Flynn core cloud environment slightly (by 3-7%). The increase in time is inevitable, because when deploying an application, in addition to creating Docker containers, compiling and launching an application (performed by Flynn), additionally a semantic search of participants is carried out using the competence ontology s and the comparison of digital contracts. However, due to this slight increase in application deployment time, the applications deployed in the implemented cloud environment gain an opportunity to access human resources. In the future, most of the operations related to the resolution of application dependencies on human resources can be performed in the background, which will save the deployment time at the level of the cloud environment.

The task ontology in the electronic tourism domain, represented in the OWL 2 language corresponding to the description logic of ALCR (D) and containing 293 axioms and 40 classes, was used for testing the IDSS. In the course of the load testing, an attempt was made to build a network of resources for the task of building a tourist route (the network assumes the fulfillment of 6 subtasks). The time of task decomposition and network construction obtained as a result of averaging over 25 tests is, on average, 1157 ms (994 ms takes the task decomposition, 163 ms takes the allocation of the subtasks to resources). It should be noted that this time only takes into account the task decomposition and the resource network organization, and does not take into account the time spent by the software services and participants on solving the subtasks assigned to them.

CONCLUSION

The chapter describes a novel human-computer cloud approach, the gist of which is to standardize human resources allocation in the manner of conventional cloud resources allocation to streamline the development of applications leveraging human information processing capabilities.

Two main components of the human-computer environment are platform, allowing to develop and deploy in the cloud human based applications, and decision support service based on dynamic resource network configuration. A unifying feature of the proposed approach is the use of ontologies for resource description and ontological mechanisms on different layers of the cloud environment. First, thanks to formal matching techniques the use of ontologies allow to reuse human resources between different applications, second, the capabilities of modern inference techniques allow to build an ad hoc decision support services employing automatic task decomposition on top of the resource management cloud layers.

The chapter also shows how some of the decision support scenarios in e-tourism can be implemented with a help of the proposed human-computer cloud concept.

ACKNOWLEDGMENT

This research was supported by the Russian Science Foundation [grant number 16-11-10253].

REFERENCES

Ahmad, S. (2011). The jabberwocky programming environment for structured social computing. *Proceedings of the 24th annual ACM symposium on User interface software and technology - UIST '11*, 53–64. 10.1145/2047196.2047203

Androcec, D., Vrcek, N., & Seva, J. (2012). Cloud computing ontologies: A systematic review. *MOPAS 2012 : The Third International Conference on Models and Ontology-based Design of Protocols, Architectures and Services*, 9–14.

Baader, F., Milicic, M., Lutz, C., Sattler, U., & Wolter, F. (2005). *Integrating description logics and action formalisms for reasoning about web services*. LTCS-Report 05-02, Chair for Automata Theory, Institute for Theoretical Computer Science, Dresden University of Technology. Retrieved from http://lat.inf.tu-dresden.de/research/reports.html

Baggio, R., & Caporarello, L. (2008). *Decision support systems in a tourism destination: literature survey and model building*. Retrieved from http://www.iby.it/turismo/papers/baggio-dss-tourism.pdf

Barta, R., Feilmayr, C., Pröll, B., Grün, C., & Werthner, H. (2009). Covering the Semantic Space of Tourism: An Approach Based on Modularized Ontologies. *Proceedings of the 1st Workshop on Context, Information and Ontologies*.

Bellini, P., Cenni, D., & Nesi, P. (2016). Cloud Knowledge Modeling and Management. In Encyclopedia of Cloud Computing. Chichester, UK: John Wiley & Sons, Ltd. doi:10.1002/9781118821930.ch52

Berka, T., & Plößnig, M. (2004). Designing recommender systems for tourism. *ENTER*. Retrieved from http://195.130.87.21:8080/dspace/handle/123456789/583

Calinescu, R., Camara, J., & Paterson, C. (2019). Socio-Cyber-Physical Systems: Models, Opportunities, Open Challenges. *2019 IEEE/ACM 5th International Workshop on Software Engineering for Smart Cyber-Physical Systems (SEsCPS)*.

Choi, C., Cho, M., Choi, J., & Hwang, M. (2009). Travel ontology for Intelligent Recommendation System. *Proc. of the 3rd Asia International Conference on Modelling and Simulation*, 637–642.

Distefano, S., Merlino, G., & Puliafito, A. (2012). SAaaS: A framework for volunteer-based sensing clouds. *Parallel and Cloud Computing*, *1*(2), 21–33.

Dolan, R. (2018). *Four Reasons Why Travel Risk Management is a Business Imperative*. Retrieved from https://www.concur.com/newsroom/article/four-reasons-why-travel-risk-management-is-a-business-imperative

Dustdar, S., & Bhattacharya, K. (2011). The social compute unit. *IEEE Internet Computing*, *15*(3), 64–69. doi:10.1109/MIC.2011.68

Ergu, D., Kou, G., Peng, Y., Shi, Y., & Shi, Y. (2013). The analytic hierarchy process: Task scheduling and resource allocation in cloud computing environment. *The Journal of Supercomputing*, *64*(3), 835–848. doi:10.100711227-011-0625-1

Euzenat, J., & Shvaiko, P. (2013). *Ontology Matching* (2nd ed.). Berlin: Springer-Verlag. doi:10.1007/978-3-642-38721-0

Faulkner, M., Cheng, M. H., Krause, A., Clayton, R., Heaton, T., Chandy, K. M., ... Olson, M. (2014). Community Sense and Response Systems: Your Phone as Quake Detector. *Communications of the ACM*, *57*(7), 66–75. doi:10.1145/2622633

Flynn. (n.d.). Retrieved from http://flynn.com

Fodor, O., & Werthner, H. (2005). Harmonise: A Step toward an Interoperable E-Tourism Merketplace. *International Journal of Electronic Commerce*, *9*(2), 11-39.

Formisano, C., Pavia, D., & Gurgen, L. (2015). The advantages of IoT and cloud applied to smart cities. *3rd International Conference Future Internet of Things and Cloud*, 325-332. 10.1109/FiCloud.2015.85

Franzoni, C., & Sauermann, H. (2014). Crowd science: The organization of scientific research in open collaborative projects. *Research Policy*, *43*(1), 1–20. doi:10.1016/j.respol.2013.07.005

GBTA. (2017). *The Five Pillars of Travel Risk Management*. Retrieved from https://www.gbta.org/blog/the-five-pillars-of-travel-risk-management/

Geonames Geographical Database. (n.d.). Retrieved from www.geonames.org/

Gretzel, U. (2011). Intelligent systems in tourism: A social science perspective. *Annals of Tourism Research*, *38*(3), 757–779. doi:10.1016/j.annals.2011.04.014

Gretzel, U., Reino, S., Kopera, S., & Koo, C. (2015). Smart tourism challenges. *Journal of Tourism*, *16*(1), 41–47.

Gruber, T. R. (1993). A translation approach to portable ontology specifications. *Knowledge Acquisition*, *5*(2), 199–220. doi:10.1006/knac.1993.1008

Guizzardi, G. (2005). *Ontological foundations for structural conceptual models* (Ph.D. thesis). Universiteit Twente.

Hozdic, E. (2019). Socio-Cyber-Physical Systems Alternative for Traditional Manufacturing Structures. *New Technologies, Development and Application II. Lecture Notes in Networks and Systems*, *76*, 15–24. doi:10.1007/978-3-030-18072-0_2

Ipsos MORI Global Business Resilience Trends Watch. (2018). Retrieved from https://www.business-wire.com/news/home/20171114005920/en/Organisations-Strides-Planning-Unknown-Risk-Perception-Remains

Kamar, E. (2012). Combining human and machine intelligence in large-scale crowdsourcing. *Proceedings of the 11th International Conference on Autonomous Agents and Multiagent Systems*.

Kim, M.H., Baik, H., & Lee, S. (2015). *Resource welfare based task allocation for UAV team with resource*. Academic Press.

Ko, R. K. L., Lee, E. W., & Lee, S. G. (2012). BusinessOWL (BOWL) - a hierarchical task network ontology for dynamic business process decomposition and formulation. *IEEE Transactions on Services Computing, 5*(2), 246–259. doi:10.1109/TSC.2011.48

Kochhar, S. (2010). The anatomy of a large-scale human computation engine. *Proceedings of the ACM SIGKDD Workshop on Human Computation - HCOMP '10.* 10.1145/1837885.1837890

Kong, Y., Zhang, M., & Ye, D. (2017). A belief propagation-based method for task allocation in open and dynamic cloud environments. *Knowledge-Based Systems, 115,* 123–132. doi:10.1016/j.knosys.2016.10.016

Korzun, D. G., Marchenkov, S. A., Vdovenko, A. S., & Petrina, O. B. (2016). A Semantic Approach to Designing Information Services for Smart Museums. *International Journal of Embedded and Real-Time Communication Systems, 7*(2), 15–34. doi:10.4018/IJERTCS.2016070102

Kulakov, K., Petrina, P., Korzun, D., & Varfolomeyev, A. (2016). Towards an understanding of smart service: the case study for cultural heritage e-Tourism. *Proceedings of the 18th Conference of FRUCT Association,* 145-152. 10.1109/FRUCT-ISPIT.2016.7561520

Lamanna, D. D., Skene, J., & Emmerich, W. (2003). SLAng: A language for defining service level agreements. *Proc. of the 9th IEEE Workshop on Future Trends in Distributed Computing Systems-FTDCS,* 100-106. 10.1109/FTDCS.2003.1204317

Little, G., Chilton, L. B., Goldman, M., & Miller, R. C. (2010). Exploring iterative and parallel human computation processes. *Proceedings of the ACM SIGKDD Workshop on Human Computation,* 68–76. 10.1145/1837885.1837907

Livieri, B. (2015). Ontology-based modeling of cloud services: Challenges and perspectives. PoEM (Short Papers). *CEUR Workshop Proceedings, 1497,* 61–70.

Ludwig, H., Keller, A., & Dan, A. (2003). *Web Service Level Agreement (WSLA) Language Specification.* Retrieved from http://www.research.ibm.com/wsla/WSLASpecV1-20030128.pdf

Masron, T., Ismail, N., & Marzuki, A. (2016). The conceptual design and application of web-based tourism decision support systems. *Theoretical and Empirical Researches in Urban Management, 11*(2), 64–75.

Meier, P. (2017). *How Crisis Mapping Saved Lives in Haiti.* Retrieved from http://voices.nationalgeographic.com/2012/07/02/crisis-mapping-haiti/

Mell, P., & Grance, T. (2011). *The NIST definition of cloud computing.* Recommendations of the National Institute of Standards and Technology, NIST Special Publication 800-145.

Merlino, G., Arkoulis, S., Distefano, S., Papagianni, C., Puliafito, A., & Papavassiliou, S. (2016). Mobile crowdsensing as a service: A platform for applications on top of sensing clouds. *Future Generation Computer Systems, 56,* 623–639. doi:10.1016/j.future.2015.09.017

OWL 2 Web Ontology Language Document Overview. (n.d.). (2nd ed.). Retrieved from https://www.w3.org/TR/owl2-overview/

Park, H., Yoon, A., & Kwon, H.-C. (2012). Task Model and Task Ontology for Intelligent Tourist Information Service. *International Journal of u- and e- Service Science and Technology, 5*(2), 43–57.

Ponomarev, A., & Parfenov, V. (2015). Verification-Enabling Interaction Model for Services in Smart Space: a TAIS Case. *Proceedings of the 17th Conference of the Open Innovations Association FRUCT*, 163-172. 10.1109/FRUCT.2015.7117988

Ra, M. (2012). Medusa: a programming framework for crowd-sensing applications categories and subject descriptors. *Proceedings of the 10th international conference on Mobile systems, applications, and services MobiSys '12*, 337–350. 10.1145/2307636.2307668

Scekic, O., Miorandi, D., Schiavinotto, T., Diochnos, D. I., Hume, A., Chenu-Abente, R., . . . Giunchiglia, F. (2015). SmartSociety – A Platform for Collaborative People-Machine Computation. *The 8th IEEE International Conference on Service Oriented Computing & Applications (SOCA'15)*.

Sengupta, B., Jain, A., Bhattacharya, K., Truong, H.-L., & Dustdar, S. (2013). Collective problem solving using social compute units. *International Journal of Cooperative Information Systems*, 22(4), 1341002. doi:10.1142/S0218843013410025

Shamir, L., Diamond, D., & Wallin, J. (2016). Leveraging Pattern Recognition Consistency Estimation for Crowdsourcing Data Analysis. *IEEE Transactions on Human-Machine Systems*, 46(3), 474–480. doi:10.1109/THMS.2015.2463082

Sheth, A., & Ranabahu, A. (2010a). Semantic Modeling for Cloud Computing, Part 1. *IEEE Internet Computing*, 14(3), 81–83. doi:10.1109/MIC.2010.77

Sheth, A., & Ranabahu, A. (2010b). Semantic Modeling for Cloud Computing, Part 2. *IEEE Internet Computing*, 14(4), 81–84. doi:10.1109/MIC.2010.98

Smirnov, A., Kashevnik, A., & Ponomarev, A. (2017). Context-based Infomobility System for Cultural Heritage Recommendation: Tourist Assistant—TAIS. *Personal and Ubiquitous Computing*, 21(2), 297–311. doi:10.100700779-016-0990-0

Smirnov, A., Ponomarev, A., Levashova, T., & Teslya, N. (2016a). Human-Computer Cloud for Decision Support in Tourism: Approach and Architecture. *Proceedings of the 19th FRUCT Conference*, 226-235. Retrieved from https://www.w3.org/TR/rdf-sparql-query/

Smirnov, A., Ponomarev, A., Levashova, T., & Teslya, N. (2016b). Decision Support in Tourism Based on Human-Computer Cloud. *Proceedings of the 18th International Conference on Information Integration and Web-based Applications & Services (iiWAS2016)*, 127-134. 10.1145/3011141.3011174

Sujit, P., George, G., & Beard, R. (2008). Multiple UAV coalition formation. *Proceedings of the American Control Conference*, 2008, 2010–2015.

Teslya, N., & Ponomarev, A. (2016). Smart Tourism Destination Support Scenario Based on Human-Computer Cloud. *Proceedings of the 19th FRUCT Conference*, 242-247. 10.23919/FRUCT.2016.7892207

TRM3. (2012). *Travel Risk Management Maturity Model (TRM3)*. Retrieved from https://www.ijet.com/sites/default/files/WP_TRM3_May2012.pdf

UNWTO. (2016). *World Tourism Organization: UNWTO Tourism Highlights 2016 Edition*. Retrieved from http://cf.cdn.unwto.org/sites/all/files/pdf/unwto_highlights16_en_hr.pdf

Ushahidi. (n.d.). Retrieved from http://www.ushahidi.com/

Wang, P., Yang, L., Li, J., Chen, J., & Hu, S. (2019). Data fusion in cyber-physical-social systems: State-of-the-art and perspectives. *Information Fusion, 51*, 42–57. doi:10.1016/j.inffus.2018.11.002

Yu, C. C. (2005). Personalized and community decision support in eTourism Intermediaries. Database and Expert Systems Applications. DEXA 2005. *Lecture Notes in Computer Science, 3588*, 900–909. doi:10.1007/11546924_88

Zhang, H. (2012). *Computational environment design* (PhD thesis). Harvard University.

Chapter 9
Smart Museum:
Semantic Approach to Generation and Presenting Information of Museum Collections

Svetlana E. Yalovitsyna

🆔 https://orcid.org/0000-0001-5024-6357

Institute of Linguistics, Literature, and History, Karelian Research Centre of the Russian Academy of Sciences, Russia

Valentina V. Volokhova

🆔 https://orcid.org/0000-0001-5486-7740

Petrozavodsk State University, Russia

Dmitry G. Korzun

🆔 https://orcid.org/0000-0003-1723-5247

Petrozavodsk State University, Russia

ABSTRACT

The chapter presents the authors' study on the smart museum concept. Semantic Web technology and ontology modeling methods are applied to construct advanced digital services, supporting the study and evolution of museum collections. The concept aims at significant increase of the information impact of museum exhibits by providing augmented annotations, identifying semantic relations, assisting the visitors to follow individual trajectories in exposition study, finding relevant information, opening the collection to knowledge from visitors. A museum collection is advanced to a knowledge base where new information is created and evolved by museum visitors and personnel. The chapter discusses reference information assistance services, which are oriented for use as mobile applications on users' smartphones. The proof-of-the-concept case study is the History Museum of Petrozavodsk State University. The pilot implementation demonstrates the feasibility of the smart museum concept in respect to the user mobility, service personalization, and collaborative work opportunity.

DOI: 10.4018/978-1-7998-1974-5.ch009

INTRODUCTION

Nowadays, the museum digitalization is a topical area for applying information and communication technology. Various information services are constructed to extend the value of existing museum collections. A typical museum collection is implemented as a database for storing descriptions on exhibits. This way, the museum information system stores the information part of collection to keep all knowledge related to and about cultural and historical heritage objects (exhibits). The basic function is an electronic archive (catalogue). Its digital extensions lead to "smart services", emphasizing a certain intelligence level in information search for and delivery to the users.

As we sequentially elaborated previously (Korzun, Marchenkov, Vdovenko, & Petrina, 2016; Petrina, Korzun, Volokhova, Yalovitsyna, & Varfolomeyev, 2017; Korzun, Yalovitsyna, & Volokhova, 2018; Yalovitsyna, Volokhova, & Korzun, 2019), the Internet of Things (IoT) enables advancing a museum information system to "a smart space" where visitors and personnel operate in the shared service-oriented information-centric environment. In particular, study activity of visitors is involved to the museum processes, hence opening many possibilities to engage the museum visitors with exhibits and available descriptive information. This chapter summarizes the authors' smart museum concept in order to form a semantic service-oriented approach to generating and presenting information of museum collections.

The semantic approach introduces an additional layer on the top of museum information system (the semantic layer). (Marchenkov, Vdovenko, Petrina, & Korzun, 2016) The layer maintains a semantic network of available digitalized descriptions (meaningful information fragments). The semantic layer connects the involved actors (museum personnel and visitors) with the physical exposition. The museum collection becomes not just a large database, where information is consumed in the traditional passive style (visitors are walking around exhibits and reading information from the database). Instead, the museum provides a digital environment where all fragments of the museum exposition become semantically related, leading to easy use and further elaboration by visitors and museum personnel.

To implement the semantic layer, the Semantic Web technology and ontology modeling methods are applied. The semantic network is represented based on the Semantic MediaWiki (SMW) technique (Krötzsch & Vrandečić, 2011). Nodes in the semantic networks are wiki-pages where information representation follows a specific format, both human- and machine- readable. Each page is augmented with semantic information in the form of tags (keywords) and links to other pages. As a result, one can search information based on keywords and connection structure, similarly as information study happens in web browsing in the Internet. This kind of information search is advanced with information ranking when a small set of the most relevant information is provided among many appropriate information fragments. The advance also follows the web technology, where the search results are sorted in accordance with certain priorities to the user (e.g., the well-known PageRank algorithm).

Our proof-of-the-concept case study is the History Museum of Petrozavodsk State University (the History Museum of PetrSU), where the focus is on everyday life history. The pilot implementation considers the following reference museum information services: 1) Visit service to support the visitor with personalized exhibition study plan, 2) Exhibition service to support the visitor with personalized delivery of knowledge on a given exhibit, and 3) Enrichment service to support the museum with a tool for extracting knowledge from visitors.

The goal of this chapter is to summarize the own authors' experience in the development of smart museum concept. The semantic approach is presented to generating and presenting information of museum collections. The presentation is structured as follows. First, to overview the existing IoT-enabled background related to smart museums. Second, to analyze the key problems of semantic layer construction on the top of a museum information system. Third, to elaborate appropriate models of Semantic Web to apply to creation of the semantic layer. Fourth, to discuss possible ranking algorithm to search the most relevant information in the museum collection. Then we summarize the key solutions and recommendations in the smart museum concept, overview possible future research directions, and conclude the chapter.

BACKGROUND

A traditional museum has a database or a museum information system, which serves as an electronic archive or catalogue, e.g., see (Kuflik, Wecker, Lanir, & Stock, 2015). Information access functions of the visitors are very limited (i.e., a kind of browsing). The Internet of Things (IoT) drastically changes this traditional way of visitor activity in museums (Chianese & Piccialli, 2014). Physical exhibits (as things) are transformed to IoT objects. The act as smart entities, i.e., providing information about themselves or even directly interacting with visitors and other objects, similarly as it happens in many IoT-based systems (Atzori, Iera, & Morabito, 2014; Chianese, Piccialli, & Jung, 2016; Poulopoulos et al., 2018; Pouryousefzadeh & Akbarzadeh, 2019).

The recent progress in information and communication technology (including IoT) supports development of on-site personalized services for museum visitors. A visitor has a personal mobile device (e.g., smartphone or tablet) accessing relevant information about surrounding exhibits and in a personalized and cognitive way (Amato et al., 2017). Information on the exhibit can be visualized on a nearby screen. The information flow become effectively go from digital cultural and historical heritage to the visitors. In particular, SMARTMUSEUM system (Ruotsalo et al., 2013) provides to its visitors much explanatory description and multimedia content associated with individual objects.

A museum exhibition can tell a story (Vassilakis et al., 2018). Objects are proactively recommended for a visitor to study based on the user profile and context information. Additional information content about some objects is retrieved from the Web. Various playful interactions with smart objects are considered in (Amaro & Oliveira, 2019). Advanced digital devices and sensor system are involved to organize such visitor-to-exhibit interactions. For instance, a mobile eye tracker is integrated into an audio guide system for museum visitors to reason about the user's focus of attention and to deliver relevant information (Mokatren, Kuflik, & Shimshoni, 2018; Raptis, Fidas, Katsini, & Avouris, 2019).

The on-site visit boundaries of cultural and historical heritage experience at the museum can be extended to assist the visitors during pre-visit planning and to follow up with post visit memories and reflections (Kuflik, Wecker, Lanir, & Stock, 2015). Information services support museum visitors to be involved into the process, e.g., using feedback when the visitor makes posts on exhibits (to read by other people, either visitors or personnel) or evaluate exhibits (i.e., a kind of collaborative activity). Services become oriented to personalized recommendations: the event is recognized when the visitor studies a certain museum exhibit. Then a set of "close" objects (information fragments) are selected, evaluated, and delivered to the visitor for further study.

The general smart spaces approach to development of service-oriented information-centric environments–including smart museum environments as a particular case–is presented in (Korzun, Balandina, Kashevnik, Balandin, & Viola, 2019). The IoT technology can be utilized in order to construct a "smart space", where exhibits can communicate with the visitors and to each other and can be organized automatically so that they can generate rich, personalized, coherent and highly stimulating experiences (Poulopoulos et al., 2018; Marshall, 2018).

A smart space defines a distributed system where many digital devices share their computational and informational resources. The considered semantic layer makes the fusion of cultural and historical heritage knowledge into a semantic network (Korzun, Varfolomeyev, Yalovitsyna, & Volokhova, 2017). All involved objects are virtually represented and interconnected, similarly as it happens in Semantic Web (Bizer et al., 2009) and interoperable IoT applications (Lakka et al. 2019). As a result, the smart space extends the museum information system. Advanced information services surround the users and have higher intelligence level (Gyrard, Zimmermann, & Sheth, 2018), following the Ambient Intelligence (AmI) paradigm.

A smart museum considers visitors as rich sources of information about collected exhibits. This kind of information can be captured using annotations (Alzahrani, Loke, & Lu, 2014). An added annotation enhances digital memory for the object, forming the secondary information layer (Torre 2013). The recommended information to a visitor can be provided based on 3D technique and other information delivery and representation methods (Sooai, Nugroho, Azam, Sumpeno, & Purnomo, 2017; Marshall, 2018).

Various information about visitors can be collected and associated with exhibits in a smart museum. The monitoring system tracks visitors' positions and movement patterns through museum art galleries with the goal of assisting museum personnel in analyzing visitors' activities, behaviors and experiences (Rashed et al., 2016). The collected behavior data are used for analysis and prediction of real museum visitors' interests and preferences (Lanir et al., 2017). In particular, service delivery to visitors is advanced based on the location information (Ahriz, Douin, & Lemoine, 2019).

The considered above systems meet with the following three problems, which define the research focus of this chapter.

1. **Semantic Layer:** Solutions to support context interaction of various objects in service construction and delivery.
2. **Ontological Model:** Solutions to collect, interlink, and share the semantic information in the museum smart space.
3. **Information Ranking:** Solutions to relevance evaluation in the collected information when constructing recommendations.

Solutions to these problems form our smart museum concept, which is summarized in the subsequent sections. The chapter summarizes our work that the authors have sequentially developed in elaborated previously (Korzun, Marchenkov, Vdovenko, & Petrina, 2016; Petrina, Korzun, Volokhova, Yalovitsyna, & Varfolomeyev, 2017; Korzun, Yalovitsyna, & Volokhova, 2018; Yalovitsyna, Volokhova, & Korzun, 2019). Early experimental proof-of-the-concept study is based on the pilot implementation in the History Museum of PetrSU. The following information services are considered.

1. Visit service to support the visitor with personalized exhibition study plan (recommended exhibits).
2. Exhibition service to support the visitor with personalized delivery of knowledge on a given exhibit (recommended facts).
3. Enrichment service to support the museum with a tool for extracting knowledge from visitors (new information about the collection).

SEMANTIC LAYER

The need of semantic integration of available information for creating smart museum services has been already well understood (Smirnov, Shilov, & Kashevnik, 2012; Mouromtsev et al., 2015). The integration supports creating new exhibitions, working with visitors on a personal or mini-group level, contributing to the realization of their expectations. An additional mediation layer is introduced–*the semantic layer*–for the integration of information retrieved and analyzed from multiple data sources, including services for semantic publishing, enrichment, search, and visualization (Simou, Chortaras, Stamou, & Kollias 2017).

The smart museum concept considers a museum as a system where three classes of information sources can be introduced, in addition to the basic collection of cultural heritage object descriptions in the museum collection.

1. Museum personnel provide expert historical knowledge related to and about the exhibits.
2. Museum visitors themselves are sources of individual (and possibly subjective) information, which can be valuable for services, similarly as it happens in social networks.
3. The today's Internet provides a lot of historical sources, as well as related cultural heritage information.

The semantic layer is responsible for integration of all these sources.

We apply the semantic network model to integration of digital content (Kalus, 2007), (Petrina, Korzun, Volokhova, Yalovitsyna, & Varfolomeyev, 2017). The concept view is shown in Figure 1, which is inherited from our work (Korzun, Yalovitsyna, & Volokhova, 2018). The same approach is used in many other similar smart IoT-based applications. Very close example can be found in the Smart City domain (Bergamini et al., 2018).

Our pilot implementation for the History Museum of PetrSU experimentally evaluates the following reference museum information services (Yalovitsyna, Volokhova, & Korzun, 2019).

1. Visit service constructs a personalized exposition of recommended exhibits for a visitor to study. For example, exhibits associated with the universities of visitor's country.
2. Exhibition service analyzes visitor profiles and situation to understand her/his personal interests. The visitor is offered with exhibits that have the highest rank in relation to the personal profile or specified interests of the visitor. The offers are displayed to the users in the exposition room (on the digital screens) or even on personal mobile devices (smartphones, tablets).
3. Enrichment service supports modification (evolution) of the information part of the collection by museum personnel or visitors. In fact, a museum visitor can enrich descriptions of studied exhibits, e.g., in the form of adding annotations or relations. Museum personnel can verify the correctness and the value of this new information.

The high-level scheme of a smart museum environment is shown in Figure 2, which is inherited from our work (Petrina, Korzun, Volokhova, Yalovitsyna, & Varfolomeyev, 2017). The system design is based on the smart space concept for implementing AmI as multiagent systems in IoT environments (Korzun, Balandina, Kashevnik, Balandin, & Viola, 2019).

The implemented services are experimental cases that show how the smart museum concept makes the museum information closer to the visitor's preferences, historical interest, and the current context. The services demonstrate a significant increase of the information impact of museum exhibits by pro-

Figure 1. Concept view on smart museum

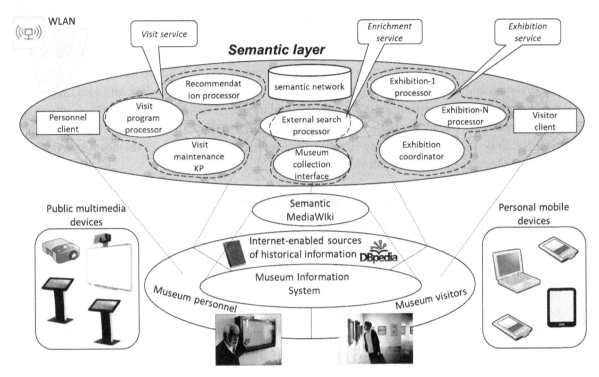

Figure 2. Smart museum environment

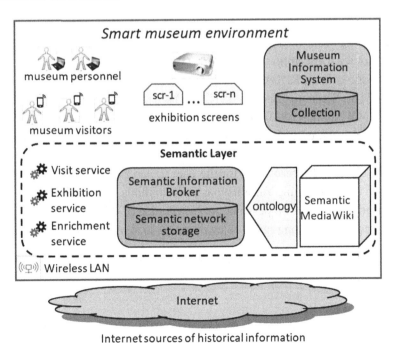

viding augmented annotations, identifying semantic relations, assisting the visitors to follow individual trajectories in exposition study, finding relevant information, opening the collection to knowledge from visitors (Korzun, Varfolomeyev, Yalovitsyna, & Volokhova, 2017).

A museum smart space is created with a semantic layer to integrate and interrelate the museum collection. The smart space opens the information for shared operation by all involved participants, including human (personnel and visitors) and machines (information collection, processing, and visualization).

We consider a museum exposition room as a particular case of indoor localized IoT environments. The localization means that although the environment is local (in a spatially restricted area) some remote components can be presented, including access to the Internet or to servers in the corporate network. The following classes of IoT-enabled devices are present.

- Public multimedia devices. For instance, they include interactive screens, media projectors, and microphones installed in the exposition room. The devices are primarily for service consumption by visualizing the information to the users. In some cases, the users can use such devices for data input and control.
- Personal mobile devices. For instance, they include smartphones, tablets, and laptops carried individually by the users. The devices can be used for personalized service consumption and participation in the activity.
- Server machines. They are responsible for data storage and processing functions. Typically, the devices are non-local, e.g., a server in the corporate network or in the Internet.
- Smart IoT devices. They represent physical things augmenting them with processing and communication capabilities. For instance, a physically presented exhibit is equipped with an RFID tag to provide textual description for any close device.
- Network communication devices. They create local area networks (LAN) such that all other participating devices can communicate locally as well as have access to external resources (e.g., to the Internet).

Semantic layer operates with data representation as a semantic network. In particular, the semantic network can use Resource Description Framework (RDF) in accordance with some ontologies. The semantic network is stored in an RDF triplestore, which is accessed and operated through a Semantic Information Broker (SIB). Semantic MediaWiki (SMW) is a mediator for a traditional Museum Information System (MIS). SMW supports RDF-aware construction of the semantic network by semantics that experts identify in records stored in MIS. This way, the implicit semantics are transformed to explicit SMW representation (as a connected set of web-pages).

A visual example of related information for the user to see and study in shown in Figure 3, which is inherited from our work (Korzun, Yalovitsyna, & Volokhova, 2018). The related information can be presented on a nearby screen or on personal mobile device of the visitor. The key problem is about which information fragments (among many relevant ones) to show to each particular visitor, based on her/his preferences and the context.

Figure 3. Example of related information about exhibits for visualization to the user (everyday life history of PetrSU)

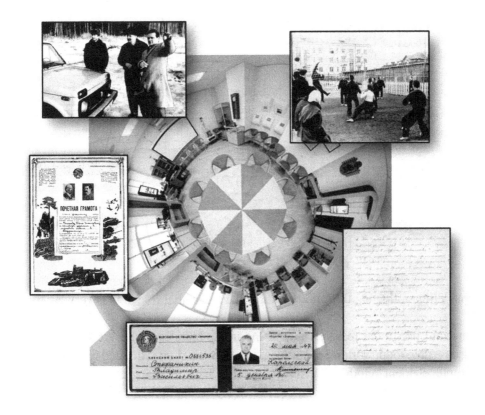

ONTOLOGICAL MODEL

Let us consider the well-known CIDOC conceptual reference model (Doerr, 2003). We apply the CIDOC model as a base for representation of historical information about exhibits. CIDOC CRM covers the major museum exhibition aspects: exhibits and other historical objects with their semantic relations between each other. The example ontology is shown in Figure 4, which is inherited from our work (Korzun, Yalovitsyna, & Volokhova, 2018).

The ontology is designed for description of objects and relations from the everyday life history domain. The everyday life history is a branch of historical research, recognized as an integral part of historical science in 1980-th. In Russia this branch began to develop at the turn of XX and XXI centuries. The study subject is the human in multiple historical, cultural, political-event, ethnic, and religious contexts. The research focus is on a comprehensive study of the repetitive "normal" or "common" way of life. For a historian, a simple description of the daily practices is not enough, and fixation of the emotional component is essential.

Figure 4. Ontological model for the museum collection about university everyday life

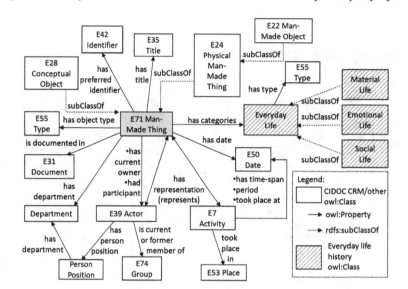

Let us consider the following three domains that have essential role in the everyday life history.

1. The Material Life: In our research way of life in the broadest sense are including such items as clothing, housing, food, working conditions, etc. Each element is divided into smaller components. For example, element "clothing" includes items such as "working clothes", "uniforms", "festive clothing". In turn, these elements can be specified. For example, the jacket as items of the student construction brigade uniform ("shtormovka") is often mentioned in the documents. This element was included in the ontology.
2. The Social Life: Event area of public daily life, including such items as holidays, academic events, special rituals, etc. It is important to note, that the project has an applied character, and semantic services will be used to the University Museum exposition. In this regard, we always recorded relationship between exhibit information and departments of the University. For example, construction brigades usually composed from one-department students
3. The Emotional Life: The emotional evaluation of events, the experience of everyday facts and domestic circumstances individuals and groups of people. The emotional evaluations are widely represented in interviews with participants of the Student construction brigades. However, emotional evaluations are extremely diverse and almost incompatible with categorization into semantic elements. We used only the class "Emotional evaluation" and the property "Has attitude to", which allow the user to find museum sources containing emotional estimates for further analysis.

The facts of the everyday life history are described in historical sources occasionally and isolated, i.e., this database is very fragmented and the fragments cannot be easily found as such. The use of the semantic network and ontology will allow systematizing the information of the different types of sources. For example, we have the opportunity to study the evolution of the clothing of student construction brigades (the block "The material life" in the list of elements of everyday life). The museum presents photographs of members of student construction brigades since 1968. Images of members in uniform are

Figure 5. Example semantic network for the museum collection about university everyday life

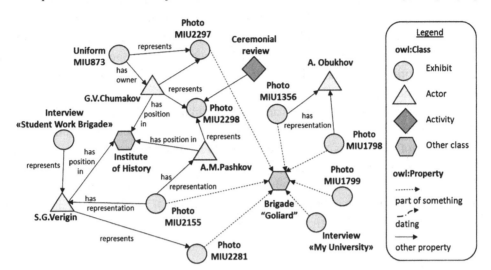

present only since 1976. The content, time and place of the creation of photographs are determined by written and oral sources. Semantic network allows combining the text sources and image for conclusion about the time of appearance of uniforms construction brigades.

The main class is *ManMade_Thing* that represents is historical information profile of a museum exhibit. This class has data properties, which describe exhibit title, museum identifier, date of create, topic, object type (e.g. photo, interview, book, etc.). Class *ManMade_Thing* property *Has attitude to* allocates emotional attitude in the interview or in the book to something. The class *ManMade_Thing* links other classes with object properties, which refer to image file, department in the university, author, owner, represented persons. All persons are represented with class *Actor*. The class *Actor* has properties, which includes open information about person: full name, date of birth, position, education, and related exhibits. Historical events are represented with class *Activity*, which can link to class *ManMade_Think* and class *Actor*.

As a result, the presented ontological model provides the following description opportunities for construction of the semantic network.

- Primary historical information about each particular exhibit (provided by experts).
- Supplementary information about collected exhibits (provided by museum personnel and visitors).
- Particular relations between exhibits and other objects to link the nodes in the semantic network.
- General construction rules for the semantic network (classes of objects, their attributes and relations).

An example semantic network is presented in Figure 5, which is inherited from (Petrina, Korzun, Volokhova, Yalovitsyna, & Varfolomeyev, 2017). In sum, the analyzed opportunities create a base for effective data mining in this kind of semantic networks. Especially note thta the role of professionals in constructing such a semantic network is essential.

Such a semantic network can be implemented using the Wiki technology for expert-based extraction of semantics from the museum collection and further transfer of the information to the semantic network. On the one hand, only an expert can identify valuable relations between different records. On the other hand, such a traditional ontology editor as Protege is difficult for use by non-professionals (in ontology modeling and engineering). In this case, the ontology development tools should be lightweight for easy use by experts in historical and cultural heritage.

Among these tools, semantic wiki systems are of especial interest, and Semantic MediaWiki (SMW) (Krötzsch & Vrandečić, 2011) is an effective candidate for use by museum personnel and historians. SMW is an extension of the famous system MediaWiki, which is a technological foundation of Wikipedia. Each object (e.g., a description of an exhibit) is represented as a web-page. The main feature is support of typified links between pages. Such typified links enable construction of simple semantic networks, which can be further automatically translated into the RDF format. In our architecture, SMW plays the role of a mediator between the museum information system and the smart space. Since the museum information system does not store directly the semantics of museum exhibits, experts extract the semantics and represent in SMW.

In SMW, objects are represented as wiki-pages. Categories play the role of ontology classes that can be assigned to the pages, thus expressing an object belonging to the class. Categories can be nested into each other, forming a class hierarchy. To describe all other relationships typified links between pages are used. The role of the subjects and objects of semantic relations in SMW always represented as wiki-pages. This model significantly limits the possibilities for information representation about the domain. That is, in SMW an expert can easily express the idea that an exhibit is addressed to a particular person. Both exhibit and person are presented as pages. Nevertheless, SMW cannot describe a logical statement about individual words or other parts of the wiki-page.

Despite the limitations, SMW can be very convenient for the rapid creation of a simplified version of a semantic network around the museum exhibits. The simplified version reflects the expert knowledge about relationships of exhibits to each other and to other objects (such as a person). In addition to expert-based work with the use of SMW, some other methods are needed for semantic network construction, including automated variants. In particular, knowledge extraction algorithms can be used for each information source (e.g., a text analyzer). In the smart spaces-based architecture, such algorithms are implemented in software agents associated with the sources (Marchenkov, Vdovenko, Petrina, & Korzun, 2016).

Recently, the developed SMW for knowledge representation of the History Museum of PertSU includes about hundred exhibitions (Petrina, Korzun, Volokhova, Yalovitsyna, & Varfolomeyev, 2017). Each exhibit is represented as own wiki-page. The latter belongs to category *Man-Made Thing* according to class in our ontology. Typified links connect wiki-pages in accordance with the ontological object properties and have type "Page". Data properties are represented as typified links with type "Text."

The ontological model covers the major museum exhibition aspects: exhibits and other historical objects, their descriptions and semantic relations. The ontology is based on CIDOC CRM, which is extended with a unique part for visit programs, exposition study, visitors, their interests, and recommendations. Note that the model applicability is not limited with the considered Visit service, Exhibition service, and Enrichment service.

INFORMATION RANKING ALGORITHMS

The ontological model from the previous section is used to collect and interlink information in the form of a semantic network. The mathematical model for this information representation is defined by ontology O. First, O describes a system of concepts C_i (ontology classes) for $i=1, ..., n$. Any particular node v in V (ontology class object, instance or individual) belongs to one or more concepts. Second, O describes the interlinking structure for L, i.e., between which concepts a relation can be and possible types of such relations. The links represent the primary semantics. Third, O describes attributes that v in V and l in L may have to reflect additional semantics (e.g., keywords).

Semantic network construction can be implemented as a collective information collection process (Korzun, Varfolomeyev, Yalovitsyna, & Volokhova, 2017). On the one hand, many nodes v are straightforwardly derived from existing descriptions (e.g., collected in the smart space or in local information systems virtualized in the smart space). Also, nodes correspond to descriptions available in various remote sources (e.g., web pages or photos in the Internet). On the other hand, for nodes v in V the expert defines semantic relations (i.e., links l in L) and their attributes.

An information service needs to find $k > 0$ the most appropriate information facts. A fact can be a node v in V, a link l in L, or a connected graph structure s in G (e.g., a path from u to v can have valued interpretation for some u and v in V). This data mining can be reduced to the ranking problem when rank values $r_v > 0$ or $r_l > 0$ are associated with nodes or links. The higher rank the better is appropriateness of the information. The rank of a connected graph structure is calculated based on ranks of the composed nodes and links.

An information service provides a search extend of the collected shared information in the smart space. The service aims at finding several the most appropriate information facts for a given problem. This property is close to the k-optimization approach (when several top solutions are used). To mention as examples, some particular semantic properties of such services are as follows.

- Semantic clustering: a set of thematically related objects.
- Semantic filtering: most appropriate descriptions for a given object.
- Semantic neighborhood: closely related objects for a given object.

The properties can be achieved based on certain information arrangements, when the order describes the relevance of information fragment. Mathematically, this way of data mining can be implemented using ranking models. Arranged information is provided with numerical rank values. Objects with similar ranks can be considered as forming a cluster. Highest-rank objects are selected in filtering. For a given objects, its rank-based neighborhood includes the objects having similar rank value.

The following three classes of ranking methods can be used for selecting top-value information in the smart space: 1) local ranking, 2) collaborative filtering, 3) structural ranking. The role of these methods for creating smart services for smart museum domain is discussed in (Petrina, Korzun, Volokhova, Yalovitsyna, & Varfolomeyev, 2017). A ranking algorithm runs within a search request when semantic network $G = \left(V, L\right)$ is traversed. The corresponding nodes $v \in V$ and links $l \in L$ are assigned with rank values $r_v \geq 0$ and $r_l \geq 0$. Then k highest-rank facts are extracted to be used in service construction as the most relevant to the current need of the user.

Local ranking: Two or more objects are analyzed for similarity based on their content and overlapping of this content. In this case, the rank is computed in respect to some fixed node u in V and reflects distance of other nodes from u.

$$r_v(u) = \frac{1}{\rho(u,v)},$$

where u and v are nodes, links, or even some connected substructures in G.

For instance, if u and v have sets K_u and K_v of annotating keywords (or tags, or other discrete semantic attributes associated with the stored content) then the rank reflects the size of content overlapping for u and v:

$$\rho(u,v) = |K_u \cap K_v|,$$

i.e., the larger the number of shared keywords the higher is the similarity.

In particular, from the service construction point of view, if u is the recent object that the user studies then the information service can provide the highest rank nodes $v_1, v_2, ..., v_k$ as a multi-option recommendation for the further study. In addition to the mathematical rank-based evaluation of the information relevance, the role of delivery of the information (service) to the user is essential. The latter problem needs problem-oriented visual models. In particular, a star graph model can be used with u in the central node and $v_1, v_2, ..., v_k$ are rays of length $r_{v1}, r_{v2}, ..., r_{vk}$. The angle position of rays can be used for reflecting geo-location information about objects $v_1, v_2, ..., v_k$.

Collaborative filtering: This ranking model assumes that many users generate opinions about each object. The opinions are transformed to some community-based scores (normalized $0 \leq r_v^* \leq 1$). Then the scores can be combined with other ranking requirements. For instance,

$$r_v = \alpha r_v^* + (1-\alpha)\left(1 - \frac{d_v}{\max\limits_{w \in W} d_w}\right)$$

where W is a set of objects of potential interest for the user, $d_w > 0$ is an individual (personalized) user's interest for object w, $0 \leq \alpha \leq 1$ is a tradeoff parameter between community scores and individual interest.

In particular, if W is a set of points of interest for the tourist and d_w is the time to reach w from the current location then the information service can provide the highest rank nodes $v_1, v_2, ..., v_k$ as recommendation for the next object to study.

Structural ranking: This ranking model utilizes the connectivity properties of the semantic network $G = (V, L)$, similarly as it happens in the well-known PageRank algorithm (for web networks analysis).

For instance, node ranks r_v for all $v \in V$ are computed iteratively starting from some initial values $r_u^{(0)}$:

$$r_v^{(i+1)} = \alpha \sum_{\forall v \to w} p_{wv} r_w^{(i)} + \left(1-\alpha\right)\pi_v$$

where p_{wv} is weight of the link $l = \left(v \to w\right)$, $0 \le \alpha \le 1$ is the damping factor denoting the probability of following the connectivity structure of G, and π is a jump probability vector for all $v \in V$.

In particular, if p_{vu} is relative weight of v's role to u then the information service can provide the highest rank objects v_1, v_2, ..., v_k as recommendation for the most appropriate information facts to study.

The presented three information ranking models lead to appropriate ranking algorithms; each is implemented as a distributed system of agents accessing the semantic network. The models have already showed their effectiveness and quality in Internet applications. In particular, local ranking is a generalization of web search based on keywords. Collaborative filtering is a mandatory element of artificial intelligence in social networks. Structural ranking is applied in many web search and recommender engines.

SOLUTIONS AND RECOMMENDATIONS

The presented smart museum concept covers solutions to the following problems that smart museum development meets.

1. The semantic layer supports information-driven interaction in service construction and delivery by extending the ontology with the subscription-based notification model. For the considered case of pilot museum services, the typical number of participating objects (distributed system size in users and machines) is not more than several dozen interacting elements.
2. The ontological model describes information sharing and integration, including available descriptions of museum exhibits and facts. This way the model provides structural rules for creating the required semantic network. For the considered case of pilot museum services, the typical semantic network size is about a few hundreds or thousands information fragments.
3. The information ranking is based on attribute and connection structure in semantic network. This way, the required algorithms are implemented for information search, exhibits and descriptions ranking, and reasoning for discovery of complex semantic relations. For the considered case of pilot museum services, the typical size of selected top-information is about 10..15% in respect to the whole amount of relevant (non-zero rank) information.

Although the proposed solutions are based the particular assumptions, the solutions have a generic character and they can serve for designing other smart museum services as well as for various museums and cultural heritage environments.

FUTURE RESEARCH DIRECTIONS

The discussed smart museum concept is based on creating an additional (semantic) layer for operation with information and knowledge in the museum collection. As we showed above, the semantic layer provides an effective data mining function for the museum collection: search for relevant information, selection of the top-relevant information based on ranking, and provision of information as a recommendation. Actually, the semantic layer is on the top of many small descriptions, each is an annotation of object in the collection. The same semantic approach is promising for other domains where data are represented as a large set of many small descriptions (Korzun, Balandina, Kashevnik, Balandin, & Viola, 2019). The following applied directions we consider as very interesting for research on digitalization opportunities and impact.

Biographies. Descriptions are voluminous text fragments (e.g., biographies, newspaper materials). They can be a part of the museum collection or stored in a separate system (e.g., a family archive). For instance, a number of German researchers in recent years have turned to the methodology of working with biographies (Bukow, Ottersbach, Tuider, & Yildiz, 2006). They consider the great potential for understanding the role of memory in the functioning of modern societies. There is a wide variety of versions of historical events recorded in the memoirs. The study of such data can be supported with information services similar to the considered reference smart museum services. The user has an opportunity to discover and analyze personalized versions of the history.

Use of data from narrative processes model. In particular, narrative coding systems are developed in (Friese, 2019). Such a system can transform the events of everyday life into a meaningful story (text description) that both organizes and represents the person's sense of self and others in the world. Clearly, this information can be used by museum personnel, sociologists, and historians in solving their practical research studies. Moreover, in sociology, an important problem is extracting information from questionnaires with open questions (Saganenko, 2000), i.e., when the answer is formulated as an arbitrary text by the questionnaire respondent.

Information about a person in open Internet sources. Fragments of open personalized information are distributed among many web pages in the Internet. They can be in the form of text descriptions, photographs, audio- and video- records. Nevertheless, modern person recognition algorithms potential can find "the relation" of a given person to the fragment, so making a building block for a semantic network. Actually, the same is implemented now manually when one search information about a given person using a web search engine (e.g., Google or Yandex). To summarize, an interesting question to implement its answer as a service: "Are you interested to know your digital footprint in the Internet?", "Or for someone who are of your interest?"

CONCLUSION

This chapter summarized our development on the smart museum concept, which was incrementally elaborated in our previous work. The development is multidiscipline. On the one hand, expert work is presented on historical and cultural heritage information as a service provided to museum visitors and personnel. On the other hand, appropriate mathematical models and algorithms are needed to develop a museum information system with smart services. The proof-of-the-concept case study was implemented and experimented in the History Museum of PetrSU with the scope of university everyday life history. The implemented pilot prototype demonstrates the following museum information services:

1. Visit service to support the visitor with personalized exhibition study plan (recommending the most interesting exhibits),
2. Exhibition service to support the visitor with personalized delivery of knowledge on a given exhibit (recommending high-relevant facts to study),
3. Enrichment service to support the museum with a tool for extracting knowledge from visitors (generating new information for the collection).

The services can be considered as particular references for research and development in the area of digitalizing the cultural and historical heritage for effective use by non-professionals and professionals.

ACKNOWLEDGMENT

This research is supported by the Program of Presidium of RAS "Ethno-national policy Realization in the Republic of Karelia in the XX–XXI centuries in the context of changes in the information environment of the region" (AHH-A18-118020990109-0) and by the State research assignment to Karelian Research Centre RAS (AAAA-A18-118030190093-9). The reported study on mathematical modeling and algorithms was funded from Russian Fund for Basic Research according to research project # 19-07-01027. The results were implemented within the Government Program of Flagship University Development for Petrozavodsk State University in 2017-2021.

REFERENCES

Ahriz, I., Douin, J., & Lemoine, F. (2019). Location-based Service Sharing for Smart Museum. In *Proc. International Conference on Software, Telecommunications and Computer Networks (SoftCOM)* (pp. 1-6). Academic Press.

Alzahrani, A. A., Loke, S. W., & Lu, H. (2014). An advanced location-aware physical annotation system: From models to implementation. *Journal of Ambient Intelligence and Smart Environments*, 6(1), 71–91. doi:10.3233/AIS-130238

Amaro, A. C., & Oliveira, L. (2019). Playful Interactions with Smart and Social Objects. In *Proc. 14th Iberian Conference on Information Systems and Technologies (CISTI)* (pp. 1-6). 10.23919/CISTI.2019.8760920

Amato, F., Moscato, V., Picariello, A., Colace, F., Santo, M.D., Schreiber, F.A., & Tanca, L. (2017). Big data meets digital cultural heritage: Design and implementation of scrabs, a smart context-aware browsing assistant for cultural environments. *J. Comput. Cult. Herit. 10*(1), 6:1-6:23.

Atzori, L., Iera, A., & Morabito, G. (2014). From smart objects to social objects: The next evolutionary step of the internet of things. *IEEE Communications Magazine*, 52(1), 97–105. doi:10.1109/MCOM.2014.6710070

Bergamini, C., Bosi, F., Corradi, A., Rolt, C. R. D., Foschini, L., Monti, S., & Seralessandri, M. (2018). LocalFocus: A Big Data Service Platform for Local Communities and Smarter Cities. *IEEE Communications Magazine*, 56(7), 116–123. doi:10.1109/MCOM.2018.1700597

Bizer, C., Lehmann, J., Kobilarov, G., Auer, S., Becker, C., Cyganiak, R., & Hellmann, S. (2009). DBpedia – a crystallization point for the Web of Data. *Journal of Web Semantics*, 7(3), 154–165. doi:10.1016/j.websem.2009.07.002

Bukow, W.-D., Ottersbach, M., Tuider, E., & Yildiz, E. (2006). *Biographische Konstruktionen im multikulturellen Bildungsprozess: Individuelle Standortsicherung im globalisierten Alltag*. Springer-Verlag. doi:10.1007/978-3-531-90071-1

Chianese, A., Piccialli, F., & Jung, J. E. (2016). The Internet of Cultural Things: Towards a Smart Cultural Heritage. In *Proc 12th International Conference on Signal-Image Technology & Internet-Based Systems (SITIS)* (pp. 493-496). 10.1109/SITIS.2016.83

Chianese, A., Piccialli, F., & Valente, I. (2015). Smart environments and cultural heritage: A novel approach to create intelligent cultural spaces. *Journal of Location Based Services*, 9(3), 209–234. doi:10.1080/17489725.2015.1099752

Doerr, M. (2003). The CIDOC conceptual reference module: An ontological approach to semantic interoperability of metadata. *AI Magazine*, 24(3), 75–92.

Friese, S. (2019). *Qualitative Data Analysis with ATLAS.ti* (3rd ed.). Max-Planck Institute.

Gyrard, A., Zimmermann, A., & Sheth, A. (2018). Building IoT-Based Applications for Smart Cities: How Can Ontology Catalogs Help? *IEEE Internet of Things Journal*, 5(5), 3978–3990. doi:10.1109/JIOT.2018.2854278

Harkovchuk, A., & Korzun, D. (2019). Semantic Information Search Service by Person's Face Photo. In *Proceedings of the 24th Conference of Open Innovations Association FRUCT* (pp. 821-823). Academic Press.

Kalus, M. (2007). Semantic networks and historical knowledge management: Introducing new methods of computer-based research. *The Journal of the Association for History and Computing*, 10.

Korzun, D., Balandina, E., Kashevnik, A., Balandin, S., & Viola, F. (2019). *Ambient Intelligence Services in IoT Environments: Emerging Research and Opportunities*. IGI Global. doi:10.4018/978-1-5225-8973-0

Korzun, D., Varfolomeyev, A., Yalovitsyna, S., & Volokhova, V. (2017). Semantic infrastructure of a smart museum: Toward making cultural heritage knowledge usable and creatable by visitors and professionals. *Personal and Ubiquitous Computing*, 21(2), 345–354. doi:10.100700779-016-0996-7

Korzun, D., Yalovitsyna, S., & Volokhova, V. (2018). Smart Services as Cultural and Historical Heritage Information Assistance for Museum Visitors and Personnel. *Baltic J. Modern Computing*, 6(4), 418–433.

Korzun, D. G., Marchenkov, S. A., Vdovenko, A. S., & Petrina, O. B. (2016). Semantic Approach to Designing Information Services for Smart Museums. *International Journal of Embedded and Real-Time Communication Systems*, 7(2), 15–34. doi:10.4018/IJERTCS.2016070102

Krötzsch, M., & Vrandečić, D. (2011). Semantic MediaWiki. In D. Fensel (Ed.), *Foundations for the web of information and services: A review of 20 years of semantic web research* (pp. 311–326). doi:10.1007/978-3-642-19797-0_16

Kuflik, T., Wecker, A., Lanir, J., & Stock, O. (2015). An integrative framework for extending the boundaries of the museum visit experience: Linking the pre, during and post visit phases. *Information Technology & Tourism, 15*(1), 17–47. doi:10.100740558-014-0018-4

Lakka, E. (2019). End-to-End Semantic Interoperability Mechanisms for IoT. In *Proc. 2019 IEEE 24th International Workshop on Computer Aided Modeling and Design of Communication Links and Networks (CAMAD)* (pp. 1-6). IEEE.

Lanir, J., Kuflik, T., Sheidin, J., Yavin, N., Leiderman, K., & Segal, M. (2017). Visualizing museum visitors' behavior: Where do they go and what do they do there? *Personal and Ubiquitous Computing, 21*(2), 313–326. doi:10.100700779-016-0994-9

Marchenkov, S. A., Vdovenko, A. S., Petrina, O. B., & Korzun, D. G. (2016). A smart space-based design of semantic layer for advancing museum information services. In S. Balandin, & T. Tyutina (Eds.), *Proc. 19th Conf. Open Innovations Association FRUCT* (pp. 159-166). 10.23919/FRUCT.2016.7892196

Marshall, M. T. (2018). Interacting with Heritage: On the Use and Potential of IoT Within the Cultural Heritage Sector. In *Proc. Fifth International Conference on Internet of Things: Systems, Management and Security* (pp. 15-22). 10.1109/IoTSMS.2018.8554899

Mokatren, M., Kuflik, T., & Shimshoni, I. (2018). Exploring the potential of a mobile eye tracker as an intuitive indoor pointing device: A case study in cultural heritage. *Future Generation Computer Systems, 81*, 528–541. doi:10.1016/j.future.2017.07.007

Mouromtsev, D., Haase, P., Pavlov, D., Cherny, E., Andreev, A., & Spiridonova, A. (2015). Towards the linked Russian heritage cloud: Data enrichment and publishing. In The Semantic Web. Latest Advances and New Domains (ESWC2015, LNCS 9088, pp. 637-651). Springer.

Petrina, O. B., Korzun, D. G., Volokhova, V. V., Yalovitsyna, S. E., & Varfolomeyev, A. G. (2017). Semantic Approach to Opening Museum Collections of Everyday Life History for Services in Internet of Things Environments. *International Journal of Embedded and Real-Time Communication Systems, 8*(1), 31–44. doi:10.4018/IJERTCS.2017010103

Poulopoulos, V., Vassilakis, C., Antoniou, A., Wallace, M., Lepouras, G., & Nores, M. L. (2018). ExhiSTORY: IoT in the service of Cultural Heritage. In *Proc. 2018 Global Information Infrastructure and Networking Symposium (GIIS)* (pp. 1-4). 10.1109/GIIS.2018.8635759

Pouryousefzadeh, S., & Akbarzadeh, R. (2019). Internet of Things (IoT) systems in future Cultural Heritage. In *Proc. 3rd International Conference on Internet of Things and Applications (IoT)* (pp. 1-5). 10.1109/IICITA.2019.8808838

Raptis, G. E., Fidas, C., Katsini, C., & Avouris, N. (2019). A cognition-centered personalization framework for cultural-heritage content. *User Modeling and User-Adapted Interaction, 29*(1), 9–65. doi:10.100711257-019-09226-7

Rashed, M. G., Suzuki, R., Yonezawa, T., Lam, A., Kobayashi, Y., & Kuno, Y. (2016). Tracking Visitors in a Real Museum for Behavioral Analysis. In *Proc. Joint 8th International Conference on Soft Computing and Intelligent Systems (SCIS) and 17th International Symposium on Advanced Intelligent Systems (ISIS)* (pp. 80-85). 10.1109/SCIS-ISIS.2016.0030

Ruotsalo, T., Haav, K., Stoyanov, A., Roche, S., Fani, E., Deliai, R., ... Hyvonen, E. (2013). SMART-MUSEUM: A mobile recommender system for the Web of Data. *Journal of Web Semantics*, *20*, 50–67. doi:10.1016/j.websem.2013.03.001

Saganenko, G. (2000). General Methodology. *Bulletin of Sociological Methodology. Bulletin de Methodologie Sociologique*, *68*(1), 79–80. doi:10.1177/075910630006800127

Simou, N., Chortaras, A., Stamou, G., & Kollias, S. (2017). Enriching and Publishing Cultural Heritage as Linked Open Data. In Mixed Reality and Gamification for Cultural Heritage (pp. 201-223). doi:10.1007/978-3-319-49607-8_7

Smirnov, A., Shilov, N., & Kashevnik, A. (2012). Ontology-based mobile smart museums service, approach for small & medium museums. In *Proc. of the 4th Int'l Conf. on Advances in Future Internet* (AFIN 2012, pp. 48-54). Academic Press.

Sooai, A. G., Nugroho, A., Azam, M. N. A., Sumpeno, S., & Purnomo, M. H. (2017). Virtual artifact: Enhancing museum exhibit using 3D virtual reality. In *Proc. 2017 TRON Symposium (TRONSHOW)* (pp. 1-5). 10.23919/TRONSHOW.2017.8275078

Torre, I. (2013). Interaction with linked digital memories. In *Proceedings of the 21st Conf. on User Modeling, Adaptation, and Personalization (UMAP 2013). Workshop on Personal Access to Cultural Heritage (PATCH 2013)* (*vol. 997*, pp. 80-87). Academic Press.

Vassilakis, C., Poulopoulos, V., Antoniou, A., Wallace, M., Lepouras, G., & Nores, M. L. (2018). exhiSTORY: Smart exhibits that tell their own stories. *Future Generation Computer Systems*, *81*, 542–556. doi:10.1016/j.future.2017.10.038

Yalovitsyna, S. E., Volokhova, V. V., & Korzun, D. G. (2019). Semantic Approach to Presenting Information of Thematic Museum Collections [In Russian]. *Harald of an Archivist*, *1*, 235–246. doi:10.28995/2073-0101-2019-1-235-246

KEY TERMS AND DEFINITIONS

Context: Any information that can be used to characterize the situation of a person or the object the person is studying.

Information Ranking: Arrangement of information fragments based on their relevance. Each rank value quantitatively reflects the relevance (i.e., a fragment of zero rank is irrelevant to the considered problem).

Museum Collection: A set of physical exhibits as well as all information descriptions associated with the collected exhibits.

Museum Information System: An information system to store the information part of the museum collection as well as to access information about the museum collection.

Ontology: Formal representation of knowledge as a set of concepts within a domain, using a shared vocabulary to denote the types, properties, and interrelationships of those concepts.

Recommendation: Information that can be interpreted by the user in order to make reasoned decisions.

Semantic MediaWiki (SMW): A full-fledged framework to create a powerful and flexible knowledge management system. All data created within SMW are easily exported or published via the Semantic Web, allowing other systems to use this data seamlessly.

Semantic Network: A knowledge base that represents semantic relations between concepts in a network. The model of knowledge representation is based on a directed or undirected graph consisting of vertices, which represent concepts, and edges, which represent semantic relations between concepts, mapping or connecting semantic fields.

Semantic Web: A technology extending the world wide web (WWW) through the standards by the world wide web consortium (W3C). The technology provides a common framework that allows data to be shared and reused across application, enterprise, and community boundaries. The technology is regarded as an integrator across different content, information applications, and systems.

Service: The process of information search, selection, and reasoning to provide meaningful information (typically in a visual form) to the user in respect to the current user's needs and context.

Smart Space: A search extend of information fused from many resources in computational networked environment (computer devices, databases, information systems, data sensors, information processors, etc.).

Chapter 10
Internet of Things Technologies for Smart Grid

Imed Saad Ben Dhaou
Qassim University, Saudi Arabia & The University of Monastir, Tunisia

Aron Kondoro
University of Dar es Salaam, Tanzania

Syed Rameez Ullah Kakakhel
https://orcid.org/0000-0001-5901-2477
University of Turku, Finland

Tomi Westerlund
https://orcid.org/0000-0002-1793-2694
University of Turku, Finland

Hannu Tenhunen
Royal Institute of Technology, Sweden

ABSTRACT

Smart grid is a new revolution in the energy sector in which the aging utility grid will be replaced with a grid that supports two-way communication between customers and the utility company. There are two popular smart-grid reference architectures. NIST (National Institute for Standards and Technology) has drafted a reference architecture in which seven domains and actors have been identified. The second reference architecture is elaborated by ETSI (European Telecommunications Standards Institute), which is an extension of the NIST model where a new domain named distributed energy resources has been added. This chapter aims at identifying the use of IoT and IoT-enabled technologies in the design of a secure smart grid using the ETSI reference model. Based on the discussion and analysis in the chapter, the authors offer two collaborative and development frameworks. One framework draws parallels' between IoT and smart grids and the second one between smart grids and edge computing. These frameworks can be used to broaden collaboration between the stakeholders and identify research gaps.

DOI: 10.4018/978-1-7998-1974-5.ch010

Figure 1. Smart grid ingredients proposed
Source: Fang, Misra, Xue, & Yang, 2012

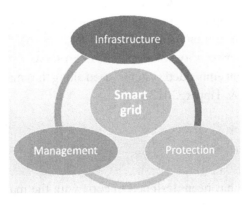

INTRODUCTION

Smart grid is a new paradigm that aims at making the legacy utility grid, efficient, green, reliable and secure. The term was coined in 2007 by the US congress in a bid to modernize the US power grid system (Energy Independence and Security Act of 2007, 2007). As stated in the 2007 Act on energy Independence and Security, a smart grid should have the following ten features: (1) Wide-scale deployment of ICT (Information and communication technologies) to shape-up performance, reliability, and trustworthiness of the utility grid, (2) dynamic optimization of grid operations and resources, (3) integration of effective renewable energy resources, (4) endorsement of advanced demand response scheme, (5) amalgamation of smart technologies for controlling and monitoring the grid operations, (6) consolidation of intelligent appliances, (7) integration of cutting-edge electricity storage and peak-abatement technologies, (8) purveying consumers with timeous information and control options, (9) development of standards for communication and interoperability of appliances and equipment, and (10) battling barriers and obstacles that prevent the adoption of smart grid technologies, practices, and services.

The legacy grid has been built using outdated technologies which cannot address existing shortcomings. Further, the current grid suffers from the interoperability issues among systems and devices which makes the need for a better and efficient grid a hard mission. For instance, the report published by NIST has identified more than 70 gaps in the current grid standards that need to be addressed (National Institute of Standards and Technology, 2014). During recent years, discernible efforts have been put forward to establish a smart grid with the characteristics stated heretofore. A good survey that summarizes the research effort on the permissive technologies for the smart grid until the year 2011 is reported in (Fang, Misra, Xue, & Yang, 2012). The authors reviewed advances in the following three axes: infrastructure, management, and protection. Finally, the researchers digested the omnifarious projects, legislations, programs, standards and trials worldwide in the area of smart grid. Figure 1 elaborates the three essential ingredients in a smart grid.

Communication is a key enabling technology for the smart grid infrastructure. It is believed that the smart grid will integrate multifarious communication technologies like cellular communication, fiberoptic, short-range communication, wireless mesh networks, power-line communication, and satellite communication. The assorted deployment of communication technologies in the smart grid is attributed to factors like the application requirements, the geographic locations, environments, legislations, cost, and so forth. In (Gungor, et al., A Survey on Smart Grid Potential Applications and Communication Requirements, 2013), the authors summarized the communication requirements for fourteen smart grid applications. They further road mapped future smart grid services and applications.

The intensive deployment of communication technologies in the smart grid has precipitated the need for cyber security. The cyber security solution aims to preserve consumer privacy, protect the data against eavesdropping and prevent embedded systems, used along the smart grid, from running malicious software (Yan Y., Qian, Sharif, & Tipper, 2012).

BACKGROUND

Legacy power grid architecture has been designed to cope with the maximum power demands. It is a centralized architecture in which the power is generated in one place, transported over long distances and then distributed to customers. The traditional power grid is a vertical business, highly deregulated, and monopolized. The snowballing operation costs associated with other epidemic factors such as carbon dioxide emission, increasing demands on electricity, have pushed the power industry and the associated stakeholders to upgrade the power grid to address the challenges, meet the market expansion, and create new business models.

Smart-grid concept evolved from the modernization effort of the legacy grid. Its focal features are the two-way communication between the end-user (customer) and the utility company, bidirectional power flow, and the heavy deployment of ICT to improve grid reliability and efficiency. Smart-gird is viewed as system of systems in which real-time communication is indispensable in achieving distributed intelligence, outage detection, demand-side management, Distributed Generation (DG), remote control, tele-protection, Advanced Metering Infrastructure (AMI), distributed automation, Home Energy Management System (HEMS), Distributed Storage (DS), etc., (Sendin, Sanchez-Fornie, Berganza, Simon, & Urrutia, 2016).

In 2010, NIST released the first smart grid roadmap for interoperability. The ultimate aim is to devise a framework to solve and guide the interoperability smart Grid devices and systems used in the smart grid. The reference model conceived by NIST identified seven major domains that constitute the smart grid. Those domains are as follows: customer, markets, service providers, operations, bulk generation, transmission, and distribution. Each domain has key features such as inter and intra-domain communication requirements, services, and actors. Figure 2 depicted the NIST conceptual reference model.

In an effort to remedy the interoperability concerns, NIST through a specialized group has proposed a stack of eight layers. The arrangement of the stack from the bottom up is as follows: basic connectivity, network interoperability, syntactic interoperability, semantics, business context, business procedures, business objectives, and policies (economic/ regulatory).

The classification of the communication platform deployed in the smart grid is essential to identify the competing solutions. The authors of (Farhangi, 2010) (Yu, et al., 2011) (Yan Y., Qian, Sharif, & Tipper, 2013) (Khan, Rehmani, & Reisslein, 2016) (Erol-Kantarci & Mouftah, 2015) classified the smart grid communication technologies based on the coverage area. This type of classification allows the projection of the existing communication standards to serve the needed communication requirements in the smart grid. Indeed, the distance between the interconnected devices, the QoS requirements, latency, power consumption, operating environments, and other factors guide the suitable communication architecture.

Figure 2. NIST smart grid reference model
Source: National Institute of Standards and Technology, 2014

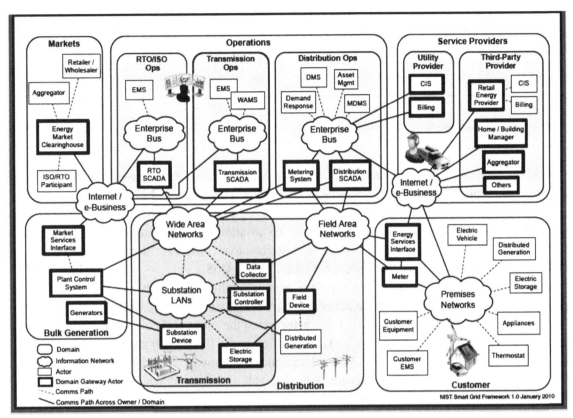

For instance, home appliances are placed close to each other, which makes the local area network as the preferred communication architecture.

In (Farhangi, 2010), the author described the nascent standards for wide area, local area and home area networks.

Table 1 summarizes the preferred network type for various standards. For HAN, the author claimed that ZigBee as a potential winner as a standard for home energy system, an emerging standard, named oneM2M, is purging its way (Elmangoush, Steinke, Al-Hezmi, & Magedanz, 2014). The third column in Table 1 summarizes the application and preferred communication protocol for oneM2M.

The generic communication architecture presented in (Yan Y., Qian, Sharif, & Tipper, 2013) is inspired from (Yu, et al., 2011). The architecture engenders home area networks (HANs), business area network (BANs), neighborhood area networks (NANs), and wide area networks (WAN). The survey paper written by (Erol-Kantarci & Mouftah, 2015) added field area networks (FAN) and argued that the topology of FAN is similar to NAN.

The works by (Gungor, Sahin, Kocak, & Ergut, Smart grid technologies: communication technologies and standards, 2011) and (Fang, Misra, Xue, & Yang, 2012) categorized the grid communication platform based on the communication medium. This type of classification permits to further select the communication architecture based on the QoS requirements, cost and the environments. For instance,

Table 1. Preferred communication for HAN, NAN and WAN

Standard	Network Type	Preferred communication	Application
IEC 61850	WAN	fiber optic WiMax	Substation automation
ANSI C12.22	LAN	IEEE 802.11 PLC	Smart meter
oneM2M	HAN	BLE, RFID/NFC, WiFi	Home automation

wireless communication in local area network is preferred over wired LAN in case the application needs flexible connectivity, shorter installation time, high mobility (Wickelgren, 1996).

In (Gungor, Sahin, Kocak, & Ergut, Smart grid technologies: communication technologies and standards, 2011), the authors compared and contrasted six available communication technologies: GSM, GPRS, 3G, WiMAX, PLC and Zigbee. They also described four communication requirements security, system reliability, robustness and availability, scalability, and QoS.

(Fang, Misra, Xue, & Yang, 2012) surveyed the interoperability between the various communication technologies to meet end-to-end requirements and described open research problems.

(Nafi, Ahmed, Gregory, & Datta, 2016) also categorized the smart grid communication architecture based on the standard model of a smart grid as identified in the IEEE 2030 standard (IEEE Std 2030-2011, 2011). This resulted in a three layers' communication network architecture. The core network which covers the generation and transmission domains, wide area network which covers the distribution network, and the private network which involves the customer domain.

(Ma, Chen, Huang, & Meng, 2013) described categories of communication technologies depending on the task they perform in the overall process of delivering power from the supply to demand side. In this way, an electric grid can be viewed as consisting of two systems, transmission and distribution. The authors discussed recent communication technologies such as wide area frequency monitoring networks and cognitive radio based regional area networks in the transmission domain, and 802.15 based smart utility networks, TV white space and Hybrid (WiMAX/Wireless Mesh Networks) in the distribution domain.

While many surveys have categorized the smart grid communication infrastructure and technologies in terms of various smart grid application requirements and supported features (Anzar, Nadeem, & Sohail, 2015) (Kabalci, 2016) (Khan & Khan, 2013), other studies have taken a different perspective. (Ancillotti, Bruno, & Conti, 2013) have taken a data centric approach. The authors have categorized the smart grid communication technologies according to their abilities to facilitate the collection, transmission and storage of critical data for smart grid applications. They described the communication sub-system of a smart grid being made up of mainly two parts. The first part is the communication infrastructure responsible for providing the pathway through which different components can connect. The second part is the middleware platform which sits on top of the communication network, abstracting away the underlying details, and providing a user friendly API for distributed smart grid applications (Ben Dhaou, et al., 2017).

Figure 3. Architecture of a cellular wireless Internet network

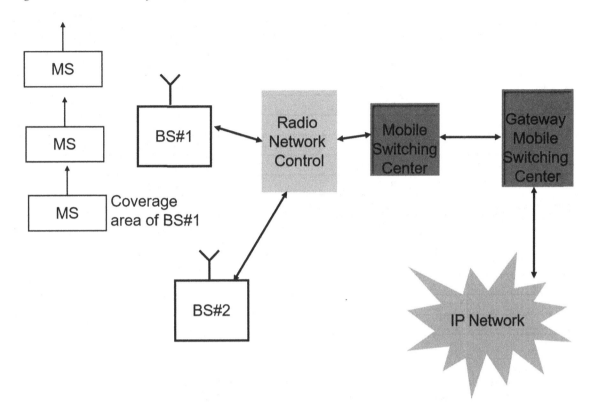

Internet of Things Technologies

Traditionally, the Internet was accessed using a fixed computer or laptop. Advances in wireless communications and silicon technologies have enabled access to the internet anywhere anytime. Nowadays, the Internet is accessible using smart-phone, WIFI or other long-range wireless communication technologies (3G, LTE, 4G, etc.). Wireless Internet access using cellular technologies is ensured by the following entities: A base-station (BS) that connects the mobile devices (MS) to cellular network for message or voice exchange, a radio network controller (RNC) is the block that is responsible for spectrum control, a mobile switching center that links the MS to the public switched network, and a gateway mobile switching center (GMSC) that interfaces the cellular network with the Internet. Figure 3 illustrates a generic architecture for wireless internet access using a cellular technology.

Advances in sensing technologies coupled with the miniaturization of the silicon devices (nanometer technologies) have enabled the development of the wireless sensor network. Wireless Sensor Network (WSN) is composed from a number of spatially distributed and communicating sensors. WSN are used to collect data from various domains such as biological system, environment, electrical appliances, machine, and city infrastructure. WSN has enabled the development of a plethora of smart and ubiquitous applications. Broadly speaking, the WSN can be used for tracking or monitoring. Table 2 cites a few applications of WSN.

Table 2. Applications of WSN

Application Name	Area	Category
ECO-driving	Vehicle engine	Monitoring
Healthcare	Human body	Monitoring
ECO-routing	Vehicle	Tracking
Surveillance	Military	Monitoring
Anti-traffic noise	Environment	Monitoring
Industrial automation	Factory	Monitoring
Traffic management system	City	Tracking
Energy saving	Building	Monitoring
Precision agriculture	Agriculture	Monitoring
Oil drilling	Underground	Monitoring
Animal tracking	Agriculture	Tracking
Corrosion monitoring	Underwater	Monitoring
Smart post	Mail system	tracking
Logistic	Production chain	tracking
Smart grid	Energy	Monitoring

Cyber-physical system, CPS, is a three-layer architecture devised to use modern ICT tools for cyber control of physical components. Figure 4. depicts the architecture for a CPS system (Lin, et al., 2017). The lower level of the architecture is the physical sensors that measure physical parameters. The measurements are then forwarded to the communication layer which is responsible for connecting the sensors to the ICT equipment for control, coordination, monitoring and managements. The application layer uses the communication layer for receiving or transmitting messages. Cyber-physical system has been used in a variety of applications such as e-health, transportation, smart-gird, building, defense, etc.

Internet of Things (IoT) is an emerging computing and communication paradigm. Though, there is not yet a globally recognized definition of the IoT, most work refer to the IoT as the interconnection of object, things and humans using Internet technology (Lin, et al., 2017). Similar to the CPS, IoT is a multilayer architecture that interconnects heterogeneous networks; hence, it is often regarded as a network of networks. Figure 5 illustrates the architecture of a service oriented IoT.

CPS and IoT have some similarities and differences. As summarized in (Lin, et al., 2017), IoT interconnects CPS systems horizontally.

IoT Architecture/Layers

There are multiple IoT architecture models available, from conceptual to technology levels. Figure 6 presents a technological and collaborative IoT architecture divided into complementary successive layers. This model is based on information flow where devices (sensors and actuators) make up the lowest layer. For the purposes of this model, a sensor is nothing more than a data generation point. This sensor can thus be a micro-device or a large water flow monitoring system. The data generated by these devices is carried via the network where it lands on edge gateways. Edge gateways are utilized to filter, normalize

Figure 4. CPS Architecture

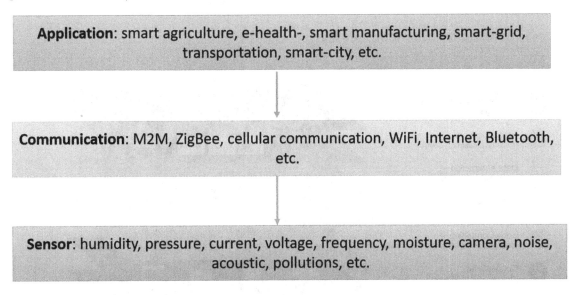

Figure 5. IoT architecture (service and application view)

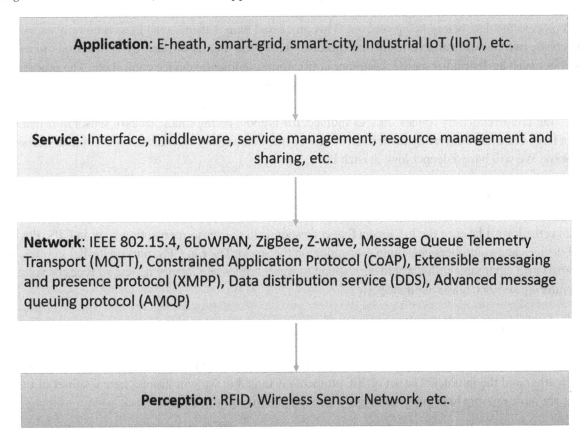

Figure 6. IoT World Forum Architecture Reference Model (device and connectivity view)

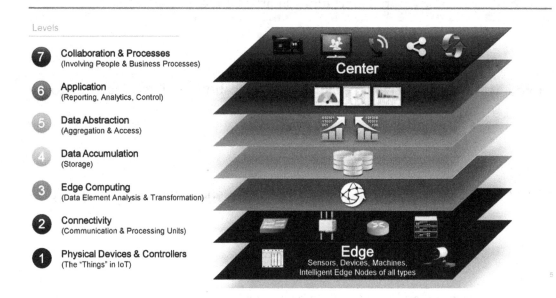

and process the data before being sent out. This processed data is then stored in a commonly accessed database, one that is available to all stakeholders. There the data is utilized by applications to offer services such as demand-response, customer notifications, automatic device control etc. The processed data in databases, combined with the decisions then enables the human decision-making process. The human decision making is complemented via visualizations based on historic or real time data, system constraints and regulatory frameworks. Combined, IoT is about taking small pieces of sensor information on a large scale and converting them into actionable information and visualizations for human decision makers. We will have a deeper look at each layer.

Physical Devices

This is the lowest layer of the IoT model that corresponds to the sensor/perception layer in CPS. Physical devices and controllers constitute everything on the sensor layer in CPS, plus controller entities. In a smart grid environment this would correspond to smart homes and factory nodes, all types of voltage monitoring sensors, home appliances etc.

Connectivity

The connectivity layer includes both network connectivity and enabling sensors and devices to talk to each other and the internet. The set of IoT protocols is large but we will discuss here a subset of them that are most relevant to smart grids. Figure 7 shows the IoT communication stack.

Figure 7. IoT communication stack

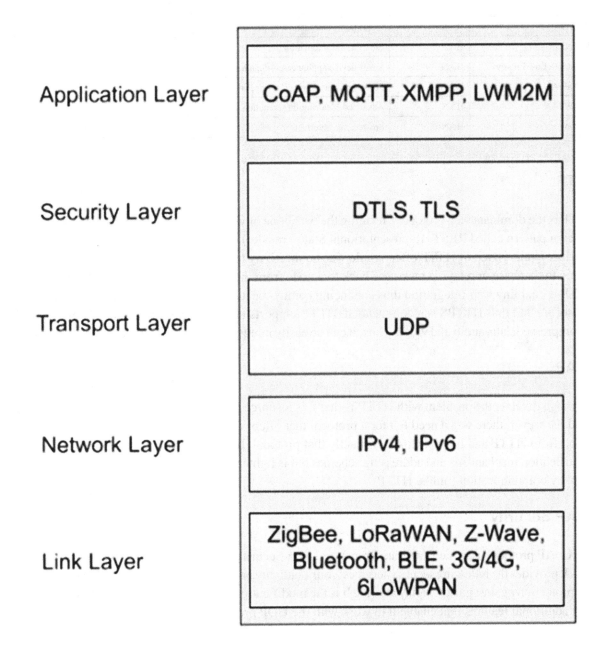

The link level protocols can be divided into three major categories: Long-Range Protocols: LoRA, NBIoT; medium range: Wi-Fi, 4G/LTE, 5G; and short Range: Bluetooth, ZigBee. Table 3 summarizes commonly known IoT wireless communication protocol.

The Application Layer Protocols are also of several types as follows:

Table 3. IoT communication protocol

IoT Protocol	SG Domain	SG Application
ZigBee	HAN	Smart home automation, Power consumption monitoring, automatic meter reading
Bluetooth	HAN	Smart home automation
Bluetooth Low Energy	HAN	Smart device/appliances automation
LoRaWAN	WAN	Power transmission monitoring, power equipment management
6LoWPAN	HAN	Advanced Metering Infrastructure, Smart home automation
Z-Wave	HAN	Smart home automation

HTTP

HTTP is the dominant web protocols, forming the backbone of world wide web. HTTP and HTTPS offer a design pattern called REST (Representational State Transfer). REST APIs (application Programming Interface) built on top of HTTP offer simple web connectivity to devices. Whether it is device to cloud, device to database or relaying messages back to a node from the cloud. The most significant benefit of HTTP is enabling web-integration thus enhancing communication and interoperability. HTTP however is insecure and thus HTTPS is recommended. HTTP supports multiple types of payload, from text files to compressed data, audio and video. Thus, it can be easily integrated into any internet connected system.

CoAP

Although diverse, the problem with HTTP is that it is resource intensive. It was not designed for IoT in mind. However, there was a need felt for a protocol that offers web-integration, can be easily translated to and from HTTP and lighter. CoAP is exactly that protocol. It follows similar syntax to HTTP, same identification mechanisms and addressing schemes but is lighter. CoAP is also designed to support one-to-many communication (unlike HTTP).

CoAP Security

The CoAP protocol uses the Datagram Transport Layer Security (DTLS) protocol as its security extension. It provides the following security services: confidentiality, integrity, authentication, non-repudiation, and protection against packet replay attacks. It is the modification of the Transport Layer Protocol (TLS) with additional features that enable it to work with the UDP protocol.

There are four defined security modes that can be used by CoAP (+DTLS):

- **NoSec:** With this mode CoAP messages are exchanged without any security
- **PreSharedKey:** In this mode, CoAP messages are protected using symmetric key encryption. Communicating devices possess shared symmetric keys that they use to encrypt messages. These symmetric keys need to be pre-configured before communication is initiated. It is a mode that is suitable for low end devices, and in small scale deployments.

Figure 8. MQTT username/password fields within CONNECT packet

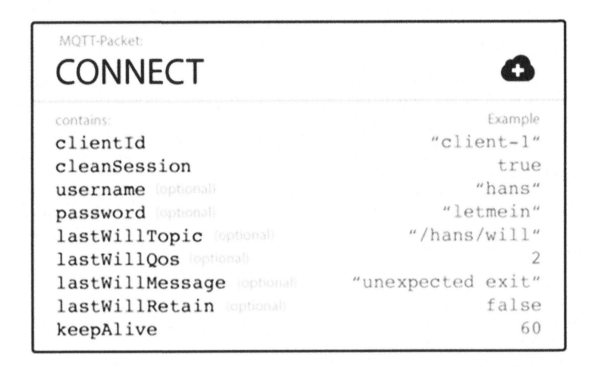

- **RawPublicKey:** In this mode, messages are protected using asymmetric key encryption. Communicating devices use pre-configured asymmetric key pair to encrypt and authenticate the messages. This mode is used for devices with more processing power but without a supporting public key infrastructure. It is defined as a mandatory mode to implement CoAP.
- **Certificate-Based:** This mode is similar to the RawPublicKey mode but with a supporting public key infrastructure. The infrastructure supports issuing, management, and validation of certificates. Each device possesses an asymmetric key pair with an X.509 certificate signed by a valid certificate authority (CA). When communicating, a device can use the key pair to secure the session, and authenticate the identity of the other party using a valid certification chain.

MQTT

MQTT was designed by IBM to be a very lightweight messaging protocol. It is a light, payload agnostic and network agnostic communication protocol. Theoretically it can even be used over SMS (short messaging service). MQTT offers higher reliability and quality of service over unreliable connections.

MQTT Security

The MQTT protocol aims to simple and lightweight. As a result, it only offers minimal security mechanisms be default. Additional security protection can be provided by standard security protocols in different layers of the communication stack. MQTT provides authentication capabilities using client identities, and username/password credentials. A client can optionally send a username and password when it connects to a broker. As Figure 8 shows, there are optional username/password fields in the MQTT CONNECT packet.

The username field is an UTF-8 encoded string while the password field is binary with a maximum of 64k bytes. When the broker receives the username/password combination, it authenticates the client and allows authorized communication to proceed. However, the username/password credentials are exchanged in plain text by default. Extra protection is needed to secure the transmission of these credentials. It can be provided in the network or transport layers.

In the network layer, standard solutions such as VPN can be used to secure the MQTT communication. This solution provides a secure tunnel through which communication can pass. It is used in situations where there are central gateways between the communicating parties.

In the transport layer, TLS/SSL is used to provide confidentiality through encryption. In addition, certificates can be used to provide authentication. In the application layer, MQTT provides client identities, and username/passwords credentials to implement authentication service. Custom encryption of payloads can also be provided by the specific application to implement further security

XMPP

XMPP started as chat/instant messaging protocol. It offers one-to-one and one-to-many communication. XMPP mandates the use of encryption (TLS/SASL) for security. For use-cases where security and node/user authentication are important XMPP is a good choice. For humans it might be a real-time communication protocol but for embedded systems it is slow.

Gateways for Interoperability

Since not all communication protocols might be supported by all the devices, gateways play an important role here. They offer internet access to the extreme low power nodes and interoperability between devices that target a different protocol.

Edge Computing

Edge computing is about bringing the computation from cloud towards the consumer edge. The consumer, in the context of smart grids, can be either home or industrial locations. Edge computing offers a distributed architecture enabling redundancy, masking cloud outages and lower response times in terms of latency. In our context, edge computing can be considered as a resource for integrating Smart Meters and distributed energy resources (DERs) into the IoT based smart grid.

Data Accumulation and Data Aggregation

IoT, in itself, does not care about what type of data is collected and why. Data collection is always context and application dependent. However, IoT architectures and solutions do offer the mechanisms to collect, store and analyze data. In the context of smart grids, data is the underlying decision metric for not only for reporting and billing but for demand predictions, load management and customer communications.

Application

Application layer in IoT deals with the tools that are enabled/envisioned based on the data aggregation from the lower layer. As stated in the previous section, these applications can be; reporting, billing, predicting load/stress and then devising algorithms for mitigating/managing the load.

Collaboration and Processes

The final layer in IoT involves people and regulatory/management processes. The end goal is to enable the business decision makers have a better insight into their operations. Enabling cross-domain and cross-industry and government collaboration. In the later section we will have an overview of how different IoT technologies can help achieve the same goals for smart grids.

IoT SECURITY

To provide the necessary security features, security mechanisms can be applied at different levels across the IoT communication stack. There exist several security extensions that have been developed for communication protocols operating at each of these levels. Each of these extensions have their own advantages and disadvantages.

The 802.15.4 standard which operates at the link layer provides eight different levels of security depending on the application needs (Alharby, Weddell, Reeve, & Harris, 2018). These levels protect each frame and provide confidentiality, authenticity, integrity, and replay detection features. Each level can provide the following security services: encryption only (AES-CTR), authentication and integrity only (AES-CBC-MAC), or all three combined (AES-CCM).

In the network layer, general-purpose security solutions such as IKEv2/IPSec (IETF) are used to provide data authentication, integrity and integrity features. They can provide host-to-host or network-to-network security by establishing secure channels through which communication can pass. The security mechanisms are transparent to all IoT applications protocols operating at the higher levels. This offers simplicity by trading off flexibility.

In the transport layers, TLS/SSL and DTLS are used to provide security services for IoT-based applications. TLS/SSL which relies on the TCP protocol is used to ensure the authenticity between communicating parties by using asymmetric encryption schemes. Certificates are used as the form of identity and a public key infrastructure is needed to support its operation. DTLS (IETF)is the modified form of TLS which operates on top of the UDP protocol. As a result, it is more lightweight and is the preferred option for many security deployments for IoT-based applications.

APPLICATION OF INTERNET OF THINGS IN SMART GRID

One of the promising approaches in the implementation of the ICT systems for powering micro-grids and smart grid has been the use of IoT technologies. These technologies have already revolutionized many other domains where they have been applied. They have allowed microprocessors and communication modules to be embedded in everyday devices, turning them into smarter devices.

In the power sector, the integration of IoT technologies has offered similar opportunities and advantages. By embedding IoT components in nodes making up the power system, the whole process of power generation, transmission, distribution, consumption, and management can be made more efficient and intelligent. These intelligent nodes can perform better by making autonomous decisions and adapting their behaviors based on the context. In addition, they can also communicate with each other and coordinate their activities in order to achieve system wide goals more efficiently.

Multi-Agent Systems

Multi-agent system, MAS, is a new promising technology for control and monitoring of the smart gird enabled by the IoT. MAS is evolved from the distributed computing environment in which agent-oriented programming has been established (Wooldridge, 2009). The development of MAS has been by promoted by the Internet technologies. An agent can be a piece of software or hardware that can collaborate to solve an optimization problem with global constraints subject to some objective function. MAS has shown great potential in WSN environment.

Three classes of agents have been established in (Dagdeviren, Korkmaz, Tekbacak, & Erciyes, 2011). Specifically, in WSN agents can be mobile software or mobile hardware or a sensor node. In the smart grid domain, MAS has been used in various levels including protection, control, FLISR (fault identification, isolation, and restoration), and substation automation (Shawon, Muyeen, Ghosh, Islam, & Baptista, 2019). The MAS is a cornerstone technology for the decentralized operation of the smart grid. Multi-level MAS based architecture has been elaborated in substation automation (Wu, Feng, Tang, & Fitch, 2005), demand-side management (Rwegasira, et al., 2019) . The lower level is often regarded as the hardware agent which is responsible for actuation, measurement, and control of hardware unit (charge controller, relay, etc.)

Figure 9 pictures physical agents that have been designed to control the operation of a DC microgrid using load-shedding techniques (Rwegasira, et al., 2019). The agents have been modeled using REPAST. The battery agent is responsible for control and monitoring the storage elements. The solar energy agent takes care of simulating the solar radiation. Finally, the load agent monitors and controls the operation of DC loads. Practical realization of the dc-microgrid necessities the incorporation of the communication protocols. A survey work of the MAS platform and the associated ICT infrastructure has been conducted in (Shawon, Muyeen, Ghosh, Islam, & Baptista, 2019). Table 4 summarizes sample work on MAS application and its associated IoT communication protocol.

Previous research has shown that the application of IoT for smart micro-grids can offer unique advantages compared to other existing ICT infrastructure. (Yu, et al., 2011) showed that IoT can help a smart-grid become more context-aware, interactive, autonomous and self-healing. It helps to achieve these goals by facilitating the collection, filtering, analysis and processing of a large amounts of contextual data. Table 5 shows the comparison between IoT based and traditional smart-grid ICT networks.

(Jabłońska, 2014) also describes the role IoT can play in powering and supporting the deployment of smart-grids and micro-grids. As cloud technologies continue to replace humans in performing data analysis, IoT through sensor technologies, can enable objects to collect contextual information and interact with their environment. The author sees these wireless sensor networks as a major part of IoT that enable wide scale collection and communication of sensor data necessary for autonomy and adaptability.

Figure 9. MAS based DSM proposed
Source: Rwegasira, et al., 2019

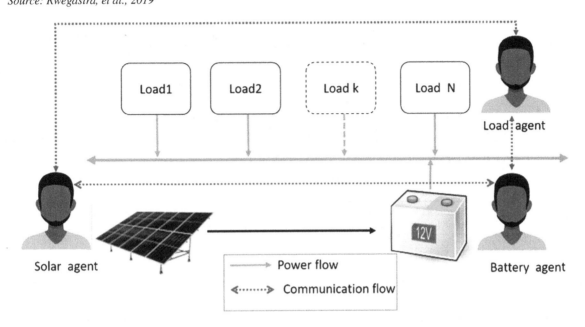

Table 4. MAS application and the associated IoT communication protocol

MAS Application	Smart-Grid Domain	IoT Communication Protocol	References
FLISR and substation automation	Distribution	TCP/IP, IEC 61850	(Ben Meskina, Doggaz, Khalgui, & Li, 2017) (Sekhavatmanesh & Cherkaoui, 2019) (Zhabelova & Vyatkin, 2012)
Energy trading and energy management	Customer	Zigbee, WiFi	(Kahrobaee, Rajabzadeh, Soh, & Asgarpoor, 2013) (Rasheed, Javaid, Hussain, Akbar, & Khan, 2017)
Microgrid control	Distribution	WiFi, Zigbee, IEC 61860	(Liang, et al., 2012) (Cintuglu & Mohammed, Multiagent-based decentralized operation of microgrids considering data interoperability, 2015) (Cintuglu, Youssef, & Mohammed, Development and Application of a Real-Time Testbed for Multiagent System Interoperability: A Case Study on Hierarchical Microgrid Control, 2018)

As IoT devices also continue to become smaller, more powerful, and consuming less power, the number and variety of functions that can be implemented in power systems can only increase. The technology has already been transforming the power grid in China turning it into a smarter system ((Liu, Li, Chen, Zhen, & Zeng, 2011). In another example, the integration of an IoT platform in a DC-based grid allowed the creation of a power system that is flexible and adaptable. This resulted in a system that is

Table 5. Comparison between IoT-based and traditional smart grid information and communication networks

	IoT Platform	Present Electric Power Communication Network Platform
Environment perception	Use sensors, RFID to collect data of all processes of electricity	Manual inspection not suited for operations in complex terrain environments
Self-healing	Network nodes have self-recovery ability. Can find, detect, remove hidden faults	Only realizes single dimension, low-level tunnel self-healing and self-recovery.
Interaction	Supports large scale both side data stream supply, both side information interaction for grid and the users	Not realized. Interaction between users and service is simple and one way.
Different character	Supports the backbone network of grid, distribution network. 3G network can also be integrated together	Can integrate many kinds of networks, however, is strictly isolated from the Internet
Security	Can realize real time monitoring, and prevent natural disaster and breakage from external factors	Has information in isolated islands, lack of information sharing, low and inefficient in processing disaster

easily upgradeable and where innovative applications can be implemented easily (Di Zenobio, Steenhaut, Thielemans, & Celidonio, 2017).

The traditional electric power system is generally divided into three main sections depending on the main function that is performed: transmission, distribution and customer (Kundur, Balu, & Lauby, 1994). In all these parts, IoT technologies have already been implemented with positive results.

In the transmission domain, IoT has been used to improve the reliability and stability of transmission lines. (Chen, Sun, Zhu, Zhen, & Chen, 2012) proposed an IoT based architecture for smart-grids (SG-IoT) that allows for the sensing and monitoring of different adverse conditions that can occur in power transmission lines. These conditions include the leaning of transmission towers, the temperature of the conducting wires, wind conditions that can disrupt power lines, and weather conditions such as temperature, humidity and rainfall that can all affect the normal operation of transmission lines. This capability was achieved by deploying small wireless sensors throughout transmission lines and towers. The data collected then passed through other two layers; network and perception, where it was exchanged and analyzed to produce useful information for decision making. A similar use case is also described by (Ou, Zhen, Li, Zhang, & Zeng, 2012) . The authors describe a similar IoT based system for monitoring power transmission lines. The system consists of sensors, a communication network, and data aggregation technologies. By fusing all these technologies together, it was possible to monitor and control the transmission system in real time. There is an opportunity for these technologies to also be applied in other parts or aspects of the smart grid.

Likewise, in the customer domain, IoT has also been applied in different use cases. To seamlessly integrate nodes in homes and buildings into the power system, (Spanò, Di Pascoli, & Iannaccone, 2015) elaborated an approach that utilizes an IoT platform that allows home devices to be embedded with computational and communication abilities. The architecture of the system which consists of sensor and actuator networks, an IoT server, and user interfaces for visualization and control, provides a mechanism for data collection, processing, and monitoring by leveraging existing devices in homes. This use of existing devices minimized the complexity of the deployment and helped with user acceptance.

All these examples highlight the potential of IoT as a driving technology behind an ICT system that can power a smart grid.

Figure 10. AMI architecture

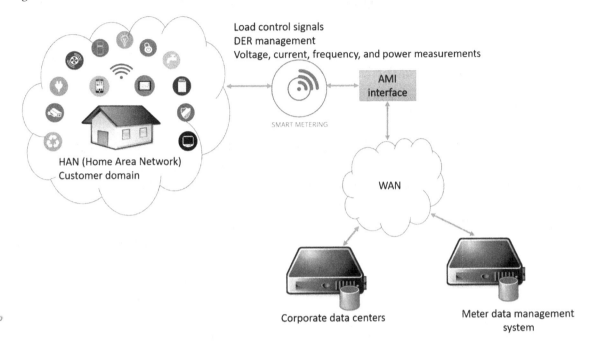

ADVANCED METERING INFRASTRUCTURE

Smart meter is the corner stone technologies for building advanced meter services that allows the customer and utility companies through the two-way communication to optimize the operation of the gird. Demand-side management along with the dynamic pricing are two significant applications of the smart-meter. Smart meter is an embedded system installed on the consumer premises to recorded various electric parameters that can be used for billing, price adjustment, situation awareness, etc.

Advanced metering infrastructure is composed of smart meters, communication network, data-management software. In the NIST reference model, energy service interface (ESI) communicates with associated domains (service providers, distribution, markets, operations, transmission) through the AMI. Figure 10: AMI architectureshows a basic architecture of an AMI.

The application of IoT in the context of AMI has been studied in several published reports. The work of (Wan, Zhang, & Wang, Demonstrability of Narrowband Internet of Things technology in advanced metering infrastructure, 2019) summarized the communication protocols used in the smart-grid. For the AMI, the authors considered the following communication protocols: cellular networks, WiMAX, PLC, wireless mesh technology, ZigBee, and digital subscriber lines. ZigBee is the winning technology in HAN. In addition to those reviewed communication standards, the author of (our work) considered Lora technology. The potential of NB-IoT in AMI has been investigated in (Wan, Zhang, & Wang, Demonstrability of Narrowband Internet of Things technology in advanced metering infrastructure, 2019). NB-IoT has a good indoor and outdoor coverage, cost efficient, and suitable for battery operated devices.

Distribution management system, DMS, monitors and controls the distribution system. It is an actor in the operations domain. Traditionally, the load at the consumer side are not managed by the DMS. To bake advanced DMS services such as demand-response program and DER, (Li, et al., 2010) proposed a middleware centric architecture for the integration of the of AMI and Distribution Management Systems. The architecture uses IoT connectivity.

SOLUTIONS AND RECOMMENDATIONS

Interoperability and Applications

In this section we will discuss how IoT can enable interoperability into the smart grid and which IoT solutions are directly applicable to the needs of smart grids. For a broader look at the technical and data interoperability between IoT models and Smart Grid, we will utilize the SGAM model (Figure 11). The SGAM is a three-dimensional smart grid model that incorporates smart grid domains, zones and interoperability. The ground grid layer encompasses the complete electrical grid from generation to customer premises. The hierarchical division into zones is based on functional separation and user philosophies. Processes include the physical equipment and energy transformation, energy management systems and microgrid management are in the operational zone all the way up to the market zone which encompasses energy trading and retail markets. The third dimension in this model is vertical interoperability, which is divided into five layers. The lower layer deals with the grid components, communication/connectivity, information, grid functionality and the business processes and policies are at the top that are enabled by the communication and information exchange from below. The SGAM offers a complete outlook at all the physical, functional, informational and associative components of a smart grid in a single framework.

Based on out previous discussion on smart grids and IoT reference models, we can draw a complementary framework between the two paradigms. Figure 12 represents the model that merges these two paradigms together.

Expanding on Figure 12, here we will list a subset of IoT technologies that will be beneficial to smart grids.

- Component Layer

The economies of scale of IoT has made it very economical to produce sensors. The proliferation of mobile devices and supply chain has further reduced the cost of electronic devices. This allows customers to acquire smarter devices and companies to blanket their premises with sensors. This sensor and smart device data are what the smart grid systems and policy makers will utilize for any type of decision making.

- Communication Layer

IoT long range protocols like LoRA and NBIoT not only reduce the cost of telemetry but increase the range of communication to kilometers, instead of meters. This is a big advantage for distributed smart grids in remote areas where telecommunications networks might not be available. Light protocols like MQTT and COAP further enhance interoperability with web applications and enterprise systems.

- Information Layer

Figure 11. The smart grid architecture model (SGAM)

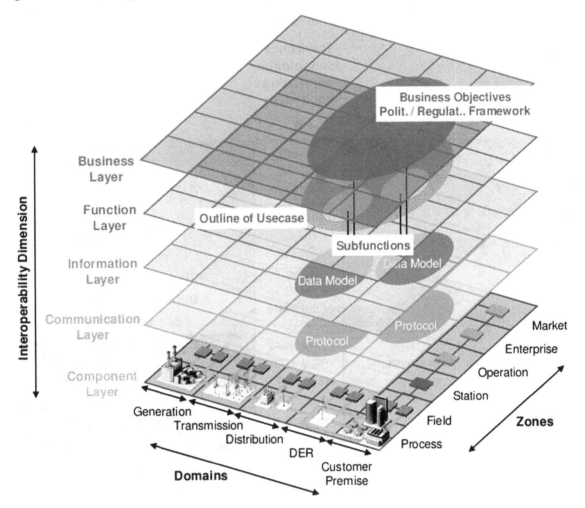

Large scale monitoring will raise the cost of computation and IT infrastructure. however, IoT supported edge computing initiatives can improve privacy (Chen, Lu, & Xiong, n.d.), reduce bandwidth costs (Aazam & Huh, 2016) and improve QoS.

- Function Layer

Middleware like KAA ("Smart Energy, Smart Lighting Solutions with the Kaa IoT Platform," n.d.) allow storage and analysis of sensor data. This enables utilities to monitor assets, perform fault detection, QoS analysis and generate health reports of the grid. Languages like OWL (web ontology language) can annotate and contextualize data by adding semantic information. SPARQL offers contextual information search over semantic links between data. Combined with ML this could enable new applications, services, predictive maintenance and load management that haven not been envisioned yet.

Figure 12. IoT technologies that can support smart grids
Smart Grid Coordination Group. Smart Grid Reference Architecture; Technical Report; CEN-CENELEC-ETSI: Brussels, Belgium, 2012. Link: ttps://ec.europa.eu/energy/sites/ener/files/documents/xpert_group1_reference_architecture.pdf

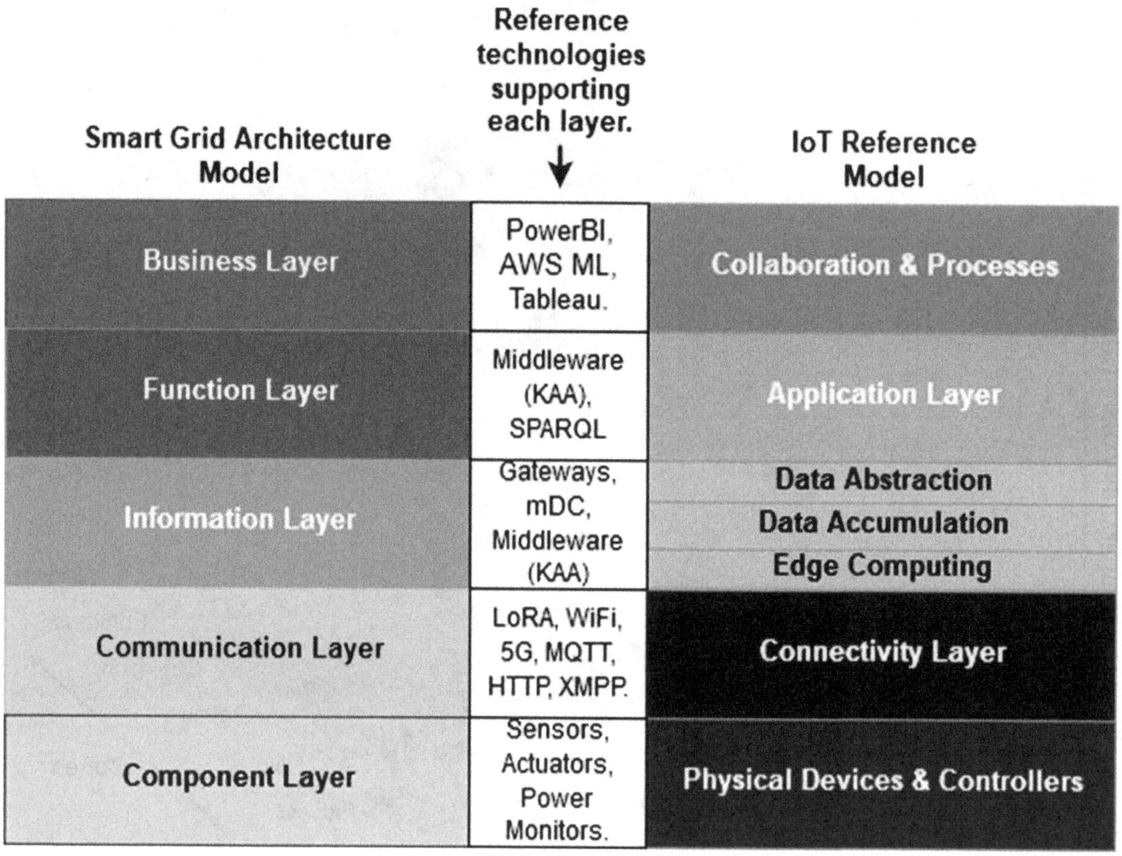

Smart Grid Architecture Model	Reference technologies supporting each layer. ↓	IoT Reference Model
Business Layer	PowerBI, AWS ML, Tableau.	Collaboration & Processes
Function Layer	Middleware (KAA), SPARQL	Application Layer
Information Layer	Gateways, mDC, Middleware (KAA)	Data Abstraction / Data Accumulation / Edge Computing
Communication Layer	LoRA, WiFi, 5G, MQTT, HTTP, XMPP.	Connectivity Layer
Component Layer	Sensors, Actuators, Power Monitors.	Physical Devices & Controllers

- Business Layer

The collection of data eventually is to provide smother operations and services. Tableau ("Business Intelligence and Analytics Software," n.d.) is a leading data visualization platform that enables analytics, data governance and collaboration in one suite. This enables board members to assess the grid and improve data collection efficiency. Governments can have better insights into energy requirements and customers will have a deeper look at their usage behaviors. Amazon AWS ML ("Machine Learning on AWS," n.d.) enables companies to use machine learning models in the cloud on their sensor data. Utilizing these services, the utility companies do not need to setup their own compute infrastructure and applications to smarten their grid/service offerings.

Edge/Fog Computing and Smart Grids

Edge computing is targeted towards using the computational elements available in the network path, from the end user devices, all the way to the cloud. The OpenFog consortium provides a definition of fog computing as "a horizontal, system-level architecture that distributes computing, storage, control and networking functions closer to the users along a cloud-to-thing continuum." (OpenFog Consortium Architecture Working Group, 2017) Fog and Edge Computing offer a solution to towards low-latency applications for a myriad of use-cases, such as, augmented and virtual reality, smart cities and infrastructure, smart healthcare and vehicular networks (Mouradian, et al., 2018). Fog/edge computing can be adapted to various paradigms because of its inherent features. It is distributed; not only fog nodes reside along the network path towards the cloud but also east-west in a peer-to-peer fashion. Proximity; Fog/Edge nodes are physically closer to the end-user whether it is a smartphone user or a smart home or a smart city control system. To support proximity and hierarchy, it must be heterogeneous in terms of computational resources. When you have many compute nodes, distributed along the network and geographical pathways, you need autonomy in operations.

Utilizing such a diverse, distributed, hierarchical and autonomic architecture would offer many benefits to Smart Grids such as:

- **Decentralization:** In the context of Fog Computing, there are no central servers. This decentralization is unlike Cloud Computing, where a large pool of resources is concentrated within a datacenter. This shift in the decentralization of computing resources aligns with the shift in distributed smart-grids. Instead of one or more large-scale energy producers, there are many, and the consumers themselves can now be producers. Similarly, in Fog Computing, the consumer's routers can be computing devices as well. The decentralized nature of fog computing nodes is a perfect fit for the decentralized smart grid. Fog computing nodes can be spread around to offer on-demand computation to the distributed smart grid applications. We see the advanced smart meter as a point for bridging the gap between the grid and fog.

- **Scalability:** Increases in smart home deployments, on-premises renewable energy solutions, a vehicle to grid-enabled cars would create scalability challenges for SG/AMI applications. Fog computing has a north-south (things to the cloud), east-west (peer-to-peer) architecture that can help mitigate those challenges. The north-south/east-west architecture means that applications and services can either move to another node in the vicinity or move upwards in the fog towards the cloud. This allows the fog itself and the applications and services to scale all-along the deployed environment. And the most significant benefit is in terms of scalability.

- **Resiliency:** Scalability and decentralization result in the resiliency of deployments. An outage at a datacenter can take out all the applications and services running there; this is not the case with fog computing. In fact, small fog nodes can offer cached services to local users whenever there is a cloud outage. A similar example would be a distributed set of storage batteries offering energy to critical local services in case of a grid outage or balancing the voltage frequency.

- **Mobility:** Decentralization allows services to exist anywhere between the end-node/things, all the way on the network path towards the cloud. Fog computing architecture allows services to be mobile. Vehicle-based fog computing is an active research area. This is in-line with vehicle-2-grid (V2G) technologies (Kester, Noel, Rubens, & Sovacool, 2018). One element of V2G technologies is the communication with the grid provider or the automation services that act as middlemen between the consumer and the grid. Cars are already being bundled with V2G capability. Adding a fog node to the car would enhance its communication, security and identity verification in a highly dynamic environment.

Figure 13. IoT assisted edge-cloud computing for smart grids

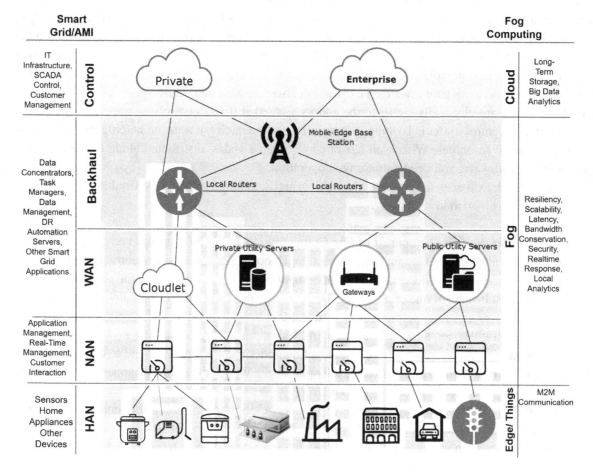

Integrating edge/fog computing into the smart grid will lift the communication infrastructure demands from the smart grid community. Furthermore, it will support the grid on each level.

Privacy, Authentication and Confidentiality

The integration of IoT within the smart grid has exposed the system to new security challenges that could impact further developments and expansions (Bekara, 2014) (Mendel, 2017). These challenges can be categorized into three main groups depending on which aspect of security they impact: privacy, confidentiality, integrity, and authentication.

Privacy-based challenges involve mechanisms that can deduce the personal behavioral patterns of users from the collection of residential and device power usage data. Smart meters and appliances generate a large amount of real time data that can used for this purpose. The fine-grained information can be used to determine personal activities of people within a resident – wake up times, sleeping times, whether they are inside or away from the house, etc., (Mármol, Sorge, Ugus, & Pérez, 2012) . To preserve the privacy this information various approaches involving anonymity, encryption, and access control have been adopted (Elmaghraby & Losavio, 2014) (He, Kumar, & Lee, 2015). (Christian, Günther, Armin, &

Dominik, 2013)propose a framework for generating privacy-related requirements for smart grid applications. It is shown that the best results can be obtained by combining and integrating privacy-enhancing approaches. Future research should focus on figuring how to do so without increasing the complexity.

Confidentiality-based challenges arise from the fact that IoT devices embedded within smart grids often communicate via publicly available networks. When data is exchanged in the clear within this environment, unauthorized third parties can access this data. If this information is sensitive in nature e.g. real time power consumption, its disclosure can lead to adverse consequences (Anzalchi & Sarwat, 2015). To tackle these issues many solutions have been proposed and adopted from existing ICT systems (Busom, Petrlic, Sebé, Sorge, & Valls, 2016) (Liu, Cheng, Gu, Jiang, & Li, 2016). These approaches typically include the use of various forms of lightweight encryption schemes such elliptic curve and homomorphic cryptography (Mahmood, et al., 2018). These approaches are preferred since they are not resource intensive. However, the efficient management of encryption/decryption keys for these schemes remains as an open research problem.

Integrity-based challenges allow attackers to intercept and modify data exchanged between nodes within the smart grid. An example of this can occur in demand response applications where an attacker can lower dynamic prices during peak hours by modifying the content of the data packets. This can lead to the opposite goal of increased consumption resulting in an overloaded power system. Other attacks involve the injection of false data within legitimate sensor and control messages (Giraldo, Cardenas, & Quijano, 2017) . A lot of research is now focused on techniques to distinguish between legitimate and illegitimate data. Machine learning and other artificial technology techniques show a lot of promise in solving these problems (Ozay, Esnaola, Yarman Vural, Kulkarni, & Poor, 2016) (Esmalifalak, Liu, Nguyen, Zheng, & Han, 2017).

Challenges involving authentication result from the ability of one smart node impersonating another by spoofing its identity. For example, a smart meter being maliciously modified to spoof another in order to shift its consumption costs (Punmiya & Choe, 2019). There is need for implementing strong authentication schemes to prevent these problems. However, existing schemes tend to increase latency of communication and involve complex key management procedures. Thus, research is focused on designing mechanisms that are simple and lightweight. For example, (Sule, Katti, & Kavasseri, 2012) have proposed a mechanism that provides strong mutual authentication between smart meters in a smart grid. The mechanism relies on use of a simple MAC instead of the typical HMAC which is more resource intensive. Similar approaches should be considered to ensure efficiency in complex smart grid systems of the future.

CONCLUSION

The utility grid is experiencing a drastic transformation towards adopting two-way communications. Smart-grid is the new generation of the utility grid that is driven by arduous factors such as the need to reduce carbon dioxide, increase the grid efficiency, decrease the cost of operation and maintenance, etc. Information and communication technology, ICT, is the disruptive technology for the realization of the smart-grid functions. The miniaturization of electronic devices coupled with the progress in sensing technology, IoT has emerged as a technological innovation that has been coined to interconnect objects, machines, humans, and systems together using the Internet technology. This chapter has described the application of IoT technologies at the five domains of the smart grid: operations, customer, generation, distribution, and transmission. IoT has enabled new forms of services and architectures such as advanced smart metering infrastructure, distributed intelligence, demand-response program, volt/var optimization, home energy management system, and substation automations. Those functions and services are enabled by key technologies such as multi-agent systems, fog/ cloud computing, middleware, and communication technologies. Notwithstanding, IoT has enabled the realization of the smart-grid, privacy and security remain one big challenge.

REFERENCES

Alharby, S., Weddell, A., Reeve, J., & Harris, N. (2018). The Cost of Link Layer Security in IoT Embedded Devices. *IFAC-PapersOnLine*, *51*(6), 72–77. doi:10.1016/j.ifacol.2018.07.132

Ancillotti, E., Bruno, R., & Conti, M. (2013). The role of communication systems in smart grids: Architectures, technical solutions and research challenges. *Computer Communications*, *36*(17-18), 1665–1697. doi:10.1016/j.comcom.2013.09.004

Anzalchi, A., & Sarwat, A. (2015). *A survey on security assessment of metering infrastructure in Smart Grid systems.* IEEE. doi:10.1109/SECON.2015.7132989

Anzar, M., Nadeem, J., & Sohail, R. (2015). A review of wireless communications for smart grid. *Renewable & Sustainable Energy Reviews*, *41*, 248–260. doi:10.1016/j.rser.2014.08.036

Bekara, C. (2014). *Security Issues and Challenges for the IoT-based Smart Grid.* IEEE. doi:10.1016/j.procs.2014.07.064

Ben Dhaou, I., Kondoro, A., Kelati, A., Rwegasira, D. S., Naiman, S., Mvungi, N. H., & Tenhunen, H. (2017, July). Communication and Security Technologies for Smart Grid. *International Journal of Embedded and Real-Time Communication Systems*, *8*(2), 40–65. doi:10.4018/IJERTCS.2017070103

Ben Meskina, S., Doggaz, N., Khalgui, M., & Li, Z. (2017). Multiagent Framework for Smart Grids Recovery. *IEEE Transactions on Systems, Man, and Cybernetics. Systems*, *47*(7), 1284–1300. doi:10.1109/TSMC.2016.2573824

Busom, N., Petrlic, R., Sebé, F., Sorge, C., & Valls, M. (2016). Efficient smart metering based on homomorphic encryption. *Computer Communications*, *82*, 95–101. doi:10.1016/j.comcom.2015.08.016

Cintuglu, M. H., & Mohammed, O. A. (2015). Multiagent-based decentralized operation of microgrids considering data interoperability. In *IEEE International Conference on Smart Grid Communications (SmartGridComm)*, (pp. 404-409). Miami, FL: IEEE. 10.1109/SmartGridComm.2015.7436334

Cintuglu, M. H., Youssef, T., & Mohammed, O. A. (2018). Development and Application of a Real-Time Testbed for Multiagent System Interoperability: A Case Study on Hierarchical Microgrid Control. *IEEE Transactions on Smart Grid*, *9*(3), 1759–1768. doi:10.1109/TSG.2016.2599265

Dagdeviren, O., Korkmaz, I., Tekbacak, F., & Erciyes, K. (2011). A Survey of Agent Technologies for Wireless Sensor Networks. *IETE Technical Review*, *28*(2), 168–184. doi:10.4103/0256-4602.72509

Dutt, N., Jantsch, A., & Sarma, S. (2016). Toward Smart Embedded Systems: A Self-aware System-on-Chip (SoC) Perspective. *ACM Transactions on Embedded Computing Systems*, 22-22:27.

Elmaghraby, A. S., & Losavio, M. M. (2014). Cyber security challenges in Smart Cities: Safety, security and privacy. *Journal of Advanced Research*, 5(4), 491–497. doi:10.1016/j.jare.2014.02.006 PMID:25685517

Elmangoush, A., Steinke, R., Al-Hezmi, A., & Magedanz, T. (Feb 2014). On the usage of standardised M2M platforms for Smart Energy management. *The International Conference on Information Networking 2014 (ICOIN2014)*, 79-84. 10.1109/ICOIN.2014.6799669

Energy Independence and Security Act of 2007. (2007). Retrieved from https://www.gpo.gov

Erol-Kantarci, M., & Mouftah, H. T. (2015). Energy-efficient information and communication infrastructures in the smart grid: A survey on interactions and open issues. *IEEE Communications Surveys and Tutorials*, 17(1), 179–197. doi:10.1109/COMST.2014.2341600

Esmalifalak, M., Liu, L., Nguyen, N., Zheng, R., & Han, Z. (2017). Detecting Stealthy False Data Injection Using Machine Learning in Smart Grid. *IEEE Systems Journal*, 11(3), 1644–1652. doi:10.1109/JSYST.2014.2341597

Fang, X., Misra, S., Xue, G., & Yang, D. (2012). Smart Grid- The New and Improved Power Grid: A Survey. *IEEE Communications Surveys & Tutorials*, 14, 944-980. doi:10.1109/SURV.2011.101911.00087

Farhangi, H. (2010). The path of the smart grid. *IEEE Power & Energy Magazine*, 8(1), 18–28. doi:10.1109/MPE.2009.934876

Giraldo, J., Cardenas, A., & Quijano, N. (2017). Integrity Attacks on Real-Time Pricing in Smart Grids: Impact and Countermeasures. *IEEE Transactions on Smart Grid*, 8(5), 2249–2257. doi:10.1109/TSG.2016.2521339

Glesner, M., & Philipp, F. (2013). Embedded Systems Design for Smart System Integration. *IEEE Computer Society Annual Symposium on VLSI (ISVLSI)*, 32-33. 10.1109/ISVLSI.2013.6654611

Gungor, V. C., Sahin, D., Kocak, T., & Ergut, S. (2011). Smart grid technologies: communication technologies and standards. *IEEE transactions*.

Gungor, V. C., Sahin, D., Kocak, T., Ergut, S., Buccella, C., Cecati, C., & Hancke, G. P. (2013, February). A Survey on Smart Grid Potential Applications and Communication Requirements. *IEEE Transactions on Industrial Informatics*, 9(1), 28–42. doi:10.1109/TII.2012.2218253

He, D., Kumar, N., & Lee, J.-H. (2015). Privacy-preserving data aggregation scheme against internal attackers in smart grids. *Wireless Networks*, 22. doi:10.100711276-015-0983-3

IEEE Std 2030-2011. (2011). *IEEE Guide for Smart Grid Interoperability of Energy Technology and Information Technology Operation with the Electric Power System (EPS), End-Use Applications, and Loads.* Retrieved from http://ieeexplore.ieee.org/stampPDF/getPDF.jsp?arnumber=6018239

IETF. (2010). *Internet Key Exchange Protocol Version 2 (IKEv2).* Retrieved from https://tools.ietf.org/html/rfc5996

IETF. (2012). *Datagram Transport Layer Security Version 1.2.* Retrieved from https://tools.ietf.org/html/rfc6347

Kabalci, Y. (2016). A survey on smart metering and smart grid communication. *Renewable & Sustainable Energy Reviews, 57,* 302–318. doi:10.1016/j.rser.2015.12.114

Kahrobaee, S., Rajabzadeh, R., Soh, L.-K., & Asgarpoor, S. (2013). A Multiagent Modeling and Investigation of Smart Homes With Power Generation, Storage, and Trading Features. *IEEE Transactions on Smart Grid, 4*(2), 659–668. doi:10.1109/TSG.2012.2215349

Khan, A. A., Rehmani, M. H., & Reisslein, M. (2016). Cognitive Radio for Smart Grids: Survey of Architectures, Spectrum Sensing Mechanisms, and Networking Protocols. *IEEE Communications Surveys Tutorials, 18,* 860-898. doi:10.1109/COMST.2015.2481722

Khan, R. H., & Khan, J. Y. (2013). A comprehensive review of the application characteristics and traffic requirements of a smart grid communications network. *Computer Networks, 57*(3), 825–845. doi:10.1016/j.comnet.2012.11.002

Korzun, D. G., & Gurtov, I. N. (2015). Service Intelligence and Communication Security for Ambient Assisted Living. *International Journal of Embedded and Real-Time Communication Systems, 6*(1), 76–100. doi:10.4018/IJERTCS.2015010104

Li, Z., Wang, Z., Tournier, J.-C., Peterson, W., Li, W., & Wang, Y. (2010). A Unified Solution for Advanced Metering Infrastructure Integration with a Distribution Management System. In *First IEEE International Conference on Smart Grid Communications* (ss. 566-571). Gaithersburg, VA: IEEE. 10.1109/SMARTGRID.2010.5621998

Liang, H., Choi, B. J., Zhuang, W., Shen, X., Awad, A. S., & Abdr, A. (2012). Multiagent coordination in microgrids via wireless networks. *IEEE Wireless Communications, 19*(3), 14–22. doi:10.1109/MWC.2012.6231155

Lin, J., Yu, W., Zhang, N., Yang, X., Zhang, H., & Zhao, W. (2017, October). A Survey on Internet of Things: Architecture, Enabling Technologies, Security and Privacy, and Applications. *IEEE Internet of Things Journal, 4*(5), 1125–1142. doi:10.1109/JIOT.2017.2683200

Liu, Y., Cheng, C., Gu, T., Jiang, T., & Li, X. (2016). A Lightweight Authenticated Communication Scheme for Smart Grid. *IEEE Sensors Journal, 16.* doi:10.1109/jsen.2015.2489258

Ma, R., Chen, H.-H., Huang, Y.-R., & Meng, W. (2013). Smart Grid Communication: Its Challenges and Opportunities. *IEEE Transactions on Smart Grid, 4*(1), 36–46. doi:10.1109/TSG.2012.2225851

Mahmood, K., Chaudhry, S. A., Naqvi, H., Kumari, S., Li, X., & Sangaiah, A. K. (2018). An elliptic curve cryptography based lightweight authentication scheme for smart grid communication. *Future Generation Computer Systems, 81,* 557–565. doi:10.1016/j.future.2017.05.002

Mármol, F., Sorge, C., Ugus, O., & Pérez, G. (2012). Do not snoop my habits: Preserving privacy in the smart grid. *IEEE Communications Magazine, 50*(5), 166–172. doi:10.1109/MCOM.2012.6194398

Mendel, J. (2017). Smart Grid Cyber Security Challenges: Overview and Classification. *e-mentor, 2017.* doi:10.15219/em68.1282

Nafi, N. S., Ahmed, K., Gregory, M. A., & Datta, M. (2016, October). A Survey of Smart Grid Architectures, Applications, Benefits and Standardization. *Journal of Network and Computer Applications*, *76*, 1–21. doi:10.1016/j.jnca.2016.10.003

National Institute of Standards and Technology. (2014). *NIST Framework and Roadmap for Smart Grid Interoperability Standards (Release 3.0)*. US Department of Commerce.

Ozay, M., Esnaola, I., Yarman Vural, F. T., Kulkarni, S. R., & Poor, H. V. (2016). Machine Learning Methods for Attack Detection in the Smart Grid. *IEEE Transactions on Neural Networks and Learning Systems*, *27*(8), 1773–1786. doi:10.1109/TNNLS.2015.2404803 PMID:25807571

Punmiya, R., & Choe, S. (2019). Energy Theft Detection Using Gradient Boosting Theft Detector With Feature Engineering-Based Preprocessing. *IEEE Transactions on Smart Grid*, *10*(2), 2326–2329. doi:10.1109/TSG.2019.2892595

Rasheed, M. B., Javaid, N., Hussain, S. M., Akbar, M., & Khan, Z. A. (2017). Multiagent Control System for Residential Energy Management under Real Time Pricing Environment. In *IEEE 31st International Conference on Advanced Information Networking and Applications (AINA)*, (pp. 120-125). Taipei: IEEE.

Rwegasira, D. S., Ben Dhaou, I. S., Kondoro, A., Anagnostou, A., Kelati, A., Naiman, S., ... Tenhunen, H. (2019). A Demand-Response Scheme Using Multi-Agent System for Smart DC Microgrid. *International Journal of Embedded and Real-Time Communication Systems*, *10*(1), 48–68. doi:10.4018/IJERTCS.2019010103

Sekhavatmanesh, H., & Cherkaoui, R. (2019). Distribution Network Restoration in a Multiagent Framework Using a Convex OPF Model. *IEEE Transactions on Smart Grid*, *10*(3), 2618–2628. doi:10.1109/TSG.2018.2805922

Sendin, A., Sanchez-Fornie, M. A., Berganza, I., Simon, J., & Urrutia, I. (2016). Telecommunication Networks for the Smart Grid. Norwood, MA: Artech House.

Shawon, M. H., Muyeen, S. M., Ghosh, A., Islam, S. M., & Baptista, M. S. (2019). Multi-Agent Systems in ICT Enabled Smart Grid: A Status Update on Technology Framework and Applications. *IEEE Access: Practical Innovations, Open Solutions*, *7*, 97959–97973. doi:10.1109/ACCESS.2019.2929577

Sule, R., Katti, R. S., & Kavasseri, R. G. (2012). *A variable length fast Message Authentication Code for secure communication in smart grids*. IEEE. doi:10.1109/PESGM.2012.6345622

Wan, L., Zhang, Z., & Wang, J. (2019). Demonstrability of Narrowband Internet of Things technology in advanced metering infrastructure. *EURASIP Journal on Wireless Communications and Networking*, (1): 1–12.

Wan, L., Zhang, Z., & Wang, J. (2019, January). Demonstrability of Narrowband Internet of Things technology in advanced metering infrastructure. *EURASIP Journal on Wireless Communications and Networking*, *2019*(1), 2–12. doi:10.118613638-018-1323-y

Wickelgren, I. J. (1996, September). Local-area networks go wireless. *IEEE Spectrum*, *33*(9), 34–40. doi:10.1109/6.535256

Wooldridge, M. (2009). An Introduction to MultiAgent Systems (2nd ed.). West Sussesx, UK: Wiley.

Wu, Q., Feng, J., Tang, W., & Fitch, J. (2005). Multi-agent Based Substation Automation Systems. In *IEEE Power Engineering Society General Meeting*, (pp. 1048-1049). San Francisco, CA: IEEE.

Yan, Y., Qian, Y., Sharif, H., & Tipper, D. (2012). A Survey on Cyber Security for Smart Grid Communications. *IEEE Communications Surveys & Tutorials, 14*, 998-1010.

Yan, Y., Qian, Y., Sharif, H., & Tipper, D. (2013). A survey on smart grid communication infrastructures: Motivations, requirements and challenges. *IEEE Communications Surveys and Tutorials, 15*(1), 5–20. doi:10.1109/SURV.2012.021312.00034

Yu, R., Zhang, Y., Gjessing, S., Yuen, C., Xie, S., & Guizani, M. (2011, September). Cognitive radio based hierarchical communications infrastructure for smart grid. *IEEE Network, 25*(5), 6–14. doi:10.1109/MNET.2011.6033030

Zhabelova, G., & Vyatkin, V. (2012). Multiagent Smart Grid Automation Architecture Based on IEC 61850/61499 Intelligent Logical Nodes. *IEEE Transactions on Industrial Electronics, 59*(5), 2351–2362. doi:10.1109/TIE.2011.2167891

Chapter 11
Internet of Things and Cyber–Physical Systems at the University

Dmitry Namiot
Lomonosov Moscow State University, Russia

Manfred Sneps-Sneppe
Ventspils University of Applied Sciences, Latvia

ABSTRACT

This chapter describes proposals for organizing university programs on the internet of things (IoT) and cyber-physical systems. The final goal is to provide a structure for a basic educational course for the internet of things and related areas. This base (template) could be used both for direct training and for building other courses, including those that are more deeply specialized in selected areas. For related areas, the authors see, for example, machine-to-machine communications and data-driven cities (smart cities) development. Obviously, the internet of things skills are in high demand nowadays, and, of course, IoT models, architectures, as well as appropriate data proceedings elements should be presented in the university courses. The purpose of the described educational course is to cover information and communication technologies used in the internet of things systems and related areas. Also, the authors discuss big data and AI issues for IoT courses and highlight the importance of data engineering.

INTRODUCTION

In our works, we addressed several times the topic of education in the field of the Internet of Things and related areas. Here you can see articles devoted to computer science and Internet of Things (IoT) education (Namiot, 2016), our paper presented on The 20th Conference of Open Innovations Association FRUCT and ISPIT 2017 seminar (Namiot, Sneps-Sneppe, & Daradkeh, 2017), and its extended version published in IJERTCS (Namiot & Sneps-Sneppe, 2017).

DOI: 10.4018/978-1-7998-1974-5.ch011

Naturally, the situation in computer science is changing rapidly. Changes should be reflected in the curriculum. One of the moments of criticism of university education now is just a weak reaction to changes and large inertia. This means, of course, that there is a need to periodically update the content of the curriculum. Also, already based on the conducted training, assessments of learning outcomes appear, both from graduates and from the industry where graduates went to work. In Russia, for example, a state program for the development of the digital economy has emerged, where the training of specialists on these issues is directly put in the forefront (Sneps-Sneppe, Namiot, & Alberts, 2018). Accordingly, this article presents our current vision on this issue.

Currently, the issues related to the Internet of Things and Machine to Machine communications (M2M) are attracting a lot of attention and IoT (M2M) skills are in high demand. At the same time, many existing presentations of IoT applications and systems contain only futuristic descriptions. They are more concentrated on the public effects and their impact on everyday life and completely ignore technical details. However, all the above-mentioned acronyms (IoT, M2M) have nowadays a full line of standards, frameworks, development tools, etc. In our opinion, it is very important to study the technical aspects of IoT (M2M). By 2020, the global demand for IoT developers is estimated at 4.5 million people (Asay, 2014). This demand naturally raises the questions of deep learning for IoT technologies.

In our opinion, currently, we cannot mention a single course on the Internet of Things that covered all the aspects discussed below. Actually, there are no even unified approaches to its content and structure. Naturally, both of these technologies – IoT and M2M (or more accurately - both of these directions) did not arise in a vacuum. They are reusing and incorporating many disciplines related to information and computer technology (Computer Science). For example, network technologies are present in the curriculum and without any connection to the Internet of Things.

However, of course, we can talk about the development of specific programming architectures and models for IoT (M2M), etc. For example, some of the top-level models for IoT and M2M programming models have been published in our papers (Namiot & Sneps-Sneppe, 2014). It seems that, at least, the navigation tool for the audience (students) in the current situation in IoT (M2M) could be very useful. In our opinion, the understanding of the architectures is a key moment for development.

In the current state of our project, we are talking about a semi-annual and an annual course (depends on the educational program) which aims to introduce students to modern information technology, standing for such areas as the M2M and IoT. In this case, it refers to students studying in areas related to Computer Science. In our practice in Russia, for example, such a course could be a part of the master's program in Faculty of Computational Mathematics and Cybernetics Lomonosov Moscow State University. Ventspils University of Applied Sciences looks for some post-graduate education. Consequently, the minimum requirements are a bachelor's degree in IT technology. Also, a significant recent trend is courses that are prepared for specific corporate customers. They can be considered as customizations of basic courses.

The big question here is debatable - it is necessary or not to include here the materials for the Smart City. Very often, it is considered in conjunction with IoT, for example. In our vision, at least for now, we should not include Smart City related questions into IoT courses. Firstly, in many aspects, it seems still more related to the processes of the organization, rather than information technologies. At the same time, our idea was to stay in computer science and computer engineering domains, which include precisely IoT and M2M. In general, Smart Cities' themes should be closer to the general sections of the digital economy. On the other hand, borders are often blurred. For example, we can mention here such a popular direction as cyber-physical systems (CPS - Sanislav, Miclea, 2012). As per definition, they are engineering systems based on the interaction of software algorithms and physical objects. CPS are integrations of computation and physical processes. In reality, there is a debatable question here. Should we consider CPS separately, or, following NIST, consider IoT as a part of CPS. The Industrial Internet of Things (IIoT) refers to interconnected things (e.g. sensors) networked together with computers' industrial applications. In this review, we make no distinction with IoT. First of all, because the courses we offer are not related to the business aspects of applications.

In summary, the questions for research can be formulated as follows. What exactly and why should be included in the course (or courses) of master's level training on the topic of the Internet of Things?

The rest of the chapter is organized as follows. First, we discuss the general content for IoT courses. This topic has already been touched upon in our previous works. Here it was seriously revised and updated based on the comments of reviewers, readers' feedback and teaching experience. In the next section, we discuss CPS courses. After that, we provide an overview of existing IoT (M2M) and CPS courses. This topic has also been extensively covered in our previous works, and it has also been seriously updated here, based on feedback from readers and new training courses found. In the last section, we describe content for our course and proposals for future development.

Some abbreviations used later in the text:

- **BLE:** Bluetooth Low energy
- **CEP:** Complex Event Processing
- **CoAP:** Constrained Application Protocol
- **CPS:** Cyber-physical Systems
- **GATT:** Generic Attribute Profile
- **IoT:** Internet of Things
- **IIoT:** Industrial Internet of Things
- **JSON:** JavaScript Object Notation
- **LPWAN:** Low-Power Wide-Area Network
- **LTE:** Long-Term Evolution (LTE) is a standard for wireless broadband communication
- **M2M:** Machine to Machine
- **MQTT:** MQ Telemetry Transport
- **Wi-Fi:** A family of wireless networking technologies, based on the IEEE 802.11 family of standards
- **WiMAX:** Worldwide Interoperability for Microwave Access is a family of wireless broadband communication standards based on the IEEE 802.16 set of standards
- **ZigBee:** An IEEE 802.15.4-based specification for a suite of high-level communication protocols

WHAT TO LEARN IN IOT COURSES

In this section, we would like to discuss the common content for IoT educational programs. According to (Holdowsky, Mahto, Raynor, & Cotteleer, 2015; Rose, 2014), IoT directions could be grouped into five topics.

1. Data measurement (sensing)
2. Data transmission (networking)
3. Data aggregation (middleware)
4. Data analysis
5. Data interaction (behavior)

It is pretty standard. At the first hand, we need to measure. The collected measurement should be transmitted. In most cases, we will need more than one measurement. So, we should be able to aggregate the measurements. As soon as data are collected, we can analyze them and make conclusions about some actions (define the behavior). In practice, this list is a perfect definition of topics in educational courses.

Sensors – here we should talk about the devices for data measurements, their working principles, and data models. The issues for discussions regarding the sensors and IoT include the multisensory data fusion (Liggins, Hall, & Llinas, 2017), the power consumption of sensors (Deepu, Heng, & Lian, 2016), the safety of measurements (Jing, Vasilakos, Wan, & Qiu 2014), and interaction with sensors (Gubbi, Buyya, Marusic, & Palaniswami, 2013). The last point is directly related to communication protocols: CoAP, MQTT, HTTP (HTTP/2), etc. (Patierno, 2014) and relates APIs. The standards are very important in this area. For example, the lack of commonly accepted standards for the connected devices' APIs caused the situation when each manufacturer or Smart Home should create its own mobile application to control their devices (Kolchin, 2016).

Network –it is the area that is best developed in terms of curriculum. Actually, it is all about network protocols and network architectures. The section related to networks should include, of course, the IP protocol (IPv6), wired and wireless networks, Bluetooth and Bluetooth Low Energy, ZigBee, Wi-Fi, WiMAX, LTE (Gubbi, Buyya, Marusic, & Palaniswami, 2013; Sneps-Sneppe & Namiot, 2012).

Integration – it is about IoT (M2M) middleware, data architectures, ETL, etc. In our opinion, based on our experience in real IoT projects, it is necessary to highlight the fact that it is about data engineering rather than about data science. Again, in our opinion, this fact is missed in many courses. Data engineering is more important for IoT education than data science. Also, it is necessary to highlight the importance of standards in this area. Consideration of standardization should include both technological standards (networking, data collection, and analysis), and regulatory aspects (e.g., security). Among technology standards that are important for IoT, we should mention the relatively isolated moments associated with the aggregation of data (ETL - extract, transform, load (Alkhamisi, Nazmudeen, & Buhari, 2016)). A negative example: among the courses that are present in the HSE program (HSE IoT, 2019) on the Internet of Things, the course on the software architecture of the Internet of Things is not mandatory.

Data analysis – it is all about data science and data mining for IoT applications. Sections related to analytical processing include descriptive analytics (with visualization), predictive analytics and recommendation systems. In this connection, it is necessary to highlight the high demand for stream analytics and real-time processing applications for IoT projects (CEP - complex event processing (Chen, Fu, Wang, Jou, & Feng, 2014)). Traditionally, this area (stream algorithms) has got a relatively poor reflection in educational programs. In our opinion, stream processing should be a key moment for IoT education (Namiot & Sneps-Sneppe, 2016a).

Data interaction - this should include end-users tools and machine to machine APIs. Note, that this topic should also include architectures, because, for example, fog computing and edge computing declare own data access models. It should include both machine to machine (M2M) and machine to human interaction (M2H). The last section (M2H) is the main section for cyber-physical systems (Sowe, Simmon, Zettsu, de Vaulx, & Bojanova, 2016).

Of course, all of this should have common background layers: standards and security. For example, Deloitte in (Holdowsky, Mahto, Raynor, & Cotteleer, 2015) proposes a similar structure. Their main IoT actions (phases) from start to end are: Create, Communicate, Aggregate, Analyze, and Act.

The first action (Create) deals with physical devices (sensors). The communicate phase is about networks. The connectivity includes processing elements, connectivity elements, and connectivity frameworks. The aggregation covers IoT middleware, data abstraction, data ingestion, and data storage. The analytics includes batch and stream analytics, data messaging, processing engines and frameworks. The similar scheme is proposed by W3C for Web of Things (W3C for Web of Things, 2016). Layers from top to down are: Application, Things, Transfer, Transport, and Network.

The application layer is about programs that either implement a thing's behavior, or which interact with a thing. The typical example of interaction is exposing or utilizing APIs for sensors. The thing here is a software object that exposes the compound state of devices or digital services. It includes data, metadata, semantic annotation, description, and interaction model.

The transfer layer addresses elements and message exchange patterns such as push, pull, publish/subscribe, etc. It provides support for devices that spend much of their time sleeping; and bindings to communication protocols such as HTTP, CoAP, MQTT, HTTP/2, Bluetooth GATT, LPWAN, etc.

The transport layer addresses of application endpoints and transmission of messages; UDP, TCP as well as non-IP based transports. Network layer addresses of network nodes and routing of packets across interconnected networks; IP (including profiles such as 6LoWPAN)

The common model for Web of Things (Web of Things, 2019) proposes a similar model, but uses a different set of names. As per this model, on the low level, we have a set of so-called Networked Things with own protocols and access models like NFC, Ethernet, Bluetooth, etc. Above that we have four layers. Their names are (from down to top): Access, Find, Share, and Compose.

The layer 1 (Access) contains access models and protocols (HTTP, MQTT, CoAP, URI/URL scheme, JSON, etc.) The layer 2 (Find) is about semantic data (e.g., RDF, JSON-LD, etc.), crawlers and search engines. The layer 3 (Share) is about security (OAuth, encryption, TLS, etc.) and social networks. The top layer 4 (Compose) is about user interfaces and mashups. As it is mentioned in many papers (e.g., (Namiot & Sneps-Sneppe, 2016a)) the most common IoT application is some mashup.

Here it is necessary to emphasize one fundamental question. The first stage - interaction with sensors at the moment is not standardized. In fact, direct work with sensors always works with software interfaces of a specific operating system (a specific vendor). Accordingly, including such issues in the university program, the university, in fact, works for a specific manufacturer. This is a real question, as will be seen, for example, even their subsequent review, many IoT courses are, in fact, sensor programming. And it is performed, of course, in a specific operating environment. Our opinion on this issue is absolutely unequivocal. Sensor programming can be part of a course for a specific corporate customer only. The main theme (direction) for the basic IoT course, in our opinion, is the system architecture. This will be reflected in the structure of the courses we offer. The main thing is to teach students to understand (choose) the system architecture of IoT systems.

As a result of this chapter, we can conclude the following. The course (program or set of courses) on the subject of the Internet of things contains four basic directions: sensors, networks, aggregation of data and data processing. The section associated with the sensors should also include APIs for working with them. We are convinced that this stage should be abstracted to the maximum extent from concrete implementations. Networks in the current state should also include software-defined networks and messaging protocols. The section of data aggregation (in practical applications often referred to as IoT middleware) is closely related to standardization. The last section (analysis and data processing) is to a lesser extent tied specifically to IoT. In general, for example, the processing of time series or machine learning remains the same for all applications, including the Internet of Things. For the same reason, cloud computing should be a separate course, in our opinion, because clouds are not only for IoT.

As per Smart Cities, in our opinion, we should follow to ITU's (International Telecommunication Union) approach, where IoT is a measuring level for Smart Cities. In other words, we discuss it separately from many Smart City related things (communications with citizens, city management, etc.).

WHAT TO LEARN IN CPS COURSES

In this section, we would like to discuss the common content for CPS educational programs. Our analysis reveals a wide range of CPS curricula. It looks like each organization understands the CPS in its own way. Initially, CPS training courses were embedded system design courses. It was considered as a synonym.

Here is a typical example from UC Santa Cruz (CMPE249: Introduction to Cyber-physical Systems 2019). This course, as per its textbook includes the following topics: modeling and analysis tools for continuous-time and discrete-time systems, finite state machines, stateflow, timed and hybrid automata, concurrency, invariants, linear temporal logic, verification, and numerical simulation. The main focus is on models in terms of differential equations for the modeling of physical processes. This course introduces for students finite state machines and stateflows. Next, they are combined with the physical models. Applications of the resulting models for design and analysis of embedded systems are discussed. The linear temporal logic, applied to specify the desired system behavior. In our case, the problem is that the courses were originally intended for IT specialties of students. And many (sometimes all) specializations (courses) on embedded systems are taught in other disciplines. E.g. differential equations usually (traditionally) are presented in separate course (or courses). That is, business turns out to be simple in changing the name of the academic discipline.

The typical master program (Stankovic, Sturges, & Eisenberg, 2017) includes the following topics:
Architectures for CPS: sensors, actuators, networks, distributed computation

Embedded and Real-Time Systems: emphasis on computing reliably and timely with noisy sensor data over wired and wireless networks

Formal Methods:

- Formal models of computation including discrete and analog computation
- Formal specifications and verification

Signal Processing:

- Digital signal processing on hardware and software
- Emphasis on distributed signal processing over networks.

Feedback Control

- Modeling of physical and computational processes
- Design techniques for stability, safety, liveness, and other specifications
- Implementation on hardware

Inference under Uncertainty: basics of modeling uncertainty, statistical inference, detection and estimation

Elective Classes include

- Computer and Network Security: how to cover attacks exploiting physical properties of computation (e.g., time, temperature, radiation)
- Hybrid Systems: modeling, verification, and control of systems containing discrete and continuous components
- Networked Control Systems
  - Control over wired and wireless networks
  - Impact of delays, packet collisions, and protocols on performance
- Computer Architecture
- Systems Engineering
- Sensor Networks
- Medical Embedded Systems
- Robotics
- Machine Learning
- Modeling from Data

Again, if you refer to the national conditions (Russian, first of all), such courses are there and the question may perhaps be simply in assembling (integrating) the program from existing training courses.

In our opinion, the future of CPS education lies in line with NIST CPS initiatives (Griffor, Greer, Wollman, & Burns, 2017). Here CPS is a natural replacement (development) of IoT. Accordingly, new IoT course options will simply include elements of physical interaction with the system. And what applies to embedded systems should remain in the IT-area, where, strictly speaking, they are now. As per NIST, the future is a unified CPS/IoT perspective. A unified components model provides 4 categories for CPS and IoT components: logical, physical, transducing, and human. The unified perspective reflects the convergence of CPS and IoT definitions. NIST describes it so: Internet of Things and cyber-physical systems comprise interacting logical, physical, transducer, and human components engineered for function through integrated logic and physics (Greer, Burns, Wollman, & Griffor, 2019).

ON IOT COURSES

This section presents some of the training programs for the Internet of Things and Smart Cities. We include Smart Cities too because IoT is the data layer for Smart Cities. IoT is the foundation for data-driven cities. At the first hand, we could mention the Master's Program for Smart Cities and Urban Analytics (Smart Cities and Urban Analytics, 2019). It covers the following issues:

- Networks and communications,
- Planning of traffic flows,
- Real-time systems,
- Geo-information systems,
- Simulation system.

The focuses are on urban planning and management. This is what it refers to the Smart Cities. As the next issue, we could mention the Master City Science program (Master in City Science, 2019). Its network-related part covers the following topics:

- New Generation Networks (NGN).
- Broadband communications.
- The Quality of Service (QoS).
- Optical and wireless networks.
- Telecommunication network architecture.
- 4G networks.
- Mesh-networks.

The main emphasis, as it can be seen from the content is Networking. In general, Masters City Science (Master in City Science, 2019) covers a wide list of areas:

- Transport and Mobility.
- Information and Communication Technologies.
- Urban and Landscape Design.
- Society and Governance.
- Environment and Sustainability.
- Economy and Business.
- Ecological Urbanism.
- Energy.

EIT Digital Master School presents a program for Embedded Systems (EIT Digital Master School, 2019). The seven specializations are:

- Embedded Platforms.
- Embedded Multicore Processing.
- Embedded Networking.
- Mobile Cyber-Physical Systems.
- Internet of Things and Energy-Efficient Computing.
- Real-Time Systems and Design of Cyber-Physical Systems.
- Critical Embedded Systems.

In our opinion, it is one of the most technically deep and elaborated programs.

Several software vendors propose IoT courses. For example, SAP provides an online course on the Internet of Things (SAP Internet of Things, 2019). In general, it is just an introduction. It covers two IoT perspectives: Societal Perspective and Business Perspective. HP also has its own training course on IoT (HP Internet of Things, 2019). This a two-day course, although, formally, it presents many topics. For example, we could mention network technologies such as RFID, WSN, and Smart-applications (Smart Cities, Smart Home, Smart Metering, and Smart Health). In general, it looks more as an introduction for managers. Intel offers an open course, called the Internet of Things (Intel IoT, 2019; Intel IoT Course, 2019), but, in fact, promotes their own programming for Edison platform.

Among other online courses can be noted here is the Open University program to IoT (My Digital Life, 2019). It uses elements of IoT for general learning computer science. In particular, it is used for teaching programming based on the Arduino. Hardware vendors are also trying to reach students in universities. For example, UCL is partnering with ARM to launch a new education kit aimed at developing students' IoT technical skills. It is a typical example of a vendor-initiated program (IoT will fire up the Next Generation of Engineers, 2015). It is about the usage of ARM IoT Device Platform, create smartphone apps and control end-devices such as a mini-robot or a wearable health device. It is a short time (one week) module. Vendor's University Program web site (ARM University, 2017) contains several examples of such programs from ARM. Kings College London offers a free survey course on IoT (Kings College London, 2019).

Oxford University offers a course on Data Science for the Internet of Things (Data Science for IoT, 2017). It includes:

- Statistics.
- Time Series analysis.
- Deep Learning.
- Real-Time processing.
- IoT Data Visualization.

Sure, time series processing is very important for IoT analytics, but this course is de-facto about data science only and uses IoT just as a name.

Coursera (Coursera IoT, 2019) offers several specializations (a set of courses, thesis projects, and a certificate) and individual courses for the Internet of Things. The specialization for IoT programming consists of the following courses:

- Introduction to the Internet of Things and Embedded Systems - an introduction to the topic, general information.
- The Arduino Platform and C Programming - course content corresponds to the name. Working with Arduino.
- Interfacing with the Arduino - work with external devices to Arduino.
- The Raspberry Pi Platform and Python Programming for the Raspberry Pi - programming for Raspberry Pi.
- Interfacing with the Raspberry Pi - working with external devices in the Raspberry Pi.

Here we can also see the influence of vendors. For example, one specialization is devoted to Qualcomm hardware exclusively, and another one is from IBM. In our opinion, the best course here is Software Architecture for the Internet of Things by EIT (IoT Software Architecture, 2017). This course will teach students how to design systems that meet the requirements of IoT systems: systems that are secure, interoperable, modifiable and scalable.

The professional training program at MIT also offers the detailed and well-elaborated training program for IoT (MIT IoT, 2019). This program includes the following sections (MIT Internet of Things Roadmap, 2019): the architecture of the IoT, processing sensor data, SLAM, stand-alone devices (cars, robots), IoT standards, wearable devices (wearables), security, Web of Things, wireless protocols, storage and analysis of data, man-machine interfaces. Course module to develop applications includes Smart Homes, Smart City, Smart materials, medical applications, and cyber-physical systems. As per our review, it is the most advanced offering for IoT education. As per the MIT model, Smart City is just an application (use case) for IoT. So, their program includes Smart Cities too (as an application and example for IoT).

Another very interesting example, in our opinion, is the IoT practical courses from the Technical University of Munich (TUM IoT, 2019). They focus mainly on cloud storage and data processing, where a great deal of attention is paid in particular to streaming processing. This is very much in line with our vision of IoT programs.

The University of Washington offers a practical course on the IoT (Raspberry Pi and other devices) (University of Washington, 2019). It includes also cloud computing part: how to store, process, present and visualize data from the internet of things, how to setup micro-services in the cloud, including data schema, database, API development and server elements, as well as simple and complex visualization tools experience (such as Tableau Public) (Sankhe-Savale, 2016). Waterford Institute of Technology (Ireland) offers an undergraduate program for the Internet of Things (WIT Internet of Things, 2019). It contains six big areas.

1. **Programming:** Includes the fundamental algorithms & data structures relevant to the field. Especially, the nature and performance of distributed, networked applications.
2. **Data Science:** The ability to select the appropriate technological components, including warehousing and analysis. The knowledge to integrate the components into a single data-analytics solution and extract meaningful insight from the IoT data.
3. **Mathematics:** Examines the formal reasoning, modeling, and analytical skills.
4. **Devices and Systems:** Explores analogue and digital interface components; insight and understanding of the components, and the integration processes.
5. **Networks and Cloud:** Provide a practical understanding of Operating Systems and the tools they require to deploy, manage and troubleshoot the underlying infrastructure required to support IoT.
6. **Project:** Deliver concrete experience IoT domain.

The summary for our review is presented in Table 1.

There are common shortcomings (problems) that we would like to mention. As far as sensors are concerned, the study almost always comes down to illustrative examples. There are no common models and the questions of programming interfaces for interaction with sensors are practically not considered. The network-related part is, probably, the most elaborated part of the education. Also, this part is more or less standard across many courses. As per IoT middleware, existing courses completely ignore current development, existing and proposed standards, and existing open source products. Data engineering is

Table 1. IoT courses and basic directions

Course	Sensing	Networking	IoT Middleware	IoT Data Mining
Smart Cities and Urban Analytics	-	-	+	+
Master in City Science	-	+	+	+
EIT Digital Master School	-	+	-	+
SAP Internet of Things	-	-	+	+
HP IoT	+	-	-	+
MIT IoT	+	+	+	+
Kings College London	+	-	-	+
WIT Internet of Things	+	+	+	+
Coursera	+	+	-	+

highly undervalued in existing courses. In our opinion, the most sensitive moment here is the lack of information about the stream processing of data and the corresponding algorithms and tools (frameworks). The data processing part in IoT courses is again more or less standard. But as we noted above, there is no critical dependence on the subject domain (IoT).

Another question on related areas is cloud computing. Perhaps, only Microsoft company puts its Azure cloud at the head of the IoT direction. But this is well within our judgment about programs targeted at the products of specific corporations. Another reason why cloud computing should be a separate course (courses) is the recent active change in systems architecture. And this is what directly concerns IoT. We are referring to the approach of clouds to data collection sites: edge, fog computing (Chiang, Zhang, 2016).

ON THE PROPOSED CONTENT FOR IOT COURSE

For several years of application, given the feedback from students and employers, the experience of writing graduation papers, we have formed the structure of the basic course. We focus on a two-year master's program. The course includes the following main areas:

1. IoT system architecture,
2. Network interoperability standards,
3. IoT data persistency
4. Principles of IoT data analysis and processing.

Accordingly, the course may include four main sections.

The first one deals with modern standards in the field of M2M and IoT. Here we should talk about oneM2M, OpenIoT, FI-WARE, OMA, ITU, etc. Actually, the amount of the proposed solutions, in varying degrees of readiness, is sufficiently large. At the same time, they can promote different approaches to building systems, data collection, and processing. It is, in fact, consideration of possible architectural solutions for building IoT systems. Course participants will need to get an idea of the existing architectural solutions, their comparative characteristics, and applicability depending on external conditions.

The second section will focus on network solutions for the IoT. This area is probably the most elaborated (in terms of education and methodology). Here, in particular, we consider network solutions such as 802.15.4, 6LoWPAN, etc. and data protocols such as COAP, MQTT, etc. It is closely related to the previous section, since the choice of network protocols can determine the application architecture. One of the best methodologically organized approaches is presented in (IoT requirements and protocols, 2017). According to this model, we should organize the education around the protocols and their features. The comparison of features will define the architectures for IoT systems. The course discusses the following protocols in connection with IoT: HTTP/REST, CoAP, MQTT, SNMP, UPnP, XMPP, Modbus. In our opinion, we should add to this list HTTP/2 at least. Finally, the following list of features is suggested: transport protocol, messaging model, mobile networks support, low power features, required resources, security, success stories, architecture. For example, CoAP supports UDP as a transport, provides request/response models (another option is publish/subscribe), has got an excellent support for mobile networks (3G/4G), medium level of security, widely used in utility field (sensing), and uses tree architecture model (other options are star, bus, client-server, P2P client). For the whole table, you can see (IoT requirements and protocols, 2017). This area is also constantly evolving. Of the recent changes, it is necessary to reflect in the course the increased interest in streaming data. Another new (relatively new) area is mesh networks. For example, it is Bluetooth mesh in IoT applications.

Interaction with a wide range of external devices (sensors) is naturally associated with the collection and storage of some of the information (measurements). Accordingly, the problems associated with the storage and processing of large data sets are among the top priority areas for the IoT applications. For IoT and M2M applications, we propose to teach students to data stream processing systems. Typically, we talk here about Apache Storm (Fox, Jha, & Ramakrishnan, 2016) and Apache Spark (Shanahan & Dai, 2017). And because the system architecture is a key moment, it is very important here to target appropriate architecture models like Lambda architecture (Namiot, 2015) and Kappa architecture (Nasir, 2016).

The Lambda Architecture targets applications built around complex asynchronous transformations that need to run with low latency (Namiot & Sneps-Sneppe, 2016b). It is a typical use case for IoT systems. The Lambda Architecture offers a dedicated real-time layer. It solves the problem with old data processing by taking its own copy of the data, processing it quickly and stores it in a fast store. This store is more complex since it has to be constantly updated. So, in this model, we have a batch processing and a real-time processing in parallel. The biggest advantage is the avoidance of the ETL process. Real-time processing can analyze the stream as it is. But it means the disadvantage also: we need several (multiple) engines for processing. It means that we will need to duplicate business logic and synchronize copies.

The next step in this direction (real-time processing) is the so-called Kappa architecture (Kappa architecture, 2016), where everything is a stream. It means that our system will proceed data "as is" in a stream and introduce some data persistence only after that. In our opinion, it is the most suitable approach for sensing data persistence. Obviously, such a group of applications constitutes a significant part of all IoT applications.

Currently, much attention is paid to data analysis (data mining), while data engineering attracts less attention in universities. However, before we can start the process of the data, we need to learn how to save them in one form or another, provide the right architecture of systems. In this connection, the course uses Big Data standards from NIST (Chang, Boyd, 2018) as a reference. Their distinguishing features are focusing on the application layer and discussions about specific use cases. Based on the fact that standards are the best practices, the NIST describes and discusses the best practices exactly.

Such documents as Big Data Use Cases and Requirements, Big Data Security and Privacy, Big Data Architecture White Paper Survey, Big Data Reference Architecture are well-organized materials that could be used as tutorials. Let us see, for example, NIST's Big Data Reference Architecture. The five main components of this architecture are:

1. System Orchestrator. It defines and integrates the required data application activities into an operational vertical system;
2. Data Provider. It introduces new data or information feeds into the Big Data system;
3. Big Data Application Provider. It executes a data life cycle to meet security and privacy requirements as well as System Orchestrator-defined requirements;
4. Big Data Framework Provider. It establishes a computing framework in which to execute certain transformation applications. Also, this provider is responsible for protecting the privacy and integrity of data;
5. Data Consumer. It includes end-users or other systems that use the results of the Big Data Application Provider

The goal of this architecture is to provide a vendor-neutral agnostic conceptual model. This model should be also technology and infrastructure-agnostic. In our opinion, in IoT education data engineering should be the top priority. Our students should understand that data engineering focuses more on design and architectures. So, data engineers are responsible for preparing the infrastructure for big data and for managing big data. Data engineering in IoT projects should design, build, and integrate data from various sources (resources). Of course, data store architecture, its support, and maintenance should precede any processing (data science, data mining). Also, data engineering targets optimization and performance issues for big data stores. The big attention should be paid to data cleaning and validation, ETL scripts and reporting tools.

Currently, in Lomonosov Moscow State University in courses on Big Data, we make extensive use of available materials from NIST (Namiot, Kupriyanovsky, Nikolaev, & Zubareva, 2016). For example, Big Data Use Cases and Requirements (NIST Big Data Public Working Group, 2018) contains detailed use cases (data architectures) including IoT examples for cargo shipping, health care, unmanned air vehicle, life science, etc.

The last section, in our opinion, is completely devoted to the consideration of data processing in real time. The main applied areas for IoT are the classification and identification of anomalies. In this particular domain, IoT requires consideration in the first place, namely streaming algorithms.

The streaming, dynamic, and distributed algorithms are key elements for analyzing big data in IoT applications. We discuss sampling and sketching as two basic techniques for designing streaming algorithms and hash functions most data streaming algorithms rely on.

In general, streaming algorithms (Gaber, Zaslavsky, & Krishnaswamy, 2009) are seriously underestimated in the existing educational courses. At the same time, there is a whole world of approaches such as data-based and task-based techniques, sampling, load shedding, sketching, creating a synopsis of data (e.g., wavelet analysis, histograms, frequency moments, etc.), aggregation, and approximation.

Finally, the described course creates the following formation of competencies:

- Understanding of the architectures and models of IoT and M2M applications;
- Knowledge of the basic models used in the design of IoT and M2M systems;
- Understanding of the network standards used in IoT;
- Understanding of data models used in IoT applications and the ability to select the data model according to the requirements;
- Knowledge of the basic streaming algorithms and understanding of real-time data processing models

In terms of practical lessons, we can present our teaching experience at Lomonosov Moscow State University and the Russian University of Transport. It is necessary to understand that there are no standards for interaction with sensors (actuators) at present. If we choose some real systems for practical training, it will always be training students to work with devices of some real manufacturer. Practically, it is the promotion of products of this manufacturer. The alternative is to try working with mobile phone sensors, as all students obviously have such devices. Of course, the set of sensors will not be very large: GPS, accelerometer, gyroscope. Sometimes it could be NFC too. We have also made extensive use of our own scientific development when wireless interfaces (Bluetooth, BLE, Wi-Fi) are considered to be sensors and used to measure network proximity (Namiot & Sneps-Sneppe, 2019). Of course, Bluetooth and Wi-Fi are presented on all mobile phones. Note also that working with sensors on phones is already possible via the W3C Web API - i.e. JavaScript. This lowers the entry threshold, reduces the complexity of programming, and allows you to focus on algorithms and architecture, rather than on the problems of client endpoint programming, which, of course, has nothing to do with IoT.

REFERENCES

W3C for Web of Things. (2016). Retrieved from https://www.w3.org/2016/09/IoTW/white-paper.pdf

Alkhamisi, A., Nazmudeen, M. S. H., & Buhari, S. M. (2016, September). A cross-layer framework for sensor data aggregation for IoT applications in smart cities. In *Smart Cities Conference (ISC2), 2016 IEEE International* (pp. 1-6). IEEE. 10.1109/ISC2.2016.7580853

Asay, M. (2014, June 27). *The Internet Of Things Will Need Millions Of Developers By 2020*. Retrieved from http://readwrite.com/2014/06/27/internet-of-things-developers-jobs-opportunity

Chang, W. L., & Boyd, D. (2018). *NIST Big Data Interoperability Framework: Volume 6, Big Data Reference Architecture* (No. Special Publication (NIST SP)-1500-6 Version 2).

Chen, C. Y., Fu, J. H., Wang, P. F., Jou, E., & Feng, M. W. (2014, August). Complex event processing for the internet of things and its applications. In *Automation Science and Engineering (CASE), 2014 IEEE International Conference on* (pp. 1144-1149). IEEE. 10.1109/CoASE.2014.6899470

Chiang, M., & Zhang, T. (2016). Fog and IoT: An overview of research opportunities. *IEEE Internet of Things Journal*, 3(6), 854–864. doi:10.1109/JIOT.2016.2584538

CMPE249: Introduction to Cyber-physical Systems. (2019). Retrieved from https://courses.soe.ucsc.edu/courses/cmpe249

Coursera IoT. (2019). Retrieved from https://ru.coursera.org/specializations/iot

Data Science for IoT. (2019). Retrieved from https://www.conted.ox.ac.uk/courses/data-science-for-the-internet-of-things-iot

Deepu, C. J., Heng, C. H., & Lian, Y. (2016). A hybrid data compression scheme for power reduction in wireless sensors for IoT. *IEEE Transactions on Biomedical Circuits and Systems*, *11*(2), 245–254. doi:10.1109/TBCAS.2016.2591923 PMID:27845673

EIT Digital Master School. (2019). Retrieved from http://www.masterschool.eitictlabs.eu/programmes/es/

Fox, G., Jha, S., & Ramakrishnan, L. (2016). *Stream2016: Streaming requirements, experience, applications and middleware workshop (No. LBNL-1006355). Lawrence Berkeley National Lab*. Berkeley, CA: LBNL. doi:10.2172/1344785

Gaber, M. M., Zaslavsky, A., & Krishnaswamy, S. (2009). Data stream mining. In *Data Mining and Knowledge Discovery Handbook* (pp. 759–787). Boston, MA: Springer. doi:10.1007/978-0-387-09823-4_39

Greer, C., Burns, M., Wollman, D., & Griffor, E. (2019). Cyber-Physical Systems & the Internet of Things. *NIST Special Publication*, *1900*, 202.

Griffor, E. R., Greer, C., Wollman, D. A., & Burns, M. J. (2017). *Framework for cyber-physical systems: Volume 2, working group reports* (No. Special Publication (NIST SP)-1500-202).

Gubbi, J., Buyya, R., Marusic, S., & Palaniswami, M. (2013). Internet of Things (IoT): A vision, architectural elements, and future directions. *Future Generation Computer Systems*, *29*(7), 1645–1660. doi:10.1016/j.future.2013.01.010

Holdowsky, J., Mahto, M., Raynor, M. E., & Cotteleer, M. (2015, August 21). *Inside the Internet of Things (IoT). A primer on the technologies building the IoT*. Retrieved from http://dupress.com/articles/iot-primer-iot-technologies-applications/

HP Internet of Things. (2019). Retrieved from http://h20195.www2.hp.com/v2/GetPDF.aspx/c04656912.pdf

HSE IoT Program. (2019). Retrieved from https://www.hse.ru/en/ma/internet/courses/index.html

Intel IoT. (2019). Retrieved from https://software.intel.com/en-us/iot/training

Intel IoT Course. (2019). Retrieved from https://github.com/guermonprez/intel-academic-IoT-course

IoT requirements and protocols. (2017). Retrieved from http://embedded-computing.com/articles/internet-things-requirements-protocols/

IoT Software Architecture. (2019). Retrieved from https://ru.coursera.org/learn/iot-software-architecture

IoT will fire up the Next Generation of Engineers. (2015, January). Retrieved from https://www.ee.ucl.ac.uk/undergraduate/newsarmiotjan2015

Jing, Q., Vasilakos, A. V., Wan, J., Lu, J., & Qiu, D. (2014). Security of the Internet of Things: Perspectives and challenges. *Wireless Networks*, *20*(8), 2481–2501. doi:10.100711276-014-0761-7

Kappa architecture. Merging Batch and Stream Processing in a Post Lambda World. (2016, June). Retrieved from https://www.datanami.com/2016/06/01/merging-batch-streaming-post-lambda-world/

Kings College London. (2019). Retrieved from https://www.futurelearn.com/courses/internet-of-things

Kolchin, M., Andreev, A., Garayzuev, D., Chursin, N., Mouromtsev, D., & Zakoldaev, D. (2016). A CoAP-Based Hypermedia Framework for Always-On and Sleepy Devices in Smart Home Environment. *International Journal of Embedded and Real-Time Communication Systems*, 7(2), 45–63. doi:10.4018/IJERTCS.2016070104

Lambda architecture. (2019). Retrieved from http://lambda-architecture.net/

Liggins, M. II, Hall, D., & Llinas, J. (Eds.). (2017). *Handbook of multisensor data fusion: theory and practice*. CRC Press. doi:10.1201/9781420053098

Master in City Science. (2019). Retrieved from http://www.citysciences.com/

MIT Internet of Things Roadmap. (2019). Retrieved from https://mitprofessionalx.mit.edu/courses/course-v1:MITProfessionalX+IOTx+2016_T1/about

MIT IoT. (2019). Retrieved from http://web.mit.edu/professional/digital-programs/courses/IoT/index.html

My Digital Life. (2019). Retrieved from http://www.open.ac.uk/courses/modules/tu100#details

Namiot, D. (2015). On big data stream processing. *International Journal of Open Information Technologies*, 3(8), 48–51.

Namiot, D. (2016). On Internet of Things and Smart Cities educational courses. *International Journal of Open Information Technologies*, 4(5), 26–38.

Namiot, D., Kupriyanovsky, V., Nikolaev, D., & Zubareva, E. (2016). On standards in Big Data area. *International Journal of Open Information Technologies*, 4(11), 12–18.

Namiot, D., & Sneps-Sneppe, M. (2014). On IoT programming. *International Journal of Open Information Technologies*, 2(10).

Namiot, D., & Sneps-Sneppe, M. (2016a, November). On Internet of Things Programming Models. In *International Conference on Distributed Computer and Communication Networks* (pp. 13-24). Springer. 10.1007/978-3-319-51917-3_2

Namiot, D., & Sneps-Sneppe, M. (2016b, October) On crowd sensing back-end. In *DAMDID/RCDL 2016 Selected Papers of the XVIII International Conference on Data Analytics and Management in Data Intensive Domains (DAMDID/RCDL 2016)* (pp. 168–175), CEUR Workshop Proceedings.

Namiot, D., & Sneps-Sneppe, M. (2017). On Internet of Things and big data in university courses. *International Journal of Embedded and Real-Time Communication Systems*, 8(1), 18–30. doi:10.4018/IJERTCS.2017010102

Namiot, D., & Sneps-Sneppe, M. (2019, April). On Content Models for Proximity Services. In *2019 24th Conference of Open Innovations Association (FRUCT)* (pp. 277-284). IEEE. 10.23919/FRUCT.2019.8711983

Namiot, D., Sneps-Sneppe, M., & Daradkeh, Y. (2017, April). On Internet of Things Education. In S. Balandin (Ed.), *Proceedings of the 20th Conference of Open Innovations Association FRUCT*. LETI University.

Nasir, M. A. U. (2016). *Fault Tolerance for Stream Processing Engines.* arXiv preprint arXiv:1605.00928

NIST Big Data Public Working Group, & the NIST Big Data Public Working Group. (2018). NIST Big Data Interoperability Framework: Volume 3, Use Cases and General Requirements. US Department of Commerce, National Institute of Standards and Technology.

Patierno, P. (2014, June) *IoT Protocols Landscape.* Retrieved from http://www.slideshare.net/paolopat/io-t-protocols-landscape

Rose, D. (2014). *Enchanted objects: Design, human desire, and the Internet of things.* Simon and Schuster.

Sanislav, T., & Miclea, L. (2012). Cyber-physical systems-concept, challenges and research areas. *Journal of Control Engineering and Applied Informatics, 14*(2), 28–33.

Sankhe-Savale, S. (2016). *Tableau Cookbook–Recipes for Data Visualization.* Packt Publishing Ltd.

SAP Internet of Things. (2019). Retrieved from https://open.sap.com/courses/iot1

Shanahan, J., & Dai, L. (2017, April). Large Scale Distributed Data Science from scratch using Apache Spark 2.0. In *Proceedings of the 26th International Conference on World Wide Web Companion* (pp. 955-957). International World Wide Web Conferences Steering Committee. 10.1145/3041021.3051108

Smart Cities and Urban Analytics. (2019). Retrieved from http://www.bartlett.ucl.ac.uk/casa/programmes/postgraduate/msc-smart-cities-and-urban-analytics

Sneps-Sneppe, M., & Namiot, D. (2012, April). About M2M standards and their possible extensions. In *Future Internet Communications (BCFIC), 2012 2nd Baltic Congress on* (pp. 187-193). IEEE. 10.1109/BCFIC.2012.6218001

Sneps-Sneppe, M., Namiot, D., & Alberts, M. (2018, May). On Digital Economy Issues Looking From the Information Systems Viewpoint. In *Proceedings of the 22st Conference of Open Innovations Association FRUCT* (p. 56). FRUCT Oy.

Sowe, S. K., Simmon, E., Zettsu, K., de Vaulx, F., & Bojanova, I. (2016). Cyber-physical-human systems: Putting people in the loop. *IT Professional, 18*(1), 10–13. doi:10.1109/MITP.2016.14 PMID:28579925

Stankovic, J. A., Sturges, J. W., & Eisenberg, J. (2017). A 21st Century Cyber-Physical Systems Education. *Computer, 50*(12), 82–85. doi:10.1109/MC.2017.4451222

Suo, H., Wan, J., Zou, C., & Liu, J. (2012, March). Security in the internet of things: a review. In Computer Science and Electronics Engineering (ICCSEE), 2012 international conference on (Vol. 3, pp. 648-651). IEEE. doi:10.1109/ICCSEE.2012.373

TUM IoT. (2019). Retrieved from https://www.caps.in.tum.de/en/teaching/ws18/practical-courses/iot/

University A. R. M. (2017) Retrieved from https://www.arm.com/support/university/

University of Washington. (2019). Retrieved from http://www.pce.uw.edu/certificates/internet-of-things.html

Web of Things. (2019). Retrieved from https://en.wikipedia.org/wiki/Web_of_Things

WIT Internet of Things. (2019). Retrieved from https://www.wit.ie/courses/type/science/department_of_computing_maths_physics/bsc-hons-in-the-internet-of-things#tab=description

Compilation of References

Abanda, A., Mori, U., & Lozano, J. A. (2019). A review on distance based time series classification. *Data Mining and Knowledge Discovery*, *33*(2), 378–412. doi:10.100710618-018-0596-4

AcqKnowledge ECG Analysis. (2017). *BIOPAC Systems Inc. official website*. Retrieved June 25, 2019 from https://www.biopac.com/knowledge-base/ecg-analysis/

Adafruit Bluefruit, L. E. SPI Friend – Bluetooth Low Energy (BLE). (2016). *Adafruit Official Website*. Retrieved October 27, 2016 from https://www.adafruit.com/product/2633

ADS129x Low-Power, 8-Channel, 24-Bit Analog Front-End for Biopotential Measurements. (2016). *Texas Instruments Official Website*. Retrieved June 25, 2019 from http://www.ti.com/lit/ds/symlink/ads1298.pdf

Ahmad, S. (2011). The jabberwocky programming environment for structured social computing. *Proceedings of the 24th annual ACM symposium on User interface software and technology - UIST '11*, 53–64. 10.1145/2047196.2047203

Ahriz, I., Douin, J., & Lemoine, F. (2019). Location-based Service Sharing for Smart Museum. In *Proc. International Conference on Software, Telecommunications and Computer Networks (SoftCOM)* (pp. 1-6). Academic Press.

Albahri, O. S., Albahri, A. S., Mohammed, K. I., Zaidan, A. A., Zaidan, B. B., Hashim, M., & Salman, O. H. (2018). Systematic review of real-time remote health monitoring system in triage and priority-based sensor technology: Taxonomy, open challenges, motivation and recommendations. *Journal of Medical Systems*, *42*(5), 80. doi:10.100710916-018-0943-4 PMID:29564649

Alcaraz, C., Cazorla, L., & Lopez, J. (2017). Cyber-physical systems for wide-area situational awareness. In *Cyber-Physical Systems* (pp. 305–317). Elsevier. doi:10.1016/B978-0-12-803801-7.00020-1

Alcaraz, C., & Lopez, J. (2013). Wide-Area Situational Awareness for Critical Infrastructure Protection. *Computer*, *46*(4), 30–37. doi:10.1109/MC.2013.72

Alharby, S., Weddell, A., Reeve, J., & Harris, N. (2018). The Cost of Link Layer Security in IoT Embedded Devices. *IFAC-PapersOnLine*, *51*(6), 72–77. doi:10.1016/j.ifacol.2018.07.132

Ali Khoudja, M., Fareh, M., & Bouarfa, H. (2019). A New Supervised Learning Based Ontology Matching Approach Using Neural Networks. In Á. Rocha & M. Serrhini (Eds.), *Smart Innovation, Systems and Technologies* (Vol. 111, pp. 542–551). Cham: Springer International Publishing.

AliveCor. (2016). *AliveCor Official Website*. Retrieved June 25, 2019 from https://www.alivecor.com/

Alkhamisi, A., Nazmudeen, M. S. H., & Buhari, S. M. (2016, September). A cross-layer framework for sensor data aggregation for IoT applications in smart cities. In *Smart Cities Conference (ISC2), 2016 IEEE International* (pp. 1-6). IEEE. 10.1109/ISC2.2016.7580853

Alkilabi, M. H. M., Narayan, A., & Tuci, E. (2017). Cooperative object transport with a swarm of e-puck robots: Robustness and scalability of evolved collective strategies. *Swarm Intelligence*, *11*(3-4), 185–209. doi:10.100711721-017-0135-8

Alzahrani, A. A., Loke, S. W., & Lu, H. (2014). An advanced location-aware physical annotation system: From models to implementation. *Journal of Ambient Intelligence and Smart Environments*, *6*(1), 71–91. doi:10.3233/AIS-130238

Amaro, A. C., & Oliveira, L. (2019). Playful Interactions with Smart and Social Objects. In *Proc. 14th Iberian Conference on Information Systems and Technologies (CISTI)* (pp. 1-6). 10.23919/CISTI.2019.8760920

Amato, F., Moscato, V., Picariello, A., Colace, F., Santo, M.D., Schreiber, F.A., & Tanca, L. (2017). Big data meets digital cultural heritage: Design and implementation of scrabs, a smart context-aware browsing assistant for cultural environments. *J. Comput. Cult. Herit. 10*(1), 6:1-6:23.

Ancillotti, E., Bruno, R., & Conti, M. (2013). The role of communication systems in smart grids: Architectures, technical solutions and research challenges. *Computer Communications*, *36*(17-18), 1665–1697. doi:10.1016/j.comcom.2013.09.004

Anda, A. (2018, August). Modeling Adaptive Socio-Cyber-Physical Systems with Goals and SysML. In *2018 IEEE 26th International Requirements Engineering Conference (RE)* (pp. 442-447). IEEE. 10.1109/RE.2018.00059

Androcec, D., Vrcek, N., & Seva, J. (2012). Cloud computing ontologies: A systematic review. *MOPAS 2012 : The Third International Conference on Models and Ontology-based Design of Protocols, Architectures and Services*, 9–14.

Antzelevitch, C., Yan, G. X., Ackerman, M. J., Borggrefe, M., Corrado, D., Guo, J., ... Wilde, A.A. (2016). J-Wave syndromes expert consensus conference report: Emerging concepts and gaps in knowledge. *Journal of Arrhythmia*, *32*(5), 315–339.

Anwary, A. R., Yu, H., & Vassallo, M. (2018). An automatic gait feature extraction method for identifying gait asymmetry using wearable sensors. *Sensors (Basel)*, *18*(2), 676. doi:10.339018020676 PMID:29495299

Anzalchi, A., & Sarwat, A. (2015). *A survey on security assessment of metering infrastructure in Smart Grid systems.* IEEE. doi:10.1109/SECON.2015.7132989

Anzar, M., Nadeem, J., & Sohail, R. (2015). A review of wireless communications for smart grid. *Renewable & Sustainable Energy Reviews*, *41*, 248–260. doi:10.1016/j.rser.2014.08.036

Arora, S., Venkataraman, V., Zhan, A., Donohue, S., Biglan, K. M., Dorsey, E. R., & Little, M. A. (2015). Detecting and monitoring the symptoms of Parkinson's disease using smartphones: A pilot study. *Parkinsonism & Related Disorders*, *21*(6), 650–553. doi:10.1016/j.parkreldis.2015.02.026 PMID:25819808

Asakawa, T., Sugiyama, K., Nozaki, T., Sameshima, T., Kobayashi, S., Wang, L., ... Namba, H. (2019). Can the latest computerized technologies revolutionize conventional assessment tools and therapies for a neurological disease? The example of Parkinson's disease. *Neurologia Medico-Chirurgica*, *59*(3), 69–78. doi:10.2176/nmc.ra.2018-0045 PMID:30760657

Asay, M. (2014, June 27). *The Internet Of Things Will Need Millions Of Developers By 2020.* Retrieved from http://readwrite.com/2014/06/27/internet-of-things-developers-jobs-opportunity

Atzori, L., Iera, A., & Morabito, G. (2014). From smart objects to social objects: The next evolutionary step of the internet of things. *IEEE Communications Magazine*, *52*(1), 97–105. doi:10.1109/MCOM.2014.6710070

Ayguadé, E. B.-O. (2009). An extension of the StarSs programming model for platforms with multiple GPUs. *European Conference on Parallel Processing*, 851-862. 10.1007/978-3-642-03869-3_79

Baader, F., Milicic, M., Lutz, C., Sattler, U., & Wolter, F. (2005). *Integrating description logics and action formalisms for reasoning about web services.* LTCS-Report 05-02, Chair for Automata Theory, Institute for Theoretical Computer Science, Dresden University of Technology. Retrieved from http://lat.inf.tu-dresden.de/research/reports.html

Baader, F., Calvanese, D., McGuinness, D., Nardi, D., & Patel-Schneider, P. (2003). *The description logic handbook: theory, implementation, and applications.* New York, NY: Cambridge University Press.

Baca, J., Pagala, P., Rossi, C., & Ferre, M. (2015). Modular robot systems towards the execution of cooperative tasks in large facilities. *Robotics and Autonomous Systems, 66,* 159–174. doi:10.1016/j.robot.2014.10.008

Baggio, R., & Caporarello, L. (2008). *Decision support systems in a tourism destination: literature survey and model building.* Retrieved from http://www.iby.it/turismo/papers/baggio-dss-tourism.pdf

Bagnall, A., Lines, J., Bostrom, A., Large, J., & Keogh, E. (2017). The great time series classification bake off: A review and experimental evaluation of recent algorithmic advances. *Data Mining and Knowledge Discovery, 31*(3), 606–660. doi:10.100710618-016-0483-9 PMID:30930678

Balandin, S., Boldyrev, S., Oliver, I., Turenko, T., Smirnov, A., Shilov, N., & Kashevnik, A. (2012). *Method and apparatus for ontology matching.* US Patent 2012/0078595 A1.

Balandin, S., & Gillet, M. (2010). Embedded Network in Mobile Devices. *International Journal of Embedded and Real-Time Communication Systems, 1*(1), 22–36. doi:10.4018/jertcs.2010103002

Barbosa, F. S., Duberg, D., Jensfelt, P., & Tumova, J. (2019). Guiding Autonomous Exploration With Signal Temporal Logic. *IEEE Robotics and Automation Letters, 4*(4), 3332–3339. doi:10.1109/LRA.2019.2926669

Barrantes, S., Egea, A. J. S., Rojas, H. A. G., & Martí, M. J. (2017). Differential diagnosis between Parkinson's disease and essential tremor using the smartphone's accelerometer. *PLoS One, 12*(8), e0183843. doi:10.1371/journal.pone.0183843 PMID:28841694

Barta, R., Feilmayr, C., Pröll, B., Grün, C., & Werthner, H. (2009). Covering the Semantic Space of Tourism: An Approach Based on Modularized Ontologies. *Proceedings of the 1st Workshop on Context, Information and Ontologies.*

Bastas, G., Fleck, J. J., Peters, R. A., & Zelik, K. E. (2018). IMU-based gait analysis in lower limb prosthesis users: Comparison of step demarcation algorithms. *Gait & Posture, 64,* 30–37. doi:10.1016/j.gaitpost.2018.05.025 PMID:29807270

Baumgartner, N., Mitsch, S., Müller, A., Retschitzegger, W., Salfinger, A., & Schwinger, W. (2014). A tour of BeAware--A situation awareness framework for control centers. *Information Fusion, 20,* 155–173. doi:10.1016/j.inffus.2014.01.008

Baumgartner, N., Retschitzegger, W., & Schwinger, W. (2008). Application Scenarios of Ontology-Driven Situation Awareness SystemsExemplified for the Road Traffic Management Domain. In S. Borgo, & L. Lesno (Eds.), *Proceedings of the 2008 Conference on Formal Ontologies Meet Industry* (pp. 77–87). Amsterdam: IOS Press.

Bazhenov, N., Korzun, D., & Balandin, S. (2018). Smartphone-Oriented Development of Video Data Based Services. In *Proceedings of the 23rd conference of FRUCT Association* (pp. 62-68). IEEE. 10.23919/FRUCT.2018.8588068

Bekara, C. (2014). *Security Issues and Challenges for the IoT-based Smart Grid.* IEEE. doi:10.1016/j.procs.2014.07.064

Bellini, P., Cenni, D., & Nesi, P. (2016). Cloud Knowledge Modeling and Management. In Encyclopedia of Cloud Computing. Chichester, UK: John Wiley & Sons, Ltd. doi:10.1002/9781118821930.ch52

Bello, J. P., Silva, C., Nov, O., Dubois, R. L., Arora, A., Salamon, J., & ... . (2018). Sonyc: A system for the monitoring, analysis and mitigation of urban noise pollution. *Communications of the ACM.*

Ben Dhaou, I., Kondoro, A., Kelati, A., Rwegasira, D. S., Naiman, S., Mvungi, N. H., & Tenhunen, H. (2017, July). Communication and Security Technologies for Smart Grid. *International Journal of Embedded and Real-Time Communication Systems, 8*(2), 40–65. doi:10.4018/IJERTCS.2017070103

Ben Meskina, S., Doggaz, N., Khalgui, M., & Li, Z. (2017). Multiagent Framework for Smart Grids Recovery. *IEEE Transactions on Systems, Man, and Cybernetics. Systems, 47*(7), 1284–1300. doi:10.1109/TSMC.2016.2573824

Bergamini, C., Bosi, F., Corradi, A., Rolt, C. R. D., Foschini, L., Monti, S., & Seralessandri, M. (2018). LocalFocus: A Big Data Service Platform for Local Communities and Smarter Cities. *IEEE Communications Magazine, 56*(7), 116–123. doi:10.1109/MCOM.2018.1700597

Berka, T., & Plößnig, M. (2004). Designing recommender systems for tourism. *ENTER*. Retrieved from http://195.130.87.21:8080/dspace/handle/123456789/583

Beyea, J., McGibbon, C. A., Sexton, A., Noble, J., & O'Connell, C. (2017). Convergent validity of a wearable sensor system for measuring sub-task performance during the timed up-and-go test. *Sensors (Basel), 17*(4), 934. doi:10.339017040934 PMID:28441748

Bini, S. A. (2018). Artificial intelligence, machine learning, deep learning, and cognitive computing: What do these terms mean and how will they impact health care? *The Journal of Arthroplasty, 33*(8), 2358–2361. doi:10.1016/j.arth.2018.02.067 PMID:29656964

Bizer, C., Lehmann, J., Kobilarov, G., Auer, S., Becker, C., Cyganiak, R., & Hellmann, S. (2009). DBpedia – a crystallization point for the Web of Data. *Journal of Web Semantics, 7*(3), 154–165. doi:10.1016/j.websem.2009.07.002

Black, D., Donovan, J., Bunton, B., & Keist, A. (2009). *SystemC: From the ground up* (Vol. 71). Springer Science & Business Media.

Blackman, S., Matlo, C., Bobrovitskiy, A., Fang, M. L., Jackson, P., Mihailidis, L., ... Sixsmith, A. (2016). Ambient assisted living technologies for aging well. *Journal of Intelligent Systems, 25*(1), 55–69. doi:10.1515/jisys-2014-0136

Blasch, E. (2016). *JDL Model (III) Updates for an Information Management Enterprise*. Academic Press.

Blasch, E. (2017). JDL Model (III) Updates for an Information Management Enterprise. In H. Fourati (Ed.), *Multisensor Data Fusion: From Algorithms and Architectural Design to Applications* (pp. 55–73). Boca Raton, FL: CRC Press. doi:10.1201/b18851-4

Bonte, P., Ongenae, F., De Backere, F., Schaballie, J., Arndt, D., Verstichel, S., ... De Turck, F. (2017). The MASSIF platform: A modular and semantic platform for the development of flexible IoT services. *Knowledge and Information Systems, 51*(1), 89–126. doi:10.100710115-016-0969-1

Borodin, A., Pogorelov, A., & Zavyalova, Y. (2013) Overview of Algorithms for Electrocardiograms Analysis. In *13th Conference of Open Innovations Association FRUCT and 2nd Seminar on e-Tourism for Karelia and Oulu Region* (pp 14-19). Helsinki, Finland: FRUCT Oy.

Borodin, A., Zavyalova, Y., Zaharov, A., & Yamushev, I. (2015). Architectural Approach to the Multisource Health Monitoring Application Design. In *17th Conference of Open Innovations Association FRUCT* (pp. 16-21). Helsinki, Finland: FRUCT Oy. 10.1109/FRUCT.2015.7117965

Bridewell, W., & Bello, P. (2015). *Incremental Object Perception in an Attention-Driven Cognitive Architecture*. CogSci.

Brito, R., Fong, S., Song, W., Cho, K., Bhatt, C., & Korzun, D. (2018). Detecting Unusual Human Activities Using GPU-Enabled Neural Network and Kinect Sensors. In Internet of Things and Big Data Technologies for Next Generation Healthcare. Series: Studies in Big Data (Vol. 23, pp. 290-296). Springer.

Bruining, N., Caiani, E., Chronaki, C., Guzik, P., & van der Velde, E. (2014). Task Force of the E-cardiology Working Group. Acquisition and Analysis of Cardiovascular Signals on Smartphones: Potential, Pitfalls and Perspectives. *European Journal of Preventive Cardiology*, *21*(2_suppl), 4–13. doi:10.1177/2047487314552604 PMID:25354948

Buckley, C., Galna, B., Rochester, L., & Mazzà, C. (2019). Upper body accelerations as a biomarker of gait impairment in the early stages of Parkinson's disease. *Gait & Posture*, *71*, 289–295. doi:10.1016/j.gaitpost.2018.06.166 PMID:30139646

Bukow, W.-D., Ottersbach, M., Tuider, E., & Yildiz, E. (2006). *Biographische Konstruktionen im multikulturellen Bildungsprozess: Individuelle Standortsicherung im globalisierten Alltag*. Springer-Verlag. doi:10.1007/978-3-531-90071-1

Busom, N., Petrlic, R., Sebé, F., Sorge, C., & Valls, M. (2016). Efficient smart metering based on homomorphic encryption. *Computer Communications*, *82*, 95–101. doi:10.1016/j.comcom.2015.08.016

Calinescu, R., Camara, J., & Paterson, C. (2019). Socio-Cyber-Physical Systems: Models, Opportunities, Open Challenges. *2019 IEEE/ACM 5th International Workshop on Software Engineering for Smart Cyber-Physical Systems (SEsCPS)*.

Calinescu, R. C., Camara Moreno, J., & Paterson, C. (2019). Socio-Cyber-Physical Systems: Models, Opportunities, Open Challenges. *5th International Workshop on Software Engineering for Smart Cyber-Physical Systems*.

CardiaCare. (2012). *CardiaCare project Official Page*. Retrieved June 25, 2019 from http://oss.fruct.org/projects/cardiacare/

Cardoso, T., Barros, E., Prado, B., & Aziz, A. (2012). Communication software synthesis from UML-ESL models. In *25th Symposium on Integrated Circuits and Systems Design (SBCCI)* (pp. 1-6). Brasilia: IEEE.

Chakravarthi, M. K., Tiwari, R. K., & Handa, S. (2015). Accelerometer based static gesture recognition and mobile monitoring system using neural networks. *Procedia Computer Science, 70*, 683-687.

Chand, P., & Carnegie, D. A. (2013). Mapping and exploration in a hierarchical heterogeneous multi-robot system using limited capability robots. *Robotics and Autonomous Systems*, *61*(6), 565–579. doi:10.1016/j.robot.2013.02.009

Chang, W. L., & Boyd, D. (2018). *NIST Big Data Interoperability Framework: Volume 6, Big Data Reference Architecture* (No. Special Publication (NIST SP)-1500-6 Version 2).

Chen, C. Y., Fu, J. H., Wang, P. F., Jou, E., & Feng, M. W. (2014, August). Complex event processing for the internet of things and its applications. In *Automation Science and Engineering (CASE), 2014 IEEE International Conference on* (pp. 1144-1149). IEEE. 10.1109/CoASE.2014.6899470

Chianese, A., Piccialli, F., & Jung, J. E. (2016). The Internet of Cultural Things: Towards a Smart Cultural Heritage. In *Proc 12th International Conference on Signal-Image Technology & Internet-Based Systems (SITIS)* (pp. 493-496). 10.1109/SITIS.2016.83

Chianese, A., Piccialli, F., & Valente, I. (2015). Smart environments and cultural heritage: A novel approach to create intelligent cultural spaces. *Journal of Location Based Services*, *9*(3), 209–234. doi:10.1080/17489725.2015.1099752

Chiang, M., & Zhang, T. (2016). Fog and IoT: An overview of research opportunities. *IEEE Internet of Things Journal*, *3*(6), 854–864. doi:10.1109/JIOT.2016.2584538

Choi, C., Cho, M., Choi, J., & Hwang, M. (2009). Travel ontology for Intelligent Recommendation System. *Proc. of the 3rd Asia International Conference on Modelling and Simulation*, 637–642.

Christofides, N. (1975). *Graph theory: An algorithmic approach (Computer science and applied mathematics)*. Academic Press, Inc.

Cintuglu, M. H., & Mohammed, O. A. (2015). Multiagent-based decentralized operation of microgrids considering data interoperability. In *IEEE International Conference on Smart Grid Communications (SmartGridComm)*, (pp. 404-409). Miami, FL: IEEE. 10.1109/SmartGridComm.2015.7436334

Cintuglu, M. H., Youssef, T., & Mohammed, O. A. (2018). Development and Application of a Real-Time Testbed for Multiagent System Interoperability: A Case Study on Hierarchical Microgrid Control. *IEEE Transactions on Smart Grid*, *9*(3), 1759–1768. doi:10.1109/TSG.2016.2599265

Ciortea, A., Mayer, S., & Michahelles, F. (2018). Repurposing manufacturing lines on the fly with multi-agent systems for the Web of Things. In *Proceedings of the 17th International Conference on Autonomous Agents and MultiAgent Systems* (pp. 813-822). International Foundation for Autonomous Agents and Multiagent Systems.

Clifford, G., Azuaje, F., & McSharry, P. (Eds.). (2006). *Advanced Methods and Tools for ECG Data Analysis*. Norwood, MA: Artech House.

CMPE249: Introduction to Cyber-physical Systems. (2019). Retrieved from https://courses.soe.ucsc.edu/courses/cmpe249

Coelho-Junior, H. J., Rodrigues, B., de Oliveira Gonzalves, I., Asano, R. Y., Uchida, M. C., & Marzetti, E. (2018). The physical capabilities underlying timed "Up and Go" test are time-dependent in community-dwelling older women. *Experimental Gerontology*, *104*, 138–146. doi:10.1016/j.exger.2018.01.025 PMID:29410234

Cornejo, A., & Lynch, N. (2010). Fault-Tolerance Through k-Connectivity. *Workshop on Network Science and Systems Issues in Multi-Robot Autonomy: ICRA*.

Coursera IoT. (2019). Retrieved from https://ru.coursera.org/specializations/iot

Criaud, M., Poisson, A., Thobois, S., Metereau, E., Redouté, J., Ibarrola, D., ... Boulinguez, P. (2016). Slowness in movement initiation is associated with proactive inhibitory network dysfunction in Parkinson's disease. *Journal of Parkinson's Disease*, *6*(2), 433–440. doi:10.3233/JPD-150750 PMID:27061065

D'Antrassi, P., Prenassi, M., Rossi, L., Ferrucci, R., Barbieri, S., Priori, A., & Marceglia, S. (2019). Personally collected health data for precision medicine and longitudinal research. *Frontiers in Medicine.*, *6*, 125. doi:10.3389/fmed.2019.00125 PMID:31231653

Dagdeviren, O., Korkmaz, I., Tekbacak, F., & Erciyes, K. (2011). A Survey of Agent Technologies for Wireless Sensor Networks. *IETE Technical Review*, *28*(2), 168–184. doi:10.4103/0256-4602.72509

Dalle Vacche, A. (2015). *Mastering Zabbix*. Packt Publishing Ltd.

Dally W. J., & Seitz C. L. (1988). *Deadlock-free message routing in multiprocessor interconnection networks*. Academic Press.

Data Science for IoT. (2019). Retrieved from https://www.conted.ox.ac.uk/courses/data-science-for-the-internet-of-things-iot

Davis, A. L. (1978). *Data Driven Nets: A Maximally Concurrent, Procedural, Parallel Process Representation for Distributed Control Systems. Computer Science Dept.* Salt Lake City, UT: University of Utah.

De Mola, F., & Quitadamo, R. (2006). Towards an Agent Model for Future Autonomic Communications. *Proceedings of the 7th WOA 2006 Workshop From Objects to Agents.*

Deepu, C. J., Heng, C. H., & Lian, Y. (2016). A hybrid data compression scheme for power reduction in wireless sensors for IoT. *IEEE Transactions on Biomedical Circuits and Systems*, *11*(2), 245–254. doi:10.1109/TBCAS.2016.2591923 PMID:27845673

Del Din, S., Godfrey, A., Mazzà, C., Lord, S., & Rochester, L. (2016). Free-living monitoring of Parkinson's disease: Lessons from the field. *Movement Disorders*, *31*(9), 1293–1313. doi:10.1002/mds.26718 PMID:27452964

Dellandrea, B., Gouin, B., Parkes, S., & Jameux, D. (2014). MOST: Modeling of SpaceWire & SpaceFiber Traffic-Applications and Operations: On-Board Segment. *Proceedings of the DASIA 2014 conference.*

Demathieu, S., Thomas, F., André, C., Gérard, S., & Terrier, F. (2008). First Experiments Using the UML Profile for MARTE. In *2008 11th IEEE International Symposium on Object and Component-Oriented Real-Time Distributed Computing (ISORC)* (pp. 50-57). Orlando, FL: IEEE.

Demiris, G. (2016). Consumer health informatics: Past, present, and future of a rapidly evolving domain. *Yearbook of Medical Informatics*, *25*(Suppl 1), S42–S47. doi:10.15265/IYS-2016-s005 PMID:27199196

Dennis, J. B., Fosseen, J. B., & Linderman, J. P. (1974). *Data flow schemas*. Springer-Verlag Berlin Heidelberg. doi:10.1007/3-540-06720-5_15

Dey, A., Salber, D., & Abowd, G. (2001). A Conceptual Framework and a Toolkit for Supporting the Rapid Prototyping of Context-Aware Applications. *Human-Computer Interaction*, *16*(2), 97–199. doi:10.1207/S15327051HCI16234_02

Distefano, S., Merlino, G., & Puliafito, A. (2012). SAaaS: A framework for volunteer-based sensing clouds. *Parallel and Cloud Computing*, *1*(2), 21–33.

Djeddi, W. E., & Khadir, M. T. (2013). Ontology alignment using artificial neural network for large-scale ontologies. *International Journal of Metadata, Semantics and Ontologies*, *8*(1), 75–92. doi:10.1504/IJMSO.2013.054180

Doerffel, T. (2009). Simulation of wireless ad-hoc sensor networks with QualNet. *Advanced Seminar on Embedded Systems, Technische Universitat Chemnitz, 16.*

Doerr, M. (2003). The CIDOC conceptual reference module: An ontological approach to semantic interoperability of metadata. *AI Magazine*, *24*(3), 75–92.

Dolan, R. (2018). *Four Reasons Why Travel Risk Management is a Business Imperative*. Retrieved from https://www.concur.com/newsroom/article/four-reasons-why-travel-risk-management-is-a-business-imperative

Douglas, K. (2012). Homo virtuous: The evolution of good and evil. *New Scientist*, *216*(2890), 42–45. doi:10.1016/S0262-4079(12)62895-4

Dovžan, D., Logar, V., & Skrjanc, I. (2015). Implementation of an evolving fuzzy model (efumo) in a monitoring system for a waste-water treatment process. *IEEE Transactions on Fuzzy Systems*, *23*(5), 1761–1776. doi:10.1109/TFUZZ.2014.2379252

Draisma, H., Swenne, C., van de Vooren, H., Maan, A., van Huysduynen, B., van der Wall, E., & Schalij, M. (2005). LEADS: An Interactive Research Oriented ECG/VCG Analysis System. *Computers in Cardiology*, *32*, 515–518.

Dunovan, K., Vich, C., Clapp, M., Verstynen, T., & Rubin, J. (2019). Reward-driven changes in striatal pathway competition shape evidence evaluation in decision-making. *PLoS Computational Biology*, *15*(5), 1–32. doi:10.1371/journal.pcbi.1006998 PMID:31060045

Dustdar, S., & Bhattacharya, K. (2011). The social compute unit. *IEEE Internet Computing*, *15*(3), 64–69. doi:10.1109/MIC.2011.68

Dutt, N., Jantsch, A., & Sarma, S. (2016). Toward Smart Embedded Systems: A Self-aware System-on-Chip (SoC) Perspective. *ACM Transactions on Embedded Computing Systems*, 22-22:27.

Eganyan, A., Suvorova, E., Sheynin, Y., Khakhulin, A., & Orlovsky, I. (2013). DCNSimulator – Software Tool for SpaceWire Networks Simulation. *Proceedings of International SpaceWire Conference*, 216-221.

EIT Digital Master School. (2019). Retrieved from http://www.masterschool.eitictlabs.eu/programmes/es/

Elers, P., Hunter, I., Whiddett, D., Lockhart, C., Guesgen, H., & Singh, A. (2018). User requirements for technology to assist aging in place: Qualitative study of older people and their informal support networks. *JMIR mHealth and uHealth*, 6(6), e10741. doi:10.2196/10741 PMID:29875083

Elfwing, S., Uchibe, E., & Doya, K. (2018). Sigmoid-weighted linear units for neural network function approximation in reinforcement learning. *Neural Networks*, 107, 3–11. doi:10.1016/j.neunet.2017.12.012 PMID:29395652

Elmaghraby, A. S., & Losavio, M. M. (2014). Cyber security challenges in Smart Cities: Safety, security and privacy. *Journal of Advanced Research*, 5(4), 491–497. doi:10.1016/j.jare.2014.02.006 PMID:25685517

Elmangoush, A., Steinke, R., Al-Hezmi, A., & Magedanz, T. (Feb 2014). On the usage of standardised M2M platforms for Smart Energy management. *The International Conference on Information Networking 2014 (ICOIN2014)*, 79-84. 10.1109/ICOIN.2014.6799669

eMotion mobile FAROS sensor for ECG, HRV. (2019). *Biomation official website*. Retrieved June 25, 2019 from http://ecg.biomation.com/faros.htm

Endsley, M. R. (2016). *Designing for situation awareness: An approach to user-centered design*. CRC Press. doi:10.1201/b11371

Energy Independence and Security Act of 2007. (2007). Retrieved from https://www.gpo.gov

Ergu, D., Kou, G., Peng, Y., Shi, Y., & Shi, Y. (2013). The analytic hierarchy process: Task scheduling and resource allocation in cloud computing environment. *The Journal of Supercomputing*, 64(3), 835–848. doi:10.100711227-011-0625-1

Erol-Kantarci, M., & Mouftah, H. T. (2015). Energy-efficient information and communication infrastructures in the smart grid: A survey on interactions and open issues. *IEEE Communications Surveys and Tutorials*, 17(1), 179–197. doi:10.1109/COMST.2014.2341600

ESA. Standard ECSS-E-ST-50-52C. (2010). *SpaceWire — Remote memory access protocol*. Noordwijk: Publications Division ESTEC.

Eskofier, B. M., Lee, S. I., Baron, M., Simon, A., Martindale, C. F., Gabner, H., & Klucken, J. (2017). An overview of smart shoes in the internet of health things: Gait and mobility assessment in health promotion and disease monitoring. *Applied Sciences*, 7(10), 986. doi:10.3390/app7100986

Esmalifalak, M., Liu, L., Nguyen, N., Zheng, R., & Han, Z. (2017). Detecting Stealthy False Data Injection Using Machine Learning in Smart Grid. *IEEE Systems Journal*, 11(3), 1644–1652. doi:10.1109/JSYST.2014.2341597

Espay, A. J., Hausdorff, J. M., Sánchez-Ferro, Á., Klucken, J., Merola, A., Bonato, P., ... Maetzler, W. (2019). Movement Disorder Society Task Force on Technology. A roadmap for implementation of patient-centered digital outcome measures in Parkinson's disease obtained using mobile health technologies. *Movement Disorders*, 34(5), 657–663. doi:10.1002/mds.27671 PMID:30901495

Euzenat, J., & Shvaiko, P. (2013). *Ontology Matching* (2nd ed.). Berlin: Springer-Verlag. doi:10.1007/978-3-642-38721-0

Evans, E. (2004). *Domain-driven design: tackling complexity in the heart of software*. Addison-Wesley Professional.

Fang, X., Misra, S., Xue, G., & Yang, D. (2012). Smart Grid- The New and Improved Power Grid: A Survey. *IEEE Communications Surveys & Tutorials, 14*, 944-980. doi:10.1109/SURV.2011.101911.00087

Farhangi, H. (2010). The path of the smart grid. *IEEE Power & Energy Magazine, 8*(1), 18–28. doi:10.1109/MPE.2009.934876

Faulkner, M., Cheng, M. H., Krause, A., Clayton, R., Heaton, T., Chandy, K. M., ... Olson, M. (2014). Community Sense and Response Systems: Your Phone as Quake Detector. *Communications of the ACM, 57*(7), 66–75. doi:10.1145/2622633

Fawaz, H. I., Forestier, G., Weber, J., Idoumghar, L., & Muller, P. A. (2019). Deep learning for time series classification: A review. *Data Mining and Knowledge Discovery, 33*(4), 917–963. doi:10.100710618-019-00619-1

Feldman, J. (2013). The neural binding problem(s). *Cognitive Neurodynamics, 7*(1), 1–11. doi:10.100711571-012-9219-8 PMID:24427186

Fernández, J. L., Sanz, R., Benayas, J. A., & Diéguez, A. R. (2004). Improving collision avoidance for mobile robots in partially known environments: The beam curvature method. *Robotics and Autonomous Systems, 46*(4), 205–219. doi:10.1016/j.robot.2004.02.004

Ferrer, E. C. (2018, November). The blockchain: a new framework for robotic swarm systems. In *Proceedings of the Future Technologies Conference* (pp. 1037-1058). Springer.

Flynn. (n.d.). Retrieved from http://flynn.com

Fodor, O., & Werthner, H. (2005). Harmonise: A Step toward an Interoperable E-Tourism Merketplace. *International Journal of Electronic Commerce, 9*(2), 11-39.

Foo, P. H., & Ng, G.-W. (2013). High-level information fusion: An overview. *Journal of Advances in Information Fusion, 8*(1), 33–72.

Formisano, C., Pavia, D., & Gurgen, L. (2015). The advantages of IoT and cloud applied to smart cities. *3rd International Conference Future Internet of Things and Cloud*, 325-332. 10.1109/FiCloud.2015.85

Fowler, M. (2010). *Domain-Specific Languages*. Pearson Education.

Fox, G., Jha, S., & Ramakrishnan, L. (2016). *Stream2016: Streaming requirements, experience, applications and middleware workshop (No. LBNL-1006355). Lawrence Berkeley National Lab*. Berkeley, CA: LBNL. doi:10.2172/1344785

Franzoni, C., & Sauermann, H. (2014). Crowd science: The organization of scientific research in open collaborative projects. *Research Policy, 43*(1), 1–20. doi:10.1016/j.respol.2013.07.005

Friese, S. (2019). *Qualitative Data Analysis with ATLAS.ti* (3rd ed.). Max-Planck Institute.

Fujino, N., Ogawa, K., & Minowa, M. (2016). Wireless network technologies to support the age of IoT. *Fujitsu Scientific and Technical Journal, 52*(4), 68–76.

Gaber, M. M., Zaslavsky, A., & Krishnaswamy, S. (2009). Data stream mining. In *Data Mining and Knowledge Discovery Handbook* (pp. 759–787). Boston, MA: Springer. doi:10.1007/978-0-387-09823-4_39

Ganapathy, K., Abdul, S. S., & Nursetyo, A. A. (2018). Artificial intelligence in neurosciences: A clinician's perspective. *Neurology India, 66*(4), 934–939. doi:10.4103/0028-3886.236971 PMID:30038071

GBTA. (2017). *The Five Pillars of Travel Risk Management*. Retrieved from https://www.gbta.org/blog/the-five-pillars-of-travel-risk-management/

Geonames Geographical Database. (n.d.). Retrieved from www.geonames.org/

Giancardo, L., Sánchez-Ferro, A., Arroyo-Gallego, T., Butterworth, I., Mendoza, C. S., Montero, P., ... Estépar, R. S. (2016). Computer keyboard interaction as an indicator of early Parkinson's disease. *Scientific Reports*, *6*(1), 34468. doi:10.1038rep34468 PMID:27703257

Giraldo, J., Cardenas, A., & Quijano, N. (2017). Integrity Attacks on Real-Time Pricing in Smart Grids: Impact and Countermeasures. *IEEE Transactions on Smart Grid*, *8*(5), 2249–2257. doi:10.1109/TSG.2016.2521339

Glesner, M., & Philipp, F. (2013). Embedded Systems Design for Smart System Integration. *IEEE Computer Society Annual Symposium on VLSI (ISVLSI)*, 32-33. 10.1109/ISVLSI.2013.6654611

Glodek, M., Honold, F., Geier, T., Krell, G., Nothdurft, F., Reuter, S., ... Biundo, S. (2015). Fusion paradigms in cognitive technical systems for human–computer interaction. *Neurocomputing*, *161*, 17–37. doi:10.1016/j.neucom.2015.01.076

Goldberger, A., Amaral, L., Glass, L., Hausdorff, J., Ivanov, P., Mark, R., ... Stanley, H. (2000). PhysioBank, PhysioToolkit, and PhysioNet: Components of a New Research Resource for Complex Physiologic Signals. *Circulation*, *101*(23), 215–220. doi:10.1161/01.CIR.101.23.e215 PMID:10851218

Gore, B. F., Hooey, B. L., Wickens, C. D., & Scott-Nash, S. (2009, July). A computational implementation of a human attention guiding mechanism in MIDAS v5. In *International conference on digital human modeling* (pp. 237-246). Springer. 10.1007/978-3-642-02809-0_26

Gorman, W. (2009). *Pentaho Reporting 3.5 for Java Developers*. Packt Publishing Ltd.

Greer, C., Burns, M., Wollman, D., & Griffor, E. (2019). Cyber-Physical Systems & the Internet of Things. *NIST Special Publication*, *1900*, 202.

Gretzel, U. (2011). Intelligent systems in tourism: A social science perspective. *Annals of Tourism Research*, *38*(3), 757–779. doi:10.1016/j.annals.2011.04.014

Gretzel, U., Reino, S., Kopera, S., & Koo, C. (2015). Smart tourism challenges. *Journal of Tourism*, *16*(1), 41–47.

Grier, J. W. (2014). Comparison and Review of Portable, Handheld, 1-lead/channel ECG / EKG Recorders. *North Dakota State University Official Website*. Retrieved October 27, 2016 from https://www.ndsu.edu/pubweb/~grier/Comparison-handheld-ECG-EKG.html

Griffor, E. R., Greer, C., Wollman, D. A., & Burns, M. J. (2017). *Framework for cyber-physical systems: Volume 2, working group reports* (No. Special Publication (NIST SP)-1500-202).

Gruber, T. R. (1993). A translation approach to portable ontology specifications. *Knowledge Acquisition*, *5*(2), 199–220. doi:10.1006/knac.1993.1008

Gubbi, J., Buyya, R., Marusic, S., & Palaniswami, M. (2013). Internet of Things (IoT): A vision, architectural elements, and future directions. *Future Generation Computer Systems*, *29*(7), 1645–1660. doi:10.1016/j.future.2013.01.010

Guizzardi, G. (2005). *Ontological foundations for structural conceptual models* (Ph.D. thesis). Universiteit Twente.

Gulwani, S., Polozov, O., & Singh, R. (2017). Program synthesis. *Foundations and Trends® in Programming Languages*, *4*(1-2), 1-119.

Gungor, V. C., Sahin, D., Kocak, T., & Ergut, S. (2011). Smart grid technologies: communication technologies and standards. *IEEE transactions*.

Gungor, V. C., Sahin, D., Kocak, T., Ergut, S., Buccella, C., Cecati, C., & Hancke, G. P. (2013, February). A Survey on Smart Grid Potential Applications and Communication Requirements. *IEEE Transactions on Industrial Informatics*, *9*(1), 28–42. doi:10.1109/TII.2012.2218253

Guth, J., Breitenbücher, U., Falkenthal, M., Fremantle, P., Kopp, O., Leymann, F., & Reinfurt, L. (2018). A detailed analysis of IoT platform architectures: concepts, similarities, and differences. In *Internet of Everything* (pp. 81–101). Springer. doi:10.1007/978-981-10-5861-5_4

Gyrard, A., Patel, P., Datta, S. K., & Ali, M. I. (2017). Semantic web meets internet of things and web of things. In *Proceedings of the 26th International Conference on World Wide Web Companion* (pp. 917-920). International World Wide Web Conferences Steering Committee. 10.1145/3041021.3051100

Gyrard, A., Zimmermann, A., & Sheth, A. (2018). Building IoT-Based Applications for Smart Cities: How Can Ontology Catalogs Help? *IEEE Internet of Things Journal, 5*(5), 3978–3990. doi:10.1109/JIOT.2018.2854278

Haas, B., Clarke, E., Elver, L., Gowman, E., Mortimer, E., & Byrd, E. (2017). The reliability and validity of the L-test in people with Parkinson's disease. *Physiotherapy, 105*(1), 84–89. doi:10.1016/j.physio.2017.11.218 PMID:29395266

Haberman, Z. C., Jahn, R. T., Bose, R., Tun, H., Shinbane, J. S., Doshi, R. N., ... Saxon, L. A. (2015). Wireless Smartphone ECG Enables Large-Scale Screening in Diverse Populations. *Journal of Cardiovascular Electrophysiology, 26*(5), 520–526. doi:10.1111/jce.12634 PMID:25651872

Haikonen, P. O. (2009). The role of associative processing in cognitive computing. *Cognitive Computation, 1*(1), 42–49. doi:10.100712559-009-9006-y

Harari, F. (1969). Graph Theory. Addison-Wesley Publishing Company.

Harkovchuk, A., & Korzun, D. (2019). Semantic Information Search Service by Person's Face Photo. In *Proceedings of the 24th Conference of Open Innovations Association FRUCT* (pp. 821-823). Academic Press.

Harper, S. (2014). Economic and social implications of aging societies. *Science, 346*(6209), 587–591. doi:10.1126cience.1254405 PMID:25359967

Hartanto, R., & Eich, M. (2014, April). Reliable, cloud-based communication for multi-robot systems. In *2014 IEEE International Conference on Technologies for Practical Robot Applications (TePRA)* (pp. 1-8). IEEE.

Hartley, R. V. L. (1928, July). Transmission of Information. *Bell System Technical Journal*.

Hasegawa, N., Shah, V. V., Carlson-Kuhta, P., Nutt, J. G., Horak, F. B., & Mancini, M. (2019). How to select balance measures sensitive to Parkinson's disease from body-worn inertial sensors-separating the trees from the forest. *Sensors (Basel), 19*(15), 3320. doi:10.339019153320 PMID:31357742

Haykin, S. (2006). Cognitive radar: A way of the future. *IEEE Signal Processing Magazine, 23*(1), 30–40. doi:10.1109/MSP.2006.1593335

Haykin, S. (Ed.). (2006). *Nonlinear methods of spectral analysis* (Vol. 34). Springer Science & Business Media.

He, D., Kumar, N., & Lee, J.-H. (2015). Privacy-preserving data aggregation scheme against internal attackers in smart grids. *Wireless Networks, 22*. doi:10.100711276-015-0983-3

Holdowsky, J., Mahto, M., Raynor, M. E., & Cotteleer, M. (2015, August 21). *Inside the Internet of Things (IoT). A primer on the technologies building the IoT.* Retrieved from http://dupress.com/articles/iot-primer-iot-technologies-applications/

Hongfei, Y., Hongjian, W., Hongli, L., & Ying, W. (2016). Research on situation awareness based on ontology for UUV. In *2016 IEEE International Conference on Mechatronics and Automation* (pp. 2500–2506). Harbin: IEEE. 10.1109/ICMA.2016.7558959

Hopcroft, J. E., Motwani, R., & Ullman, J. D. (2001, March). Introduction to automata theory, languages, and computation. *ACM SIGACT News*.

Horrocks, I. (2008). Ontologies and the semantic web. *Communications of the ACM*, *51*(12), 58–67. doi:10.1145/1409360.1409377

Hozdic, E. (2019). Socio-Cyber-Physical Systems Alternative for Traditional Manufacturing Structures. *New Technologies, Development and Application II. Lecture Notes in Networks and Systems*, *76*, 15–24. doi:10.1007/978-3-030-18072-0_2

HP Internet of Things. (2019). Retrieved from http://h20195.www2.hp.com/v2/GetPDF.aspx/c04656912.pdf

HSE IoT Program. (2019). Retrieved from https://www.hse.ru/en/ma/internet/courses/index.html

Hubble, R. P., Naughton, G. A., Silburn, P. A., & Cole, M. H. (2015). Wearable sensor use for assessing standing balance and walking stability in people with Parkinson's disease: A systematic review. *PLoS One*, *10*(4), e0123705. doi:10.1371/journal.pone.0123705 PMID:25894561

Huh, J., Le, T., Reeder, B., Thompson, H. J., & Demiris, G. (2013). Perspectives on wellness self-monitoring tools for older adults. *International Journal of Medical Informatics*, *82*(11), 1092–1103. doi:10.1016/j.ijmedinf.2013.08.009 PMID:24041452

IEEE Std 2030-2011. (2011). *IEEE Guide for Smart Grid Interoperability of Energy Technology and Information Technology Operation with the Electric Power System (EPS), End-Use Applications, and Loads*. Retrieved from http://ieeexplore.ieee.org/stampPDF/getPDF.jsp?arnumber=6018239

IETF. (2010). *Internet Key Exchange Protocol Version 2 (IKEv2)*. Retrieved from https://tools.ietf.org/html/rfc5996

IETF. (2012). *Datagram Transport Layer Security Version 1.2*. Retrieved from https://tools.ietf.org/html/rfc6347

Ingalls, D. H. H. (1986). A simple technique for handling multiple polymorphism. *ACM SIGPLAN Notices*, *21*(11), 347–349. doi:10.1145/960112.28732

Intel IoT Course. (2019). Retrieved from https://github.com/guermonprez/intel-academic-IoT-course

Intel IoT. (2019). Retrieved from https://software.intel.com/en-us/iot/training

IoT requirements and protocols. (2017). Retrieved from http://embedded-computing.com/articles/internet-things-requirements-protocols/

IoT Software Architecture. (2019). Retrieved from https://ru.coursera.org/learn/iot-software-architecture

IoT will fire up the Next Generation of Engineers. (2015, January). Retrieved from https://www.ee.ucl.ac.uk/undergraduate/newsarmiotjan2015

Ipsos MORI Global Business Resilience Trends Watch. (2018). Retrieved from https://www.businesswire.com/news/home/20171114005920/en/Organisations-Strides-Planning-Unknown-Risk-Perception-Remains

Iqbal, A., Ullah, F., Anwar, H., Kwak, K. S., Imran, M., Jamal, W., & Rahman, A. (2018). Interoperable Internet-of-Things platform for smart home system using Web-of-Objects and cloud. *Sustainable Cities and Society*, *38*, 636–646. doi:10.1016/j.scs.2018.01.044

Issariyakul, T., & Hossain, E. (2012). *Introduction to Network Simulator NS2*. Springer Science+Business Media.

Ito, K., & Matsuura, S. (2010). Model driven development for embedded systems. In *Proceedings of the 9th WSEAS international conference on Software engineering, parallel and distributed systems* (pp. 102-108). World Scientific and Engineering Academy and Society (WSEAS).

Ivanov, D. (2018, September). Decentralized planning of intelligent mobile robot's behavior in a group with limited communications. In *International Conference on Intelligent Information Technologies for Industry* (pp. 418-427). Springer.

Jantsch, E. (1975). *Design for Evolution*. New York: George Braziller.

Jianru, H., Xiaomin, C., & Huixian, S. (2012). An OPNET Model of SpaceWire and Validation. *Proceedings of the 2012 International Conference on Electronics, Communications and Control*, 792-795.

Jing, Q., Vasilakos, A. V., Wan, J., Lu, J., & Qiu, D. (2014). Security of the Internet of Things: Perspectives and challenges. *Wireless Networks*, *20*(8), 2481–2501. doi:10.100711276-014-0761-7

Joe, J., Hall, A., Chi, N. C., Thompson, H., & Demiris, G. (2018). IT-based wellness tools for older adults: Design concepts and feedback. *Informatics for Health & Social Care*, *43*(2), 142–158. doi:10.1080/17538157.2017.1290637 PMID:28350186

Johnston, W. M., Hanna, J. R., & Millar, R. J. (2004). Advances in dataflow programming languages. *ACM Computing Surveys*, *36*(1), 1–34. doi:10.1145/1013208.1013209

Joshi, A. (2016). *Embedded Systems: Technologies and Markets*. BCC Research.

Jungnickel, D. (2008). *Graphs, Networks and Algorithms* (3rd ed.). Springer-Verlag Berlin Heidelberg. doi:10.1007/978-3-540-72780-4

Kabalci, Y. (2016). A survey on smart metering and smart grid communication. *Renewable & Sustainable Energy Reviews*, *57*, 302–318. doi:10.1016/j.rser.2015.12.114

Kahrobaee, S., Rajabzadeh, R., Soh, L.-K., & Asgarpoor, S. (2013). A Multiagent Modeling and Investigation of Smart Homes With Power Generation, Storage, and Trading Features. *IEEE Transactions on Smart Grid*, *4*(2), 659–668. doi:10.1109/TSG.2012.2215349

Kalus, M. (2007). Semantic networks and historical knowledge management: Introducing new methods of computer-based research. *The Journal of the Association for History and Computing*, 10.

Kamar, E. (2012). Combining human and machine intelligence in large-scale crowdsourcing. *Proceedings of the 11th International Conference on Autonomous Agents and Multiagent Systems*.

Kappa architecture. Merging Batch and Stream Processing in a Post Lambda World. (2016, June). Retrieved from https://www.datanami.com/2016/06/01/merging-batch-streaming-post-lambda-world/

Karsai, G., Sztipanovits, J., Lédeczi, Á., & Bapty, T. (2003, January 29). Model-integrated development of embedded software. *Proceedings of the IEEE*, *91*(1), 145–164. doi:10.1109/JPROC.2002.805824

Kashevnik, A., Kalyazina, D., Parfenov, V., Shabaev, A., Baraniuc, O., Lashkov, I., & Khegai, M. (2018). Ontology-Based Human-Robot Interaction: An Approach and Case Study on Adaptive Remote Control Interface. In *Interactive Collaborative Robotics, Third International Conference on Interactive Collaborative Robotics (ICR 2018)*. Leipzig, Germany: Springer International Publishing.

Kashevnik, A., Smirnov, A., & Teslya, N. (2018). Ontology-Based Interaction of Mobile Robots for Coalition Creation. *International Journal of Embedded and Real-Time Communication Systems*, *9*(2), 63–78. doi:10.4018/IJERTCS.2018070105

Khan, A. A., Rehmani, M. H., & Reisslein, M. (2016). Cognitive Radio for Smart Grids: Survey of Architectures, Spectrum Sensing Mechanisms, and Networking Protocols. *IEEE Communications Surveys Tutorials*, *18*, 860-898. doi:10.1109/COMST.2015.2481722

Khan, R. H., & Khan, J. Y. (2013). A comprehensive review of the application characteristics and traffic requirements of a smart grid communications network. *Computer Networks*, *57*(3), 825–845. doi:10.1016/j.comnet.2012.11.002

Khronos Vision Working Group. (2017, March 10). *The OpenVX™ Specification v1.1.* Retrieved from https://www.khronos.org/registry/OpenVX/specs/1.1/OpenVX_Specification_1_1.pdf

Kim, M.H., Baik, H., & Lee, S. (2015). *Resource welfare based task allocation for UAV team with resource.* Academic Press.

Kim, A., Kim, J., Rietdyk, S., & Ziaie, B. (2015). A wearable smartphone-enabled camera-based system for gait assessment. *Gait & Posture, 42*(2), 138–144. doi:10.1016/j.gaitpost.2015.05.001 PMID:26059484

Kings College London. (2019). Retrieved from https://www.futurelearn.com/courses/internet-of-things

Klug, C., Schmalstieg, D., Gloor, T., & Arth, C. (2019). A complete workflow for automatic forward kinematics model extraction of robotic total stations using the denavit-hartenberg convention. *Journal of Intelligent & Robotic Systems, 95*(2), 311–329. doi:10.100710846-018-0931-4

Kluge, F., Gaßner, H., Hannink, J., Pasluosta, C., Klucken, J., & Eskofier, B. M. (2017). Towards mobile gait analysis: Concurrent validity and test-retest reliability of an inertial measurement system for the assessment of spatio-temporal gait parameters. *Sensors (Basel), 17*(7), 1522. doi:10.339017071522 PMID:28657587

Kocakulak, M., & Butun, I. (2017). An overview of Wireless Sensor Networks towards internet of things. In *2017 IEEE 7th Annual Computing and Communication Workshop and Conference (CCWC)* (pp. 1–6). Las Vegas, NV: IEEE. 10.1109/CCWC.2017.7868374

Kochhar, S. (2010). The anatomy of a large-scale human computation engine. *Proceedings of the ACM SIGKDD Workshop on Human Computation - HCOMP '10.* 10.1145/1837885.1837890

Koes, M., Nourbakhsh, I., Sycara, K., Koes, M., Sycara, K., Nourbakhsh, I., & Jennings, N. R. (2005, July). *Heterogeneous multirobot coordination with spatial and temporal constraints* (Vol. 5). AAAI.

Kokar, M. M., Matheus, C. J., & Baclawski, K. (2009). Ontology-based situation awareness. *Information Fusion, 10*(1), 83–98. doi:10.1016/j.inffus.2007.01.004

Kolchin, M., Andreev, A., Garayzuev, D., Chursin, N., Mouromtsev, D., & Zakoldaev, D. (2016). A CoAP-Based Hypermedia Framework for Always-On and Sleepy Devices in Smart Home Environment. *International Journal of Embedded and Real-Time Communication Systems, 7*(2), 45–63. doi:10.4018/IJERTCS.2016070104

Kolmogorov, A. N. (1965). Three approaches to the quantitative definition of information'. *Problems of Information Transmission, 1*(1), 1–7.

Kong, Y., Zhang, M., & Ye, D. (2017). A belief propagation-based method for task allocation in open and dynamic cloud environments. *Knowledge-Based Systems, 115*, 123–132. doi:10.1016/j.knosys.2016.10.016

Ko, R. K. L., Lee, E. W., & Lee, S. G. (2012). BusinessOWL (BOWL) - a hierarchical task network ontology for dynamic business process decomposition and formulation. *IEEE Transactions on Services Computing, 5*(2), 246–259. doi:10.1109/TSC.2011.48

Korzun, D. (2017). Internet of things meets mobile health systems in smart spaces: An overview. In Internet of Things and Big Data Technologies for Next Generation Healthcare. Studies in Big Data (vol. 23, pp. 111-129). Springer.

Korzun, D., Meigal, A., Borodin, A., & Gerasimova-Meigal, L. (2017). On mobile personalized healthcare services for human involvement into prevention, therapy, mutual support, and social rehabilitation. In *Proceedings of the 2017 International Multi-Conference on Engineering, Computer and Information Sciences* (pp. 276-281). IEEE. 10.1109/SIBIRCON.2017.8109888

Korzun, D. G., Borodin, A. V., Timofeev, I. A., Paramonov, I. V., & Balandin, S. I. (2015). Digital Assistance Services for Emergency Situations in Personalized Mobile Healthcare: Smart Space Based Approach. *2015 International Conference on Biomedical Engineering and Computational Technologies (SIBIRCON)*, 1-6. 10.1109/SIBIRCON.2015.7361852

Korzun, D. G., Marchenkov, S. A., Vdovenko, A. S., & Petrina, O. B. (2016). A Semantic Approach to Designing Information Services for Smart Museums. *International Journal of Embedded and Real-Time Communication Systems*, 7(2), 15–34. doi:10.4018/IJERTCS.2016070102

Korzun, D., Balandina, E., Kashevnik, A., Balandin, S., & Viola, F. (2019). *Ambient Intelligence Services in IoT Environments: Emerging Research and Opportunities*. IGI Global. doi:10.4018/978-1-5225-8973-0

Korzun, D., & Meigal, A. (2019). Multi-Source Data Sensing in Mobile Personalized Healthcare Systems: Semantic Linking and Data Mining. In *Proceedings of the 24th conference of FRUCT Association* (pp. 187-192). IEEE. 10.23919/FRUCT.2019.8711950

Korzun, D., Nikolaevskiy, I., & Gurtov, A. (2016). Service Intelligence and Communication Security for Ambient Assisted Living. *International Journal of Embedded and Real-Time Communication Systems*, 6(1), 75–100.

Korzun, D., Varfolomeyev, A., Yalovitsyna, S., & Volokhova, V. (2017). Semantic infrastructure of a smart museum: Toward making cultural heritage knowledge usable and creatable by visitors and professionals. *Personal and Ubiquitous Computing*, 21(2), 345–354. doi:10.100700779-016-0996-7

Korzun, D., Yalovitsyna, S., & Volokhova, V. (2018). Smart Services as Cultural and Historical Heritage Information Assistance for Museum Visitors and Personnel. *Baltic J. Modern Computing*, 6(4), 418–433.

Krötzsch, M., Simancik, F., & Horrocks, I. (2012). *A description logic primer*. arXiv preprint arXiv:1201.4089

Krötzsch, M., & Vrandečić, D. (2011). Semantic MediaWiki. In D. Fensel (Ed.), *Foundations for the web of information and services: A review of 20 years of semantic web research* (pp. 311–326). doi:10.1007/978-3-642-19797-0_16

Kubicek, H., & Cimander, R. (2009). Three dimensions of organizational interoperability: Insights from recent studies for improving interoperability frame-works. *European Journal of ePractice, 6*.

Kubicek, H., Cimander, R., & Scholl, H. (2011). Organizational Interoperability in E-Government: Lessons from 77 European Good-Practice Cases. Academic Press.

Kuflik, T., Wecker, A., Lanir, J., & Stock, O. (2015). An integrative framework for extending the boundaries of the museum visit experience: Linking the pre, during and post visit phases. *Information Technology & Tourism*, 15(1), 17–47. doi:10.100740558-014-0018-4

Kulakov, K., Petrina, P., Korzun, D., & Varfolomeyev, A. (2016). Towards an understanding of smart service: the case study for cultural heritage e-Tourism. *Proceedings of the 18th Conference of FRUCT Association*, 145-152. 10.1109/FRUCT-ISPIT.2016.7561520

Kurbanov, L., Rozhdestvenskaya, K., & Suvorova, E. (2018). Deadlock-Free Routing in SpaceWire Onboard Network. *2018 22nd Conference of Open Innovations Association (FRUCT)*, 107-114.

Kuzmin, A., Safronov, M., Bodin, O., Petrovsky, M., & Sergeenkov, A. (2016a). Device and Software for Mobile Heart Monitoring. In S. Balandin (Ed.), *19th Conference of Open Innovations Association FRUCT* (pp. 121-127). Helsinki, Finland: FRUCT Oy. 10.23919/FRUCT.2016.7892191

Kuzmin, A., Safronov, M., Bodin, O., Petrovsky, M., & Sergeenkov, A. (2016b). Mobile Heart Monitoring System Prototype Based on the Texas Instruments Hardware: Energy Efficiency and J-point Detection. *International Journal of Embedded and Real-Time Communication Systems*, 7(1), 64–84. doi:10.4018/IJERTCS.2016010104

LabChartECG Analysis Add-On. (2017). *ADInstruments official website*. Retrieved June 25, 2019 from https://www.adinstruments.com/products/ecg-analysis

Laird, J. E. (2012). *The Soar cognitive architecture*. MIT Press. doi:10.7551/mitpress/7688.001.0001

Lakka, E. (2019). End-to-End Semantic Interoperability Mechanisms for IoT. In *Proc. 2019 IEEE 24th International Workshop on Computer Aided Modeling and Design of Communication Links and Networks (CAMAD)* (pp. 1-6). IEEE.

Lamanna, D. D., Skene, J., & Emmerich, W. (2003). SLAng: A language for defining service level agreements. *Proc. of the 9th IEEE Workshop on Future Trends in Distributed Computing Systems-FTDCS*, 100-106. 10.1109/FTDCS.2003.1204317

Lambda architecture. (2019). Retrieved from http://lambda-architecture.net/

Langley, P., & Choi, D. (2006). Learning recursive control programs from problem solving. *Journal of Machine Learning Research*, 7(Mar), 493–518.

Lanir, J., Kuflik, T., Sheidin, J., Yavin, N., Leiderman, K., & Segal, M. (2017). Visualizing museum visitors' behavior: Where do they go and what do they do there? *Personal and Ubiquitous Computing*, 21(2), 313–326. doi:10.100700779-016-0994-9

Lara, J., Cooper, R., Nissan, J., Ginty, A. T., Khaw, K. T., Deary, I. J., ... Mathers, J. C. (2015). A proposed panel of biomarkers of healthy ageing. *BMC Medicine*, 13(1), 222. doi:10.118612916-015-0470-9 PMID:26373927

Lara, J., Godfrey, A., Evans, E., Heaven, B., Brown, L. J., Barron, E., ... Mathers, J. C. (2013). Towards measurement of the Healthy Ageing Phenotype in lifestyle-based intervention studies. *Maturitas*, 76(2), 189–199. doi:10.1016/j.maturitas.2013.07.007 PMID:23932426

Laure, D., Medvedev, O., Balandin, S., & Lagutina, K. (2015). Mobile Apps for Stimulating Healthy Life: Walky Doggy Reference Example. In *17th Conference of Open Innovations Association FRUCT*. Helsinki, Finland: FRUCT Oy.

Lavrovskaya, I., Olenev, V., & Korobkov, I. (2017). Fault-Tolerance Analysis Algorithm for SpaceWire Onboard Networks. In *Proceedings of the 21st Conference of Open Innovations Association FRUCT*. University of Helsinki.

Lazarescu, M. T. (2017). Wireless sensor networks for the internet of things: Barriers and synergies. In *Components and Services for IoT Platforms* (pp. 155–186). Springer. doi:10.1007/978-3-319-42304-3_9

Le Page, P., MacLachlan, H., Anderson, L., Penn, L., Moss, A., & Mitchell, A. (2015). The efficacy of a Smartphone ECG Application for Cardiac Screening in an Unselected Island Population. *Britain Journal Cardiology*, 22, 31–33.

Lea, P. (2018). *Internet of Things for Architects: Architecting IoT solutions by implementing sensors, communication infrastructure, edge computing, analytics, and security*. Packt Publishing Ltd.

Lebedev, S., & Panteleyev, M. (2017). Ontology-Driven Situation Assessment System Design and Development in IoT Domains. *International Journal of Embedded and Real-Time Communication Systems*, 8(1), 1–17. doi:10.4018/IJERTCS.2017010101

Lee, C. Y., Kang, S. J., Hong, S. K., Ma, H. I., Lee, U., & Kim, Y. J. (2016). A validation study of a smartphonebased finger tapping application for quantitative assessment of bradykinesia in Parkinson's disease. *PLoS One*, 11(7), 1–11. doi:10.1371/journal.pone.0158852

Lhermitte, S., Verbesselt, J., Verstraeten, W. W., & Coppin, P. (2011). A comparison of time series similarity measures for classification and change detection of ecosystem dynamics. *Remote Sensing of Environment*, 115(12), 3129–3152. doi:10.1016/j.rse.2011.06.020

Liang, H., Choi, B. J., Zhuang, W., Shen, X., Awad, A. S., & Abdr, A. (2012). Multiagent coordination in microgrids via wireless networks. *IEEE Wireless Communications*, *19*(3), 14–22. doi:10.1109/MWC.2012.6231155

Liang, X., & Xiao, Y. (2009). Studying bio-inspired coalition formation of robots for detecting intrusions using game theory. *IEEE Transactions on Systems, Man, and Cybernetics. Part B, Cybernetics*, *40*(3), 683–693. doi:10.1109/TSMCB.2009.2034976 PMID:19933008

Li, B., Moridian, B., Kamal, A., Patankar, S., & Mahmoudian, N. (2019). Multi-robot mission planning with static energy replenishment. *Journal of Intelligent & Robotic Systems*, *95*(2), 745–759. doi:10.100710846-018-0897-2

Liggins, M. II, Hall, D., & Llinas, J. (Eds.). (2017). *Handbook of multisensor data fusion: theory and practice*. CRC Press. doi:10.1201/9781420053098

Lindenberger, U. (2014). Human cognitive aging: Corriger la fortune? *Science*, *346*(6209), 572–578. doi:10.1126cience.1254403 PMID:25359964

Lin, J., Yu, W., Zhang, N., Yang, X., Zhang, H., & Zhao, W. (2017, October). A Survey on Internet of Things: Architecture, Enabling Technologies, Security and Privacy, and Applications. *IEEE Internet of Things Journal*, *4*(5), 1125–1142. doi:10.1109/JIOT.2017.2683200

Li, S., Jin, Q., Jiang, X., & Park, J. (Eds.). (2014). *Frontier and Future Development of Information Technology in Medicine and Education. Lecture Notes in Electrical Engineering 269*. Springer Science and Business Media Dordrecht. doi:10.1007/978-94-007-7618-0

Little, G., Chilton, L. B., Goldman, M., & Miller, R. C. (2010). Exploring iterative and parallel human computation processes. *Proceedings of the ACM SIGKDD Workshop on Human Computation*, 68–76. 10.1145/1837885.1837907

Liu, Y., Cheng, C., Gu, T., Jiang, T., & Li, X. (2016). A Lightweight Authenticated Communication Scheme for Smart Grid. *IEEE Sensors Journal*, *16*. doi:10.1109/jsen.2015.2489258

Livieri, B. (2015). Ontology-based modeling of cloud services: Challenges and perspectives. PoEM (Short Papers). *CEUR Workshop Proceedings*, *1497*, 61–70.

Li, W., Li, Z., Li, Y., Ding, L., Wang, J., Gao, H., & Deng, Z. (2019, November). Semi-autonomous bilateral teleoperation of six-wheeled mobile robot on soft terrains. *Mechanical Systems and Signal Processing*, *133*, 106234. doi:10.1016/j.ymssp.2019.07.015

Li, Z., Wang, Z., Tournier, J.-C., Peterson, W., Li, W., & Wang, Y. (2010). A Unified Solution for Advanced Metering Infrastructure Integration with a Distribution Management System. In *First IEEE International Conference on Smart Grid Communications* (ss. 566-571). Gaithersburg, VA: IEEE. 10.1109/SMARTGRID.2010.5621998

Loh, K. K., & Kanai, R. (2016). How has the Internet reshaped human cognition? *The Neuroscientist*, *22*(5), 506–520. doi:10.1177/1073858415595005 PMID:26170005

López, J., Pérez, D., Paz, E., & Santana, A. (2013). WatchBot: A building maintenance and surveillance system based on autonomous robots. *Robotics and Autonomous Systems*, *61*(12), 1559–1571. doi:10.1016/j.robot.2013.06.012

Lovas, R., Farkas, A., Marosi, A. C., Ács, S., Kovács, J., Szalóki, Á., & Kádár, B. (2018). Orchestrated platform for cyber-physical systems. *Complexity*.

Ludwig, H., Keller, A., & Dan, A. (2003). *Web Service Level Agreement (WSLA) Language Specification*. Retrieved from http://www.research.ibm.com/wsla/WSLASpecV1-20030128.pdf

Luo, H. (2015). *Wearable mini-size intelligent healthcare system*. U.S. Patent No. 9,044,136. Washington, DC: U.S. Patent and Trademark Office.

MacLean, P. D. (1990). *The triune brain in evolution: role in paleocerebral functions*. Springer.

Maehara, Y., Saito, S., & Towse, J. N. (2019). Joint cognition and the role of human agency in random number choices. *Psychological Research*, *83*(3), 574–589. doi:10.100700426-017-0944-9 PMID:29110078

Mahmood, K., Chaudhry, S. A., Naqvi, H., Kumari, S., Li, X., & Sangaiah, A. K. (2018). An elliptic curve cryptography based lightweight authentication scheme for smart grid communication. *Future Generation Computer Systems*, *81*, 557–565. doi:10.1016/j.future.2017.05.002

Mamun, M. A. A., Hannan, M. A., Hussain, A., & Basri, H. (2016). Theoretical model and implementation of a real time intelligent bin status monitoring system using rule based decision algorithms. *Expert Systems with Applications*, *48*(C), 76–88. doi:10.1016/j.eswa.2015.11.025

Mancini, M., King, L., Salarian, A., Holmstrom, L., McNames, J., Horak, F.B. (2011). Mobility Lab to Assess Balance and Gait with Synchronized Body-worn Sensors. *Journal of Bioengineering & Biomedical Science, S1*.

Mancini, M., Carlson-Kuhta, P., Zampieri, C., Nutt, G., Chiari, L., & Horak, F. B. (2012). Postural sway as a marker of progression in Parkinson's disease: A pilot longitudinal study. *Gait & Posture*, *36*(3), 471–476. doi:10.1016/j.gaitpost.2012.04.010 PMID:22750016

Manjula Shenoy, K., Shet, K. C., & Dinesh Acharya, U. (2013). NN based ontology mapping. *Communications in Computer and Information Science, 296*, 122–127.

Man, S., ter Haar, C., de Jongh, M., Maan, A., Schalij, M., & Swenne, C. (2017). Position of ST-Deviation Measurements Relative to the J-point: Impact for Ischemia Detection. *Journal of Electrocardiology*, *50*(1), 82–8981. doi:10.1016/j.jelectrocard.2016.10.012 PMID:27914634

Man, S., ter Haar, C., Maan, A., Schalij, M., & Swenne, C. (2015). The Dependence of the STEMI Classification on the Position of ST-deviation Measurement Instant Relative to the J point. *Computers in Cardiology*, *42*, 837–840.

Ma, R., Chen, H.-H., Huang, Y.-R., & Meng, W. (2013). Smart Grid Communication: Its Challenges and Opportunities. *IEEE Transactions on Smart Grid*, *4*(1), 36–46. doi:10.1109/TSG.2012.2225851

Marchenkov, S. A., Vdovenko, A. S., Petrina, O. B., & Korzun, D. G. (2016). A smart space-based design of semantic layer for advancing museum information services. In S. Balandin, & T. Tyutina (Eds.), *Proc. 19th Conf. Open Innovations Association FRUCT* (pp. 159-166). 10.23919/FRUCT.2016.7892196

Mármol, F., Sorge, C., Ugus, O., & Pérez, G. (2012). Do not snoop my habits: Preserving privacy in the smart grid. *IEEE Communications Magazine*, *50*(5), 166–172. doi:10.1109/MCOM.2012.6194398

Marshall, M. T. (2018). Interacting with Heritage: On the Use and Potential of IoT Within the Cultural Heritage Sector. In *Proc. Fifth International Conference on Internet of Things: Systems, Management and Security* (pp. 15-22). 10.1109/IoTSMS.2018.8554899

Masron, T., Ismail, N., & Marzuki, A. (2016). The conceptual design and application of web-based tourism decision support systems. *Theoretical and Empirical Researches in Urban Management*, *11*(2), 64–75.

Master in City Science. (2019). Retrieved from http://www.citysciences.com/

Matheus, C. J., Kokar, M. M., Baclawski, K., Letkowski, J. A., Call, C., Hinman, M. L., … Boulware, D. M. (2005). SAWA: An assistant for higher-level fusion and situation awareness. In Multisensor, Multisource Information Fusion: Architectures, Algorithms, and Applications 2005 (Vol. 5813, pp. 75–86). International Society for Optics and Photonics.

Meier, P. (2017). *How Crisis Mapping Saved Lives in Haiti.* Retrieved from http://voices.nationalgeographic.com/2012/07/02/crisis-mapping-haiti/

Meigal, A., Gerasimova-Meigal, L., Borodin, A., Voronova, N., Yelaeva, L., & Kuzmina, G. (2016). Mobile Health Service is Promising to Detect the Blood Pressure and HRV Fluctuations Across the Menstrual and the Lunar Cycle. In *19th Conference of Open Innovations Association FRUCT* (pp. 167-172). Helsinki, Finland: FRUCT Oy.

Meigal, A., Korzun, D., Gerasimova-Meigal, L., Borodin, A., & Zavialova, Y. (2019). Ambient intelligence At-Home Laboratory for human everyday life. *International Journal of Embedded and Real-Time Communication Systems, 10*(2), 117–134. doi:10.4018/IJERTCS.2019040108

Meigal, A., Prokhorov, K., Gerasimova-Meigal, L., Bazhenov, N., & Korzun, D. (2017). Towards a Personal At-Home Lab for Motion Video Tracking in Patients with Parkinson's Disease. In *Proceedings of the 21st conference of FRUCT Association* (pp. 231-237). IEEE. 10.23919/FRUCT.2017.8250187

Meigal, A., Reginya, S., Gerasimova-Meigal, L., Prochorov, K., & Moschevikin, A. (2018). Analysis of human gait based on smartphone inertial measurement unit: a feasibility study. In *Proceedings of the 22nd conference of FRUCT Association* (pp. 151-158). IEEE. 10.23919/FRUCT.2018.8468264

Meiling, S., Purnomo, D., Shiraishi, J.-A., Fischer, M., & Schmid, T. C. (2018). MONICA in Hamburg: Towards Large-Scale IoT Deployments in a Smart City (18-21 June 2018, Ljubljana, Slovenia). In *2018 European Conference on Networks and Communications (EuCNC)* (pp. 224–229). IEEE. 10.1109/EuCNC.2018.8443213

Melgaard, J., Struijk, J. J., Hansen, J., Kanters, J. K., Jensen, A. S., Schmidt, S., & Graff, C. (2014). Automatic J-point Location in Subjects with Electrocardiographic Early Repolarization. *Computers in Cardiology, 41*, 585–588.

Mell, P., & Grance, T. (2011). *The NIST definition of cloud computing.* Recommendations of the National Institute of Standards and Technology, NIST Special Publication 800-145.

Mellor, S., Balcer, M., & Jacoboson, I. (2002). *Executable UML: A foundation for model-driven architectures.* Addison-Wesley Professional.

Mendel, J. (2017). Smart Grid Cyber Security Challenges: Overview and Classification. *e-mentor, 2017.* doi:10.15219/em68.1282

Merlino, G., Arkoulis, S., Distefano, S., Papagianni, C., Puliafito, A., & Papavassiliou, S. (2016). Mobile crowdsensing as a service: A platform for applications on top of sensing clouds. *Future Generation Computer Systems, 56*, 623–639. doi:10.1016/j.future.2015.09.017

Meulpolder, M., Pouwelse, J., Epema, D., & Sips, H. (2009). BarterCast: A practical approach to prevent lazy freeriding in P2P networks. *IEEE International Symposium on Parallel & Distributed Processing.*

Micó-Amigo, M. E., Kingma, I., Faber, G. S., Kunikoshi, A., van Uem, J. M. T., van Lummel, R. C., ... van Dieлn, J. H. (2017). Is the Assessment of 5 Meters of Gait with a Single Body-Fixed-Sensor Enough to Recognize Idiopathic Parkinson's Disease-Associated Gait? *Annals of Biomedical Engineering, 45*(5), 1266–1278. doi:10.100710439-017-1794-8 PMID:28108943

Mischkalla, F., He, D., & Mueller, W. (2010). Closing the gap between UML-based modeling, simulation and synthesis of combined HW/SW systems. In *Proceedings of the Conference on Design, Automation and Test in Europe* (pp. 1201-1206). Dresden: European Design and Automation Association. 10.1109/DATE.2010.5456990

MIT Internet of Things Roadmap. (2019). Retrieved from https://mitprofessionalx.mit.edu/courses/course-v1:MITProfessionalX+IOTx+2016_T1/about

MIT IoT. (2019). Retrieved from http://web.mit.edu/professional/digital-programs/courses/IoT/index.html

Mokatren, M., Kuflik, T., & Shimshoni, I. (2018). Exploring the potential of a mobile eye tracker as an intuitive indoor pointing device: A case study in cultural heritage. *Future Generation Computer Systems*, *81*, 528–541. doi:10.1016/j.future.2017.07.007

Moral-Munoz, J. A., Esteban-Moreno, B., Herrera-Viedma, E., Cobo, M. J., & Pérez, I. J. (2018). Smartphone Applications to Perform Body Balance Assessment: A Standardized Review. *Journal of Medical Systems*, *42*(7), 119. doi:10.100710916-018-0970-1 PMID:29845455

Morrison, J. P. (2010). *Flow-Based Programming: A New Approach To Application Development* (2nd ed.). Charleston: Createspace Independent.

Mosterman, P. J. (2007). *MATLAB and Simulink for Embedded System Design*. The MathWorks.

Mouromtsev, D., Haase, P., Pavlov, D., Cherny, E., Andreev, A., & Spiridonova, A. (2015). Towards the linked Russian heritage cloud: Data enrichment and publishing. In The Semantic Web. Latest Advances and New Domains (ESWC2015, LNCS 9088, pp. 637-651). Springer.

My Digital Life. (2019). Retrieved from http://www.open.ac.uk/courses/modules/tu100#details

Nadim, I., Elghayam, Y., & Sadiq, A. (2018, April). Semantic discovery architecture for dynamic environments of Web of Things. In *2018 International Conference on Advanced Communication Technologies and Networking (CommNet)* (pp. 1-6). IEEE. 10.1109/COMMNET.2018.8360269

Nafi, N. S., Ahmed, K., Gregory, M. A., & Datta, M. (2016, October). A Survey of Smart Grid Architectures, Applications, Benefits and Standardization. *Journal of Network and Computer Applications*, *76*, 1–21. doi:10.1016/j.jnca.2016.10.003

Namiot, D., & Sneps-Sneppe, M. (2016b, October) On crowd sensing back-end. In *DAMDID/RCDL 2016 Selected Papers of the XVIII International Conference on Data Analytics and Management in Data Intensive Domains (DAMDID/RCDL 2016)* (pp. 168–175), CEUR Workshop Proceedings.

Namiot, D., & Sneps-Sneppe, M. (2019, April). On Content Models for Proximity Services. In *2019 24th Conference of Open Innovations Association (FRUCT)* (pp. 277-284). IEEE. 10.23919/FRUCT.2019.8711983

Namiot, D. (2015). On big data stream processing. *International Journal of Open Information Technologies*, *3*(8), 48–51.

Namiot, D. (2016). On Internet of Things and Smart Cities educational courses. *International Journal of Open Information Technologies*, *4*(5), 26–38.

Namiot, D., Kupriyanovsky, V., Nikolaev, D., & Zubareva, E. (2016). On standards in Big Data area. *International Journal of Open Information Technologies*, *4*(11), 12–18.

Namiot, D., & Sneps-Sneppe, M. (2014). On IoT programming. *International Journal of Open Information Technologies*, *2*(10).

Namiot, D., & Sneps-Sneppe, M. (2016a, November). On Internet of Things Programming Models. In *International Conference on Distributed Computer and Communication Networks* (pp. 13-24). Springer. 10.1007/978-3-319-51917-3_2

Namiot, D., & Sneps-Sneppe, M. (2017). On Internet of Things and big data in university courses. *International Journal of Embedded and Real-Time Communication Systems, 8*(1), 18–30. doi:10.4018/IJERTCS.2017010102

Namiot, D., Sneps-Sneppe, M., & Daradkeh, Y. (2017, April). On Internet of Things Education. In S. Balandin (Ed.), *Proceedings of the 20th Conference of Open Innovations Association FRUCT*. LETI University.

Nasir, M. A. U. (2016). *Fault Tolerance for Stream Processing Engines.* arXiv preprint arXiv:1605.00928

Nasle, A. (2017). *Real-time predictive systems for intelligent energy monitoring and management of electrical power networks.* U.S. Patent No. 9,557,723. Washington, DC: U.S. Patent and Trademark Office.

National Institute of Standards and Technology. (2014). *NIST Framework and Roadmap for Smart Grid Interoperability Standards (Release 3.0).* US Department of Commerce.

Negash, B., Westerlund, T., & Tenhunen, H. (2019). Towards an interoperable Internet of Things through a web of virtual things at the Fog layer. *Future Generation Computer Systems, 91*, 96–107. doi:10.1016/j.future.2018.07.053

Nguyen, T. (2017, May). A modeling & simulation based engineering approach for socio-cyber-physical systems. In *2017 IEEE 14th International Conference on Networking, Sensing and Control (ICNSC)* (pp. 702-707). IEEE.

Nicolas, A., Posadas, H., Peñil, P., & Villar, E. (2014). Automatic deployment of component-based embedded systems from UML/MARTE models using MCAPI. In *Design of Circuits and Integrated Systems* (pp. 1-6). Madrid: IEEE.

NIST Big Data Public Working Group, & the NIST Big Data Public Working Group. (2018). NIST Big Data Interoperability Framework: Volume 3, Use Cases and General Requirements. US Department of Commerce, National Institute of Standards and Technology.

nRF52832. (2018). *Nordic Semiconductor Official Website.* Retrieved June 25, 2019 from https://www.nordicsemi.com/Products/Low-power-short-range-wireless/nRF52832

NS-3 Manual. (2017). *NS-3 Network Simulator, 165.* doi:10.23919/FRUCT.2017.8250185

Nuevo, J. (2004). A Comprehensible GloMoSim Tutorial. *INRS, 34.*

Olenev, V., Lavrovskaya, I., Korobkov, I., & Sheynin, Y. (2019). Design and Simulation of Onboard SpaceWire Networks. *2019 24th Conference of Open Innovations Association (FRUCT)*, 291-299.

Olenev, V., Lavrovskaya, I., Morozkin, P., Rabin, A., Balandin, S., & Gillet, M. (2014). Co-Modeling of Embedded Networks Using SystemC and SDL: From theory to practice. Advancing Embedded systems and real-time communications with emerging technologies, 206-233.

Olenev, V. (2009). Different approaches for the stacks of protocols SystemC modelling analysis. *Proceedings of the Saint-Petersburg University of Aerospace Instrumentation scientific conference*, 112-113.

Ono, K., & Ogawa, H. (2014). Personal Robot Using Android Smartphone. *Procedia Technology, 18*, 37–41. doi:10.1016/j.protcy.2014.11.009

Osipov, V. (2017). Structure and basic functions of cognitive neural network machine. In *MATEC Web of Conferences* (Vol. 113, p. 02011). EDP Sciences. 10.1051/matecconf/201711302011

Osipov, V., Vodyaho, A., & Zhukova, N. (2017). About one approach to multilevel behavioral program synthesis for television devices. *International Journal of Computers and Communications, 11*, 17-25.

Osipov, V. (2016, July). Space-time structures of recurrent neural networks with controlled synapses. In *International Symposium on Neural Networks* (pp. 177-184). Springer. 10.1007/978-3-319-40663-3_21

Osipov, V. Y. (2016). Automatic synthesis of action programs for intelligent robots. *Programming and Computer Software*, *42*(3), 155–160. doi:10.1134/S0361768816030063

Osipov, V. Y., Vodyaho, A. I., Zhukova, N. A., & Glebovsky, P. A. (2017, May). Multilevel automatic synthesis of behavioral programs for smart devices. In *2017 International Conference on Control, Artificial Intelligence, Robotics & Optimization (ICCAIRO)* (pp. 335-340). IEEE. 10.1109/ICCAIRO.2017.68

Osipov, V. Y., Zhukova, N. A., Vodyaho, A. I., Kalmatsky, A., & Mustafin, N. G. (2017). Towards building of cable TV content-sensitive adaptive monitoring and management systems. *Int. J. Comput. Commun*, *11*, 75–81.

Osipov, V., & Nikiforov, V. (2018, June). Formal aspects of streaming recurrent neural networks. In *International Symposium on Neural Networks* (pp. 29-36). Springer. 10.1007/978-3-319-92537-0_4

Osipov, V., & Osipova, M. (2018). Space–time signal binding in recurrent neural networks with controlled elements. *Neurocomputing*, *308*, 194–204. doi:10.1016/j.neucom.2018.05.009

Osipov, V., Stankova, E., Vodyaho, A., Lushnov, M., Shichkina, Y., & Zhukova, N. (2019, July). Automatic Synthesis of Multilevel Automata Models of Biological Objects. In *International Conference on Computational Science and Its Applications* (pp. 441-456). Springer. 10.1007/978-3-030-24296-1_35

OTcl Official website. (2019). *OTcl and TclCL*. Retrieved from https://sourceforge.net/projects/otcl-tclcl/

OWL 2 Web Ontology Language Document Overview. (n.d.). (2nd ed.). Retrieved from https://www.w3.org/TR/owl2-overview/

Ozay, M., Esnaola, I., Yarman Vural, F. T., Kulkarni, S. R., & Poor, H. V. (2016). Machine Learning Methods for Attack Detection in the Smart Grid. *IEEE Transactions on Neural Networks and Learning Systems*, *27*(8), 1773–1786. doi:10.1109/TNNLS.2015.2404803 PMID:25807571

Pai, F.-P., Yang, L.-J., & Chung, Y.-C. (2017). Multi-layer ontology based information fusion for situation awareness. *Applied Intelligence*, *46*(2), 285–307. doi:10.100710489-016-0834-7

Palm, G. (2013). Neural associative memories and sparse coding. *Neural Networks*, *37*, 165–171. doi:10.1016/j.neunet.2012.08.013 PMID:23043727

Park, D. C., & Reuter-Lorenz, P. (2009). The adaptive brain: Aging and neurocognitive scaffolding. *Annual Review of Psychology*, *60*(1), 173–196. doi:10.1146/annurev.psych.59.103006.093656 PMID:19035823

Parkes, S., & Ferrer-Florit, A. (2010). *SpaceWire-D – Deterministic Control and Data Delivery Over SpaceWire Networks*. Draft B.

Park, H., Yoon, A., & Kwon, H.-C. (2012). Task Model and Task Ontology for Intelligent Tourist Information Service. *International Journal of u- and e- Service Science and Technology*, *5*(2), 43–57.

Pasluosta, C. F., Gassner, H., Winkler, J., Klucken, J., & Eskofier, B. (2015). Parkinson's disease as a working model for global healthcare restructuration. In *Proceedings of the 5th EAI International Conference on Wireless Mobile Communication and Healthcare* (pp. 162-165). ACM.

Pasluosta, C. F., Gassner, H., Winkler, J., Klucken, J., & Eskofier, B. M. (2015). An emerging era in the management of Parkinson's disease: Wearable technologies and the internet of things. *IEEE Journal of Biomedical and Health Informatics*, *19*(6), 1873–1881. doi:10.1109/JBHI.2015.2461555 PMID:26241979

Patierno, P. (2014, June) *IoT Protocols Landscape*. Retrieved from http://www.slideshare.net/paolopat/io-t-protocols-landscape

Peñil, P., Posadas, H., Nicolás, A., & Villar, E. (2012). Automatic synthesis from UML/MARTE models using channel semantics. In *Proceedings of the 5th International Workshop on Model Based Architecting and Construction of Embedded Systems* (pp. 49-54). Innsbruck: Association for Computing Machinery.

Perlovsky, L. I. (2007). Cognitive high level information fusion. *Information Sciences, 177*(10), 2099–2118. doi:10.1016/j.ins.2006.12.026

Petrina, O. B., Korzun, D. G., Volokhova, V. V., Yalovitsyna, S. E., & Varfolomeyev, A. G. (2017). Semantic Approach to Opening Museum Collections of Everyday Life History for Services in Internet of Things Environments. *International Journal of Embedded and Real-Time Communication Systems, 8*(1), 31–44. doi:10.4018/IJERTCS.2017010103

Petrov, V., Mikhaylov, K., Moltchanov, D., Andreev, S., Fodor, G., Torsner, J., ... Koucheryavy, Y. (2018). When IoT keeps people in the loop: A path towards a new global utility. *IEEE Communications Magazine, 57*(1), 114–121. doi:10.1109/MCOM.2018.1700018

Plaza, B. (2009, September). Monitoring web traffic source effectiveness with Google Analytics: An experiment with time series. *Aslib Proceedings, 61*(5), 474–482. doi:10.1108/00012530910989625

Ponomarev, A., & Parfenov, V. (2015). Verification-Enabling Interaction Model for Services in Smart Space: a TAIS Case. *Proceedings of the 17th Conference of the Open Innovations Association FRUCT*, 163-172. 10.1109/FRUCT.2015.7117988

Poulopoulos, V., Vassilakis, C., Antoniou, A., Wallace, M., Lepouras, G., & Nores, M. L. (2018). ExhiSTORY: IoT in the service of Cultural Heritage. In *Proc. 2018 Global Information Infrastructure and Networking Symposium (GIIS)* (pp. 1-4). 10.1109/GIIS.2018.8635759

Pouryousefzadeh, S., & Akbarzadeh, R. (2019). Internet of Things (IoT) systems in future Cultural Heritage. In *Proc. 3rd International Conference on Internet of Things and Applications (IoT)* (pp. 1-5). 10.1109/IICITA.2019.8808838

Prateek, G. V., Skog, I., McNeely, M. E., Duncan, R. P., Earhart, G. M., & Nehorai, A. (2017). Modeling, detecting, and tracking freezing of gait in Parkinson disease using inertial sensors. *IEEE Transactions on Biomedical Engineering*. doi:10.1109/TBME.2017.2785625 PMID:29989948

Proessl, F., Swanson, C. W., Rudroff, T., Fling, B. W., & Tracy, B. L. (2018). Good agreement between smart device and inertial sensor-based gait parameters during a 6-min walk. *Gait & Posture, 64*, 63–67. doi:10.1016/j.gaitpost.2018.05.030 PMID:29859414

Punmiya, R., & Choe, S. (2019). Energy Theft Detection Using Gradient Boosting Theft Detector With Feature Engineering-Based Preprocessing. *IEEE Transactions on Smart Grid, 10*(2), 2326–2329. doi:10.1109/TSG.2019.2892595

Puschel, M. M., Moura, J. M. F., Johnson, J. R., Padua, D., Veloso, M. M., Singer, B. W., ... Rizzolo, N. (2005). SPIRAL: Code Generation for DSP Transforms. *SPIRAL: Code generation for DSP transforms. Proceedings of the IEEE, 93*(2), 232–275. doi:10.1109/JPROC.2004.840306

Qian, B., & Cheng, H. H. (2018). Bio-Inspired Coalition Formation Algorithms for Multirobot Systems. *Journal of Computing and Information Science in Engineering, 18*(2), 021010. doi:10.1115/1.4039638

Ra, M. (2012). Medusa: a programming framework for crowd-sensing applications categories and subject descriptors. *Proceedings of the 10th international conference on Mobile systems, applications, and services MobiSys '12*, 337–350. 10.1145/2307636.2307668

Raptis, G. E., Fidas, C., Katsini, C., & Avouris, N. (2019). A cognition-centered personalization framework for cultural-heritage content. *User Modeling and User-Adapted Interaction, 29*(1), 9–65. doi:10.100711257-019-09226-7

Rashed, M. G., Suzuki, R., Yonezawa, T., Lam, A., Kobayashi, Y., & Kuno, Y. (2016). Tracking Visitors in a Real Museum for Behavioral Analysis. In *Proc. Joint 8th International Conference on Soft Computing and Intelligent Systems (SCIS) and 17th International Symposium on Advanced Intelligent Systems (ISIS)* (pp. 80-85). 10.1109/SCIS-ISIS.2016.0030

Rasheed, M. B., Javaid, N., Hussain, S. M., Akbar, M., & Khan, Z. A. (2017). Multiagent Control System for Residential Energy Management under Real Time Pricing Environment. In *IEEE 31st International Conference on Advanced Information Networking and Applications (AINA)*, (pp. 120-125). Taipei: IEEE.

Raymond, E. S. (2003). *The art of Unix programming*. Addison-Wesley.

Reginya, S., Meigal, A., Gerasimova-Meigal, L., Prokhorov, K., & Moschevikin, A. (2019). Using Smartphone Inertial Measurement Unit for Analysis of Human Gait. *International Journal of Embedded and Real-Time Communication Systems*, *10*(3), 101–117. doi:10.4018/IJERTCS.2019070107

Reyss, A., & Balandin, S. (2010). Healthcare, Medical Support and Consultancy Applications and Services for Mobile Devices. *IEEE Region 8 International Conference on Computational Technologies in Electrical and Electronics Engineering (SIBIRCON)*, 300–305.

Riva, D., Fani, M., Benedetti, M. G., Scarsini, A., Rocca, F., & Mamo, C. (2019). Effects of high-frequency proprioceptive training on single stance stability in older adults: Implications for fall prevention. *BioMed Research International*, *2019*(2382747), 1–11. doi:10.1155/2019/2382747 PMID:31240206

Rodić, A., Jovanović, M., Stevanović, I., Karan, B., & Potkonjak, V. (2015). *Building Technology Platform Aimed to Develop Service Robot with Embedded Personality and Enhanced Communication with Social Environment*. Digital Communications and Networks.

Rose, D. (2014). *Enchanted objects: Design, human desire, and the Internet of things*. Simon and Schuster.

Rosenberg, D., & Mancarella, S. (2010). *Embedded system development using SysML*. Academic Press.

Rudnitckaia, J. (2015). Process Mining. Data science in action. University of Technology, Faculty of Information Technology.

Ruotsalo, T., Haav, K., Stoyanov, A., Roche, S., Fani, E., Deliai, R., ... Hyvonen, E. (2013). SMARTMUSEUM: A mobile recommender system for the Web of Data. *Journal of Web Semantics*, *20*, 50–67. doi:10.1016/j.websem.2013.03.001

Rwegasira, D. S., Ben Dhaou, I. S., Kondoro, A., Anagnostou, A., Kelati, A., Naiman, S., ... Tenhunen, H. (2019). A Demand-Response Scheme Using Multi-Agent System for Smart DC Microgrid. *International Journal of Embedded and Real-Time Communication Systems*, *10*(1), 48–68. doi:10.4018/IJERTCS.2019010103

Sadri, F. (2011). Ambient intelligence: A survey. *ACM Computing Surveys*, *43*(4), 36:1-36:66.

Safronov, M., Kuzmin, A., Bodin, O., Baranov, V., Trofimov, A., & Tychkov, A. (2019). Mobile ECG Monitoring Device with Bioimpedance Measurement and Analysis. In S. Balandin (Ed.), *24th Conference of Open Innovations Association FRUCT* (pp. 375-380). Helsinki, Finland: FRUCT Oy. 10.23919/FRUCT.2019.8711944

Saganenko, G. (2000). General Methodology. *Bulletin of Sociological Methodology. Bulletin de Methodologie Sociologique*, *68*(1), 79–80. doi:10.1177/075910630006800127

Saini, I., Singh, D., & Khosla, A. (2013). QRS Detection Using K-Nearest Neighbor Algorithm (KNN) and Evaluation on Standard ECG Databases. *Journal of Advanced Research*, *4*(4), 331–344. doi:10.1016/j.jare.2012.05.007 PMID:25685438

Sancho, J., Robles, A., & Duato, J. (2000). A new methodology to compute deadlock-free routing tables for irregular networks. *Network-Based Parallel Computing. Communication, Architecture, and Applications*, 45-60.

Sancho, J., & Robles, A. (2000). Improving the up*/down* routing scheme for networks of workstations. *European Conference on Parallel Processing*, 882-889. 10.1007/3-540-44520-X_123

Sanislav, T., & Miclea, L. (2012). Cyber-physical systems-concept, challenges and research areas. *Journal of Control Engineering and Applied Informatics*, *14*(2), 28–33.

Sankhe-Savale, S. (2016). *Tableau Cookbook–Recipes for Data Visualization*. Packt Publishing Ltd.

SAP Internet of Things. (2019). Retrieved from https://open.sap.com/courses/iot1

Sato, A., Tanabe, Y., Chinushi, M., Hayashi, Y., Yoshida, T., Ito, E., ... Aizawa, Y. (2012). Analysis of J Waves During Myocardial Ischaemia. *Europace*, *14*(5), 715–723. doi:10.1093/europace/eur323 PMID:22037542

SCALABLE Network Technologies. (2014). Make Networks Work. Network modeling software for Development and Analysis. *QualNet Datasheet, 4*.

Scekic, O., Miorandi, D., Schiavinotto, T., Diochnos, D. I., Hume, A., Chenu-Abente, R., . . . Giunchiglia, F. (2015). SmartSociety – A Platform for Collaborative People-Machine Computation. *The 8th IEEE International Conference on Service Oriented Computing & Applications (SOCA'15)*.

Schlachetzki, J. C., Barth, J., Marxreiter, F., Gossler, J., Kohl, Z., Reinfelder, S., ... Klucken, J. (2017). Wearable sensors objectively measure gait parameters in Parkinson's disease. *PLoS One*, *12*(10), e0183989. doi:10.1371/journal.pone.0183989 PMID:29020012

Sedgewick, R. (2002). *Algorithms in C++. Part 5 Graph Algorithms* (3rd ed.). Addison-Wesley.

Seiger, R., Huber, S., Heisig, P., & Assmann, U. (2016). Enabling self-adaptive workflows for cyber-physical systems. In Enterprise, Business-Process and Information Systems Modeling (pp. 3–17). Springer. doi:10.1007/978-3-319-39429-9_1

Sekhavatmanesh, H., & Cherkaoui, R. (2019). Distribution Network Restoration in a Multiagent Framework Using a Convex OPF Model. *IEEE Transactions on Smart Grid*, *10*(3), 2618–2628. doi:10.1109/TSG.2018.2805922

Sendin, A., Sanchez-Fornie, M. A., Berganza, I., Simon, J., & Urrutia, I. (2016). Telecommunication Networks for the Smart Grid. Norwood, MA: Artech House.

Sengupta, B., Jain, A., Bhattacharya, K., Truong, H.-L., & Dustdar, S. (2013). Collective problem solving using social compute units. *International Journal of Cooperative Information Systems*, *22*(4), 1341002. doi:10.1142/S0218843013410025

Serena, F., Poveda-Villalón, M., & García-Castro, R. (2017, June). Semantic discovery in the web of things. In *International Conference on Web Engineering* (pp. 19-31). Springer.

Shabanov, V., & Ivanov, D. (2019, March). Organization of Information Exchange in Coalitions of Intelligent Mobile Robots. In *2019 International Conference on Industrial Engineering, Applications and Manufacturing (ICIEAM)* (pp. 1-5). IEEE. 10.1109/ICIEAM.2019.8743043

Shamir, L., Diamond, D., & Wallin, J. (2016). Leveraging Pattern Recognition Consistency Estimation for Crowdsourcing Data Analysis. *IEEE Transactions on Human-Machine Systems*, *46*(3), 474–480. doi:10.1109/THMS.2015.2463082

Shanahan, J., & Dai, L. (2017, April). Large Scale Distributed Data Science from scratch using Apache Spark 2.0. In *Proceedings of the 26th International Conference on World Wide Web Companion* (pp. 955-957). International World Wide Web Conferences Steering Committee. 10.1145/3041021.3051108

Shannon, C. E. (1948). A mathematical theory of communication. *The Bell System Technical Journal*, *27*(3), 379–423. doi:10.1002/j.1538-7305.1948.tb01338.x

Shawon, M. H., Muyeen, S. M., Ghosh, A., Islam, S. M., & Baptista, M. S. (2019). Multi-Agent Systems in ICT Enabled Smart Grid: A Status Update on Technology Framework and Applications. *IEEE Access: Practical Innovations, Open Solutions, 7*, 97959–97973. doi:10.1109/ACCESS.2019.2929577

Sheth, A., & Ranabahu, A. (2010a). Semantic Modeling for Cloud Computing, Part 1. *IEEE Internet Computing, 14*(3), 81–83. doi:10.1109/MIC.2010.77

Sheth, A., & Ranabahu, A. (2010b). Semantic Modeling for Cloud Computing, Part 2. *IEEE Internet Computing, 14*(4), 81–84. doi:10.1109/MIC.2010.98

Sheynin, Y. (1998). Asynchronous Growing Processes - the formal model of parallel computations in distributed computing structures (in Russian). In *Proceedings of the International Conference "Distributed information processing" (DIP-98)* (pp. 111-115). Novosibirsk: ISP SO RAN.

Sheynin, Y., Olenev, V., Lavrovskaya, I., Korobkov, I., & Dymov, D. (2014). STP-ISS Transport Protocol for Spacecraft On-board Networks. *Proceedings of 6th International SpaceWire Conference 2014 Program*, 26-31. 10.1109/SpaceWire.2014.6936226

Shin, Y.-S., Wee, J.-K., Song, I., & Lee, S. (2014). Small-area low-power heart condition monitoring system using dual-mode SAR-ADC for low-cost wearable healthcare systems. In *3rd International Conference on Biomedical Engineering and Technology (iCBEB 2014)* (pp. S277-S284). Beijing, China: Metapress.

Shooman, M. L. (2002). *Reliability of Computer Systems and Networks. Fault Tolerance, Analysis, and Design.* New York: Wiley.

Shull, P. B., Jirattigalachote, W., Hunt, M. A., Cutkosky, M. R., & Delp, S. L. (2014). Quantified self and human movement: A review on the clinical impact of wearable sensing and feedback for gait analysis and intervention. *Gait & Posture, 40*(1), 11–19. doi:10.1016/j.gaitpost.2014.03.189 PMID:24768525

Silsupadol, P., Teja, K., & Lugade, V. (2017). Reliability and validity of a smartphone-based assessment of gait parameters across walking speed and smartphone locations: Body, bag, belt, hand, and pocket. *Gait & Posture, 58*, 516–522. doi:10.1016/j.gaitpost.2017.09.030 PMID:28961548

Simou, N., Chortaras, A., Stamou, G., & Kollias, S. (2017). Enriching and Publishing Cultural Heritage as Linked Open Data. In Mixed Reality and Gamification for Cultural Heritage (pp. 201-223). doi:10.1007/978-3-319-49607-8_7

Siraj, S., Gupta, A. K., & Rinku-Badgujar. (2012). Network Simulation Tools Survey. *International Journal of Advanced Research in Computer and Communication Engineering, 1*(4), 201-210.

Smart Cities and Urban Analytics. (2019). Retrieved from http://www.bartlett.ucl.ac.uk/casa/programmes/postgraduate/msc-smart-cities-and-urban-analytics

Smart, P. R., Russell, A., Shadbolt, N. R., Carr, L. A., & ... (2007). Aktivesa: A technical demonstrator system for enhanced situation awareness. *The Computer Journal, 50*(6), 703–716. doi:10.1093/comjnl/bxm067

Smirnov, A., Kashevnik, A., & Shilov, N. (2015). *Cyber-Physical-Social System Self-Organization: Ontology-Based Multi-level Approach and Case Study.* 2015 IEEE 9th International Conference on Self-Adaptive and Self-Organizing Systems, Cambridge, MA.

Smirnov, A., Kashevnik, A., Teslya, N., Mikhailov, S., & Shabaev, A. (2015, April). Smart-M3-based robots self-organization in pick-and-place system. In *2015 17th Conference of Open Innovations Association (FRUCT)* (pp. 210-215). IEEE. 10.1109/FRUCT.2015.7117994

Smirnov, A., Ponomarev, A., Levashova, T., & Teslya, N. (2016a). Human-Computer Cloud for Decision Support in Tourism: Approach and Architecture. *Proceedings of the 19th FRUCT Conference*, 226-235. Retrieved from https://www.w3.org/TR/rdf-sparql-query/

Smirnov, A., Shilov, N., & Kashevnik, A. (2012). Ontology-based mobile smart museums service, approach for small & medium museums. In *Proc. of the 4th Int'l Conf. on Advances in Future Internet* (AFIN 2012, pp. 48-54). Academic Press.

Smirnov, A., Kashevnik, A., & Ponomarev, A. (2017). Context-based Infomobility System for Cultural Heritage Recommendation: Tourist Assistant—TAIS. *Personal and Ubiquitous Computing, 21*(2), 297–311. doi:10.100700779-016-0990-0

Smirnov, A., Kashevnik, A., Ponomarev, A., & Shilov, N. (2017, June). Context-aware decision support in socio-cyber-physical systems: From smart space-based applications to human-computer cloud services. In *International Conference on Practical Applications of Agents and Multi-Agent Systems* (pp. 3-15). Springer. 10.1007/978-3-319-59930-4_1

Smirnov, A., Kashevnik, A., Shilov, N., Balandin, S., Oliver, I., & Boldyrev, S. (2010). On-the-Fly Ontology Matching in Smart Spaces: A Multi-Model Approach. *Proceedings of the Third Conference on Smart Spaces*, 72-83. 10.1007/978-3-642-14891-0_7

Smirnov, A., Ponomarev, A., Levashova, T., & Teslya, N. (2016b). Decision Support in Tourism Based on Human-Computer Cloud. *Proceedings of the 18th International Conference on Information Integration and Web-based Applications & Services (iiWAS2016)*, 127-134. 10.1145/3011141.3011174

Sneps-Sneppe, M., & Namiot, D. (2012, April). About M2M standards and their possible extensions. In *Future Internet Communications (BCFIC), 2012 2nd Baltic Congress on* (pp. 187-193). IEEE. 10.1109/BCFIC.2012.6218001

Sneps-Sneppe, M., Namiot, D., & Alberts, M. (2018, May). On Digital Economy Issues Looking From the Information Systems Viewpoint. In *Proceedings of the 22st Conference of Open Innovations Association FRUCT* (p. 56). FRUCT Oy.

Sooai, A. G., Nugroho, A., Azam, M. N. A., Sumpeno, S., & Purnomo, M. H. (2017). Virtual artifact: Enhancing museum exhibit using 3D virtual reality. In *Proc. 2017 TRON Symposium (TRONSHOW)* (pp. 1-5). 10.23919/TRONSHOW.2017.8275078

Sowe, S. K., Simmon, E., Zettsu, K., de Vaulx, F., & Bojanova, I. (2016). Cyber-physical-human systems: Putting people in the loop. *IT Professional, 18*(1), 10–13. doi:10.1109/MITP.2016.14 PMID:28579925

SpaceWire Standard. (2008). *ECSS – Space Engineering. SpaceWire – Links, Nodes, Routers and Networks*. ECSS-E-ST.

Spector, L. (2006). Evolution of artificial intelligence. *Artificial Intelligence, 170*(18), 1251–1253. doi:10.1016/j.artint.2006.10.009

SSFNet Official website. (2019). *Scalable Simulation Network*. Retrieved from http://www.ssfnet.org/internetPage.html

Stankovic, J. A., Sturges, J. W., & Eisenberg, J. (2017). A 21st Century Cyber-Physical Systems Education. *Computer, 50*(12), 82–85. doi:10.1109/MC.2017.4451222

Stefanov, K., Voevodin, V., Zhumatiy, S., & Voevodin, V. (2015). Dynamically reconfigurable distributed modular monitoring system for supercomputers (dimmon). *Procedia Computer Science, 66*, 625–634. doi:10.1016/j.procs.2015.11.071

Steinberg, J. S., Varma, N., Cygankiewicz, I., Aziz, P., Balsam, P., Baranchuk, A., ... Piotrowicz, R. (2017). ISHNE-HRS Expert Consensus Statement on Ambulatory ECG and External Cardiac Monitoring/Telemetry. *Annals of Noninvasive Electrocardiology, 22*(3), 1–40. doi:10.1111/anec.12447 PMID:28480632

Sujit, P., George, G., & Beard, R. (2008). Multiple UAV coalition formation. *Proceedings of the American Control Conference, 2008*, 2010–2015.

Sule, R., Katti, R. S., & Kavasseri, R. G. (2012). *A variable length fast Message Authentication Code for secure communication in smart grids*. IEEE. doi:10.1109/PESGM.2012.6345622

Sun, Y., Yang, G., & Zhou, X. (2017). A survey on run-time supporting platforms for cyber physical systems. *Frontiers of Information Technology & Electronic Engineering*, *18*(10), 1458–1478. doi:10.1631/FITEE.1601579

Suo, H., Wan, J., Zou, C., & Liu, J. (2012, March). Security in the internet of things: a review. In Computer Science and Electronics Engineering (ICCSEE), 2012 international conference on (Vol. 3, pp. 648-651). IEEE. doi:10.1109/ICCSEE.2012.373

Susto, G. A., Cenedese, A., & Terzi, M. (2018). Time-series classification methods: Review and applications to power systems data. In *Big data application in power systems* (pp. 179–220). Elsevier. doi:10.1016/B978-0-12-811968-6.00009-7

Svennberg, E., Engdahl, J., Al-Khalili, F., Friberg, L., Frykman, V., & Rosenqvist, M. (2015). Mass Screening for Untreated Atrial Fibrillation: The STROKESTOP Study. *Circulation*, *131*(25), 2176–2184. doi:10.1161/CIRCULATIONAHA.114.014343 PMID:25910800

Syschikov, A., Sedov, B., Nedovodeev, K., & Pakharev, S. (2017). Visual Development Environment for OpenVX. *Proceedings of the 20th Conference of Open Innovations Association FRUCT.*

Syschikov, A., Sedov, B., & Sheynin, Y. (2016). Domain-Specific Programming Technology for Heterogeneous Many-core Platforms. In *Proceedings of the 12th Central and Eastern European Software Engineering Conference in Russia* (p. 15). ACM. 10.1145/3022211.3022224

Syschikov, A., Sheynin, Y., Sedov, B., & Ivanova, V. (2014). Domain-specific programming environment for heterogeneous multicore embedded systems. *International Journal of Embedded and Real-Time Communication Systems*, *5*(4), 1–23. doi:10.4018/IJERTCS.2014100101

Sztipanovits, J., Bapty, T., Koutsoukos, X., Lattmann, Z., Neema, S., & Jackson, E. (2018). Model and tool integration platforms for cyber-physical system design. *Proceedings of the IEEE*, (99), 1–26. 10.1109/JPROC.2018.2838530

Tagliabue, A., Kamel, M., Siegwart, R., & Nieto, J. (2019). Robust collaborative object transportation using multiple mavs. *The International Journal of Robotics Research*, *38*(9), 1020–1044. doi:10.1177/0278364919854131

Tamura, K., Kocher, M., Finer, L., Murata, N., & Stickley, C. (2018). Reliability of clinically feasible dual-task tests: Expanded timed get up and go test as a motor task on young healthy individuals. *Gait & Posture*, *60*, 22–27. doi:10.1016/j.gaitpost.2017.11.002 PMID:29132071

Tecuci, G., Boicu, M., Bowman, M., Marcu, D., Shyr, P., & Cascaval, C. (2000). An experiment in agent teaching by subject matter experts. *International Journal of Human-Computer Studies*, *53*(4), 583–610. doi:10.1006/ijhc.2000.0401

Teslya, N., & Ponomarev, A. (2016). Smart Tourism Destination Support Scenario Based on Human-Computer Cloud. *Proceedings of the 19th FRUCT Conference*, 242-247. 10.23919/FRUCT.2016.7892207

Thales Alenia Space. (2011). *Modeling Of SpaceWire Traffic*. Project Executive Summary & Final Report, 25. Author.

Theodoropoulos, D., Mazumdar, S., Ayguade, E., Bettin, N., Bueno, J., Ermini, S., ... Giorgi, R. (2017). The AXIOM platform for next-generation cyber physical systems. *Microprocessors and Microsystems*, *52*, 540–555. doi:10.1016/j.micpro.2017.05.018

Tianxing, M., & Zhukova, N. (2018). An Ontology of Machine Learning Algorithms for Human Activity Data Processing. *Learning*, *10*, 12.

TINA Circuit Simulator for Analog RF, Digital, MCU, HDL, Symbolic & Mixed Circuit Simulation with Integrated PCB Design. (2019) *Designsoft official website*. Retrieved June 25, 2019 from https://www.tina.com

Torre, I. (2013). Interaction with linked digital memories. In *Proceedings of the 21st Conf. on User Modeling, Adaptation, and Personalization (UMAP 2013). Workshop on Personal Access to Cultural Heritage (PATCH 2013) (vol. 997*, pp. 80-87). Academic Press.

Tosello, E., Fan, Z., Castro, A. G., & Pagello, E. (2016, July). Cloud-based task planning for smart robots. In *International Conference on Intelligent Autonomous Systems* (pp. 285-300). Springer.

Treisman, A. (1996). The binding problem. *Current Opinion in Neurobiology, 6*(2), 171–178. doi:10.1016/S0959-4388(96)80070-5 PMID:8725958

Triberti, S., & Barello, S. (2016). The quest for engaging AmI: Patient engagement and experience design tools to promote effective assisted living. *Journal of Biomedical Informatics, 63*, 150–156. doi:10.1016/j.jbi.2016.08.010 PMID:27515924

TRM3. (2012). *Travel Risk Management Maturity Model (TRM3)*. Retrieved from https://www.ijet.com/sites/default/files/WP_TRM3_May2012.pdf

Trombetti, G., Gokhale, A., Schmidt, D. C., Greenwald, J., Hatcliff, J., Jung, G., & Singh, G. (2005). An Integrated Model-Driven Development Environment for Composing and Validating Distributed Real-Time and Embedded Systems. In S. Beydeda, M. Book, & V. Gruhn (Eds.), Model-Driven Software Development (pp. 329-361). Springer-Verlag Berlin Heidelberg. doi:10.1007/3-540-28554-7_15

Tsotsos, J. K., Kotseruba, I., Rasouli, A., & Solbach, M. D. (2018). Visual attention and its intimate links to spatial cognition. *Cognitive Processing, 19*(1), 121–130. doi:10.100710339-018-0881-6 PMID:30094803

TUM IoT. (2019). Retrieved from https://www.caps.in.tum.de/en/teaching/ws18/practical-courses/iot/

Tysnes, O. B., & Storstein, A. (2017). Epidemiology of Parkinson's disease. *Journal of Neural Transmission (Vienna, Austria), 124*(8), 901–905. doi:10.100700702-017-1686-y PMID:28150045

Tyugu, E., Matskin, M., & Penjam, J. (1999). Applications of structural synthesis of programs. In *International Symposium on Formal Methods* (pp. 551–569). Toulouse, France: Academic Press.

University of Washington. (2019). Retrieved from http://www.pce.uw.edu/certificates/internet-of-things.html

UniversityA. R. M. (2017) Retrieved from https://www.arm.com/support/university/

UNWTO. (2016). *World Tourism Organization: UNWTO Tourism Highlights 2016 Edition*. Retrieved from http://cf.cdn.unwto.org/sites/all/files/pdf/unwto_highlights16_en_hr.pdf

Ushahidi. (n.d.). Retrieved from http://www.ushahidi.com/

van Leeuwen, B., Eldridge, J., & Leemaster, J. (2011). SpaceWire Model Development Technology for Satellite Architecture. *Sandia Report. Sandia National Laboratories, 2011*, 30.

Vangheluwe, H. (2018, May). Multi-paradigm modeling of cyber-physical systems. In *Proceedings of the 4th International Workshop on Software Engineering for Smart Cyber-Physical Systems* (pp. 1-1). ACM.

Van-Roy, P., & Harid, S. (2004). *Concepts, Techniques, and Models of Computer Programming*. MIT Press.

Varga, A., & Hornig, R. (2008). An overview of the OMNeT++ simulation environment. *Proceedings of the 1st international conference on Simulation tools and techniques for communications, networks and systems & workshops.* 10.4108/ICST.SIMUTOOLS2008.3027

Vassilakis, C., Poulopoulos, V., Antoniou, A., Wallace, M., Lepouras, G., & Nores, M. L. (2018). exhiSTORY: Smart exhibits that tell their own stories. *Future Generation Computer Systems*, *81*, 542–556. doi:10.1016/j.future.2017.10.038

Verma, D., Desai, N., Preece, A., & Taylor, I. (2017, May). A block chain based architecture for asset management in coalition operations. In *Ground/Air Multisensor Interoperability, Integration, and Networking for Persistent ISR VIII* (Vol. 10190, p. 101900Y). International Society for Optics and Photonics. doi:10.1117/12.2264911

Vervoort, D., Vuillerme, N., Kosse, N., Hortobágyi, T., & Lamoth, C. J. (2016). Multivariate analyses and classification of inertial sensor data to identify aging effects on the Timed-Up-and-Go test. *PLoS One*, *11*(6), e0155984. doi:10.1371/journal.pone.0155984 PMID:27271994

Vicente, J., Johannesen, L., Galeotti, L., & Strauss, D. (2013). ECGlab: User Friendly ECG/VCG Analysis Tool for Research Environments. *Computers in Cardiology*, *40*, 775–778.

Vienne, A., Barrois, R. P., Buffat, S., Ricard, D., & Vidal, P. P. (2017). Inertial sensors to assess gait quality in patients with neurological disorders: A systematic review of technical and analytical challenges. *Frontiers in Psychology*, *8*, 817. doi:10.3389/fpsyg.2017.00817 PMID:28572784

Vlagsma, T. T., Koerts, J., Tucha, O., Dijkstra, H. T., Duits, A. A., van Laar, T., & Spikman, J. M. (2016). Mental slowness in patients with Parkinson's disease: Associations with cognitive functions? *Journal of Clinical and Experimental Neuropsychology*, *38*(8), 844–852. doi:10.1080/13803395.2016.1167840 PMID:27132647

W3C for Web of Things. (2016). Retrieved from https://www.w3.org/2016/09/IoTW/white-paper.pdf

Walsh, J. A. III, Topol, E. J., & Steinhubl, S. R. (2014). Novel Wireless Devices for Cardiac Monitoring. *Circulation*, *130*(7), 573–575. doi:10.1161/CIRCULATIONAHA.114.009024 PMID:25114186

Wang, P., Yang, L. T., Li, J., Chen, J., & Hu, S. (2019). Data fusion in cyber-physical-social systems: State-of-the-art and perspectives. *Information Fusion*, *51*, 42–57. doi:10.1016/j.inffus.2018.11.002

Wang, Y., Tan, G., Wang, Y., & Yin, Y. (2012). Perceptual control architecture for cyber–physical systems in traffic incident management. *Journal of Systems Architecture*, *58*(10), 398–411. doi:10.1016/j.sysarc.2012.06.004

Wan, L., Zhang, Z., & Wang, J. (2019). Demonstrability of Narrowband Internet of Things technology in advanced metering infrastructure. *EURASIP Journal on Wireless Communications and Networking*, (1): 1–12.

Web of Things. (2019). Retrieved from https://en.wikipedia.org/wiki/Web_of_Things

Weiser, M. (1991). The Computer for the Twenty-First Century. *Scientific American*, *256*(3), 94–104. doi:10.1038cientificamerican0991-94 PMID:1675486

Weiser, M., & Brown, J. S. (1995). Designing Calm Technology. *Powergrid Journal*, *1*, 1–5.

Wickelgren, I. J. (1996, September). Local-area networks go wireless. *IEEE Spectrum*, *33*(9), 34–40. doi:10.1109/6.535256

Wilson, E. O. (2012). *The Social Conquest of Earth*. New York: Live right Publishing Corporation.

Wirdefeldt, K., Adami, H. O., Cole, P., Trichopoulos, D., & Mandel, J. (2011). Epidemiology and etiology of Parkinson's disease: A review of the evidence. *European Journal of Epidemiology*, *26*(S1Suppl. 1), S1–S58. doi:10.100710654-011-9581-6 PMID:21626386

WIT Internet of Things. (2019). Retrieved from https://www.wit.ie/courses/type/science/department_of_computing_maths_physics/bsc-hons-in-the-internet-of-things#tab=description

Wolf, W. H. (2009). Cyber-physical systems. *IEEE Computer*, *42*(3), 88–89. doi:10.1109/MC.2009.81

Wooldridge, M. (2009). An Introduction to MultiAgent Systems (2nd ed.). West Sussesx, UK: Wiley.

Wu, Q., Feng, J., Tang, W., & Fitch, J. (2005). Multi-agent Based Substation Automation Systems. In *IEEE Power Engineering Society General Meeting*, (pp. 1048-1049). San Francisco, CA: IEEE.

Wyma, J. M., Woods, D. L., Yund, E. W., Herron, T. J., & Reed, B. (2015). Age-related slowing of response selection and production in a visual choice reaction time task. *Frontiers in Human Neuroscience, 9*, 193:1-193:12.

Xiang, C., Jiang, T., Chang, B., & Sui, Z. (2015). ERSOM: A structural ontology matching approach using automatically learned entity representation. In *Conference Proceedings - EMNLP 2015: Conference on Empirical Methods in Natural Language Processing* (pp. 2419–2429). 10.18653/v1/D15-1289

Xue, F., Tang, H., Su, Q., & Li, T. (2019). Task Allocation of Intelligent Warehouse Picking System based on Multi-robot Coalition. *Transactions on Internet and Information Systems (Seoul), 13*(7).

Xu, J. (2001). *Topological Structure and Analysis of Interconnection Networks*. Kluwer Academic publishers. doi:10.1007/978-1-4757-3387-7

Yalovitsyna, S. E., Volokhova, V. V., & Korzun, D. G. (2019). Semantic Approach to Presenting Information of Thematic Museum Collections [In Russian]. *Harald of an Archivist, 1*, 235–246. doi:10.28995/2073-0101-2019-1-235-246

Yan, Y., Qian, Y., Sharif, H., & Tipper, D. (2012). A Survey on Cyber Security for Smart Grid Communications. *IEEE Communications Surveys & Tutorials, 14*, 998-1010.

Yang, L., Yang, S.-H., & Plotnick, L. (2013). How the internet of things technology enhances emergency response operations. *Technological Forecasting and Social Change, 80*(9), 1854–1867. doi:10.1016/j.techfore.2012.07.011

Yan, Y., Qian, Y., Sharif, H., & Tipper, D. (2013). A survey on smart grid communication infrastructures: Motivations, requirements and challenges. *IEEE Communications Surveys and Tutorials, 15*(1), 5–20. doi:10.1109/SURV.2012.021312.00034

Yu, C. C. (2005). Personalized and community decision support in eTourism Intermediaries. Database and Expert Systems Applications. DEXA 2005. *Lecture Notes in Computer Science, 3588*, 900–909. doi:10.1007/11546924_88

Yu, L., & Cai, Z. (2009, August). Robot exploration mission planning based on heterogeneous interactive cultural hybrid algorithm. In *2009 Fifth International Conference on Natural Computation* (Vol. 5, pp. 583-587). IEEE. 10.1109/ICNC.2009.15

Yu, R., Zhang, Y., Gjessing, S., Yuen, C., Xie, S., & Guizani, M. (2011, September). Cognitive radio based hierarchical communications infrastructure for smart grid. *IEEE Network, 25*(5), 6–14. doi:10.1109/MNET.2011.6033030

Zago, M., Sforza, C., Pacifici, I., Cimolin, V., Camerota, F., Celletti, C., ... Galli, M. (2018). Gait evaluation using Inertial Measurement Units in subjects with Parkinson's disease. *Journal of Electromyography and Kinesiology, 42*, 44–48. doi:10.1016/j.jelekin.2018.06.009 PMID:29940494

Zavyalova, Y. V., Korzun, D. G., Meigal, A. Y., & Borodin, A. V. (2017). Towards the development of smart spaces-based socio-cyber-medicine systems. *International Journal of Embedded and Real-Time Communication Systems, 8*(1), 45–63. doi:10.4018/IJERTCS.2017010104

Zavyalova, Y., Kuznetsova, T., Korzun, D., Borodin, A., & Meigal, A. (2018). Designing a Mobile Recommender System for Treatment Adherence Improvement among Hypertensives. In *Proceedings of the 22nd conference of FRUCT Association* (pp. 290-296). IEEE. 10.23919/FRUCT.2018.8468269

Zhabelova, G., & Vyatkin, V. (2012). Multiagent Smart Grid Automation Architecture Based on IEC 61850/61499 Intelligent Logical Nodes. *IEEE Transactions on Industrial Electronics, 59*(5), 2351–2362. doi:10.1109/TIE.2011.2167891

Zhang, H. (2012). *Computational environment design* (PhD thesis). Harvard University.

Zhang, T., & Ueno, H. (2007). Knowledge model-based heterogeneous multi-robot system implemented by a software platform. *Knowledge-Based Systems*, *20*(3), 310–319. doi:10.1016/j.knosys.2006.04.019

Zhukova, N., Baimuratov, I., Than, N., & Mustafin, N. (2019, April). The Information Estimation System for Data Processing Results. In *Proceedings of the 24th Conference of Open Innovations Association FRUCT* (p. 117). FRUCT Oy.

Zhu, Y., Zhang, T., Song, J., & Li, X. (2013). A hybrid navigation strategy for multiple mobile robots. *Robotics and Computer-integrated Manufacturing*, *29*(4), 129–141. doi:10.1016/j.rcim.2012.11.007

Zimmer, C. (2006). *Evolution: The Triumph of an Idea*. Harper Perennial.

About the Contributors

Sergey Balandin received M.Sc. in Computer Science from St.-Petersburg Electro-Technical University "LETI" (Russia, 1999) and in Telecommunications from Lappeenranta University of Technology (Finland, 2000). In 2003 graduated from PhD School of Nokia Research Center and got PhD degree in Telecommunications and Control Theory from St.-Petersburg Electro Technical University "LETI". In 2012 Sergey got MBA degree in Finland. He is a founder and president of FRUCT Association and Adjunct Professor at the Tampere University. In 1999-2011 Sergey Balandin worked for Nokia Research Center, his last position was Principal Scientist of Ubiquities Architectures team. Sergey is IARIA Fellow, Editor-in-Chief of IJERTCS journal, invited professor at ITMO University, and author of 100+ papers and 29 international patents. He holds expert position in various organizations and international programs, including, EURIPIDES[2], Skolkovo Foundation, Russian Academy of Science, National State Scientific Center of Kazakhstan, etc. He co-edited several books published in LNCS, IEEE Xplore and IGI. His current research interests include various aspects of Smart Spaces, network and services performance evaluation, and IoT.

Ekaterina Balandina received her Dipl.-Ing. (2011) and M.Sc. (2013) degrees in Mathematical Provision and Administration of Information Systems. In 2010 Ekaterina won personal Presidential scholar for studies abroad and started her PhD studies at University of Oulu. Later she moved to the Tampere University of Technology, where she is currently finalizing the dissertation. Her research interests include intelligent networks, smart spaces, Internet of Things, location-aware solutions, and protocol design. She is an author of over 25 research publications.

* * *

Ildar Baimuratov is a Ph.D. student in ITMO University.

Viktor Baranov, PhD (candidate of Engineering Science), Associate Professor of Information and Measurement Technique and Metrology Sub-Department at Penza State University. PhD degree in 2004, scientific specialty "Instruments and Methods of Measurements."

Imed Ben Dhaou (S'97-M'02, SM'2011) was born in 1972 in Tunisia. He received Master's degree in Electrical Engineering from the Tampere University of Technology, Tampere, Finland, the Ph.D. degree from the Royal Institute of Technology, Stockholm, Sweden, and the docent degree from University of Turku in 1997, 2002, 2019, respectively. His research interests are in the areas of embedded systems for

IoT, interconnect optimization, low-power circuit design, high-level power estimation, robust estimation, Intelligent Transportation Systems, and VLSI for DSP and wireless systems. He has authored and co-authored more than 60 journals and conference papers in these areas. Dr. Ben Dhaou received the Best Paper Award from the 1997 Finnish Symposium on Signal Processing and a travel grant from the Ph.D. forum at DAC, Los Angeles in 2000. Since September 2014, Dr. Ben Dhaou has been serving as editor to the microelectronics journal, Elsevier. He was the Guest Editor for the special issue of on-chip signaling in deep-submicron technology, Journal of Analog Integrated Circuits and Signal Processing.

Oleg Bodin, PhD (Doctor of Engineering Science), Professor of Information and Measurement Technique and Metrology Sub-Department at Penza State University. Doctor degree in 2008, scientific specialties "Instruments, Systems and Products for Medical Usage" and "System Analysis, Control and Information Processing". Professor since 2012.

Nadezhda Chumakova is an engineer in the EmCoMobile Lab of the Institute of High Performance Computer and Network Technologies at the Saint-Petersburg State University of Aerospace Instrumentation (SUAI). She holds an MSc in Computer Science from Saint-Petersburg State University of Aerospace Instrumentation, the main research subject: "Conformance testing of the spacecraft on-board network equipment". Nadezhda Chumakova has over 4 years industrial experience. She currently participates in the development of a new scheduling tables design method for STP-ISS transport protocol. Also she currently participates software implementation of this method, a part of the SpaceWire Automated Network Design and Simulation (SANDS) tool. Her main research interests are conformance testing, on-board networks, SystemC modeling language, and scheduling tables design.

Liudmila I. Gerasimova-Meigal graduated from the Medical School of Petrozavodsk State University (PetrSU) in 1993. In 2008 received degree of Doctor of medical sciences in Pathophysiology. Currently she occupies the position of Professor of Pathophysiology in PetrSU. She collaborates with the department of applied physics (University of Eastern Finland, Kuopio) on mathematical methods for early diagnostics of parkinsonism by means of electromyography. In 1999 she was awarded a Gold medal and Prize of Russian Academy of Sciences for the best study in the field of physiology for young Doctor of Sciences. The research interest is environmental pathophysiology and novel methods of diagnostics of circulation and motor systems. Currently studies the effect of analogue microgravity on healthy subjects and patients with Parkinson's disease.

Vera Ivanova graduated State University of Aerospace Instrumentation, Russia (2014, Master in Techniques and Technology). Has 6 years programming exprerience in C/C#, WPF, main accent on the creating of Integrated Development Environment for Visual Parallel Programming.

Syed Rameez Ullah Kakakhel received his bachelor's in Computer Engineering in 2010 and Masters in Embedded Computing Systems in 2015. He is currently pursuing his PhD from the Department of Future Technologies at the University of Turku. His research is focused on fog computing and distributed autonomic edge computing. He has an interest in Internet of Things and distributed smart systems.

Alexey Kashevnik is a senior researcher in Computer Aided Integrated Systems Laboratory at St.Petersburg Institute for Informatics and Automation of the Russian Academy of Sciences (SPIIRAS) from 2003 and associate professor in Information Technologies and Programming Faculty at ITMO University, Russia from 2014. He is associate editor of the International Journal of Embedded and Real-Time Communication Systems (IJERTCS), advisory board member of Open Innovation Association FRUCT, and program committee member of the several international conferences. He received his PhD in computer science at SPIIRAS in 2008. His research interests include intelligent transportation systems, human-computer interaction, driver assistant, knowledge management, profiling, ontologies, smart-spaces, knowledge-based systems, Internet of Things, cloud computing, context management, robotics, and decision support systems. He has published more than 200 research papers in reviewed international journals, proceedings of international conferences, and books.

Aron Kondoro received his Master of Science degree in Information and Communication Systems Security from the Royal Institute of Technology (KTH - Sweden) in 2012 and Bachelor of Science in Computer Science from the University of Dar-es-Salaam in 2007. He is an Assistant Lecturer in the Computer Science and Engineering (CSE) Department at the University of Dar-es-Salaam (UDSM), Tanzania. Currently, he is a PhD student at KTH/UDSM doing research in using smart grid technologies to design and implement more efficient, reliable and autonomous solar-driven microgrids for off-grid rural communities. His other research and consultancy activities are focused on analyzing ICT systems security and using mobile technologies to design applications for educational and financial use-cases.

Ilya Korobkov is a Junior Researcher in the EmCoMobile Lab of the Institute of High Performance Computer and Network Technologies at the Saint-Petersburg State University of Aerospace Instrumentation (SUAI). He holds an MSc in Computer Science from Saint-Petersburg State University of Aerospace Instrumentation, the main research subject: "Network simulation and evaluation performance of embedded systems communication protocols". He is preparing PhD thesis on scheduling methods in real-time onboard spacecraft networks. Ilya korobkov has over 10 years of industrial experience. He participated in the development of simulation models such standards like as PIE, UniPro, SpaceWire, SpaceWire-RT, SpaceFibre, STP-ISS. He currently participates in the development of the simulation part of the SpaceWire Automated Network Design and Simulation (SANDS) tool and new scheduling tables design methods for STP-ISS transport protocol and SpaceFibre networks. Also he currently participates software implementation of these methods, a part of the SpaceWire Automated Network Design and Simulation (SANDS) tool. His main research interests are modeling, embedded onboard systems and networks, C++, System modeling language, virtual prototyping, TLM 2.0, scheduling tables design, math methods to estimate networks bandwidth by Queuing Theory.

Dmitry G. Korzun received B.Sc. (1997) and M.Sc (1999) degrees in Applied Mathematics and Computer Science from the Petrozavodsk State University (PetrSU, Russia). He received Ph.D. degree in Physics and Mathematics from the St.-Petersburg State University (Russia) in 2002. He is an Associate Professor at the Department of Computer Science of PetrSU (since 2003) and a part-time Research Scientist at the Helsinki Institute for Information Technology HIIT, Aalto University, Finland (2005-2014). Since 2014 he acts as Vice-dean for Research at the Faculty of Mathematics of PetrSU (now Faculty of Mathematics and Information Technology) of PetrSU and as Leading Research Scientist. Dmitry Korzun serves on technical program committees and editorial boards of a number of international conferences and journals. His research interests include analysis and evaluation of distributed systems, discrete modeling, ubiquitous computing and smart spaces, Internet of Things, software engineering, algorithm design and complexity, linear Diophantine analysis and its applications, theory of formal languages and parsing. More than 150 research and educational works have been published since 1997.

Lev Kurbanov is an engineer in the EmCoMobile Lab of the Institute of High Performance Computer and Network Technologies at the Saint-Petersburg State University of Aerospace Instrumentation (SUAI). He is an engineer in the field of Automated Information Processing and Control Systems and holds an MSc in Computer Science from Saint-Petersburg State University of Aerospace Instrumentation, the main research subject: "Deadlock-free routing in onboard SapceWire network". Lev Kurbanov has over 5 years of industrial experience. He participated in the development of software Network-on-Chip design solutions. He currently participates in the development of the routing design part of the SpaceWire Automated Network Design and Simulation (SANDS) tool. His main research interests are embedded systems, routing in networks, graph theory and operation research.

Andrey Kuzmin, PhD (candidate of engineering science), Associate Professor of Information and Computing Systems Sub-Department at Penza State University. Graduated from computing technique department of Penza state university in 2004. PhD degree in 2007, scientific specialties "System Analysis, Control and Information Processing" and "Instruments, Systems and Products for Medical usage."

Irina Lavrovskaya is a Researcher in a Embedded Computing for Mobile Communications Lab at the Saint-Petersburg State University of Aerospace Instrumentation (SUAI). She holds an MSc in Computer Science from Saint-Petersburg State University of Aerospace Instrumentation, the main research subject: "Modeling of formally specified embedded systems communication protocols". Irina Lavrovskaya has over 10 years of industrial experience. She participated in the development of such standards as UniPro and SpaceWire. The last project she took part in was SpaceWire-RT project funded under the EU's Seventh Framework Programme. She currently participates in the development of a new transport protocol STP-ISS operating over SpaceWire. Her main research interests are embedded systems, modeling, SDL and SystemC modeling languages and development of communication protocols for on-board and spacecraft systems.

Sergey Lebedev graduated from the Saint Petersburg Electrotechnical University "LETI" (ETU) in 2010. He is an assistant at ETU (Department of Computer Science and Engineering). He is co-author of more than 10 publications in the field of multi-agent systems and semantic web technologies.

Alexander Yu Meigal graduated from Medical Institute of Petrozavodsk State University(PetrSU) on 1987. Researcher (1987-1990), senior researcher (1990-1991) at the Laboratory for Heat Exchange and Thermoregulation (PetrSU), in 1997 received degree of Doctor of medical sciences in Physiology. Since the year 1998 - professor, and since the year 2018 - Head of the Department of Physiology of PetrSU. In 1991-1999 led joint projects with the University of Eastern Finland (Kuopio) and Finnish Institute of Occupational Health (Oulu, Finland) testing the human motor system under cold conditions. Since the year 2006 collaborates with the department of applied physics (University of Eastern Finland, Kuopio) on mathematical methods for early diagnostics of parkinsonism by means of electromyography. Participated in the project of simulation of interplanetary space flight to Mars (2010) as a specialist in electromyography Starting from 2012 has organized and leads the laboratory for novel methods in physiology (Institute of Advanced biomedical technologies, PetrSU). In 1999 he was awarded a Gold medal and Prize of Russian Academy of Sciences for the best study in the field of physiology for young Doctor of Sciences. Gold medal for the invention of the "Microgravity-based rehabilitation of parkinsonian patients by the method of "dry immersion" (2016). Currently leads the projects on the influence of analogue microgravity on healthy subjects and patients with Parkinson's disease, and role of microgravity in the ontogenesis of the motor function in term and preterm infants.

Alex P. Moschevikin defended PhD in Physics (Laser two-step photoionization of Lithium isotopes) in 1999, since that time works as associate professor at Institute of Physics and Technology of Petrozavodsk State University. Since 2005 leads the team of researchers and developers of applications and technologies in wireless communication, inertial navigation, industrial automation and Internet. Worked as principal investigator in several large projects including international programs: "Development of new local positioning technology on the basis of RealTrac featuring improved accuracy", ""Autonomous Self-Calibrated Inertial Measurement Unit", "Research and educational center Plasma", etc. The RealTrac local positioning technology won the 1st place in International competition "Evaluating AAL Systems through Competitive Benchmarking, EvAAL-2013".

Dmitry Namiot is a senior scientist Faculty of Computational Mathematics and Cybernetics, Lomonosov Moscow State University, Moscow, Russia.

Konstantin Nedovodeev is a senior researcher in the Institute for High-Performance Computer and Network Technologies laboratory at St. Petersburg State University of Aerospace Instrumentation, currently working on VIPE. His research interests include models of parallel computation, compiler and tasking runtime design. He received his PhD degree in computer science from Peter the Great St. Petersburg Polytechnic University.

Valentin Olenev is a Head of the laboratory for Embedded Computing for Mobile Communications of the Saint-Petersburg State University of Aerospace Instrumentation (SUAI). He holds M. Sc. in Computer Science from Saint-Petersburg State University of Aerospace Instrumentation, the main research subject: "Research and development of a system for Wi-Fi networks security increase"; and Ph.D in Mathematical support for computers, complexes and computer networks from Saint-Petersburg State University of Aerospace Instrumentation, the main research subject: "Design of communication protocols models for embedded systems". Valentin Olenev has about 10 years of industrial experience and his main research interests are: networking, embedded systems, modeling, SDL and SystemC modeling languages, models architecture, Petri Nets, SpaceWire, on-board systems. He has over 30 scientific publications. Also Valentin Olenev is an associate professor at Aerospace Computer and Software Systems Department at SUAI.

Sergey Pakharev graduated State University of Aerospace Instrumentation, Russia (2017, Master of engineering and technology). Has 5 years of programming experience in C/C++ with the main accent on the software architecture for embedded and distributed systems.

Michail Panteleyev graduated from the Penza Polytechnical Institute in 1982. Ph.D (1988), Associate Professor, Saint Petersburg Electrotechnical University "LETI" (Department of Computer Engineering). He is coauthor of more than 100 publications in the field of artificial intelligence, multi-agent systems and semantic web technologies.

Andrew Ponomarev is a senior researcher in Computer Aided Integrated Systems Laboratory at St.Peterburg Institute for Informatics and Automation of the Russian Academy of Sciences (SPIIRAS) since 2008. He is also an associate professor at St.Petersburg State Electrotechnical University "LETI". He received his BSc (2002) and engineering diploma (2003) from Tyumen State Oil and Gas University, and PhD in system analysis from SPIIRAS in 2012. His research interests include human computation systems, crowd computing, recommendation systems, operations research and data analysis. He published more than 40 research papers in reviewed journals and proceedings of international conferences, books, manuals.

Sergey Reginya received the B.Tech and M.Tech degrees at Faculty of Physical Engineering of Petrozavodsk State University, Russian Federation, in 2010 and 2012, respectively. In 2011 he joined the Lab127 research team in PetrSU which carried out several projects on real time location systems, wireless sensors networks, automation and distributed remote software and hardware development. Currently he is a software engineer at innovative company Nanonets Ltd, Russian Federation. His research interests include strapdown inertial navigation, multi-sensor integrated navigation, wireless sensors networks, local positioning systems algorithms, and experiment automation.

Maxim Safronov is a Ph.D. student at Penza State University. Master degree in Penza State University in 2018. Current educational profile is "Measurement and Information Technologies."

Boris Sedov graduated State University of Aerospace Instrumentation, Russia (2011, Master of Science). Has 8 years research experience in parallel programming area with main accent on the Integrated Development Environment for Visual Parallel Programming, Domain-Specific language development, Generating and Modelling tool flows for DSLs and embedded systems.

Yuriy Sheynin graduated Leningrad Instituted of Aerospace Instrumentation, USSR (1973, Engineer in Computer Science), Candidate of Science (equal to PhD, 1979, Computer Science), Doctor of Science (2002, Computer Science and Software Engineering), Professor (2012). Scientific interests: Computer Architectures; Embedded computing, System Level Integration, Systems-on-Chip (SoC), VLSI Architectures, NoC. Real-time and embedded software. Networks, protocols. Parallel computations formal models; Parallel programming. Operating systems for parallel and distributed computers.

Nikolay Shilov received his ME at St.Petersburg State Technical University, Russia, in 1998 and his PhD at SPIIRAS in 2005. He is a senior researcher at the Computer Aided Integrated Systems Laboratory of SPIIRAS. His current research interests belong to areas of virtual enterprise configuration, supply chain management, knowledge management, ontology engineering and socio-cyberphysical systems.

Nikolai Sinyov is an engineer in the EmCoMobile Lab of the Institute of High Performance Computer and Network Technologies at the Saint-Petersburg State University of Aerospace Instrumentation (SUAI). He is an engineer in the field of Automated Information Processing and Control Systems and holds an MSc in Computer Science from Saint-Petersburg State University of Aerospace Instrumentation, the main research subject: "Research and Analysis of Flow Control Mechanism for Transport Protocols of the SpaceWire Onboard Networks". Nikolai Sinyov has over 6 years of industrial experience. He participated in the development of simulation models such standards like as SpaceWire, SpaceWire-RT and STP-ISS. He currently participates in the development of the simulation part of the SpaceWire Automated Network Design and Simulation (SANDS) tool. His main research interests are modeling, embedded systems, C++ and SystemC modeling languages and implemetation of communication protocols for onboard and spacecraft systems.

Manfred Sneps-Sneppe is a professor at Ventspils University of Applied Sciences, Ventspils, Latvia.

Alexey Syschikov graduated State University of Aerospace Instrumentation, Russian Federation (2003, Master of Science). Has 12 years of research experience in parallel programming and embedded systems area with main accent on Models of Computation, Domain-Specific language development, Generating and Modelling tool flows for DSLs and embedded systems.

Hannu Tenhunen received the Diploma Engineer degree in electrical engineering and computer sciences from Helsinki University of Technology, Helsinki, Finland, in 1982 and Ph.D. degree in microelectronics from Cornell University, Ithaca, NY, in 1986. During 1978–1982, he was with Electron Physics Laboratory, Helsinki University of Technology. From 1983 to 1985, he was with Cornell University as a Fulbright Scholar. From September 1985, he was with the Signal Processing Laboratory, Tampere University of Technology, Finland, as an Associate Professor. He was also a Coordinator of the National Microelectronics Program of Finland during 1987–1991. Since January 1992, he has been with Royal Institute of Technology, Sweden, where he is a Chair Professor in electronic system design. His current research interests are VLSI circuits and systems for autonomic and smart systems and IoT. He has been actively involved in several EU programs on VLSI/system-on-a-chip. He was education director of European Institute of Innovation and Technology EIT Digital. He has published over 825 reviewed publications and holds 9 international patents in areas relevant to this project.

Nikolay Teslya is a senior researcher in Computer Aided Integrated Systems Laboratory at St. Petersburg Institute for Informatics and Automation of the Russian Academy of Sciences (SPIIRAS). He works at SPIIRAS since 2010. He is a senior researcher at International Laboratory on Intelligent Technologies for Socio-Cyberphysical Systems, ITMO University since 2014. He received his engineering diploma in field of mathematics and computer science (2013) in St. Petersburg Electrotechnical University "LETI", and PhD in software engineering at SPIIRAS in 2015. His research interests includes infomobility, knowledge management, ontologies, ontology matching, internet of things, e-Tourism applications. He is a member of technical program committee of the International Conferences of Open Innovations Association FRUCT (http://fruct.org/) since 2017. He published more than 40 research papers in reviewed journals and proceedings of international conferences.

Man Tianxing is a Ph.D. student in ITMO University.

Osipov Vasiliy received the qualification of a radio engineer at the Higher Naval School of Radio Electronics in 1981. He obtained his Ph.D. in 1990 and his Doctor's degree (Dr. in Engineering) in 2000. He is currently Professor, Head of the Laboratory of Computing & Information Systems and Software Engineering at St. Petersburg Institute for Informatics and Automation of the Russian Academy of Sciences. His research interests include associative intelligent machines, neural networks, automatic program synthesis, system modeling.

Alexander Vodyaho obtained his PhD degree from Saint-Petersburg Electrotechnical University "LETI", Saint-Petersburg in 1977 and his Doctor of Philosophy also from Saint-Petersburg Electrotechnical University "LETI", Saint-Petersburg in 1992. He is a Vice Head of the Department of Computer Science and Engineering of Saint-Petersburg Electrotechnical University. His research interest includes enterprise systems, software architecture and knowledge management.

Valentina V. Volokhova received her MSc (1998) degree in Historical Science from the Petrozavodsk State University (PetrSU, Russia). She received a PhD degree in Russian History from the Petrozavodsk State University (PetrSU, Russia) in 2002. She is an Associate Professor at the Department of Russian History of PetrSU (since 2003). Her research interests include memory studies, commemorative practices, methods of historical research. Her educational activity started in 2001 at the Faculty of History of PetrSU (now Institute of History, Political and Social Sciences). Since that time, she has taught more than 20 study courses on hot topics in Russian History

Tomi Westerlund is a University Research Fellow at the University of Turku and a Research Professor at Wuxi Institute of Fudan University, Wuxi, China. He has yearly acted as a visiting scholar at Fudan University, Shanghai, China. Dr. Westerlund leads the Turku Intelligent Robotics and Embedded Systems (TIERS) research group (tiers.utu.fi). TIERS is part of the Finnish Centre of Excellence in Research of Sustainable Space (Academy of Finland). His current research interest is in the areas of Industrial IoT, smart cities and autonomous vehicles (aerial, ground and surface) as well as (co-)robots. In all these application areas, the core research interests are in energy efficiency, dependability, interoperability, for/edge computing, swarm intelligence and edge AI. Orcid 0000-0002-1793-2694.

Svetlana E. Yalovitsyna graduated from the history department of Petrozavodsk state University (1992). Since 1998 Svetlana has been a lecturer of PetrSU. In 2002 she defended the dissertation (degree of candidate of history). Since 2007 she has been an associate Professor of the University. Among the training courses were subjects related to the use of quantitative methods and IT-technologies in historical research. In 2015, she managed the Museum of History (PetrSU), creating a new design of information presentation and data storage. In 2016 she became Deputy Director on scientific work of Institute of language, literature and History at Karelian Research Center, Russian Academy of Sciences.

Nataly Zhukova is a researcher at the laboratory of computing & information systems and programming technologies, St. Petersburg Institute for Informatics and Automation of Russian Academy of Sciences (SPIIRAS).

Index

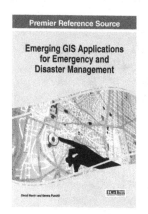

IGI Global Proudly Partners With eContent Pro International

Receive a 25% Discount on all Editorial Services

Editorial Services

IGI Global expects all final manuscripts submitted for publication to be in their final form. This means they must be reviewed, revised, and professionally copy edited prior to their final submission. Not only does this support with accelerating the publication process, but it also ensures that the highest quality scholarly work can be disseminated.

English Language Copy Editing

Let eContent Pro International's expert copy editors perform edits on your manuscript to resolve spelling, punctuaion, grammar, syntax, flow, formatting issues and more.

Scientific and Scholarly Editing

Allow colleagues in your research area to examine the content of your manuscript and provide you with valuable feedback and suggestions before submission.

Figure, Table, Chart & Equation Conversions

Do you have poor quality figures? Do you need visual elements in your manuscript created or converted? A design expert can help!

Translation

Need your documjent translated into English? eContent Pro International's expert translators are fluent in English and more than 40 different languages.

Email: customerservice@econtentpro.com   **www.igi-global.com/editorial-service-partners**

Publisher of Peer-Reviewed, Timely, and
Innovative Academic Research Since 1988

IGI Global's Transformative Open Access (OA) Model:
How to Turn Your University Library's Database Acquisitions Into a Source of OA Funding

In response to the OA movement and well in advance of Plan S, IGI Global, early last year, unveiled their OA Fee Waiver (Offset Model) Initiative.

Under this initiative, librarians who invest in IGI Global's InfoSci-Books (5,300+ reference books) and/or InfoSci-Journals (185+ scholarly journals) databases will be able to subsidize their patron's OA article processing charges (APC) when their work is submitted and accepted (after the peer review process) into an IGI Global journal.*

How Does it Work?

1. When a library subscribes or perpetually purchases IGI Global's InfoSci-Databases including InfoSci-Books (5,300+ e-books), InfoSci-Journals (185+ e-journals), and/or their discipline/subject-focused subsets, IGI Global will match the library's investment with a fund of equal value to go toward subsidizing the OA article processing charges (APCs) for their patrons.

   Researchers: Be sure to recommend the InfoSci-Books and InfoSci-Journals to take advantage of this initiative.

2. When a student, faculty, or staff member submits a paper and it is accepted (following the peer review) into one of IGI Global's 185+ scholarly journals, the author will have the option to have their paper published under a traditional publishing model or as OA.

3. When the author chooses to have their paper published under OA, IGI Global will notify them of the OA Fee Waiver (Offset Model) Initiative. If the author decides they would like to take advantage of this initiative, IGI Global will deduct the US$ 1,500 APC from the created fund.

4. This fund will be offered on an annual basis and will renew as the subscription is renewed for each year thereafter. IGI Global will manage the fund and award the APC waivers unless the librarian has a preference as to how the funds should be managed.

Hear From the Experts on This Initiative:

"I'm very happy to have been able to make one of my recent research contributions, 'Visualizing the Social Media Conversations of a National Information Technology Professional Association' featured in the *International Journal of Human Capital and Information Technology Professionals*, freely available along with having access to the valuable resources found within IGI Global's InfoSci-Journals database."

– Prof. Stuart Palmer,
Deakin University, Australia

For More Information, Visit: www.igi-global.com/publish/contributor-resources/open-access or contact IGI Global's Database Team at eresources@igi-global.com.

Printed in the United States
By Bookmasters